Clerical Marriage
and the English Reformation

Clerical Marriage and the English Reformation

Precedent Policy and Practice

HELEN L. PARISH

Ashgate

Aldershot • Burlington USA • Singapore • Sydney

© Helen L. Parish, 2000

Published by
Ashgate Publishing Limited
Gower House
Croft Road
Aldershot
Hants GU11 3HR
England

Ashgate Publishing Company
131 Main Street
Burlington
Vermont 05401–5600
USA

Ashgate website: http://www.ashgate.com

British Library Cataloguing in Publication Data

Parish, Helen L.
    Clerical Marriage and the English Reformation: Precedent
    Policy and Practice.
    (St Andrews Studies in Reformation History)
    1. Catholic Church—Clergy—Family relationships.
    2. Reformation—England.
    I. Title.
    253.2'09031

Library of Congress Cataloging-in-Publication Data

Parish, Helen L.
    Clerical marriage and the English Reformation: precedent policy and
    practice/Helen L. Parish.
        p.   cm. (St Andrews Studies in Reformation History)
    Includes bibliographical references and index.
    ISBN 0–7546–0038–6 (alk. paper)
    1. Reformation—England. 2. England—Church history—16th century.
    3. Clergy—Family relationships. 4. Marriage—History—16th century.
    5. Celibacy—History—16th century. I. Title. II. Series.
    BR377.H37   2000
    253'.25'094209031—dc21   00–20648

ISBN 0 7546 0038 6

This book is printed on acid free paper.

Typeset in Sabon by Express Typesetters, Farnham, Surrey and
Printed and bound in Great Britain by MPG Books Ltd, Bodmin, Cornwall

Contents

St Andrews Studies in Reformation History

*The Shaping of a Community: The Rise and Reformation of the
English Parish c. 1400–1560*
Beat Kümin

*Seminary or University? The Genevan Academy and
Reformed Higher Education, 1560–1620*
Karin Maag

Marian Protestantism: Six Studies
Andrew Pettegree

Protestant History and Identity in Sixteenth-Century Europe
(2 volumes) edited by Bruce Gordon

*Antifraternalism and Anticlericalism in the German Reformation:
Johann Eberlin von Günzburg and the Campaign against the Friars*
Geoffrey Dipple

*Reformations Old and New: Essays on the Socio-Economic
Impact of Religious Change c. 1470–1630*
edited by Beat Kümin

Piety and the People: Religious Printing in French, 1511–1551
Francis M. Higman

The Reformation in Eastern and Central Europe
edited by Karin Maag

John Foxe and the English Reformation
edited by David Loades

The Reformation and the Book
Jean-François Gilmont, edited and translated by Karin Maag

Foreword

There is a history in all men's lives,
Figuring the nature of the times deceased.

William Shakespeare, *Henry IV, Part II* (1597), Act 3, Scene 1

History never looks like history when you are living through it.
It always looks confusing and messy and it always feels
uncomfortable.

John W. Gardner

At times the sixteenth century can seem no less confusing and messy for
those who write about it than it was for those who lived through it. As
those who made the Reformation sought to understand the events of the
past and the present, those who were affected by religious and political
change saw the securities of the mediaeval past subside, and watched the
collapse of the certainties of daily life. Few groups were as susceptible to
the changing fortunes of the Reformation in England as the clergy. The
sacraments which underpinned the nature and function of the priesthood
were redefined, and messages preached from the pulpit were subjected to
the vagaries of political change and doctrinal debate. Priests who had
made a perpetual promise of celibacy were granted the freedom to
marry, only to find that freedom revoked four years later. Clerical
marriage was a highly visible sign of religious revolution, and the
changing demands of legislation on the subject led to disruption and
dislocation on a national scale. In the course of researching and writing
the history of clerical marriage during the Reformation, it is impossible
to ignore the polemical passions and personal struggles which governed
thought and action, and which brought the issue to the fore.

The debate on clerical marriage in the sixteenth century encompassed
almost every major theme in Reformation controversy, and sheds light
upon the nature and motivations behind religious change. Biblical and
patristic texts became the language of debate, records of past centuries
were plundered, and the present became a hunting ground for those who
sought to convince or convert. However, the certainties of polemical
debate were not always borne out by events in the parishes, and image
and reality in the English Reformation did not always coincide. The
response of the clergy to legislation that attempted to control their public
and private lives gives some indication of the struggle which faced those
who sought to capture hearts and minds, and suggests a variety of
influences which may have governed individual reactions to religious
change. As a result, a study of clerical marriage in England is also a study

of questions of authority, the place of history, and the understanding of the nature of the church and its sacraments. Against the reformation demanded by polemicists stands the reformation enacted by church and state and the reformation accepted, rejected or ignored by the laity and the clergy. Confronted with this multiplicity of opinion, action and reaction, it is the task of the historian to 'figure the nature of the times deceased'.

Acknowledgements

Many debts have been accumulated in the process of researching and writing this book. I am grateful for the assistance of the staff of the Bodleian Library, the Public Record Office, the British Library, the Lincoln Archives Office, the Wiltshire Record Office, the Berkshire Record Office, the Hampshire Record Office, the East Sussex Record Office, and the West Sussex Record Office. Special thanks are also due to those who have given up their time to read parts of this text, and generously shared their knowledge with me, especially Christopher Haigh, Andrew Pettegree, Andrew Hope, Tom Freeman, Tim McCann, Peter Wilkinson, John Watson and Christopher Bradshaw, and to John Guy, who first suggested the project. Their advice and comments have much improved what follows; any errors, of course, remain my own. Particular thanks are due to my supervisor, Dr Felicity Heal, for her help and support throughout the last years. Her comments and criticisms have helped to shape what follows, and have contributed to my continued enthusiasm for research in the sixteenth century. Thanks are also due to the members of Jesus College Oxford and Wolfson College Oxford, whose support, both financial and personal, did much to make research on this book possible.

I have also been fortunate to enjoy the company of many friends and colleagues both in Oxford and elsewhere, both fellow historians, and those whose spare time has been encroached upon by unknown writers and clergy from the sixteenth century. However, my greatest debt is to my parents and to Gavin: without their unfailing support and encouragement this book might never have been written. I hope that they enjoy what follows.

Abbreviations

AM, 1563	J. Foxe, *The Actes and Monumentes of these latter and perillous dayes* (1563), RSTC 11222
AM, 1570	J. Foxe, *The Actes and Monumentes of these latter and perillous dayes* (1570), RSTC 11223
APC	*Acts of the Privy Council*, ed. J.R. Dasent, 32 vols (1890–1907)
ARG	*Archiv Für Reformationsgeschichte*
BIHR	*Bulletin of the Institute of Historical Research*
BL	*British Library*
CCCC	*Corpus Christi College Cambridge*
CPR	*Calendar of the Patent Rolls Preserved in the Public Record Office* (1901–66)
CW	*The Yale Edition of the Complete Works of St Thomas More*, ed. J.M. Headley (New Haven and London, 1963–)
DNB	*Dictionary of National Biography*
EETS	*Early English Text Society*
EHR	*English Historical Review*
ESRO	*East Sussex Record Office*
HRO	*Hampshire Record Office*
JEH	*Journal of Ecclesiastical History*
LAO	*Lincolnshire Archives Office*
LNQ	*Lincolnshire Notes and Queries*
LP	*Letters and Papers, Foreign and Domestic of the Reign of Henry VIII*, eds S. Brewer, J. Gairdner, 21 vols (1862–1932)
LW	*Luther's Works. American Edition*, eds J. Pelikan, H.C. Oswald, 56 volumes (St Louis, 1955–82)
PRO	*Public Record Office*
TRHS	*Transactions of the Royal Historical Society*
TRP	*Tudor Royal Proclamations*, eds P.L. Hughes and J.F. Larkin, 3 vols (New Haven and London, 1964–69)
WRO	*Wiltshire Record Office*
WSRO	*West Sussex Record Office*
WW	*The Whole Worckes of W.Tyndall, Iohn Frith, and Doct. Barnes, three worthy martyrs and principall teachers of this churche of Englande*, (1573), RSTC 24436

Introduction

Since the pontificate of Gregory VII, the clergy in the western church, in theory at least, had been separated from the laity by their obligation to celibacy. The exaltation of virginity over marriage had roots in biblical and patristic writings, and built upon the division of the sacred and the profane, the human and the divine. Clerical celibacy was visible testimony to the sacrificial function of the priest at Mass, and to the elevated nature of the priestly caste, which stood astride the divide between earth and heaven.[1] This image was shattered by the Reformation. In what amounted to a highly visible act of doctrinal iconoclasm, votaries left the cloister and parish clergy took wives. If Martin Luther was surprised to find 'pigtails on the pillow', the shock to the majority of the laity must have been greater still.[2] Luther's marriage, and the Protestant attack on monastic vows and morality, gave clerical celibacy and clerical marriage a prominent role in Reformation debate both in England and on the Continent, attracting the attention of Protestant and Catholic polemicists from More and Luther to Harding and Jewel.

The debate on clerical marriage was not conducted in a vacuum. Legislation on clerical marriage, most notably the Six Articles of 1539, the lifting of the prohibition on clerical marriage in 1549, and the condemnation of such marriages in 1553, clearly influenced the nature and tone of religious polemic. However, it also had profound effects upon the many clergy, both secular and regular, who had chosen to marry, and the implications of the ideological debate may be seen in their actions. Of all the acts of the Edwardian Reformation, the lifting of the prohibition on clerical marriage was surely the one in which participation was most clearly voluntary. Clergy were offered a free choice in the rejection of one of the most visible aspects of the mediaeval heritage of Catholicism, the celibate priesthood, and a significant proportion chose marriage. The actions of the married clergy raise important questions

---

[1] G. Sloyan, 'Biblical and Patristic Motives for Celibacy of Church Ministers', *Concilium*, 8 (1972), pp. 13–29; E. Schillebeeckx, *Clerical Celibacy Under Fire. A Critical Appraisal*, tr. C.A.L. Jarrott (London and Sydney, 1968), pp. 51–6; A.L. Barstow, *Married Priests and the Reforming Papacy: The Eleventh Century Debate*, Texts and Studies in Religion, 12 (1982); J. Bugge, *Virginitas. An Essay in the History of a Medieval Ideal* (The Hague, 1975); D. Callum, 'The Origins of Clerical Celibacy', unpublished D.Phil., University of Oxford (1977); R. Cholij, *Clerical Celibacy in East and West* (Worcester, 1989).

[2] *Table Talk*, *LW*, 54, p. 191, June 1532.

about the spread of the Reformation in England, and the effect of local and national influences upon the belief and conduct of this one section of society.

'God hath opened the press to preach': Printed Books and the Reformation

From the perspective of the mid-sixteenth century, John Foxe could still find cause to rejoice in the death of John Hus, over a century before. In the condemnation of Hus, the church might have silenced one individual, Foxe claimed, but divine providence had ensured that the cause for which Hus had died would not perish with him. 'God hath opened the press to preach,' Foxe declared, 'whose voice the Pope is never able to stop with all the puissance of his triple crown.'[3] Foxe was not alone in his appreciation of the importance of printing to the dissemination of reform, or indeed in believing that such a fortuitous invention was a sign that the Reformation was in accordance with the divine will. Martin Luther had drawn the same conclusion, proclaiming that printing was 'God's highest and extremest act of grace whereby the business of the Gospel is driven forward'.[4] The use of the printing presses by German reformers attracted praise from Nicholas Udall, and the early printed books of the English Reformation were regarded as a means by which to 'help the rude and ignorant people to more knowledge of God and his holy word'.[5] The opponents of reform were quick to recognize the challenge that the reformers' use of printing posed to the preservation of unity and orthodoxy. Roland Phillips, the vicar of Croydon, predicted, 'we must root out printing or printing will root us out', and at the burning of Luther's books in London in May 1521, Bishop Nix of Norwich warned that 'if this continue much longer it will undo us all'.[6] The events of the following decades did little to allay such

---

[3] AM, 1570, p. 837; When Martin Bucer suggested that the Wittenberg reformers would do well do bring their message to the people by preaching, Luther retorted 'we do that with our books'. E. Eisenstein, *The Printing Press as an Agent of Change: Communications and Cultural Transformations in Early Modern Europe*, 2 vols (Cambridge, 1979), 1, p. 373. John Rastell declared that printing was 'the cause of many strau[n]ge thynges here after to come'. E.J. Devereux, 'John Rastell's Press in the English Reformation', *Moreana*, 49 (1976), p. 29.

[4] Eisenstein, *Printing Press*, 1, p. 309.

[5] *The First tome or volume of the Paraphrases of Erasmus* (1549), RSTC 2854, sig. B3v; W.A. Clebsch, *England's Earliest Protestants 1520–1535* (New Haven, 1964), p. 72; L. Ridley, *Commentary in Englyshe vpon ... epystle to the Ephysyans* (1540), RSTC 21038, sig. *1r.

[6] Clebsch, *England's Earliest Protestants*, p. 72; D.M. Loades, 'The Press Under the

fears. Writing in the reign of Mary, Edmund Bonner claimed that 'pernicious and evylle doctryne' had been advanced by the reformers in their sermons, and 'by ther prynted treatyses', and the Catholic writer Miles Huggarde complained that the Marian martyrs would soon be forgotten were it not for the 'three half-penny books that steal out of Germany'.[7]

It was not only the writers themselves who accorded such importance to printing and the written word. The arrival of Lutheran literature and ideas in England in the reign of Henry VIII heralded a campaign of censorship and book-burning which was revived by his daughter Mary. In January 1521, Tunstall wrote to Wolsey with the urgent recommendation that printers and booksellers be forbidden to import or translate Luther's works.[8] Luther's books were burned in Cambridge in 1520, and in London in 1521 and 1526;[9] a list of prohibited literature was issued in 1526, and further enlarged in March 1529.[10] The 1529 proclamation listed 14 heretical works by English and European authors, including Tyndale's *The Practice of Prelates*, and Bullinger's *The Christian State of Matrimony*. A further proclamation in 1530 added to the list, and ordered that no literature should be either printed or imported without episcopal licence. Print was a powerful force: in 1543 the ignorance of the people in matters of religion was blamed upon heretical preaching, ballads and books.[11] In July 1546 a lengthy proclamation for the prohibition of heretical literature was issued, setting forth a list of condemned works which reads as a roll-call of early English evangelical writers, including Tyndale, Wycliffe, Frith,

---

Tudors. A Study in Censorship and Sedition', *Transactions of the Cambridge Bibliographical Society*, 4 (1964), pp. 31–2. Miles Coverdale suggested that the survival of papist literature posed a similar threat to the success of reform, and, presenting Cromwell with a list of such works, offered to purchase and destroy them. *LP*, XIV, i, 444; *LP*, XIV, ii, 782.

[7] M. Huggarde, *The Displaying of the Protestantes* (1556), RSTC 13558, p. 70; E. Bonner, *A Profitable and Necessary Doctrine*, quoted in E. Duffy, *The Stripping of the Altars. Traditional Religion in England 1400–1580* (New Haven, 1992), p. 529.

[8] R. Rex, 'The English Campaign Against Luther in the 1520s', *TRHS*, fifth series, 39 (1989), p. 86; S. Brigden, *London and the Reformation* (Oxford, 1989), p. 157.

[9] Clebsch, *England's Earliest Protestants*, p. 26ff.; D. Daniell, *William Tyndale. A Biography* (New Haven, 1994), pp. 189ff.; Rex, 'Campaign Against Luther', p. 102; C.R. Gillet, *Burned Books. Neglected Chapters in British History and Literature* (New York, 1932), p. 19; C.S. Meyer, 'Henry VIII burns Luther's Books 12 May 1521', *JEH*, 9 (1958), pp. 173–87.

[10] Gillet, *Burned Books*, p. 20; Loades, 'Press Under the Tudors', 32; *TRP*, I, no. 122, 6 March 1529.

[11] *TRP*, I, no. 129, 22 June 1530; Act for the Advancement of True Religion, in Duffy, *Stripping of the Altars*, pp. 432–3; 35 Henry VIII c.1.

Joye, Roy, Becon, Bale and Turner.[12] Within 18 months of her accession, Mary Tudor had issued three proclamations against heretical literature, and in June 1558 the council sanctioned the death penalty for the possession of any heretical or treasonable work, whether English or imported.[13] A proclamation 'prohibiting seditious and heretical books' in July 1555 included the works of 24 prominent reformers, including several who had been condemned by Henry VIII in 1546.[14] The main threat came from the evangelical polemicists in exile, in the form of Latin and English tracts intended for both a domestic and a wider audience.[15] The success of these attempts to control the production and circulation of reformist literature is still disputed, but the fact that such measures were deemed necessary is testimony to the influence that such works were believed to exercise over the people.[16]

The attitude of the Tudors to print was not always hostile. After the initial flurry of censorship and book-burning in the 1520s, Henry VIII was persuaded that official policy and views, not least over the matter of the divorce, could be promulgated effectively in print. The potential of the press in advancing the views of the government was recognized and exploited by Thomas Cromwell in the decade following the break with Rome, and the relaxation of censorship under Protector Somerset encouraged a flood of polemical literature favourable to the Protestant

---

[12] *TRP*, I, no. 272, 8 July 1546; Loades, 'Press Under the Tudors', p. 33; Gillet argues, 'upon these authors and titles a whole history of the attempted reformation might be hung', *Burned Books*, p. 29.

[13] D.M. Loades, *The Reign of Mary Tudor. Politics, Government and Religion in England 1553–1558* (London, 1979), p. 337; *TRP*, II, 4, 5, 41, 90.

[14] *TRP*, II, no. 422, including Bale, Barnes, Tyndale, Coverdale, Becon and Turner.

[15] J. Loach, 'Pamphlets and Politics 1553–1558', *BIHR*, 48 (1975), pp. 35–7; Loades, 'Press Under the Tudors', pp. 37–9; A. Pettegree, 'The Latin Polemic of the Marian Exiles', *Humanism and Reform. The Church in Europe, England and Scotland 1400–1643*, Studies in Church History, Subsidia 8 (1991), pp. 305–39; E. Baskerville, *A Chronological Bibliography of Propaganda and Polemic Published in English between 1553 and 1558* (Philadelphia, 1979).

[16] Loades argues that the 1529 proclamation was fairly effective, although notes that the repeated attempts at censorship in the first years of Mary's reign amount to a confession of failure. 'The Press Under the Tudors', pp. 32, 43–4; *idem, Reign of Mary Tudor*, p. 336. Loach reads a sense of defeat in the wording of the 1558 proclamation: 'Pamphlets and Politics', p. 33, and Gillet suggests that the claim the 'blood of the martyrs is the seed of the church' has parallels in attempts to inhibit book circulation, given that the burning of books automatically attracted more attention than they might otherwise have enjoyed: *Burned Books*, p. 3. There were some notable failures, including Tunstall's efforts to purchase the entire run of English Bibles which merely served to give financial support to the venture, and Thomas More's inclusion of sections of his opponents' works in his own books which made More's work popular among the Brethren, giving them access to the very ideas that he condemned; Brigden, *London*, pp. 181–2.

Reformation.[17] This respect for the power of the printed word, however grudging, has not always been shared by subsequent generations of historians of the Reformation. Where Reformation literature has been studied in detail, the mechanics of the book trade and attempts at official censorship have often attracted more attention than the themes and contents of the books themselves.[18] While Cromwell's contribution to the patronage of Protestant preaching and printed propaganda has long been recognized, Protestant and Catholic literature in the 1540s has often been ignored.[19] Such analysis as there is has often focused upon strident personalities including Thomas More and William Tyndale, and their polemical writings are all too frequently used to analyse the state of mind of the author.[20]

The works of Protestant and Catholic polemicists in the mid-Tudor period often receive only superficial treatment in biographies of the authors, where polemical writings are glossed over as embarrassing

---

[17] G.R. Elton, *Reform and Renewal. Thomas Cromwell and the Common Weal* (Cambridge, 1977), pp. 160ff. For Somerset see pp. 6–7 below.

[18] The importance of the print to the Reformation has, however, been recognized in studies of the printing revolution. See for example Eisenstein, *The Printing Press*, especially ch. 4; S.H. Steinberg, *Five Hundred Years of Printing* (Harmondsworth, 1961). Historians of the continental Protestant Reformation have shown a greater willingness to emphasize the links between print and Protestantism. M.U. Chrisman argues that printed books are 'cultural artefacts which reflect the questions, doubts, assumptions, and certainties of their time', *Lay Culture, Learned Culture. Books and Social Change in Strasbourg 1480–1599* (New Haven, CT and London, 1982), p. xix. Studies of official censorship, and attempts to evade such restriction, include Loades, 'Press Under the Tudors'; Loach, 'Pamphlets and Politics'; M.E. Kronenberg, 'Forged Addresses in Low Country Books in the Period of the Reformation', *The Library*, fifth series, 2 (1947), pp. 81–94.

[19] J. Block, 'Thomas Cromwell's Patronage of Preaching', *Sixteenth Century Journal*, 8 (1977) pp. 37–50; D.M. Loades, *Politics and the Nation 1450–1660*, fourth edition (1992), pp. 180–89; J.N. King, *English Reformation Literature. The Tudor Origins of the Protestant Tradition* (Princeton, 1982), pp. 48–9; G.R. Elton, *Reform and Reformation. England 1509–1558* (London, 1977), pp. 157–68 notes that printing and propaganda boomed during the 1530s, and offers a brief account of the works produced. However, Protestant polemic produced after the relaxation of printing restrictions under Protector Somerset receives only cursory treatment, ibid., p. 343. Dickens allocates six pages to the discussion of Protestant propaganda under Edward VI, much of which is devoted to a study of the social criticisms of the so-called 'Commonwealth men'. However, Dickens does argue that access to printing allowed the Protestant Reformation to succeed where late mediaeval reform movements had failed: *The English Reformation*, second edition (London, 1989), pp. 247–53, 31, 56ff.

[20] Alistair Fox argues that polemical writings provide the 'vital material' for the study of More, but uses these works to argue for a deterioration in the character of the author: *Thomas More, History and Providence* (Oxford, 1982), pp. 3, 111, 117, 122; R. Marius, *Thomas More* (London, 1993); Daniell, *William Tyndale*, especially pp. 250–80; Clebsch, *England's Earliest Protestants*, also adopts an essentially biographical approach, treating the key figures in separate chapters.

lapses into populism. George Joye's biographers devote only 30 pages to his controversial literature, including the debate with Stephen Gardiner, and the polemical works of Coverdale in the period 1535–40 are relegated to the appendix in Mozley's biography.[21] McConica's determination to argue for the continuity of Erasmian reform in the Henrician and Edwardian Reformations leads him to ignore the works of more radical evangelical writers, including Bale, Turner and Joye, and the exile literature that dominated Reformation polemic in the 1540s.[22] Recent biographies of such writers have done something to remedy this deficiency, and give a more prominent role to their controversial writings. William Turner's polemic is described in detail by Whitney Jones, although with little comparative analysis, Thomas Becon's prolific writings from the 1540s feature heavily in D.S. Bailey's biography, and the polemic of John Bale has undergone something of a rehabilitation in recent years.[23]

It is only recently that the literature of the Reformation between 1540 and 1553 has begun to receive greater attention in comparative rather than biographical studies.[24] The work of J.N. King, while written from a literary rather than historical background, has demonstrated the centrality of the printed word in its various forms to the Edwardian Reformation. With the lifting of censorship restrictions, the printing of Protestant polemic soared dramatically, encouraged by the patronage of the duke of Somerset. Protestant writers found posts in the Protector's

---

[21] C.C. Butterworth and A.G. Chester, *George Joye 1495? –1553. A Chapter in the History of the English Bible and the English Reformation* (Philadelphia, 1962), pp. 205–33; J.F. Mozley, *Coverdale and his Bibles* (London, 1953).

[22] J.K. McConica, *English Humanists and Reformation Politics* (Oxford, 1968).

[23] W.R.D. Jones, *William Turner: Tudor Naturalist, Physician, and Divine* (London, 1988); D.S. Bailey, *Thomas Becon and the Reformation of the Church of England* (Edinburgh, 1952); L.P. Fairfield, *John Bale, Mythmaker for the English Reformation* (West Lafayette, Indiana, 1976); *idem*, 'John Bale and the Development of Protestant Hagiography in England', *JEH*, 24 (1973), pp. 145–60; H. McCusker, *John Bale: Dramatist and Antiquary* (Bryn Mawr, 1942); W.T. Davies, 'A Bibliography of John Bale', *Papers and Proceedings of the Oxford Bibliographical Society*, 5 (1936), pp. 201–80; J.W. Harris, *John Bale: A Study in the Minor Literature of the Reformation* (Urbana, Illinois, 1940).

[24] M.R. Powell, 'The Polemical Literature of the English Protestant Reformers *c*. 1534–1547', unpublished Ph.D., University of Edinburgh (1984); Catherine M.F. Davies, 'Towards a Godly Commonwealth. The Public Ideology of Protestantism c1546–1553', unpublished Ph.D., University of London (1988); *idem*, '"Poor Persecuted Little Flock" or "Commonwealth of Christians". Edwardian Protestant Concepts of the Church', in P. Lake and M. Dowling, eds, *Protestantism and the National Church in Sixteenth Century England* (London, 1987), pp. 78–102; King, *English Reformation Literature*; L.E.C. Wooding, 'From Humanists to Heretics: English Catholic Theology and Ideology c.1530–1570', unpublished D.Phil., University of Oxford (1995).

household, dedicated their works to him, and produced popular literature which paralleled the needs and objectives of the Reformation in the first years of the reign of Edward VI.[25] The first months of the reign witnessed a dramatic upsurge in debate on the theology of the Eucharist, preceding the publication of the first Edwardian Prayer Book in 1549. Over 30 tracts were printed in 1548, launching a vitriolic attack on the doctrine of transubstantiation, and often advancing radical Protestant doctrines. Indeed the content of these works cast doubt upon McConica's argument for the continuity of Erasmianism in the Edwardian Reformation.[26] Although Stephen Gardiner complained that Somerset was unable to control this flood of literature, it is clear that the Edwardian government recognized the value of print to the dissemination of reform. Evangelical polemic set forth defences of the government programme of reform, and created an image of the young Edward as a king in the mould of reforming Old Testament monarchs, most notably the boy king Josiah.[27]

In the works of such writers, the Reformation itself was represented as a clash of literary cultures. The narrator of *A Pore Helpe* cast himself in the role of the reactionary by his preference for superstitious practices over the English Bible and Paraphrases, and Shepherd set the two armies in this battle of the books face to face in a catalogue of contemporary Catholic and Protestant writers.[28] The polemical literature of the Reformation is of great value to the historian attempting to identify the ideology, ambitions and achievements of Reformation protagonists. For the first time in history, a propaganda campaign was conducted through the medium of print; as W.A. Clebsch suggests, the character of English-

[25] King, *English Reformation Literature*, chs 2–4; *idem,*'Protector Somerset, Patron of the English Renaissance', *The Papers of the Bibliographical Society of America*, 70 (1976), pp. 307–31; *idem*, 'Freedom of the Press, Protestant Propaganda, and Protector Somerset', *Huntingdon Library Quarterly*, 40 (1976–77), pp. 1–10. Luke Shepherd's *John Bon and Mast Person* appeared on the eve of Corpus Christi in 1548, a move which appeared timed to coincide with the suppression of the feast. However, Duffy notes that its appearance did land its publishers in trouble: *Stripping of the Altars*, p. 460; King, *English Reformation Literature*, pp. 258–9. Of the 394 extant English works from the Protectorate, some 274 dealt with religious matters, of which 160 propounded controversial doctrines. Forty-nine of these were by authors whose works had been prohibited by Henry VIII. King, 'Freedom of the Press', pp. 2–3. Works by authors such as Bale, Barnes, Becon, Turner and Tyndale were reprinted and allowed to circulate freely. King, *English Reformation Literature*, pp. 88–9.
[26] King, 'Freedom of the Press', pp. 3–5.
[27] King, *English Reformation Literature*, pp. 52–4, 161–206; *idem, Tudor Royal Iconography. Literature and Art in an Age of Religious Crisis* (Princeton, 1989), pp. 90–101. See Chapter 6 below.
[28] L. Shepherd, *A Pore Helpe* (1548), RSTC 13051.7, sig. A3r; King, *English Reformation Literature*, p. 257.

speaking Christianity was formed by 'England's earliest Protestants and their books'.[29] The works of Reformation polemicists, both Protestant and Catholic, offer a sense of the objectives of their authors, their preoccupations and their attitudes to contemporary events. Printed books provide a link between idea and event, between policy and practice. If the written word is considered not as autonomous, but as something inseparable from its specific historical context, it becomes invaluable to the historian for the insights which it can offer into literary, political and religious culture of the time. The aspirations of Reformation writers are manifested in their works, which provide a testimony of personal belief and popular attitudes in many cases unmatched by the official records of the Reformation.[30]

Clerical Marriage and the Reformation

Despite its importance in the eyes of theologians, polemicists and even monarchs in the sixteenth century, the lifting of the prohibition on clerical marriage, and particularly the debate that sustained it, has attracted little attention from historians. The work of H.C. Lea, now nearly a century old, has remained the standard study of the history of sacerdotal celibacy, although its treatment of the Reformation period is patchy and somewhat polemical. Lea presents a summary of the process by which compulsory clerical celibacy was introduced in the church, and offers a straightforward account of views and legislation on clerical marriage during the era of Reformation in England and Europe. His treatment of the printed debate on clerical celibacy is somewhat scanty, however, and his analysis of the tone of the Edwardian Act which legalized clerical marriage has exerted undue influence over subsequent historians.[31] In recent years, the English debate on clerical marriage has received rather more attention. J.K. Yost has provided a brief summary of reformist arguments in favour of clerical marriage in the first half of the sixteenth century, largely based upon the works of Barnes, Joye and Ponet. However, the analysis of a limited number of works cannot do justice to the complexity of the debate. The polemicists under consideration were clearly not the only evangelical writers active in the

---

[29] L.P. Febvre (tr. D. Gerard), *The Coming of the Book. The Impact of Printing 1450–1800* (London, 1976), p. 288; Clebsch, *England's Earliest Protestants*, pp. 2–3.

[30] Davies, '"Poor Persecuted Little Flock"', *passim*; Stephen Greenblatt, *Renaissance Self-Fashioning From More to Shakespeare* (Chicago, 1980).

[31] H.C. Lea, *History of Sacerdotal Celibacy in the Christian Church* third edition (1907). For an account of Tudor legislation on clerical marriage, including the 1549 statute, see Chapters 1 and 8 below.

mid-sixteenth century, but more importantly, Yost offers no analysis of Catholic defences of celibacy in the same period.[32]

The most recent study of the impact of the Reformation upon attitudes to marriage in general, and clerical marriage in particular, is Eric Carlson's *Marriage and the English Reformation*.[33] The thrust of Carlson's argument is that the English Reformation was not followed by a transformation of attitudes to marriage and marriage law to the same degree as took place in Protestant churches on the Continent. Moving to the subject of clerical marriage in particular, Carlson claims that 'the celibate ideal was not attacked in England with either the vigour or immediate success that characterised such attacks elsewhere'.[34] Those who participated in the polemical debate on clerical marriage, with the exception of Thomas Becon, had little positive to say about marriage, and all remained unmarried themselves.[35] This lack of enthusiasm for a married priesthood spawned 'an English reformed tradition of ambivalence' to clerical marriage which persisted into the reign of Elizabeth.[36] While Carlson's detailed analysis of marriage law is clearly important, the chapter that examines clerical marriage is not without flaws. Carlson fails to place the controversy over clerical marriage within the context of other Reformation debates, and the contention that English polemicists were ambivalent towards marriage is not supported by their words and actions. Several writers on clerical marriage were in fact married themselves, most notably Thomas Cranmer, William Turner, John Ponet and Miles Coverdale. John Bale is ignored almost entirely, despite his prolific outpourings on the subject. The reappraisal of marriage in the works of continental reformers to which Carlson refers has long been recognized, and English polemicists clearly sympathized with their views.[37] A variety of works were published in English in praise of marriage, and the numerous editions of Coverdale's translation of Bullinger's *Der Christliche Ehestand* suggests that the work was popular, and in accordance with the general attitude of the reformers. In 1540, George

---

[32] J.K. Yost, 'The Reformation Defence of Clerical Marriage in the Reign of Henry VIII and Edward VI', *Church History*, 50 (1981), pp. 52–65.

[33] E. Carlson, *Marriage and the English Reformation* (Oxford, 1994); *idem*, 'Clerical Marriage and the English Reformation', *Journal of British Studies*, 31 (1992), pp. 1–31.

[34] Carlson, *Marriage and the English Reformation*, pp. 3, 7.

[35] Ibid., p. 54. Becon was clearly married, and was deprived of his benefices as a married priest in the reign of Mary, despite Carlson's assertion in the earlier article that 'Becon himself never married': 'Clerical Marriage', pp. 9–10. Bailey, *Thomas Becon*.

[36] Carlson, *Clerical Marriage*, 2.

[37] For the reappraisal of marriage in the continental Reformation see S. Ozment, *When Fathers Ruled. Family Life in Reformation Europe* (Cambridge, Mass., 1983).

Joye translated Philip Melanchthon's *Defensio Conjugii Sacerdotum*, a vehement attack on the enforcement of clerical celibacy, which also included a lengthy defence of the estate of marriage. Melanchthon's work clearly influenced the content, if not the tone, of Joye's *Defence of the Mariage of Preistes* of 1541, and in his translation of Zwingli's *Christianae Fidei*, Joye added a text, 'the complaining prayer of the poor persecuted marriage priests', an impassioned plea on behalf of the exiled reformers, married clergy and their families.[38] If English Protestants were not writing extensively on marriage themselves, they were at least active in bringing the opinions of their European associates to the attention of an English audience.

Contrary to Carlson's contention, there are many positive affirmations of marriage in English polemical literature. References to the honour of marriage abound in such works, and the frequent assertion in the works of English writers that marriage was a form of chastity suggests that they held both marriage and chastity in high esteem.[39] William Tyndale, for example, who Carlson claims held a strong preference for the single life, argued that marriage made available the merits of the death of Christ, 'and the man by that marriage is pure as Christ, and cleane wythout sinne, and honourable, and in fauour thorow ye grace of that mariage'.[40] Carlson's argument that the English attack on clerical celibacy lacked the vigour of continental demands for a married priesthood is contradicted by the vehemence of the language in native

---

[38] W. Harrington, *The Commendacions of Matrymony* (1528), RSTC 12799; D. Erasmus (tr. Richard Taverner), *A ryght fruteful Epystle in laude and Praise of Matrymony* (1536), RSTC 10492; *The Commendation of Matrimony made by Cornelius Agrippa & translated into English by David Clapam* (1545), RSTC 202; Coverdale's translation appeared in 1541 as *The Christian State of Matrimony*, and was reprinted in 1543 with a preface by Becon as *The Golden Book of Christian Matrimony*. It ran to nine editions between 1541 and 1575; P. Melanchthon (tr. G. Joye), *A very godly defense ... defending the mariage of preistes* (Antwerp, 1541), RSTC 17798; G. Joye, *The Rekening and declaratio[n] of the faith of H. Zwingly* (Antwerp, 1543), RSTC 26138.

[39] Becon, *Book of Matrimony*, in Becon, *Worckes* (1564), RSTC 1710, fols GGg4r, GGg5r, HHh5v–6r, PPp3v; G. Joye, *The Letters whych Johan Ashwell ... sente secretly to the byshope of Lincolne* (Antwerp, 1531), RSTC 845, sig. F1v; G. Joye, *The Defence of the Mariage of Preistes* (Antwerp, 1541), RSTC 21804, sig. A4r; J. Bale, *The Actes of the Englysh Votaries*, pt I (Antwerp, 1546), RSTC 1270, fol. 13r; H. Latimer, 'A Sermon Preached ... the 17th day Janurary Anno 1552', in G.E. Corrie ed., *The sermons of Hugh Latimer sometime bishop of Worcester*, Parker Society (Cambridge, 1844), pp. 160–66; J. Ponet, *A defence for the mariage of Preistes* (1549), RSTC 20176, sig. A6vff.

[40] Tyndale, *Answer to More's Dialogue*, WW, p. 312. While the focus of this book is the treatment of clerical marriage in Reformation polemic, there are occasions on which the discussion will touch upon the debate over the value of marriage in general terms. The Protestant defence of clerical marriage from Scripture (Chapter 2 below) depended heavily upon biblical verses which praised marriage *per se*.

evangelical polemic, and by the almost disproportionate attention paid to the issue in such literature.

Attacks on clerical celibacy featured in anti-Mass tracts, in commentaries on the Apocalypse, and were a pivotal part of the emergent Protestant history of the English and Roman church.[41] Promises of celibacy were condemned as acts of idolatry, and the continued existence of a celibate priesthood under Henry VIII led Protestant writers to draw parallels between his actions and the rule of idolatrous Old Testament kings.[42] It is something of a distortion to search for declarations of the superiority of marriage over virginity in Protestant polemic on clerical celibacy, and unreasonable to expect all defenders of clerical marriage themselves to marry. It was the enforcement of compulsory celibacy, and not chastity itself, that was inherently wrong in the eyes of Protestant writers. God might call an individual to chastity or to marriage, and it was outside the authority of the church on earth to compel man to live in one state or another. Marriage vows did not offer a short cut to salvation any more than did vows of chastity. To expect the whole of the first generation of English reformers to marry, and to praise marriage over virginity, as Carlson appears to do, is to expect them to renounce their determination to follow biblical models and injunctions. Thus while Carlson's work may be useful for the insights which it offers into marriage law and practice in sixteenth-century England, it does little to improve modern knowledge of the vigorous debate on clerical marriage.

The Reformation Debate on Clerical Marriage

It was not until 1549 that clerical marriage was legalized in England. However, the issue of clerical celibacy had attracted the attention of both Catholic and Protestant polemicists for at least twenty years before this date, and the debate continued throughout the reigns of Edward and Mary and beyond. Clerical celibacy was discussed in both popular English works and Latin treatises. The tone of polemical debate in the Reformation, and particularly the debate on clerical marriage, was frequently abusive, and the language crude, with the result that such works have been largely dismissed by literary critics, and censored in

---

[41] See Chapters 4, 5 and 7 below. For more general comments on the development of Protestant history see R. Pineas, 'William Tyndale's Use of History as a Weapon of Religious Controversy', *Harvard Theological Review*, 55 (1962), pp. 121–41; 'William Tyndale's Influence on John Bale's Polemical Use of History', *ARG*, 53 (1962), pp. 79–96.

[42] See Chapter 6 below.

their nineteenth-century Parker Society reprints.[43] However, such language was often part of the controversy itself. Bale's condemnation of the Catholic clergy with the declaration 'beastly are they in ther doctrine and their lyuyng' was not just an ill-considered accusation, but an idea that was a central feature of Reformation polemic.[44] Issues of morality and theology were inextricably linked in the minds of many polemicists, both Catholic and Protestant, and allegations of sexual misconduct added weight to doctrinal debate. While Thomas More attempted to use Luther's marriage to discredit his teaching, Protestant polemicists constructed a historical narrative of the misdeeds of the Catholic clergy to demonstrate that celibacy was an impossible ideal, and to argue that the theology which underpinned it was flawed. In terms of polemical capital, attacks on the morality of opponents could be as fruitful as detailed theological argument, and the language of debate reflected this. The moral conduct of the clergy was immediately obvious to the majority of the faithful in a way in which the intricacies of doctrinal debate were not. The argument that Christ would not be made present on the altar at Mass by the words of an unchaste priest was more firmly grounded in reality than a detailed scriptural exegesis on the subject of the Real Presence, even if theological precision was sacrificed in the process.

Polemical literature was fundamentally divisive. In the minds of Reformation writers, there could be no compromise between truth and falsehood, between Christ and Antichrist. Stephen Greenblatt has argued that Renaissance identity was defined in terms of another alien entity, a suggestion borne out in Thomas More's equation of the heretic with that which was most foreign: the bestial, the chaotic and the demonic.[45] Certainly, the polemical debate on clerical marriage was conducted in terms of opposing extremes. Chastity was set against unchastity; scriptural truth against the doctrines of men; the persecuted against the persecutor; the spouse of Christ against the whore of Babylon; and the godly king against the idolater. This contrast between truth and error was to become a central feature of Protestant history, finding its clearest expression in Bale's *Image of Both Churches* and Foxe's *Actes and Monuments*. However, these stark polarities were commonplace in the literature of the English Reformation from the earliest years, and Bale's delineation of the true church and the false has clear parallels

---

[43] Duffy refers to the 'blustering scurrilities' of Bale and Becon: *Stripping of the Altars*, p. 529. The language of polemic has parallels in the visual imagery of the Reformation: R. Scribner, *Popular Culture and Popular Movements in Reformation Germany* (London, 1987), especially ch. 13.

[44] J. Bale, *Yet a Course at the Romyshe Foxe* (Antwerp, 1543), RSTC 1309.

[45] Greenblatt, *Self-Fashioning*, pp. 9, 65, 86.

with Thomas More's invitation to the reader to choose between the teachings of an unchaste monk and those of the holy saints of the church.[46]

It was Luther's marriage, and the Catholic reaction to it, that opened the floodgates in the debate on clerical marriage. Luther's marriage provided Thomas More with the opening for an attack on Reformation morality and doctrine, and the marriage of leading reformers was to play a vital role in the conservative villification of their teachings.[47] The whole of Luther's teaching should be prohibited, More argued, on the grounds that people would benefit by listening to the teachings of the pure angels rather than those of 'an open incestuouse lechour / a playne limme of the devil / and a manyfest messenger of hell'.[48] Luther was cast in the role of 'Luder', the self-contradictory simpleton, promulgating doctrines which were ill considered and which threatened to bring chaos and disorder to the church. His marriage, and the breaking of his vow of chastity, were an indication of his shameless impiety and the error of his teachings.[49]

Late in 1528, Tunstall warned of the threat which heretical literature posed to the English church, and called upon More to produce a defence of the institutional church. More was to write 'for the common man some books that would help him see through the cunning malice of the heretics, and so keep him alerted and better fortified against these traitorous subverters of the church'.[50] The *Dialogue Concerning Heresies*, More's response to Tunstall's request, appeared in June 1529. William Tyndale replied with the *Answer to Sir Thomas More's Dialogue* (1531), and clerical marriage – and Luther's marriage in particular – were a prominent feature of the ensuing debate. More attempted to use Luther's marriage to discredit Tyndale's writings, while Tyndale argued that the prohibition of clerical marriage proved that the Roman church was not the church of Christ. In contrast, More's constant references to married clergy and religious, particularly Luther, did much to establish broken vows of celibacy as the mark of the heretic.

---

[46] T. More, *Dialogue Concerning Heresies*, CW, 6, p. 434.

[47] More, *Responsio ad Lutherum* (1523), CW, 5; *Dialogue* (1529), CW, 6; *Confutation of Tyndale's Answer* (1532), CW, 8. For the discussion of these works by recent historians see Marius, *Thomas More*, pp. 281ff., 340–50; Daniell, *William Tyndale*, pp. 262–9; Fox, *Thomas More*; Clebsch, *England's Earliest Protestants*, ch. 15; L.A. Schuster, 'Thomas More's Polemical Career 1523–1533', CW, 8, pp. 1137–268; J.M. Headley, 'Thomas More and Luther's Revolt', *ARG*, 60 (1969), pp. 145–60.

[48] More, *Dialogue*, p. 346.

[49] Fox, *Thomas More*, pp. 141ff.

[50] E.F. Rogers, *The Correspondence of Sir Thomas More* (Princeton, 1947), pp. 387, 19–26.

By the close of the decade, clerical marriage had become a central feature of Reformation controversy.[51]

In the two decades that followed, polemical literature on clerical marriage was almost totally dominated by original works by evangelical writers, and translations of the works of continental reformers.[52] Several of the first generation of reformers at Cambridge were to become involved in the debate on clerical marriage. After his arrest in 1525 and subsequent abjuration, Robert Barnes fled to Antwerp, and by the summer of 1530 was a guest of Bugenhagen in Wittenberg.[53] In 1530 he published the *Sentenciae ex Doctoribus Collectae*, a section of which was devoted to biblical, patristic and historical evidence in favour of the marriage of priests. Much of this material was to feature in his later writings on clerical marriage. In 1534 Barnes added a defence of such marriages to the revised edition of the *Supplication*, arguing that they were in accordance with the law of God, and justified by Scripture, the Fathers, and the 'examples and practyse of holy and vertuous men'.[54] The *Vitae Romanorum Pontificum* included a detailed account of the enforcement of clerical celibacy in the pontificate of Gregory VII, and Barnes's history of the church, and especially his history of the papacy, was to exert considerable influence over the debate on clerical marriage

---

[51] Other works from the 1520s which discuss clerical marriage include Joye, *Letters whych Johan Ashwell ... sente secretly to the byshope of Lincolne* (Antwerp, 1531), RSTC 845; W. Roy, *Rede me and be nott wroth* (n.p., 1528), RSTC 21427; J. Frith, *A Pistle to the Christen reader: The Reuelacion of Antichrist* (Antwerp, 1529), RSTC 11394.

[52] On the Catholic side, Richard Whitford's *Pype or Tonne* was printed in 1532 (RSTC 25421). Whitford, a close friend of Erasmus, had composed the work several years before as a refutation of the teachings of Martin Luther, and a defence of the religious life and vows, and J. Hogg suggests that the work had already circulated in manuscript before its publication by Redman. *Richard Whitford's 'The Pype or Tonne of the Lyfe of Perfection' with an Introductory Study on Whitford's Works* (Salzburg, 1979), pp. 20, 100–102. Dionysius, *The Lyfe of Prestes* was reprinted in 1533 (RSTC 6894). Dionysius was a Carthusian monk, active in the first half of the fifteenth century, but his works on the religious life, and particularly his defence of the purity of priesthood, had much to offer those who took to the defence of the religious life in the 1530s in England. R. Macken, 'Denys the Carthusian. Commentator on Boethius "De Consolatione Philosophiae"', *Analecta Carthusiana*, 118 (1984). *Dives and Pauper*, an exposition of the Ten Commandments, which dated from the first half of the fifteenth century, was reissued in 1536 (RSTC 19214). However, such works hardly constituted an effective response to the Protestant attack on clerical celibacy. Miles Huggarde followed More in ridiculing married priests and their wives in *The Displaying of the Protestantes* (1556), RSTC 13558, but only Stephen Gardiner and Richard Smith produced forceful defences of clerical celibacy. See pp. 18ff. below.

[53] Clebsch, *England's Earliest Protestants*, p. 42.

[54] R. Barnes, *A Supplication unto the most gracious prince Henry VIII* (1534), RSTC 1471, sig. Q2v.

in future years.[55] The *Vitae Romanorum Pontificum* was expanded by
John Bale, and Bale's history of the enforcement of clerical celibacy has
much in common with details provided by Barnes in the *Supplication*.[56]

Among the English writers of the 1540s, the figure of John Bale looms
large in polemical debate, particularly in arguments against clerical
celibacy. A former Carmelite, Bale had been converted to the Reformation by the mid-1530s, and turned to writing vitriolic and profuse
polemic against the Catholic church.[57] Bale enjoyed the protection and
patronage of Cromwell, but fled abroad after the passing of the Act of
Six Articles in 1539. In exile he produced a string of polemical treatises
highly critical of the state of the church in England, and of the English
bishops in particular.[58] Despite the initial promise of reform, Bale
contested, the pope had been banished from the realm in name alone,
while the bishops upheld popish doctrines and ceremonies. In the eyes of
Bale, clerical celibacy was not only the doctrine of the Antichrist and the
root cause of abundant clerical immorality, but also evidence that the
English church was not the true congregation. Bale's approach to church
history owed much to the work of Tyndale, but Bale was to add new
emphases, particularly in the central role which he accorded to clerical
celibacy and morality.[59] The *Image of Both Churches*, Bale's commentary on the Book of Revelation, was first printed in Antwerp in 1545,
reprinted in 1548, twice in 1550, and again in 1570. The work formed
the basis of the notes on Revelation in the Geneva Bible in 1560, and was
translated into Dutch in Emden in 1555. The first part of *The Actes of
the Englysh Votaries* was reprinted three times, and the first two parts
were printed together in 1551 and 1560.[60] Bale's history of the church,
and particularly the separation and identification of the true and false
churches, exerted a powerful influence over other writers, especially
John Foxe.[61]

[55] Barnes, *Sentenciae ex Doctoribus Collectae* (Wittenberg, 1536), sigs F2v–G1v; *Vitae Romanorum Pontificum* (Basle, 1555), fols 186–216.

[56] Barnes, *Vitae Romanorum Pontificum*; J. Bale, *Acta Romanorum Pontificum* (Basle, 1558). See Chapter 4 below.

[57] Fairfield, *John Bale*, p. 31.

[58] Bale, *Romyshe Foxe*; *A Mystery of Inyquyte* (Antwerp, 1545), RSTC 1303; *The Image of Both Churches* (1550), RSTC 1298; *The First Examinacyon of Anne Askewe* (Wesel, 1546), RSTC 848; *The Lattre Examinacyon of Anne Askewe* (Wesel, 1547), RSTC 850; *Actes of the Votaries*.

[59] Pineas, 'William Tyndale's influence on John Bale', pp. 79–96. Bale's concern to place clerical celibacy and morality at the centre of his history of the church is clearest in *The Actes of the Englysh Votaries*, but also has a strong influence on his apocalyptic interpretation of the past in *The Image of Both Churches*; see Chapters 4 and 5 below.

[60] STC 1296.5, 1297, 1298, 1299, 1301.

[61] In Foxe's account of the imposition of clerical celibacy in the eleventh century, there

Bale's obsession with clerical celibacy and clerical morality ensures him a dominant role in the polemical literature on the subject during the Reformation. However, Bale was far from alone among evangelical writers in his hostility to clerical celibacy, and the Act of Six Articles prompted a further upsurge in the volume of English Protestant polemic. English exiles, including George Joye and William Turner, produced works that were highly critical of the religious situation in England, and the prohibition of clerical marriage featured high on their list of complaints. The English church, it was claimed, was as yet unreformed, and Catholic doctrine, the 'Romish Fox', was preserved in England by the bishops, and by the failure of the king to effect a complete break with the church of Antichrist.[62] The period of exile in the last years of Henry VIII's reign was to exert a powerful influence over the development of Protestant identity among this group of writers, and further strengthened the ideological links between England and the Continent.[63]

The literature of the Henrician exiles shared common themes and ideals, and its authors enjoyed relative freedom from persecution while they remained abroad. Other evangelical writers remained in England, and the tone of their work is more cautious. Thomas Becon was arrested in 1541, after preaching in defence of the Reformation in Norwich. Although there are no surviving copies of this recantation, Becon admitted in his second recantation that he had preached against prayer to the saints, the sacrament of the altar, and 'against the contynencie of prysts'. His books were burned at his recantation in March 1541, and Becon retired to Kent.[64] In the period after the recantation, Becon continued to publish under the name of Theodore Basille, although the majority of his printed works were devotional rather than polemical. Becon also provided the preface to Coverdale's translation of Bullinger's

are clear similarities with Bale's history. It was Bale who first associated the prohibition of marriage to the clergy with Silvester II and his alleged witchcraft, and Foxe adopted Bale's condemnation of Gregory VII as a necromancer. See pp. 110–12, 124–7 below.

[62] Bale, *Romyshe Foxe*; *A Mysterye of Inyquyte*; *The Actes of the Votaries*; G. Joye, *The Exposiction of Daniel the Prophete* (Antwerp, 1545), RSTC 14823; *George Ioye confuteth Winchesters false Articles* (Antwerp, 1543); *The Refutation of the byshop of Winchesters derke declaration* (1546); *Defence of the Mariage of Preistes*; Butterworth, *George Joye*, pp. 26–36. Joye's exact movements are unclear. His early works used a Strasbourg colophon, possibly to confuse his opponents, and Butterworth suggests that it is likely that they were printed in Antwerp; Jones, *William Turner*; W. Turner, *The Huntyng & fyndyng out of the Romishe fox* (Antwerp, 1543), RSTC 24354; *The Rescuynge of the Romishe Fox* (Bonn, 1545), RSTC 24355.

[63] Turner's friendship with John a Lasco encouraged Cranmer to invite him to England. H. Robinson, *Original Letters*, Parker Society, 2 vols (Cambridge, 1846), I, pp. 16–18. The influence of exile in the development of justifications for the Reformation is discussed in A. Pettegree, *Marian Protestantism. Six Studies* (Aldershot, 1996), Introduction.

[64] Bailey, *Thomas Becon*, pp. 14–16.

Der Christliche Ehestand, which appeared as *The Golden Book of Christian Matrimony* in 1543. While the work was primarily in praise of marriage, Becon's preface was highly critical of those who spurned marriage.[65] The translation of Bullinger's work was clearly relevant to the situation in England, and carried implied criticism of the continued prohibition on clerical marriage. The appearance of the work on lists of prohibited books, and the fact that it ran to at least nine editions, testify to its popularity and importance. The attribution of the translation to Becon on the title page suggests that he was a well-respected writer; Becon himself claimed that the printer had set forth the work in his name believing that to do so would increase its sales.[66]

The legalization of clerical marriage in 1549, and the action taken against married priests in 1553, prompted further debate on clerical celibacy.[67] John Ponet entered into the fray with the *Defence for the mariage of Preistes* of 1549, which elicited a reply from Thomas Martin in 1554.[68] Ponet responded in 1555, claiming that the name of Thomas Martin was merely a pseudonym for Stephen Gardiner, and promised that his work would allow the papists to 'see their own impudency and confusion'.[69] The debate between Ponet and Martin was in effect a battle for the possession of Scripture and the heritage of the early church. Both writers argued that their position could be justified by reference to Scripture, and claimed the example of the Apostles and the primitive church as their own. Where Ponet claimed that the prohibition of clerical marriage was a departure from the pure faith of the primitive church, Martin argued that clerical marriage had been the mark of the heretic from the earliest Christian centuries. Martin exploited the unfortunate circumstances of Ponet's marriage to his own advantage, while Ponet argued that the forced separation of married priests from their wives in the reign of Mary gave the lie to Martin's assertion that they were 'pretensed marriages'.

Martin was one of the few Catholic controversialists active in the

---

[65] Bullinger (tr. Coverdale/Becon), *The Golden Book of Christian Matrimony* (Antwerp, 1543), RSTC 4046, sig. A2rff. Becon's major original work on marriage and clerical celibacy, *The Booke of Matrimony*, was not printed until the appearance of the folio edition of his works.

[66] Becon's claim was made in the preface to the folio edition of his works.

[67] A. Gilby, *An Answer to the Deuillish Detection of Stephane Gardiner* (1547), RSTC 11884. The lifting of printing restrictions was followed by a flood of publications on the Mass, many of which touched upon the issue of clerical celibacy. See Chapter 7 below.

[68] J. Ponet, *A defence for the mariage of Preistes, by Scripture and Aunciente Wryters* (1549), RSTC 20176; T. Martin, *A Treatise declarying and plainly provyng that the pretensed marriage of priestes ... is no mariage* (1554), RSTC 17517.

[69] J. Ponet, *An Apologie fully aunsweringe ... D. Steph. Gardiner* (Strasbourg, 1555), RSTC 20175.

middle decades of the sixteenth century to take an active part in the debate on clerical marriage.[70] The literature of the evangelical exiles in the later years of Henry VIII's reign had prompted Stephen Gardiner to enter the debate (although his work now survives only in Turner's answer to it, *The Rescuynge of the Romishe Fox*), and Miles Huggarde launched a spirited attack on Protestant morality and doctrine in 1556.[71] While the subject of clerical marriage clearly lent itself to the scurrilous style of popular polemic, several treatises were printed in Latin, presumably for a specifically clerical or international readership.[72] In the 1540s, Stephen Gardiner had entered into a literary exchange with Martin Bucer, in which the celibacy of the clergy was a dominant feature. The debate was opened in 1544, with Gardiner claiming that Bucer, in a debate with Latomus, had misrepresented Gardiner's views on clerical celibacy as expressed at Ratisbon.[73] Bucer did not produce a reply immediately, leading Gardiner to reissue the letter in 1545, and to publish a second work against Bucer in 1546, in which he repeated his defence of clerical celibacy.[74] Bucer eventually entered into the debate in 1548 with the *Gratulatio*,[75] translated into English in 1549. Gardiner replied almost immediately, although the text of his reply was not printed until 1554.[76]

Bucer was not the only continental theologian to influence the debate on clerical marriage in England. Peter Martyr entered into a Latin controversy with Richard Smith in the 1550s,[77] and the works of other foreign Protestants were translated by English reformers. Coverdale's translation of Bullinger's work on marriage circulated widely in England, and a string of works by other continental writers on marriage were also translated into English. In 1529 William Roy published a translation of

---

[70] For Catholic literature in general see Wooding, 'From Humanists to Heretics'.

[71] Huggarde, *Dislaying of the Protestantes*.

[72] Pettegree, 'Latin Polemic', pp. 305–6.

[73] *Stephani Vvinton. Episcopi Angli ad Martin Bucerum Epistola de impudente eiusdem Pseudologia Conquestio* (Louvain, 1544). Gardiner drew attention to Paul's statement 'Bonum est hominem mulierem non tangere', while Bucer argued from the apparently contradictory advice 'it is better to marry than to burn'. For a further discussion of the debate over the meaning of these texts see Chapter 2 below.

[74] *Ad Martin Bucerum Epistola* (Louvain, 1545).

[75] M. Bucer, *Gratulatio Martini Buceri ad ecclesiam Anglicanam* (Basle, 1548), translated into English by Sir Thomas Hoby as the *Gratulation of ... Martin Bucer ... unto the church of England* (1549), RSTC 3963.

[76] *Exetasis Testimoniorvm quae Martinus Bucerus ex sanctis patribus non sancte edidit* (Louvain, 1554).

[77] Smith published his *Defensio sacri Episcoporu[m] & sacerdotum coelibatus* (Paris, 1550); Martyr's reply came with the *Defensio de Petri Martyris Vermilii florentini divinarum literarum in schola Tigurina* (Basle, 1559).

Luther's commentary on 1 Corinthians 7, a crucial text in the debate on clerical marriage, and John Frith translated Luther's *de Antichristo* in the same year. Frith added the 'Pistle to the Christen reader' to Luther's discussion of Antichrist, but this was the only part of the work which was original.[78] The commentary established clerical celibacy as an invention of the Antichrist, a theme expounded at length in the treatment of Daniel 11:37.[79] From the outset, the treatment of clerical celibacy in English polemic was heavily influenced by the ideology of the continental Reformation.

William Turner's polemic in the 1540s owed much to the works that he had translated in the previous decade. The criticism of ritual, ceremonial and doctrinal innovation in Turner's later work has strong parallels with *Vom Alten und Neuen Gott*, which Turner translated in 1534, and in the *Co[m]parison betwene the olde learnynge & the newe*, translated from Urbanus Rhegius in 1537.[80] In 1541, George Joye published a translation of Melanchthon's work on clerical marriage, as *A very godly defence ... of the mariage of preistes*, which Melanchthon had addressed to the king in the aftermath of the Act of Six Articles. While Joye claimed that he had written his own defence of clerical marriage before this was printed, the two writers shared the same concerns. Both condemned the oppressive nature of the 1539 legislation, criticized vows of chastity, and complained that the church tolerated clerical fornication while forbidding the godly state of matrimony to its priests. The exchange of material relating to clerical marriage between English and continental reformers was to continue. In April 1556, Ponet asked Bullinger to send him 'a transcript from the epistle to the Philadelphians respecting the marriage of Paul and the other apostles', which Ponet wished to use in his controversy with 'a most impudent papist', probably Thomas Martin.[81] Peter Martyr carried the letter to Bullinger, who duly supplied a copy of the letter of Ignatius, which he had procured from Conrad Gesner. Ponet expressed his gratitude to Bullinger, and his admiration for Gesner, declaring that the papers provided by Gesner would be numbered 'among my choicest treasures', and admitting that he preserved the 'memorials' of such great men.[82] The

---

[78] M. Luther, *Das Siebend capitel S Pauli zu den Chorinthern* (Wittenberg, 1523); W.A. Clebsch, 'The earliest translations of Luther into English', *Harvard Theological Review*, 55 (1963), pp. 75–86; *idem, England's Earliest Protestants*, pp. 72, 86.

[79] See below, Chapter 5.

[80] J. von Watt (tr. W. Turner), *A Worke entytled of ye olde god & the newe* (1534), RSTC 25127; *The Olde Learnynge & the Newe* (Southwark,1537), RSTC 20840. A further edition of *The Olde Learnynge & the Newe* was printed in 1538.

[81] *Original Letters*, I, p. 116.

[82] Ibid., p. 117. Ponet's connections with Martyr were to cause problems for his wife. Ponet had apparently borrowed a number of books from Martyr, which his wife had sold

debate on clerical marriage in English polemic was not conducted in a vacuum.

Melanchthon's defence of clerical marriage was not Joye's only venture into the works of continental writers. In 1545 he published *The Exposicion of Daniel the Prophete*, using material that he claimed to have gathered from the works of Melanchthon, Oecolampadius, Conrad Pelikan and John Draconite.[83] The work included Melanchthon's dedication to the duke of Saxony, but was printed in English for a English audience, and was heavily laden with references to the state of the English church.[84] Both Joye and Bale had demonstrated the polemical value of biblical prophecy, and Luther's work on Antichrist was to be only the first of several continental commentaries on biblical prophecies to be translated into English. John Old printed two discussions of the Antichrist in the reign of Mary. The first, *A short description of Antichrist vnto the nobilitie of Englande*, was issued in Emden in 1555, and the second, a translation of the Swiss reformer Rudolph Gualter's work, appeared in 1556.[85] The condemnation of clerical celibacy as the invention of the Antichrist featured heavily in both works, with Old arguing that the pope, by the prohibition of marriage to the clergy, had revealed himself as the vicar of Satan rather than the vicar of Christ.[86]

Gualter's work, when published in Switzerland, was intended not as an attack on the papal Antichrist, but as an admonition to the reformed church.[87] The translation of the text into English is not altogether surprising, given that Gualter was already familiar with several of the English reformers, and had spent time in England in 1537. Richard Masters praised 'the most godly Bullinger and his like-minded disciple Gualter' in 1551, and Gualter himself corresponded with Christopher

---

after his death: ibid., p. 118. The material that Bullinger supplied to Ponet, the letter of Ignatius to the Philadelphians, was to be the focus of a controversy between John Jewel and Thomas Harding, with both claiming that the letter supported their (opposing) views on clerical marriage. J. Booty, *John Jewel as Apologist of the Church of England* (London, 1963), pp. 106ff. There are different versions of the letter of Ignatius, and Booty argues that the passage of the letter which deals with the marriage of the Apostles is likely to be a fourth-century interpolation. See Chapter 2 below, pp. 39ff.

[83] Joye, *The Exposicion of Daniel the Prophete* (Antwerp, 1545), RSTC 14823.

[84] See Chapter 5 below. Joye declared on the title page that he hoped that the work would be studied by emperors and kings. R. Pineas, 'George Joye's "Exposicion of Daniel"', *Renaissance Quarterly*, 28 (1975), pp. 332–43; Butterworth, *George Joye*, pp. 235–44.

[85] R. Gualter (tr. J. Old), *Antichrist. That is to say a true reporte that Antichriste is come ...* (Zürich, 1556), RSTC 25009.

[86] *A Short Description of Antichrist vnto the Nobilite of Englande* (Emden, 1555), RSTC 673; sig. D6r.

[87] I am grateful to Dr Kurt Jakob Rüetschi for this information.

Hales in 1550.[88] Pilkington and Lever both had cause to thank him for his hospitality during their exile in Mary's reign.[89] Thomas Sampson told Bullinger that he had intended to translate Gualter's sermons on Antichrist himself, but 'was informed that some other Englishman had not only undertaken the same task, but had completed it'.[90] Gualter's sermons clearly suited Old's purpose, outlining the evidence for the presence of Antichrist in the church, and calling for further reform. Christ had purged the church of ceremonies, but Antichrist had reintroduced them, the text declared, in what must have seemed to Old to be an accurate assessment of the religious situation in England in 1555.[91] The Swiss influence over English apocalyptic literature continued into the following decade, with the publication of Bullinger's *A Hvndred Sermons vpo[n] the Apocalips* in 1561, in which the issue of vows of celibacy continued to loom large. Despite its application to the history of their native church, the apocalyptic thought of English Protestants was heavily influenced by their contemporaries in Europe.[92]

The polemical literature on clerical marriage in England was plentiful and varied. Several English writers, most notably John Bale, made forceful and influential contributions to the debate, and to the literature of the Reformation in general. However, the contact between English and continental reformers, the number of tracts by foreign writers that were translated into English, and the influence of evangelical writers in exile upon the nature and tone of polemic, make it impossible to consider the work of English polemicists in isolation from their European contemporaries.[93] The debate on clerical marriage supports Gordon Rupp's assertion that the English Reformation 'neither began nor ended at the white cliffs of Dover'.[94] Luther's marriage was the intellectual property of Thomas More, and the actions of Henry VIII and

---

[88] *Original Letters*, I, pp. 124; II, 359–60; I, 185–7.

[89] Ibid., pp. 134–5, 166–8.

[90] Ibid., p. 174.

[91] Gualter, *Antichrist*, sig. N8r.

[92] R. Bauckham, *Tudor Apocalypse. Sixteenth Century Apocalypticism, Millennarianism, and the English Reformation from John Bale to John Foxe and Thomas Brightman* (Sutton Courtenay, 1978), p. 14. John Bale's apocalyptic thought was influenced by Thomas Kirchmeyer, Joachim von Watt and Luther. Fairfield, *John Bale*, pp. 70–72. Bullinger was a respected figure; Archbishop Whitgift recommended that the clergy in the province who were not preachers should study one of Bullinger's sermons from the *Decades* each week: D. MacCulloch, *The Later Reformation in England: 1547–1603* (Basingstoke, 1990), p. 71.

[93] See Chapter 4 below.

[94] E.G. Rupp, 'The Battle of the Books: The ferment of ideas and the beginning of the Reformation', in P.N. Brooks, ed., *Reformation Principle and Practice. Essays in Honour of Arthur Geoffrey Dickens* (London, 1980), pp. 1–19, 4. For continental influences on the English Reformation see W.K. Jordan, *Edward VI. The Young King* (London, 1968),

Mary against married priests attracted the attention of foreign writers. The defence of clerical celibacy was a central feature of Catholic polemic, and the marriage of the leaders of the Reformation in England and abroad was central to the conservative attack on their theology. In the eyes of evangelical writers, clerical marriage was not merely a remedy for clerical fornication, but a vital issue of doctrine and morality which was relevant to almost every Reformation controversy.

Ideology and Action: Clerical Marriage in England c. 1500–c. 1570

The debate on clerical celibacy cannot be considered in isolation from other key Reformation controversies; most obviously the polemical literature on clerical marriage was heavily influenced by the dispute over the relative authority of Scripture and tradition in Reformation polemic. Both Catholic and evangelical writers drew heavily upon biblical texts to justify their opposing positions, in a debate which challenges the traditional assumption that while Catholic polemicists drew upon the tradition of the church, Scripture was the preserve of Protestants. An examination of the use of Scripture by both sides in the polemical debate reveals a willingness to argue from common ground, and to engage in detailed analysis of opposing viewpoints.[95] The reformist principle of *sola scriptura* did little to narrow the boundaries of the debate on clerical marriage. Catholic polemicists frequently argued from Scripture, and their evangelical counterparts were equally willing to turn to the history and traditions of the church to support their contention that clerical celibacy was a recent innovation. The church of the Apostles, and the history of the primitive church, became a moral and theological hunting ground for Reformation writers on both sides of the debate. In rewriting the history of the church, reformist polemicists drew upon a variety of mediaeval chronicles and letters, but their work clearly owed much to the interchange of ideas and information with continental Protestant writers. An investigation of the debate over clerical celibacy reveals the process by which Protestant history was constructed, and the effective and persuasive research which several writers undertook.[96]

The enforcement of clerical celibacy offered a clear chronological framework on which evangelical polemicists could base their interpretations of history. Having established the roots of the married

---

pp. 189ff.; Pettegree, *Marian Protestantism*, p. 7; D. MacCulloch, *Thomas Cranmer. A Life* (New Haven, CT, 1996), pp. 447ff.

[95] See Chapter 2 below.

[96] See Chapters 3 and 4 below.

priesthood in the primitive church, John Bale and other writers set out to demonstrate the process by which the Roman church had come to prohibit marriage to its clergy. History revealed the growth of doctrinal error in the institutional church, and the enforcement of the celibate ideal was clear evidence of the perversion of Christianity by the addition of false, unscriptural doctrines. The prohibition of marriage to the clergy became the mark of the false congregation, the body of the Antichrist, throughout the history of the church. This theme was developed at length in commentaries on Revelation, and clerical celibacy became an integral part of the redefinition of Antichrist in moral and doctrinal terms.[97] The separation of the two churches on the issue of clerical marriage allowed the identification of the members of the true church and the false throughout history, from the earliest centuries to the unfolding conflict between good and evil in the Reformation. Thus clerical celibacy was central both to the identification of the true church and the false in the sixteenth century, and to the assessment of the progress of reform in England.

Catholic writers claimed that their opponents, unable to keep to the moral strictures of Catholicism, had invented a theological system that allowed their followers to sin freely, to reject the traditions of the church, and to break vows of chastity. The vow of chastity, and the question of whether or not it could be broken, was therefore a central feature in the debate on clerical marriage.[98] Both before and after the Reformation, Catholic authors argued that such vows were pleasing to God, and could be broken only under pain of damnation. In contrast, evangelical writers claimed that promises of celibacy, particularly where they were regarded as efficacious in the process of salvation, were doctrinally insupportable. Marriage was a state ordained by God, but monastic vows were the invention of men, an idol of the heart. Such arguments certainly helped to legitimate clerical marriage, but also had much broader implications. The destruction of idols had been the mark of the reforming kings of the Old Testament, and became the sign of the godly ruler in the sixteenth century. By their attitude to clerical marriage, therefore, individual monarchs placed themselves in the historical company of either the reforming kings of the Old Testament, or the idolatrous and ungodly rulers who suffered the wrath of God. In the eyes of Protestant polemicists, attitudes to clerical marriage offered an indication of success and failure in the Reformation, and justified their criticism of the king, as the prophets of the Old Testament had chastised their rulers.

---

[97] See Chapter 5 below.
[98] See Chapter 6 below.

24   CLERICAL MARRIAGE AND THE ENGLISH REFORMATION

Celibacy was inextricably linked with the nature and function of the priesthood, and in particular with the theology of the Mass. This correlation between the character and function of the priest was expressed vehemently in the works of Catholic writers, and exerted a strong influence over subsequent debate. However, while it might be expected that the rejection of the sacrificial function of the priest would lead to a relaxation of the obligation to celibacy, this was not the main argument of reformist writers. Evangelical polemicists drew upon the argument that the theology of the Mass necessitated a celibate priesthood to claim that the moral conduct of the clergy revealed the error of the doctrines which they preached. Such arguments featured heavily in the flood of literature against the Mass in the early months of Edward's reign, fuelled by the characterization of the Mass as a debauched woman. Where Catholic writers were at pains to argue that the ministry of an impure priest did not contaminate the sacraments, Protestant writers exploited their fears and claimed that the moral laxity of the clergy cast doubt upon the whole Eucharistic theology of the Roman church.[99]

While the debate on clerical marriage has been somewhat neglected, the impact of the legalization of clerical marriage in England in 1549 has received rather more attention, in a series of local studies that put flesh on the bones of W.H. Frere's work on the Marian reaction. Frere's statistical study of the deprivation of married clergy in England has been supported and augmented by the work of Hilda Grieve on the married clergy of Essex, along with more recent studies of clergy and clerical marriage, and the fate of clergy wives.[100] A more detailed analysis of attitudes to reform, and to the married priesthood on a national scale, can be formulated by an investigation of the impact of legislation on

[99] See Chapter 7 below.

[100] W.H. Frere, *The Marian Reaction in its Relation to the English Clergy. A Study of the Episcopal Registers* (London, 1896); R. Spielmann, 'The Beginning of Clerical Marriage in the English Reformation. The Reigns of Edward and Mary', *Anglican and Episcopal History*, 56 (1987), pp. 251–263; R. Baskerville, 'Married Clergy and Pensioned Religious in the Norwich Diocese', *EHR*, 48 (1933), pp. 43–64, 199–228; J.F. Williams, 'The Married Clergy of the Marian Period', *Norfolk Archaeology*, 32 (1961), pp. 85–95; M. Zell, 'The Personnel of the Clergy in Kent in the Reformation Period', *EHR*, 84 (1994), pp. 513–33; F. Heal, 'The Parish Clergy and the Reformation in the Diocese of Ely', *Proceedings of the Cambridge Antiquarian Society*, 66 (1976), pp. 141–63; C. Cross, 'Priests into Ministers: The Establishment of Protestant Practice in the Diocese of York', in Brooks, ed., *Reformation Principle and Practice*, pp 203–25; H. Grieve, 'The Deprived Married Clergy in Essex 1553–1561', *TRHS*, fourth series, 22 (1940), pp. 141–69; A.L. Barstow, 'The First Generation of Anglican Clergy Wives: Heroines or Whores?', *Historical Magazine of the Protestant Episcopal Church*, 15 (1983), pp. 3–16; M. Prior, 'Reviled and Crucified Marriages. The Position of Tudor Bishops' Wives', in Prior, ed., *Women in English Society, 1500–1800* (London, 1985), pp. 118–48.

clerical marriage.[101] The religious changes of the 1530s were seen by some clergy as an invitation to break their promises of chastity, in anticipation of the legalization of clerical marriage. However, Henry VIII continued to insist that the priesthood should remain celibate, and the Act of Six Articles of 1539 (which was to remain in effect until the accession of Edward VI) included a vigorous expression of the king's opposition to clerical marriage. The events of the last decade of Henry's reign were a powerful influence upon the polemical debate on clerical marriage, but the number of clergy affected by the king's actions remained small. However, a more significant number of clergy took advantage of the lifting of the prohibition of clerical marriage in 1549, and it is the fate of these clergy in particular that forms the basis of this study.

In March 1553/54, Mary issued a proclamation ordering that all married clergy be deprived of their benefices, and separated from their wives.[102] The records of these deprivation proceedings are the best available assessment of the number of clergy who had married since 1549, and offer some insight into the attitude to religious change expressed by the clergy involved in the middle decades of the sixteenth century. The behaviour of the married clergy between 1549 and 1570 raises several questions. In the eyes of Reformation polemicists, the true church and the false could be identified by their teaching on clerical celibacy, and among the higher clergy of the mid-sixteenth century, marriage was often indicative of Protestant belief. The evidence for a similar correlation between clerical marriage and clerical Protestantism at a local level is harder to quantify, but tentative conclusions may be drawn, based upon the actions and experiences of married clergy in the middle decades of the century. On a practical level, the possibility that a clergyman could marry might have been limited by the wealth of the cure; those with a low income may have feared that they would be unable to support a family, while for others, with glebe lands to farm, a wife and family may have been an economic asset. Using the *Valor Ecclesiasticus*, the value of the livings of the married priests can be compared with the value of livings in the dioceses as a whole, to test the hypothesis that clerical wealth influenced levels of clerical marriage.

The polemical debate on clerical marriage might be expected to have exerted a greater influence over those clergy who were able to absorb the arguments set forth in these works. A useful comparison may be made between the educational standards of married clergy and those of their

---

[101] The four dioceses are described in greater detail in Chapter 8 below.

[102] The legislation on clerical marriage under Henry VIII, Edward VI and Mary is described in detail and discussed in Chapters 1 and 8 below.

unmarried contemporaries, based upon the matriculation records of the two universities. However, for those clergy who could not appreciate the doctrinal subtleties of the debate over clerical marriage, it is likely that the example of neighbouring priests who married may have been a powerful incentive to follow suit. The possibility that the decision of a priest to marry was influenced by the conduct of other clergy has therefore been investigated, and the results of this study are shown in the series of maps (see Appendix). Whatever factors influenced the decision of priests to break their promise of chastity, their marriages were to have profound consequences for the Marian church and the first months of Elizabeth's reign. Many of the deprived Marian clergy were restored to their benefices after the accession of Elizabeth, and many clergy married in the first months of the new regime, despite the legal uncertainty that surrounded clerical marriages, not least the attitude of the queen herself. Clerical marriage, hardly a dogmatic certainty in 1559, rapidly became an established feature of the Elizabethan church.

Whatever the motivations for their marriages, the clergy who married under Edward VI were a visible expression of doctrinal change. Even if they were not totally committed to the Reformation themselves, the fact that they were able to marry was concrete evidence of the break with the Catholic past. The rejection of clerical celibacy did much to consolidate Protestant identity among the reformers themselves and in the eyes of their opponents. Catholic polemicists argued that clerical marriage was the mark of the heretic, while their opponents pointed to the celibate priesthood as evidence that the institutional church was not the church of Christ. The polemical debate on clerical marriage during the Reformation offers insights into the attitudes of Protestant and Catholic writers both to the past and to the events unfolding before them, while the clergy who married present the historian with the response of at least one section of society to the religious changes of the mid-sixteenth century. In the eyes of John Ponet, there was only one question to answer:

> The Apostles taught one thing: the byshop of Rome brought in another. Nowe iudge you whether it is beste for vs which professe to follow the Apostles, or the Romish Antichriste. The laws of God, whych wylleth bishopes and priests to mary: or the doctrine of the deuyll as Paul calleth it, which forbyddeth theym marryge.[103]

---

[103] Ponet, *Defence of the Mariage of Preistes*, sig. C1r.

CHAPTER ONE

'This act is in this country a monster': Clerical Marriage in England during the Reformation

The legalization of clerical marriage in England was, in the words of H.C. Lea, 'a process of far more intricacy than in any other country which adopted the Reformation'.[1] For the best part of a century, Lea's work has been the standard history of celibacy in the church, and his account of sixteenth-century legislation on the issue is still widely accepted. The prohibition on clerical marriage, it is argued, persisted as a consequence of Henry VIII's doctrinal conservatism, and was lifted only reluctantly in 1549.[2] The discipline of celibacy was enforced in the English church for the best part of two decades after the break with Rome, and was tolerated rather than welcomed in the Elizabethan church. However, the question of the validity of clerical marriage remained controversial throughout the period. Thomas More's pre-occupation with Luther's marriage ensured that the issue of clerical marriage was a central feature of the polemical literature of the 1520s. The official policy of the Henrician church was made clear in the following decade: throughout the 1530s, celibacy was enjoined upon the clergy in successive statutes and proclamations. Preaching and polemic in defence of clerical marriage continued, and a number of clergy, both secular and regular, took wives. In 1534, John Rastell petitioned Cromwell for the lifting of the prohibition on clerical marriage,[3] and such demands became increasingly vociferous. Writing to Lady Lisle in November 1535, Anthony Waite claimed, 'it is preached here that priests must have wives', alongside unorthodox opinions on purgatory, and demands for communion in both kinds.[4] Two months later, in a description of the state of the English church, the imperial ambassador drew attention to the publication of Gardiner's *De Vera Obedientia*, and

---

[1] H.C. Lea, *History of Sacerdotal Celibacy in the Christian Church*, third edition, 2 vols (London, 1907), II, p. 77.

[2] E. Carlson, 'Clerical Marriage and the English Reformation', *Journal of British Studies*, 31 (1992), pp. 1–31.

[3] E. Carlson, *Marriage and the English Reformation*, Ph.D., University of Harvard (1987), p. 160; S. Brigden, *London and the Reformation* (Oxford 1989), p. 28.

[4] *LP*, IX, 812.

noted 'clerks are allowed to marry'.[5] Ortiz was only half right. Clerks had indeed married, but there is nothing to suggest that they were permitted in law to do so. A royal proclamation of 1535 threatened to deprive married priests of their benefices, and further condemnation of clerical marriage was to follow.[6]

In June 1536, the Lower House of Convocation protested against the spread of heresy, listing the belief 'that Priests shuld have wiffes' among the most contentious errors.[7] Their fears were grounded in reality. When deprived of his benefice and examined for heresy in the reign of Mary, the parson of Hadleigh, Rowland Taylor, confirmed that he had been married for some twenty-nine years, making him one of the first priests in England to marry.[8] Hadleigh had a longstanding tradition of heterodox dissent by 1554, and Diarmaid MacCulloch argues that the Marian regime rapidly identified the community as a threat.[9] In 1528, John Tyball confessed that he had preached that every priest should have a wife, and had persuaded Friar Meadow, a Greyfriar of Colchester, to abandon his religion and marry.[10] Other religious houses were similarly affected. John ap Rice wrote to Cromwell in October 1535, describing the situation in the abbey of Walden and the conduct of the abbot, 'a man of good learning', who had 'secretly contracted marriage, because, though he might not do it by the laws of men, he might do it lawfully by the laws of God for avoiding of more inconvenience'. Only seven monks remained in the house, the abbot having persuaded the rest that there was 'no sanctity in monkery'.[11] Appealing to Cromwell for mercy, the abbot described his wife, identified by Wriothesley as one 'mistress Bures, nun of the minories', as his 'remedy'.[12] Such assertions would not

---

[5] *LP*, X, 82.

[6] D. Wilkins, *Concilia Magnae Britanniae et Hiberniae*, 4 vols (1776), I, p. 776; D. Peet, 'The Mid-Sixteenth Century Parish Clergy with particular consideration of the diocese of Norwich and York', unpublished Ph.D., University of Cambridge (1980), p. 293.

[7] J. Strype, *Ecclesiastical Memorials Relating Chiefly to Religion and the Reformation of it*, 3 vols (Oxford, 1822), I, appendix, p. 176.

[8] W.H. Frere, *The Marian Reaction in its Relation to the English Clergy. A Study of the Episcopal Registers* (Church Historical Society, London, 1896), p. 67; Carlson, 'Clerical Marriage', p. 6.

[9] D. MacCulloch, *Suffolk and the Tudors. Politics and Religion in an English County 1500–1600* (Oxford, 1986), pp. 155–71. Bilney had preached in the area, and as a peculiar of the archbishop of Canterbury, Hadleigh provided a refuge for Nicholas Shaxton after he resigned the bishopric of Salisbury.

[10] *LP*, IV, ii, 4218.

[11] *LP*, IX, 661.

[12] Ibid. Charles Wriothesley, *A Chronicle of England during the reigns of the Tudors from AD 1485 to 1559*, ed. W.D. Hamilton, Camden Society, n.s., 11 (1875), 1, p. 63; E. Baskerville, 'English Monks and the Suppression of the Monasteries', *Bedford Historical Series*, 7 (1958), p. 137.

have been out of place in the works of Luther or Tyndale. Monastic vows were condemned as idolatrous by evangelical polemicists, and the argument from 1 Corinthians 7 that marriage was a remedy for fornication was a favoured text.[13]

In a letter to the duke of Suffolk in June 1537, Sir Thomas Tyrell protested that the vicar of Mendlesham 'brought home his woman and children to his vicarage, openly declaring he is married to her. This act is in this country a monster, and many grudge at it.' The vicar, he claimed, had stated that the king was aware that he was married, and therefore no action had been taken to separate him from his 'wife'. Tyrell was concerned that the 'crime' should be dealt with, on the grounds that it offered a poor example to other 'carnal priests', and might encourage others to marry.[14] In August 1538, Adam Lewes, another priest with Mendlesham connections, informed the authorities in Rye that he knew of a hundred other priests who had married.[15] Such reports were almost certainly exaggerated, but Lewes's statement suggests that the fears of conservatives, and the king himself, were not unfounded; more recently, the inhabitants of Mendlesham in Suffolk have been described as 'striking in their continuity of religious dissent', perhaps encouraged by the attitude of their preists towards the traditions of the church.[16]

The vicar of Mendlesham was clearly mistaken in the belief that the king would sanction his marriage. Henry VIII's attitude to clerical marriage had been set out in no uncertain terms throughout the 1530s. In 1536 the bishops were ordered to investigate incidents of clerical marriage in their dioceses, and Henry VIII condemned those clergy who 'have p[re]sumed to mary themselfs, contrarye to the custome of o[u]r churche of England'.[17] The break with Rome was not to be accompanied by the relaxation of all Roman discipline, and clerical celibacy was established as a feature of the historical English church. The bishops were instructed to make 'secret enquiry', and any married clergy were to be apprehended, or brought to the attention of the Council. The duty of the bishops to investigate clerical marriage was hardly compatible with the archbishop of Canterbury's own situation.[18] However, the enforcement of clerical celibacy is in keeping with the sentiments expressed in the article on marriage in the *Bishops' Book* of 1537:

---

[13] See Chapters 6 and 2, pp. 138ff. and 39ff.

[14] *LP*, XII, ii, 81. BL Cotton MS Cleo E iv fol. 124.

[15] *LP*, XII, i, 990, *LP*, XII, ii, 450.

[16] MacCulloch, *Suffolk and the Tudors*, p. 178.

[17] BL Cotton MS Cleo E v fol. 299r.

[18] D. MacCulloch, *Thomas Cranmer: A Life* (New Haven, CT, 1996), p. 171.

> Christ seemeth to exhort such as he shall endue with the grace and
> virtue of continence, wherby they shall be able to abstain from the
> works of matrimony to continue sole and unmarried.[19]

The passage was not a ringing endorsement of clerical celibacy, but it
did assert that celibacy was a state which some could attain. Further
action was taken against married clergy in November 1538. A royal
proclamation prohibited marriage to the clergy, and threatened those
who had already married with the loss of their benefices.[20] The king's
personal concern over the issue is clear from the alterations that he made
to the draft of the proclamation. The original draft opened with a
declaration that the king was aware that a 'fewe nombre' of clergy,
'being prestes as well religious', had taken it upon themselves to marry,
contrary to the vow they had made on receiving orders. Henry amended
the text, adding that such marriages were contrary to 'the holsu[m]e
monission off saint Palle ad Thimotheu[m] ad Titu[m] and ad
Cori[n]theos bothe first and seco[n]de and also to the opinions of meny
of the olde faders and expositers of Scripture'.[21] Fearing that their
example would encourage other clergy to marry, Henry ordered that
priests who had already married should be expelled from their benefices
and 'reputed as laye p[er]sonnes', and threatened those clergy who
married after 1538 with imprisonment.

Despite the proclamation of 1538, the debate on clerical marriage
continued. Wriothesley claimed that preachers continued to defend
clerical marriage, even in the presence of the king, and clergy continued
to marry.[22] Indeed, the actions of Cromwell were not altogether
consistent with the policy of his king. In 1536, the Welsh clergy
petitioned Cromwell, requesting that they be allowed to retain their
'hearth companions', in accordance with tradition. While clerical
marriage was technically illegal in Wales, it is clear that some clergy had
at least entered into a 'civil marriage' through public betrothal, and that
they regarded these marriages as binding. Such unions were sometimes
welcomed by the laity; in their petition, the priests complained that they

---

[19] C. Lloyd, *Formularies of Faith Put Forth by Authority During the Reign of Henry VIII* (Oxford, 1825), p. 88.

[20] P.L. Hughes and J.F. Larkin, eds, *TRP*, I, p. 274.

[21] BL Cotton MS Cleo E v fol. 382.

[22] Wriothesley, *Chronicle*, I, p. 83; *Original Letters Relevant to the English Reformation*, ed. H. Robinson, Parker Society, 2 vols (1846), II, p. 624. Letter from John Butler, Nicholas Eliot, Nicholas Partridge and Bartholomew Traheron to Conrad Pellican, Leo Jud and Heinrich Bullinger, 8 March 1539. The English writers seem somewhat over-optimistic about the prospect of the legalization of clerical marriage, writing that 'Nothing has yet been settled as to the marriage of the clergy, although some have freely preached before the king on the subject.'

could find no lodging because men feared for the safety of their wives and daughters. The Welsh clergy presumably believed that Cromwell would be sympathetic to their plight.[23]

Their hopes would have been boosted by Cromwell's action in commending the preaching of a married priest who had been deprived of his orders to the abbot of Reading. In his reply, the abbot argued that while the man might be learned, 'he cannot but instil like persuasion of marriage, and that would be but occasion of slander, the laws standing as they do yet', and refused to act upon the recommendation.[24] The following year, a Winchester priest wrote to Cromwell, presumably expecting support for his marriage. John Palmes argued that the king had delivered him from the bondage brought into the church by the pope, and claimed that since the letters patent concerning his appointment to his benefice did not specifically forbid marriage, there was no just reason why he should not marry. After his marriage, however, he had been summoned to appear before his bishop, and in January 1539 appealed to Cromwell for assistance. A month later, he wrote to Cromwell again, declaring that he alone preached against Rome in Hampshire, and claiming that he feared that the laws of the bishop of Rome, the 'stinking Anti-Christ' would be brought to bear upon him. In his defence, Palmes contrasted his marriage with the actions of the parson of Burfield, who he claimed had kept a concubine for 20 years, and had children by her.[25] The protest was of no avail, and was unlikely to impress either the bishop of Winchester, Stephen Gardiner, who was later to enter the polemical debate on clerical marriage on the opposing side, or the king, given the views that he expressed in 1538.

The significance of the 1538 proclamation was not lost on evangelical reformers. John Foxe accompanied his description of the proclamation, and the later Act of Six Articles, with the declaration 'Here followeth how religion began to go backward'.[26] The reaction of foreign Protestants was no more enthusiastic. In a letter to Cranmer in March 1539, Philip Melanchthon appealed that the tyranny of Rome be overthrown, and that the abuses which had followed from it should be reformed. He had heard 'with great sorrow' of the recent prohibition of marriage to the clergy, and criticized the arguments set forth in defence of vows. On 1 April 1539 he wrote to the king, expressing his

---

[23] *LP*, X, 215; G. Williams, *The Welsh Church from Conquest to Reformation* (Fayetteville, 1993), pp. 341–5.

[24] *LP*, XIII, i, 147, 26 January 1538.

[25] *LP*, XIV, i, 120, 206, 412, 890.

[26] *AM*, 1570, p. 1259.

disappointment that superstitious rites remained in England, and again urged that priests be given the freedom to marry.[27] Clerical celibacy had already been identified by the German ambassadors as one of the 'three heads of idolatry' which remained unreformed in the English church, and which were an obstacle to closer union with the Lutherans.[28] However, by 1538, the discipline of the Henrician church had been rigorously defined, and the hostility of the king to clerical marriage made abundantly clear. Indeed, Henry had already expressed his views on these key issues in a letter to the German ambassadors in 1538, in a lengthy defence of private Masses, communion in one kind, and clerical celibacy,[29] and the king's refusal to make concessions on these points led to the termination of the negotiations with the Lutherans.

The Act of Six Articles, passed in June 1539, was regarded by contemporary writers as the key piece of legislation on clerical celibacy in the reign of Henry VIII, and their sentiments have been shared by subsequent historians. Opposition to the article enforcing celibacy on the clergy was punishable by imprisonment, and those priests who married were to be adjudged felons, and could be put to death without the right to the benefit of clergy.[30] The penalty was reduced by the king in the following year, but this did little to improve the situation of married clergy.[31] Contemporaries identified Stephen Gardiner as the driving force behind the Act. William Turner referred to the articles as 'Gardiner's gospel',[32] Henry Brinkelow made the same identification in the *Complaynt of Roderick Mors*, and the attribution was repeated by Foxe.[33] Martin Bucer claimed that Gardiner had convinced the king that the hope of a French alliance rested upon signs that reform in England would proceed no further. In an attempt to appease Francis, Henry VIII prohibited clerical marriage, 'for both kings hate the marriage of priests'.[34] More recently, historians have played down the influence of Gardiner over the king in 1539, and present the Act as the policy and

---

[27] *LP*, XIV, i, 631, 666.

[28] *LP*, XIII ii, 37, 5 August 1538; BL Cotton MS Cleo E v fol. 173; MacCulloch, *Cranmer*, pp. 220–21.

[29] BL Cotton MS Cleo E v fol. 215ff.

[30] 31 Henry VIII c.14; *LP*, XIV, i, 1065. The prohibition of clerical marriage was opposed by a group of the spiritual lords, namely Cranmer, Shaxton, Hilsey, Barlow and Latimer. Goodrich of Ely remained undecided.

[31] 32 Henry VIII c.10.

[32] W. Turner, *The Rescuynge of the Romishe Fox* (Bonn, 1545), RSTC 24355, sig. A3.

[33] Henry Brinklow, *The Complaynt of Roderyck Mors*, ed. J.M. Cowper, *EETS*, extra series XXII (1874), p. 60; *AM*, 1570, pp. 1295–6.

[34] *LP*, XIV, ii, 186. Letter to the Landgrave of Hesse, 16 September 1539.

initiative of Henry VIII.[35] John Guy argues that 'from the beginning of 1539, Henry planned a religious settlement of his own choosing', and Glyn Redworth has drawn attention both to the roots of the articles in the events of preceding months, and to the key role of the king in the determination of doctrine.[36] The prohibition of clerical marriage was entirely consistent with royal pronouncements in the 1530s and Henry VIII's correspondence with the Lutherans in the preceding months. Thus with the exception of the defence of auricular confession, Redworth argues, each of the Six Articles had been anticipated in the royal pronouncements of the previous six months.[37] The king was sufficiently interested in the issue of clerical marriage to amend the draft article on vows, to make it clear that such vows were 'made to God advisedly' and could not therefore be broken.[38] Henry's concern to maintain the prohibition on clerical marriage throughout the 1530s strengthens Redworth's argument further, and suggests that the position adopted in June 1539 reflected the views of the king as much as those of the bishop of Winchester.

The prohibition of clerical marriage in the Act of Six Articles, and the penalties laid down for those clergy who married, attracted widespread comment and criticism. George Joye, in his *Defence of the Mariage of Preistes* (1541), claimed that the article on clerical celibacy merely served to protect the interests of the nobility. Encouraged by the duke of Norfolk, Joye claimed, the nobility had feared that clergy would marry their daughters, and appropriate secular wealth to themselves. Not only did the enforcement of clerical celibacy protect the position of the nobility, but the forced separation of married clergy from their wives also offered them the opportunity to take these women as their concubines.[39] Joye's views echo the sentiments expressed in a letter from Marillac to Montmorency, in June 1539, which described reactions to the Act. 'The people', he claimed,

> show great joy at the king's declaration touching the sacrament, being much more inclined to the old religion than to the new

---

[35] C.S.L. Davies, *Peace, Print and Protestantism* (1977), p. 211; A.G. Dickens, *The English Reformation*, second edition (1989), p. 201; MacCulloch, *Cranmer*, pp. 240–41; in contrast to the view of G. Elton, *Studies in Tudor and Stuart Politics and Government* (1974), I, p. 205, and S.E. Lehmberg, *The Later Parliaments of Henry VIII* (1977), pp. 57–8.

[36] J. Guy, *Tudor England* (Oxford, 1988), p. 185. G. Redworth, 'A Study in the Formulation of Policy. The Genesis and Evolution of the Act of Six Articles', *JEH*, 37 (1986), pp. 42–67.

[37] Redworth, 'Six Articles', pp. 46–7.

[38] BL Cotton MS Cleo E v fols 327–30; Redworth, 'Six Articles', p. 67.

[39] G. Joye, *Defence of the mariage of Preistes* (Antwerp, 1541), RSTC 21804, sig. C2r.

> opinions, which are sustained only by some bishops who are little
> content at the refusal of their request to marry in order afterwards
> to convert the property of the church into patrimony and
> succession.[40]

Mary Prior, following Chapuys and Marillac, argues that this prospect
of intermarriage between the clergy and the nobility was a key influence
in the decision of the king to uphold clerical celibacy,[41] but it is clear
from his own words, and involvement in the legislation of the 1530s,
that Henry himself had other objections to married priests.

The king's opinions were well known: English Protestant exiles in the
last decade of the reign of Henry VIIII used the example of the idolatrous
kings of the Old Testament to draw unfavourable comparisons with the
state of the Henrician church, and other writers were more direct in their
criticism.[42] Philip Melanchthon addressed a lengthy refutation of the
articles to the king. The letter was first printed by Richard Grafton, who
was imprisoned for his actions, but later appeared in Foxe's *Actes and
Monuments*.[43] Melanchthon composed a detailed defence of clerical
marriage from Scripture and the history of the church, before turning his
attention to the king. Henry was praised for his actions against the
Roman Antichrist, but Melanchthon then demanded that the king
explain why 'in the meane time you defende & maintayne those laws of
that Romishe Antichrist, whiche be the strength and the sinowes of all
hys power, as priuate masses, single lyfe of Priestes, and other
superstitions'. In enforcing celibacy upon the clergy, he argued, Henry
VIII threatened the spread of the truth of the Gospel, since 'this is not to
abolishe Antichrist, but to establishe hym'.[44]

The Act created problems for Henry's archbishop of Canterbury.
Cranmer had been married briefly during his time in Cambridge, but in
the summer of 1532 he married again, this time in violation of his
promise of celibacy.[45] After taking up his role as ambassador to the
emperor, Cranmer, like his predecessor Thomas Elyot, had been
impressed by the abolition of compulsory clerical celibacy in the city,
and Elyot noted Cranmer's interest in the Lutheran liturgy. In July,
Cranmer married Margaret, the niece of the wife of the Nuremberg
reformer Osiander, in a ceremony at which Osiander officiated. Some

---

[40] *LP*, XIV, i, 1092; BL Add.MSS 33514, fol. 22.

[41] M. Prior, 'Reviled and Crucified Marriages. The Position of Tudor Bishops' Wives',
in Prior, ed., *Women in English Society 1500–1800* (1991), p. 122; *LP*, XVI, 733, 737.

[42] This is discussed at length in Chapter 6, pp. 155–60.

[43] S. Brigden, *London and the Reformation* (Oxford, 1989), p. 354; *APC*, I, p. 107
(8 April 1542); *AM*, 1570, p. 1340–44.

[44] *AM*, 1570, p. 1343.

[45] MacCulloch, *Cranmer*, pp. 69, 72.

eight years later, the Polish ambassador to Spain made a somewhat indelicate enquiry into the place of marriage in the English church, asking whether Cranmer was leading the life of the Apostle Paul.[46] MacCulloch comments that Cranmer would certainly not have found the joke amusing, but Cranmer's predicament is a clear demonstration of the differences in opinion between Henry VIII and those who anticipated that the English church would be purged of the influence of Rome in the 1530s.[47]

Responses to the Six Articles varied, from married clergy who admitted that they had erred, to those who were determined enough to break the law in defence of their theological or personal convictions. In London, John Duffet of St Mary Magdalene in Milk Street was prosecuted under the Act for marrying a woman thought to have been a nun.[48] Robert Ward, a friar, who had married in 1538, was accused of contracting marriage in breach of his vow of chastity. Ward had already demonstrated beliefs that were less than orthodox; in 1535 he had argued that the priests deluded the people by claiming that they could 'have forgiveness by their absolution'.[49] John Foster admitted to Cromwell that he had married a nun, claiming that he had believed such marriages to be legal by the law of God. 'My disfortune [sic] has been to have conceived untruly God's word,' Foster confessed, 'and not only with my intellect to have thought it, but externally and really I have fulfilled the same.' Foster assured Cromwell that when he had become aware of Henry VIII's views on clerical marriage, he had sent his wife sixty miles away.[50] When confronted with the law of the king, Foster was prepared to admit that the law of God could be open to misinterpretation.

Others were less willing to accept the law of the king. Eric Carlson has drawn attention to the case of William Turner, who married in the aftermath of the Six Articles.[51] The marriage was solemnized at the

---

[46] Ibid., p. 73.

[47] George Browne, the married archbishop of Dublin, was to face a similar predicament in the 1540s. Although no equivalent of the Act of Six Articles was enforced in Ireland, Browne's marriage was a focus for the hostility of his opponents. The archbishop eventually married his wife to one of his servants. Browne's situation is discussed in J. Murray, 'Ecclesiastical Justice and the Enforcement of the Reformation: The case of Archbishop Browne and the Clergy of Dublin', in A. Ford, J. McGuire and K. Milne, eds, *As By Law Established. The Church of Ireland Since the Reformation* (Dublin, 1995), pp. 33–51.

[48] *AM*, 1570, p. 1377.

[49] *LP*, VIII, 625; Wriothesley, *Chronicle*, I, p. 83; *LP*, XIII, ii, 571.

[50] BL Cotton MS Cleo E iv fol. 116.

[51] E. Carlson, 'The marriage of William Turner', *Historical Research*, 65 (1992), pp. 336–9.

chapel of the Hospital of Bethlehem in London, a favoured church for clergy determined to enter into 'illegal' marriages.[52] When the case reached the bishop's court, Turner's wife denied that she knew that he had received orders which were an impediment to marry. Carlson states that this was a prudent claim to make, given that under the Six Articles she would be counted as guilty as Turner; the fact that the couple married in London rather than Cambridge suggests that they were well aware of the illegality of their actions.[53] Turner and his wife fled abroad, from where he argued the case for clerical marriage in a vitriolic and prolonged debate with Stephen Gardiner over the progress of the Reformation in England.[54] Despite their effect on individual clerical marriages, the Six Articles did not put an end to preaching and polemic on the subject.

Few clergy were prepared to follow the example of Turner and risk prosecution under the 1539 legislation. The polemical debate continued, however, fuelled by the activity of Protestant exiles, including Turner himself, John Bale and George Joye. There was little realistic prospect that Henry VIII would be persuaded to lift the prohibition on clerical marriage, although the passage on celibacy which had been included in the *Institution of a Christian Man* was removed from the *King's Book* of 1543.[55] The legalization of clerical marriage appeared further away than ever, given the nature of official religion in England in the last years of Henry's reign. In 1546 Hooper complained to Bullinger that 'as far as true religion is concerned, idolatry is nowhere in greater vigour. Our king has destroyed the pope but not popery', and included clerical celibacy among the list of doctrines and practices 'never before held by the people in greater esteem than at the present moment'.[56] The prospect of a married priesthood was not attractive either to the king or, it appeared, to many of his people.

Both the king and his people were targeted by a barrage of polemical literature on the subject of clerical marriage in the 1530s and 1540s. Jonathan Barry has suggested that despite its popularity, such literature

---

[52] In March 1543, one Margaret, formerly a nun of Norfolk, confessed in the consistory court of London that she had married John Clerice in the Bethlehem chapel. W. Hale, *A Series of Precedents and Proceedings in Criminal Causes* (1847), pp. 134–5.

[53] Carlson, 'William Turner', pp. 337–8.

[54] W. Turner, *The Huntyng & fyndyng out of the Romishe fox* (Basle, 1543), RSTC 24354; *The Rescuynge of the Romishe Fox* (Bonn, 1545), RSTC 24355; *The Huntyng of the Romyshe Vuolfe* (Emden, 1554), RSTC 24356.

[55] Lloyd, *Formularies of Faith*, p. 274.

[56] *Original Letters*, I, pp. 36–7. January 1546.

reflected the views of its authors as much as its intended readers.[57] In the case of the literature in defence of clerical marriage, this is certainly true: the frequently cited examples of lay hostility to clerical wives suggest that evangelical writers in the 1530s and 1540s had a large audience to convince, including the king himself.[58] Both church and state clearly believed in the power of print to influence the people, and the authors of sixteenth-century printed books often claimed that they had written for the benefit of the nation and its people.[59] H.S. Bennett has argued that this was particularly true of the religious book, in which authors openly addressed 'the christen reader', or 'all chrysten people'. Walter Lynne wrote in the hope that his work would be read by 'al men, women, and chyldren', who would then be persuaded to abandon 'newe errours (grounded upon the Romeish rocke)'.[60] Such comments are in keeping with Tunstall's request that Thomas More should refute Luther in the vernacular, and Bale's declaration that *The Image of Both Churches* provided all people with the means with which they could identify the true church.[61]

Writers on both sides of the religious divide clearly believed that there were people who were open to persuasion. Those who were obstinate in their opposition to the theology of the Reformation may have been beyond the reach of even the most ardent polemicist, but for the converted and the lukewarm, it has been suggested that evangelical polemic stiffened morale, and presented a persuasive and coherent world view.[62] By 1549, English Protestant polemicists had done much to establish the married priesthood as a central part of this world view. The central role of the celibate priesthood in Catholic theology ensured that the issue of clerical marriage would play a prominent role in Reformation debate. A married priest was a highly visible manifestation

---

[57] J. Barry, 'Literacy and Literature in Popular Culture: Reading and Writing in Historical Perspective', in T. Harris, ed., *Popular Culture in England c1500–1850* (Basingstoke, 1995), pp. 72–3.

[58] For examples of lay hostility to clerical marriage see M. Prior, 'Reviled and Crucified Marriages', pp. 118–48; A.L. Barstow, 'The First Generation of Anglican Clergy Wives: Heroines or Whores?', *Historical Magazine of the Protestant Episcopal Church*, 52 (1983), pp. 3–16; P. Marshall, *The Catholic Priesthood and the English Reformation* (Oxford, 1994), pp. 165–73.

[59] See above, Introduction, pp. 2–5; R. O'Day, *Education and Society 1500–1800. The Social Foundations of Education in Early Modern Britain* (1982), ch. 2; H.S. Bennett, *English Books and Readers 1475–1557* (Cambridge, 1952), pp. 55–7.

[60] Ibid., p. 58.

[61] See above, Introduction, and Chapter 5 below.

[62] A. Ryrie, 'The Problem of Legitimacy and Precedent in English Protestantism 1539–1547', in B. Gordon ed., *Protestant History and Identity in Sixteenth-Century Europe*, 2 vols (Aldershot, 1996), I, p. 81.

of the Reformation, and one which many were unwilling to accept. The debate was not yet over, as the events of the 1550s were to show; indeed, the importance attached to the enforcement of clerical celibacy by the Marian regime is in keeping with the breadth and depth of the debate on clerical marriage in the preceding decades.

CHAPTER TWO

Celibate Priesthood or Married Ministry? The Testimony of the Bible

In 1528 William Tyndale completed the first edition of *The Parable of the Wicked Mammon*, in which he avowed his intention to 'bringe the Scripture into the right sense & to digge againe the wells of Abraham, & to purge and clense them of the erth of worldly wisdome / wherewith these Philistines haue stopped them'.[1] Tyndale's declaration touches upon a key theme in Reformation debate.[2] Protestant writers claimed that divine revelation had ended with the apostolic period, and, with the exception of the eschaton, the promises of God in Scripture had been fulfilled. If Christ returned to earth, Tyndale suggested, He would add nothing to the corpus of revealed truths contained in the two testaments.[3] There was therefore no licence to augment the words of Scripture, or turn to other sources to settle theological disputes.[4] Indeed, to give priority to the words of the Fathers, Tyndale claimed, was to rest the word of God on the foundation of the words of men, subjecting the

[1] W. Tyndale, *The Parable of the Wicked Mammon*, WW, pp. 61–2; J.A.R. Dick, '"To Dig Again the Wells of Abraham": Philology, Theology, and Scripture in Tyndale's *The Parable of the Wicked Mammon*', *Moreana*, 108 (1991), p. 40.

[2] The reformation debate on the authority of Scripture and tradition is discussed in several important works: G.R. Evans, *Problems of Authority in Reformation Debates* (Cambridge, 1992); B. Gerrish, *The Old Protestantism and the New. Essays on the Reformation Heritage* (Edinburgh, 1982); G.H. Tavard, *Holy Writ or Holy Church. The Crisis of the Protestant Reformation* (London, 1959); E. Flesseman van Leer, 'The Controversy about Ecclesiology between Thomas More and William Tyndale', *Nederlands Archief voor Kerkesgeschiedenis*, 44 (1960), pp. 65–86; *idem*, 'The Controversy about Scripture and Tradition Between Thomas More and William Tyndale', *Nederlands Archief voor Kerkesgeschiedenis*, 43 (1959), pp. 143–64; B. Gogan, *The Common Corps of Christendom. Ecclesiological Themes in the Writings of Sir Thomas More* (Leiden, 1982); J.M. Headley, 'The Reformation as a Crisis in the Understanding of Tradition', *ARG*, 78 (1987), pp. 5–22; *idem, Luther's View of Church History* (1963); *idem*, 'Thomas Murner, Thomas More, and the first Expression of More's Ecclesiology', *Studies in the Renaissance*, 14 (1967), pp. 73–92; R.C. Marius, 'Thomas More and the Early Church Fathers', *Traditio*, 24 (1968), pp. 379–407; *idem*, 'Thomas More's View of the Church', *CW*, 8, pp. 1269–363; P. Marshall, 'The Debate over "Unwritten Verities" in Early Reformation England', in B. Gordon ed., *Protestant History and Identity in Sixteenth-Century Europe vol. I The Medieval Inheritance* (Aldershot, 1996), pp. 60–77.

[3] Tyndale, *Answer to More's Dialogue*, WW, pp. 385–6.

[4] Tyndale, *Obedience of a Christian Man*, WW, p. 128. 2. Thess. 2.

divine will to human authority. Tyndale's belief in the sufficiency of Scripture as a repository of divine revelation was the foundation of an attack on what he regarded as the non-scriptural teachings of the church, most notably ceremonies, the sacramental system and the celibacy of the clergy. Where the opponents of the Reformation could cite only the authority of the human and institutional church in their defence, Tyndale argued, the reformers could turn to the higher authority of the complete record of the word of God.[5] The Bible provided the means of passing judgement upon the teachings of the church, and for this reason the clergy had withheld it from the people, and clouded its message with human traditions and ordinances.[6] The denial of the supreme authority of the word of God was a sign of the disordering of the world by Antichrist, who 'turneth the rotes of the trees vpwarde', making the truth of Scripture dependent upon the doctors.[7]

In reply, Catholic writers pointed to the insufficiency of Scripture as a repository of necessary doctrine, its ambiguities on key issues, and argued for the validity of the traditional teachings of the church as a complementary source of divine revelation. The adumbration of truth was incomplete, as Scripture itself testified. Not only had one of the evangelists written that the Gospels did not record all the deeds of Christ, but Christ had promised that the Spirit would remain with the church until the end of time, leading it into truth.[8] The intrinsic authority of the Bible as the written word of God was never called into question; rather it was argued that the Bible was not the only source of doctrine and rule of life. God's continued presence in the world would take a different form. Thomas More challenged the foundations of Tyndale's argument. The process of revelation had not been completed in the

---

[5] Tyndale, *Answer*, p. 297.

[6] Tyndale, *Obedience*, pp. 177, 128; R. Pineas, 'William Tyndale's Polemical Use of the Scriptures', *Nederlands Archief voor Kerkesgeschichte*, 45 (1962), pp. 65–78; A. Richardson, 'Scripture as evidence in Tyndale's *The Obedience of a Christian Man*', *Moreana*, 106 (1991), p. 85. Tyndale was not the only writer to defend the supremacy of Scripture over the traditions of the church: see also A. Gilby, *An Answer to the Deuellish Detection of Stephane Gardiner* (1547), RSTC 11884; U. Rhegius (tr. W. Turner), *A Co[m]parison Betwene the Olde Learnynge & The Newe* (Southwark, 1537), RSTC 20840; J. von Watt (tr. W. Turner), *A worke entytled of ye olde god & the newe of the old doctryne and ye newe* (1534), RSTC 25127; E.P., *A Confutatio[n] of Unwritten Verities* (Wesel, 1558), RSTC 5996. The same concerns are reflected in the omission of four 'non-scriptural' sacraments from the Bishops' Book of 1537. C. Lloyd, *Formularies of Faith put forth by Authority during the Reign of Henry VIII* (Oxford, 1825).

[7] Ibid., p. 103.

[8] John 21:25: 'There were many other things that Jesus did; if all that were written down, the world itself, I suppose, would not hold all the books that would have to be written.' John 16:12–13: 'I still have many things to say to you, but they would be too much for you now. But when the Spirit of truth comes, he will lead you to a complete truth.'

apostolic age, but had continued throughout the history of the church. Christ had promised the Holy Spirit, and not a book, as a guide for His followers, and in accordance with the text of John 16:12–13, it was inconceivable that the church should err in the introduction of traditions, since these traditions were the fruits of this inspiration of the Spirit.[9] The 'public faith' of the Catholic church, by which it had been recognized through history, was in sharp contrast to the diversity of belief among successive generations of heretics, 'of all whych euery one contraryeth his felow in great articles of the faith'. There were as many heretical sects as there were heretics, but only one church.[10] Consensus provided a measure of truth; therefore the individual should refer his beliefs to the greater authority of the church.[11]

The sufficiency of Scripture, and its correct interpretation, were not new problems in the sixteenth century. By the dawn of the Reformation it was possible to identify two strands in mediaeval thought: one in which Scripture was interpreted against the backdrop of the historical continuity of the church which defined the parameters of interpretation, and a second in which tradition was seen as a providentially ordained source of revelation which compensated for the silence of Scripture on key matters.[12] Even where disputes could be settled by recourse to Scripture alone, it was argued that the word of God must be interpreted through the guidance of the Spirit, and in accordance with the determinations of the Father who had been duly inspired to provide the faithful with a correct understanding. In this understanding of revelation, the writings of the Fathers and the pronouncements of the church were not to be set up in opposition to the written word of Scripture, but were rather part of a broader understanding of *scriptura sacra*, which included not only the Old and New Testaments, but also the works of the Fathers and the canons and decrees of the church.[13] Scripture was not a separate entity either above or outside the

---

[9] T. More, *Responsio ad Lutherum*, CW, 5, pp. 236–7.

[10] More, *Confutation of Tyndale's Answer*, CW, 8, pp. 728, 772. For the assertion of Catholic unity see *Dialogue Concerning Heresies*, CW, 6, p. 166.

[11] The centrality of consensus on More's arguments casts doubts upon William Clebsch's assertion that More believed that 'the determination of the official Church's teaching was easily settled by reference to the papacy': W.A. Clebsch, *England's Earliest Protestants 1520–1535* (New Haven, 1964), p. 296. The defence of tradition and unwritten verities in More's work rests upon the shared beliefs of the common corps of Christendom, past and present, to a much greater extent than Clebsch allows.

[12] H. Oberman, *The Dawn of the Reformation: Essays in Late Medieval and Early Reformation Thought* (Edinburgh, 1986), pp. 289–96; A. McGrath, *Reformation Thought. An Introduction* (Oxford, 1988), p. 97.

[13] Y. Congar, *Tradition and Traditions: An Historical and a Theological Essay* (London, 1966), p. 91.

church, but rather a constituent part of divine revelation mediated and interpreted by the church of God, with the result that any choice between Scripture and tradition was a choice with little real meaning.

When this model was challenged, however, the balance and inclusiveness which had supported it gave way under the pressure of polemical assault. Wycliffe's attack upon the traditions and ceremonies of the church not only implied a separation of Scripture from tradition, but also encouraged the conclusion that once the constituent parts of the *scriptura sacra* were separated, the words of the Bible could be turned to judge traditional interpretations and unwritten revelations. The response to Wycliffe from the pens of Thomas Netter and William of Waterford deepened divisions further, by defending the authority of tradition on the basis that certain truths necessary for salvation were not contained in Scripture, but were known only through revelation in the church. Such an approach underpinned grandiose assertions of ecclesiastical power and privilege in the fourteenth and fifteenth centuries, imbuing the church with an infallibility in identifying and determining the content of faith. This clash between the image of a church founded upon a broad understanding of revelation and those who sought reform on the premise of Scripture alone gained added momentum in the first years of the Reformation. The circulation of vernacular Bibles, both in England and abroad, ensured that the appeal to the primacy of the written word was rarely uncontroversial, while with the *ad fontes* appeal to the original text, the nature, content and authority of Scripture were hotly disputed, and the framework of religious debate was remodelled.

The opposition of divine and human law, witnessed either in the context of the theology of salvation or in disputes over the authority of Scripture and tradition, caused fractures which ran deep. One historian has gone so far as to argue that the whole of the Reformation movement developed from conflict over the submission of man to divine or human bidding. Obedience to God alone denied the role of the institutional church in the covenant between God and man, rejected the interpretative authority of the church in the preaching of Scripture, and amounted to a repudiation of its sacramental nature.[14] While this fragmentation of Scripture and tradition contributed in part to the divisive character of printed debate, polemical modes of thought in the Reformation helped to make these divisions more concrete. Polemical literature thrived upon exclusivity and opposition, dictating modes of thought in which either/or alternatives predominated and the possibility of compromise was denied. Thus the principle of *sola scriptura* was pitted against a caricature of *sola ecclesia*, and the authority of the individual conscience was raised above

---

[14] Ibid., p. 142.

the authority of the institutional church.[15] Evangelical writers offered a choice between the word of God and the word of the pope, suggesting that the doctrine and practice of the pre-Reformation church were built upon the arbitrary pronouncements of its human hierarchy, and presenting a picture of the reformed churches founded upon the faith of Scripture alone. Those who leapt to the defence of the Church argued more strongly for the authenticity and necessity of extra-scriptural revelation, and for the unique interpretative powers which the church possessed, guiding the faithful in the correct reading of Scripture, and guided itself by the inspiration of the Holy Spirit. The determination of Tyndale and others to 'dig again the wells of Abraham' was to exert a powerful influence over both the polemic of the Reformation, and the formulation of theology and identity in the nascent reformed churches.

Writing against the Lutheran rejection of the traditions and cere-monies of mediaeval Catholicism, Thomas More argued that the visible and enduring practices of the church marked out its identity as the true church of Christ. The Catholic church, he claimed, enjoyed both unity of faith in the present and continuity of faith with the past, as 'that true church which has been by a certain unbroken succession from the one which Christ long ago established and which has ever remained uncor-rupted in the faith of its origin'.[16] It was this continuity of faith and practice that defined the identity of the church, and left those outside with no solid foundation: when the reformers attacked the teaching of the church, they challenged not only the authority of the contemporary body of believers, but also doctrines received, preserved and handed down from the patristic era.[17] Truth had crystallized slowly in the teachings of the institutional church, with the result that for More the present-day faith of the church provided the starting-point from which a doctrinal line could be traced to the earliest days of Christianity.[18] To deny the continuity of revelation and the permanent guidance of the Holy Spirit was to deny the historical identity of the church, which had been the custodian of this revelation and recipient of divine inspiration through the centuries. The challenge of the Reformation was therefore not simply a challenge to certain traditional practices, but was all the more serious for the threat that it posed to the whole ecclesiastical framework. Brian Gogan has drawn attention to the notion prevalent in Thomas More's thought that there was a fundamental unity in

---

[15] L. Schuster, 'Reformation Polemic and Renaissance Values', *Moreana*, 43–4 (1974), p. 50. See also chapter 5 below.

[16] More, *Responsio*, pp. 191/39–193/2.

[17] More, *Confutation*, p. 310/25–7.

[18] Flesseman van Leer, 'Controversy about Ecclesiology', p. 78.

revelation, which linked the various earthly phases of the working out of the eternal plan for salvation.[19] Just as there would be no longstanding contradictions in the faith revealed to the church, so there could be no break in the chain of revelation, and no cessation of the divine guidance in the interpretation of Scripture. Viewed in this way, the threat posed by the Reformation was cataclysmic, because it implied that the promise that the Holy Spirit would reside in the church until the end of time had been false.[20]

The belief that God was continually active in human history and understanding provided the backbone of the argument for the insufficiency of Scripture in matters pertaining to salvation. If the guidance of the Holy Spirit was required to reveal the divine truth in the post-apostolic age, the content of the written word of God in Scripture appeared incomplete. In the writings of Thomas More, the Holy Spirit was both a source of divine revelation and a record of that revelation, whether in tablets of stone, on paper, or in the hearts of men.[21] The word of God, he claimed, 'is parte wryten in the Scrypture and part unwryten that appereth not proved therein'.[22] Revelation not contained in Scripture was still of divine origin, however: this body of practice had been taught by Christ to the Apostles, and passed by them to the church, which had preached it to the faithful. These unwritten verities were not unrelated to Scripture, or antagonistic to it, but were rather part of the one fount of revelation from which Scripture flowed. Whereas Henry VIII defended tradition as an alternative source of knowledge, Gogan argues that the origins of More's argument lay more firmly in the mainstream of mediaeval thought on the coinherence of Scripture and tradition.[23] All essential truth was contained in the sacred texts, but tradition was the explication of the hidden truths of the written word of God that were necessary for full Christian understanding. Tradition, properly seen, was the 'authoritative exegesis' of Scripture, which could only be understood fully when illuminated by the traditions of the church.[24]

The authority of the church to interpret and mediate the word of God stemmed from its role in the determination of the correct biblical canon. Thomas More argued that while it was clearly possible for heretics to attempt to validate their assertions by an appeal to Scripture, their

---

[19] Gogan, *Common Corps*, p. 66.

[20] John 16.

[21] Gogan, *Common Corps*, p. 194, More; *Confutation*, p. 45/6–15, p. 332/36–7, pp. 752/30–753/28.

[22] Flesseman van Leer, 'Scripture and Tradition', p. 146.

[23] Gogan, *Common Corps*, pp. 310–11.

[24] Marshall, 'Unwritten Verities', p. 61.

knowledge of Scripture had been acquired through the church, which had made an infallible declaration of the true canon.[25] Because the church had authenticated Scripture, and had determined its correct interpretation, it was impossible that this authentic text could contain anything that ran contrary to the faith of the church. It was the faith of the church that had determined the content of the written text, and the faith of the church preceded the text and governed its meaning. This hypothesis was neatly summarized in the often-quoted declaration of Augustine that he would not have believed the Gospel were it not for the church.[26] More was prepared to concede that the word had been preached before the existence of the church, but argued that it was the living church in the past, now embodied in the institutional church of the present, that had provided the context for the correct and faithful understanding of the Bible.[27] If the church had been empowered and guided to the determination of the true text of Scripture, it made little sense to deny the authority of that church to interpret the text. The interpretation of the individual could not be raised above that of the church in its history; for More the exegesis of Scripture was 'never a matter of purely private intuition. It takes place within a living community and a living tradition.'[28] Scripture and tradition stood side by side in the revelation of truth, but it was the right and the responsibility of the church to safeguard that truth as the final authority. In times of doubt, therefore, the individual should cleave to the faith of the church, and allow God to elaborate the true meaning of revelation.[29] By arguing with reference to Scripture alone it was possible to turn the Bible against itself, and the diversity of heretical sects belied any substantive argument for the perspicuity of Scripture, or the assertion that the written word had only one meaning. However, the guidance of the spirit in the historical church ensured the correct interpretation, and because God spoke through the word and the church there was no possibility of error.

The interpretative authority of the church was also under threat, however, from those such as Tyndale who argued for the autopisty of the written word of Scripture, denying that any further clarification or elaboration was required. For Thomas More, however, it was clear that the whole of divine revelation was not contained in Scripture alone, but was complemented by the faith of the church which preserved what had been heard and received from the mouths of the Apostles. Scripture was

---

[25] Flesseman van Leer, 'Scripture and Tradition', p. 152.

[26] Augustine, *Contra Epistola Manichaei*, quoted in Marshall, 'Unwritten Verities', p. 68.

[27] More, *Responsio*, I, pp. 133/31–134/2; Gogan, *Common Corps*, p. 198.

[28] Gogan, *Common Corps*, p. 199.

[29] Flesseman van Leer, 'Scripture and Tradition', 160.

an incomplete revelation of the divine plan, but the insufficiency of the written word was balanced by the so-called 'gospel in the heart'. The old law, he claimed, had been written in tablets of stone, but the new law was written inwardly, in the 'book' of the heart.[30] To confine the activity and revelation of God to the written word was to limit the divine power and deny the possibility of divine activity beyond the text of Scripture. John Fisher argued from Augustine that there was a three-fold distinction in the development of doctrine, between those matters that were contained in Scripture, those that were found in the unwritten apostolic tradition, and those that were loosely defined as customs confirmed by approved practice.[31] Catholic polemic in the sixteenth century sought to demonstrate the key role of extra-scriptural practices in the life of the community of believers. Thomas More identified three clear illustrations of divine revelation outside Scripture: the commandments given to Adam and Eve, those given to the patriarchs and prophets, and the preaching of the Apostles which had helped to shape the oral traditions transmitted through the church.[32] Luther, it was alleged, had failed to appreciate that the Bible had never been intended as a vehicle by which all knowledge of the divine could be conveyed; rather it had been written to provide its readers with a model of virtue in the life of Jesus. The text of the Scriptures was not itself Christ, but rather had been written about Christ, and could therefore be augmented by the will of God.[33] To deny the possibility of further revelation was to deny all other parts of the Christian faith which were not obviously contained in this written record.

These 'unwritten verities' were strongly defended by Catholic polemicists from the early years of the Reformation. The term covered a multitude of dogmas, practices and customs which were to fall victim to the doctrinal iconoclasm of the reformers, prompting the application of the general defence of extra-scriptural revelation to key features of traditional religion, including the celibacy of the clergy. In the theology of Fisher, unwritten verities had been transmitted through the prophets and the Apostles, and clarified by the Fathers of the church, the councils and the popes, whose collective authority clearly outweighed that of questioning individuals.[34] The defence of unwritten verities amounted to

---

[30] More, *Responsio*, p. 101/12–28 Jer. 31:31–4; *Confutation*, p. 257/33–7; p. 270/18–23.

[31] E. Surtz, *The Works and Days of John Fisher* (Cambridge, Mass., 1967), p. 102.

[32] A.B. Ferguson, *Clio Unbound. Perceptions of the Social and Cultural Past in Renaissance England* (Durham, North Carolina, 1979), p. 155.

[33] R.R. McCutcheon, 'The Responsio ad Lutherum. Thomas More's Inchoate Dialogue with Heresy', *Sixteenth Century Journal*, 22 (1991), pp. 88–9.

[34] Ferguson, *Clio Unbound*, p. 151.

a vindication of progressive revelation, of God's continued communication with mankind, and the interpretation of that revelation by the church. Yet this was a defence of divine traditions rather than the laws of man, and the focus of the argument was the evident action of an omnipotent God in communicating with His people outside the fixed medium of the written word. From the patristic period it had been possible to identify beliefs and practices that were founded upon the developing faith and authority of the church, although no effort had been made in definition or codification. By the later Middle Ages, however, such 'unwritten verities' had acquired a normative authority, and the importance of these traditions was enshrined in the decrees of the Council of Trent. The Gospel, defined by the decree, was to be found 'contained in the written books and in unwritten traditions which were received by the Apostles from the lips of Christ himself, or, by the same Apostles, at the dictation of the Holy Spirit, and were handed on and have come down to us ... '.[35] The council confirmed that extra-scriptural traditions were an essential part of the Christian message, but the exact formulation of its pronouncement caused some debate. The initial decree had included a 'partim ... partim' formula, which left the way open for assertions or accusations that this implied the existence of two independent sources of revelation. The removal of the clause, which had echoed the interpretation of Scripture and tradition favoured by Thomas More and Henry VIII, avoided locating divine revelation in Scripture alone or tradition alone, and affirmed the existence of one source of faith, identifying Scripture and tradition as the two channels through which this source was carried to the faithful.[36]

The *locus classicus* for the attack on the evangelical position on unwritten verities was the teaching of the church on the perpetual virginity of Mary. Writing against Luther, Thomas More argued that the whole article of faith depended upon the teaching of the church: there was no incontrovertible text of Scripture which could be used to underpin the doctrine.[37] This approach was not unique to More: John Fisher had used the same argument to demonstrate the authority of the church in the determination of doctrine. Scripture was indeed notably silent on the subject, and, if anything, appeared to support an alternative hypothesis, with references to the brothers and sisters of Christ. For Fisher, the only positive proof that could be adduced in defence of the belief was therefore the constant teaching authority of the church. Both Erasmus and Rhenanus had also used the debate between Jerome and

---

[35] Quoted in Marshall, 'Unwritten Verities', p. 60.
[36] Congar, *Tradition*, p. 157–68.
[37] *Responsio*, pp. 102/27–104/7.

Helvidius in discussing the question, and had noted that Jerome's argument in favour of the perpetual virginity rested upon the traditions of the church alone. Rex notes that Fisher added a new twist to the argument by applying the case to the emerging conflict over the sufficiency of Scripture, and this certainly touched a nerve with evangelical writers.[38] With no obvious scriptural warrant for the teaching, if the reformed churches continued to uphold the doctrine they would thereby be compelled to accept the general validity of extra-scriptural revelation. The case was made all the more sensitive by the repudiation of the cult of the Virgin by reformers on both sides of the Channel; the destruction of a key element of Catholic piety was unlikely to succeed if part of the theology which underpinned it was allowed to survive. To reject all those practices that did not have a transparent foundation in Scripture would be to reject other key aspects of mainstream evangelical practice, such as infant baptism, making its position against Anabaptism untenable. Yet to accept the traditional teaching on the perpetual virginity would be to open the floodgates to other beliefs and practices condemned as unscriptural but which were taught on the authority of the church, most obviously purgatory and the theology of the afterlife.

This potential for conflict in the principle of *sola scriptura* was visible from the first stirrings of evangelical criticism and political reformation. The early pronouncements of the Henrician Reformation against the papal power of dispensation amounted to an attack on the traditional authority of the church to interpret and apply the word of God in Scripture. Yet as Peter Marshall has demonstrated, the Bible was not the sole source of authority in the Henrician church.[39] Whilst claiming a foundation in the word of God, the Henrician church still defined and enforced non-scriptural practice, but by making such matters dependent upon the will of the king and not the will of the pontiff. The implication might have been that these laws were not necessary for salvation, but Marshall notes the semantic nature of the distinction: obedience was not demanded by the law of God, but the duty of obedience to the laws of the kings meant that such formulations were still binding upon the conscience. The distinction was blurred further by the declaration in 1539 that vows of chastity, condemned as unscriptural by evangelicals, were in fact 'binding by the law of God'.[40] If the official Reformation failed to produce a watertight definition of the locus of authority in the church, the efforts of evangelical writers could generate further conflict.

The defence of *sola scriptura* depended upon the assumption that the

---

[38] Rex, *Theology of John Fisher*, p. 98, quoting ALC proem 8v (col. 285).

[39] Marshall, 'Unwritten Verities', *passim*.

[40] Ibid., p. 71.

language of the Bible was clear and self-evident, and indeed that every reader would be able to comprehend from Scripture that message which was essential to salvation. William Tyndale had upheld the right of the individual to read and interpret the word of God, but was forced to concede that there would be some passages which were too complex to understand. These, he suggested, should be studied in the broadest context, and interpreted with this general meaning in mind. Others, however, were to be read against the general articles of faith, an argument that came close to admitting the need for, and the existence of, an authority external to the text. Tyndale's suggestion that it was the duty of the curate to teach the people perhaps suggests a declining optimism concerning the capacity of the laity to receive and comprehend the truth.[41] Flesseman van Leer has questioned the validity of equating the Reformation with the message of *sola scriptura* in light of such admissions of the apparent need for an interpretative framework outside the mind of the reader.[42] One writer goes further still, suggesting that far from encouraging the free interpretation of the Bible, Tyndale sought to replace the interpretations of the infallible church with his own 'infallible' understanding of Scripture.[43] Similar tensions can be traced within the continental magisterial Reformation. The Reformation, McGrath argues, was characterized by the belief that it could be understood what the Bible had to say on every subject, an attitude expressed in Erasmus's *Enchiridion*, Zwingli's *On the Clarity and the Certainty of the Word of God* (1522), and Luther's *To the Christian Nobility of the German Nation*. Luther argued that the word of God could act as its own exegete: 'scriptura sui ipsius interpres'.[44]

For McGrath, however, there are fundamental problems in assuming an identity between the image and reality of this 'exegetical optimism'.[45] There were clear differences of opinion in crucial matters of faith, not least the theology of the Eucharist, and the ability to understand the word of God in its totality appeared predicated upon a correct reading of Greek and Hebrew texts, which was unlikely to find popular appeal. For Catholic polemicists, the appeal to the interpretative authority of the church offered a resolution to conflict, but this did not fit easily with the evangelical emphasis upon the freedom of the individual to read Scripture. For evangelicals to turn to the authority of the Christian community to validate interpretations would be to concede ground to

---

[41] Richardson, 'Scripture as evidence', p. 87.

[42] Flesseman van Leer, 'Scripture and Tradition', 157–9.

[43] R. Pineas, 'William Tyndale's Polemical Use of the Scriptures', *Nederlands Archiv voor Kerkesgeschiedenis* 45 (1962), p. 67.

[44] Quoted in Marshall, 'Unwritten Verities', p. 67.

[45] McGrath, *Reformation Thought*, pp. 111–12.

the traditional structures of authority. Alternative means or 'filters' were therefore found, either in the form of catechisms which could introduce the reader to the correct meaning of Scripture, or in the formulation of what McGrath calls a 'political hermeneutic', in which the city emerged as the body in which the power to interpret was vested.[46] In reformed apologetic, however, the authority of religious or secular powers was firmly that of interpretation: it was the duty of the church to expound the word of God but not to augment it or introduce new doctrines.[47] In Tyndale's eyes the Catholic church had failed in its obligation of stewardship of the Gospel, by suppressing the Bible in order that it might not be judged by comparison with the divine plan. The same was true in the early decades of the evangelical movement in England, and Tyndale's complaint that it was considered heresy and treason to read the Scriptures applied as much to his king as to the pope. If the cry of *sola scriptura* undermined the historical edifice of Catholicism, it could be as much of a challenge to the structures of the nascent English church.

The challenge was all the more real when the appeal to Scripture alone was used to pass judgement upon the structures of secular and ecclesiastical authority. Tyndale argued that just as the Israelites had been instructed to read Scripture to determine whether their priesthood fulfilled its obligations, so the Christian faithful should measure their church against the model of the church in the days of the Apostles.[48] By 1528 and the publication of the *Obedience*, the Bible was being set forth as the sole model and authority for Christian behaviour, and the mirror in which all conduct was to be examined.[49] Such assertions were supported by the evangelical belief in the sufficiency of Scripture, and the doctrinal formularies of the official church which argued that nothing necessary to salvation could be added to the faith of Scripture.[50] In the words of John Jewel, Scripture was the rule 'whereby all truth and Catholic doctrine may be proved and all heresy may be disproved and confuted'.[51] Such a model still left the way open for development in doctrine and practice, but such innovations and customs were not to be held as essentials of faith. However, the assertion of the sufficiency of Scripture did not put an end to debate within the evangelical movement. Peter Marshall notes that there was still a 'hermeneutic dimension' to the

---

[46] Ibid., pp. 112–13.

[47] Gerrish, *Old Protestantism and the New*, p. 67.

[48] Pineas, 'Tyndale's Polemical Use of the Scriptures', p. 65.

[49] Richardson, 'Scripture as evidence', p. 83.

[50] Evans, *Problems of Authority*, p. 75, quoting the English Articles of 1553, 1571; Marshall, 'Unwritten Verities', pp. 68–71.

[51] W. Southgate, *John Jewel and the Problem of Doctrinal Authority* (Cambridge, Mass., 1962), p. 152, quoting Jewel's *Apology*.

debate: even if Scripture did contain all that was true and condemned all that was false, the question of who decided what was condemned and what was commended still remained unanswered.[52] Further opportunities for conflict arose over those practices that were not explicitly recommended in Scripture. Was obedience to these traditional beliefs and practices to be decided at the level of the individual conscience, or that of the national church, or was it legitimate to assume that those matters which were not enjoined in Scripture were therefore prohibited?[53] Different understandings of the sufficiency and supremacy of Scripture were to find a clear expression in the vestiarian controversies in the English church in the reigns of Edward VI and Elizabeth, but were also to feature in the debate over the exact meaning and implications of key passages in the debate over clerical celibacy. While there was nothing here to suggest that Scripture did not have authority, and indeed priority over other Christian texts, there was a clear difference between those who believed that Scripture was the word of God, and those who argued that Scripture contained the word of God, thus allowing a greater degree of interpretative authority.[54]

The initial attack upon the place of tradition in the Christian church had been launched with the aim of distinguishing between the divine and the temporal, the eternal promise and the mutable laws of man. The optimistic appeal to Scripture alone, in the first years of evangelical reform, seemed to offer the clearest measure of truth and falsehood, and promised to throw into sharp relief divisions between the laws of God and the customs of the church. However, the insistence upon the right of the individual to read and interpret the word of God opened the door to a multitude of different understandings of the message of the Gospel and raised questions about the need for an external interpretative authority. While it was possible to deny the legitimacy of human innovation in matters of doctrine, English reformers turned increasingly to the duty of obedience to the king to validate the structure and customs of the national church. Models of godly rule by kings were plentiful, and the propagandists of the English Reformation turned to the kings of the Old Testament, David and Josiah, to root the supremacy in the events of the Christian past. The necessity of obedience was presented to the people by William Tyndale's *Obedience of a Christian Man*, and Stephen Gardiner's *De Vera Obedientia*, and preached from the pulpit in the *Homily on Obedience* (1547). John Jewel argued that while the truth of Christian doctrine existed independently of secular powers and human

---

[52] Marshall, 'Unwritten Verities', p. 67.
[53] See for example Calvin, *Institutes*, 4.7.10.
[54] McGrath, *Reformation Thought*, p. 104.

actions, the monarch in parliament still held rightful authority in matters temporal and spiritual, an authority that legitimated the enforcement of right faith and practice.[55] However, the use of Scripture to judge the faith and actions of the mediaeval church encouraged a similar appeal to biblical texts in the face of opposition from figures of authority in post-Reformation church and government. The will of the king and his parliament might be the legitimate power in determining the nature of the newly reformed church, but as the debate over clerical marriage indicates, polemicists on both sides of the religious divide were prepared to argue from Scripture against the pronouncements of the monarch.

Despite their opposing views on the relative authority of Scripture and tradition, neither side in the debate questioned the ultimate authority of the Bible. The assault of the reformers, the rejection of doctrines and practices that were deemed unscriptural, was met with a barrage of biblical citations from the pens of Catholic controversialists in defence of such teachings. The centrality of Scripture to Reformation debates made the Bible a fertile hunting ground for polemicists seeking justification for their views on all questions of doctrine and practice, and the debate on clerical marriage provides a clear demonstration of the exploitation of Scripture by Catholic and evangelical polemicists alike. Both claimed the testimony of Scripture as their own, disputing the interpretation of key texts, and adducing apparently contradictory passages to undermine the position of their opponents. In evangelical polemic, Scripture provided the foundation for both the defence of clerical marriage, and for the denunciation of compulsory clerical celibacy. References were made to the marriage of priests under the old law, the marriage of the Apostles, and the holiness of the married state, to justify the legalization of clerical marriage in the sixteenth century. In contrast, Catholic propagandists, led by Thomas More in the 1520s, and Richard Smith and Thomas Martin in the 1550s, rallied to the defence of clerical celibacy, claiming that the testimony of Scripture confirmed that the decrees of the church were in accordance with the law of God.

The debate over the validity of clerical marriage focused on key passages in the Old and New Testaments, and highlights some of the uncertainties and tensions creations by the appeal to *sola scriptura*. The nature of the Levitical priesthood was debated at length, with both Catholic and Protestant writers drawing heavily upon the examples of priests and holy men of the Old Testament. Tyndale claimed that despite the injunctions to purity, there was no specific statement anywhere in the Old Testament that denied marriage to the clergy. If the priests were ordered to abstain from their wives at all 'it was but for a tyme, to geue

---

[55] Southgate, *John Jewel*, pp. 215–17.

them to prayer'.[56] Bale echoed Tyndale's argument, claiming that God had appointed wives 'by hys seruant Moses, unto the Leuytycall prestes in the sacred posteryte of Aaron', although he admitted that it was a 'labour lost' to convince the Catholic clergy of this. The injunctions of Leviticus 21, and Ezekiel 44, which stipulated that a priest was not to marry a prostitute or a widow, clearly confirmed that the priests of the old law had been allowed to marry. The prohibitions were laid upon certain groups of women, rather than marriage itself.[57] Thomas Becon used the same argument, based on the Deuteronomic code, to confirm that marriage was not forbidden to the priests of the old law.[58] In fact, God had commanded men to multiply, Becon argued, 'but the vowe of chastitie sayeth "encrease not, multiply not, and replenishe not the earthe"'.[59] There was nothing to suggest that God had intended that priests should remain unmarried, in violation of this injunction, and those who spurned marriage in order to be priests could not cite the law of Moses in their defence. Indeed, the example of the priests of the old law suggested that the godly were in fact married. Those who embraced matrimony, Becon argued, 'bothe please God and are also inheritours of euerlastinge glorie' along with Noah, Lot, Seth, Abraham, Isaac, Jacob, Josias and the Apostles.[60] Marriage was a sign of God's blessing, and a destiny ordained for man.

The Old Testament was replete with examples of godly marriage. Becon referred to Sarah and Tobias, Abraham and Sarah, Agar, the mother of Ishmael, and Jacob's search for a wife in Mesopotamia.[61] In contrast, a vow of chastity was a poor show of holiness. Becon argued from the text of Proverbs 30, a condemnation of the pretence of purity, which could be interpreted as an indictment of the unmarried and unchaste clergy of the sixteenth century.[62] The later verses of Proverbs 30 also include a warning against the locusts 'who have no king, and yet

---

[56] Tyndale, *Answer*, p. 317.

[57] J. Bale, *The Actes of the Englysh Votaries*, pt. I (Wesel, 1546), RSTC 1270, fols 8v–9r; Lev. 21, Ezek. 44; *Yet a Course at the Romyshe Foxe* (Antwerp, 1543), RSTC 1309, sig. K2v.

[58] T. Becon, *Book of matrimony*, in *Workes*, I, fol. HHh3r.

[59] Ibid., fol. OOo1v–2r.

[60] Becon, *Matrimony*, fol. IIi6v. Bullinger offered a similar list in *The Golden Boke of Christen Matrimonye* (1543), RSTC 4046, fol. 23r–v. Becon provided a preface to the work.

[61] Becon, *Matrimony*, fol. HHh5r. Becon coupled this with a reference to Prov. 19, arguing that while man received riches from his parents, he received his wife from God, Hhh6r, Gen. 28, Gen. 21, Gen. 32.

[62] Ibid., fol. HHh3r–v. The image of the Catholic clergy as locusts was common in Protestant polemic, especially in commentaries on Revelation 9, where the identification afforded apocalyptic possibilities. See chapter 5, pp. 126ff.

they all march in good order; the lizard which you can catch in your hand, yet it frequents the palaces of kings'. Far from being a sign of holiness among the priests and prophets of the old law, abstaining from marriage was an attempt on the part of the clergy to exert influence in the affairs of princes. In an argument intended to attract the attention of secular authorities, Becon suggested that clerical celibacy presented a real threat to the rule of princes. Philip Melanchthon had made the same point in the aftermath of the prohibition of clerical marriage in England in the Six Articles of 1539. A celibate priesthood provided princes with a 'fayre flock' from which to choose their ministers and ambassadors, but also promoted greed and licentiousness. Melanchthon had appealed to Henry VIII to revoke the legislation, arguing 'it pertayneth to the offices of princes to abolysshe and destroye this theyr uniust and tyrannical prohibicion'.[63] The lessons and examples of Scripture could only be brought to fruition through the authority of the king.

In contrast, Catholic writers defended the correlation between the laws of Leviticus and the celibacy of the contemporary clergy. Under the old law, purity had been expected in the presence of the sacred, and abstinence from women was deemed a necessity.[64] Thomas Martin argued that the priests of the old law had abstained from their wives before performing their sacrifices, indicating that chastity was expected of those who approached the sacred. Ahimelech told David that 'If the men ... be pure & cleare from wemen, let the[m] eat', but that the sacrificial loaves would be withheld if the men were not chaste.[65] Thus, Richard Smith argued, if such purity was expected of those who would eat the holy bread of the Old Testament, then it was all the more necessary in the priests of the new law, who sacrificed the body of Christ.[66] Smith claimed that the whole argument in favour of clerical marriage rested upon the words of Genesis, 'Crescite (inquit Deus), multiplicamini & replete terram.' Marriage, however, was not the only state pleasing to God. The Old Testament was rich with examples of celibate men of God, including Melchisedech, Joshua, Jeremiah and Daniel.[67] Chastity was indeed a sign of holiness, and one which ensured that the sacrifices of men would be pleasing to God. Smith quoted Solomon, and the warning that 'the sacrifice of wicked men is

---

[63] P. Melanchthon (tr. G. Joye), *A very godly defense ... defending the mariage of preistes* (Antwerp, 1541), RSTC 17798, sig. A2v–4r.

[64] Dionysius Carthusianus, *The Lyfe of Prestes* (1533), RSTC 6894, sig. G4r.

[65] T. Martin, *A Treatise declaryng and plainly provyng that the pretensed marriage of priestes ... is no mariage* (1554), RSTC 17517, sig. B4v. I Sam. 21:4.

[66] R. Smith, *Defensio sacri Episcoporu[m] & sacerdotum coelibatus, contra impias & indoctas Petri Martyris Vermilii* (Paris, 1551), sig. A8r.

[67] Ibid., sig. E4v–5r.

abhorrent', and cited Isaiah 8 and Psalms 75 (76)[68] against those who broke the chastity of the priesthood.[69] Psalms 75 (76) included the injunction to fulfil the promises made to God (v.11), which Smith interpreted as an injunction to keep vows, and vows of chastity in particular. The following verse, however, carried the warning that God 'snuffs out the life of princes, he is terrible to the kings of the earth'. If, as Becon argued, the celibacy of the clergy allowed them to infiltrate the palaces of princes, in the eyes of Smith, the breaking of such vows posed an even greater threat to the rule of the king.

The use of the Old Testament by Catholic and evangelical writers alike raised the question of whether the law of Moses was still binding upon priests and people after the coming of Christ. Catholic controversialists claimed that the holiness expected of a priest of the old law was all the more necessary for a Christian priest who handled the body of Christ in the Mass.[70] The fact that Christ was born of a virgin, and lived as such, further increased the expectation that the priests of the new law should be pure. The distinction between the priests of the Old and New Testament lay not in the lifting of their obligation to purity, but in the added force behind such a demand. Thomas Martin declared that the clergy should make and keep a vow of perpetual chastity, since 'their character, their dignity, their function and office is continuall', in contrast to the Levitical priesthood, where the office of the priest was exercised for only 12 days of the year.[71] Adam had come to 'replenish the earth', but Christ had come 'to multiply in the worlde the spirituall generacion of the sonnes of God'. This contrast between the old law and the new, it was argued, should be reflected in the attributes of the ministry. The Levitical priesthood was a priesthood of hereditary succession, but the priesthood of the New Testament was founded upon succession in the Spirit. Any function that the marriage of priests might have served under the old law was unnecessary in the Christian church.[72]

In contrast, evangelical polemicists suggested that the abrogation of the old law by the coming of Christ was evidence that all observances of the Levitical law, including priestly abstinence, were of no effect or value. Robert Crowley argued that the Levitical code was a 'ded cano[n]', which could not be used to support the prohibition of clerical

---

[68] The Psalter contains 150 psalms. From Psalm 10 to Psalm 148 the re-numbering in the Hebrew Bible is one figure ahead of the Greek and the Vulgate. The Greek and Vulgate divide into two Psalms 116 and 147, but join together Psalms 9 and 10 and Psalms 114 and 115.

[69] R. Smith, *Defensio*, sig. C2v, Prov. 21. sig. D8r.

[70] More, *Dialogue*, p. 312. Luke 1:8, 23.

[71] Martin, *Pretensed marriage*, sigs B8v–C1r, K4v.

[72] Ibid., sig. MM1r.

marriage in present times. In any case, the priests of the Old Testament were only prohibited from marriage to widows and divorcees. Thus 'the dedication of priestes in the olde law was not of enough force to restrayne the mariage of Prestes: ergo it is not of force nowe to wyth holde our priestes from mariage'. Furthermore, Paul had written of the irrelevance of the old law after the coming of Christ, an irrelevance which Crowley believed extended to the constraints placed upon the priesthood.[73] Thomas Becon argued the same point from the epistle of James. If the priests of the old law could marry, the priests of the new law could clearly do the same, freed from the constraints of the law of Moses. The law of the Old Testament was a ceremonial law, 'an ordynaunce for a time', which did not prohibit marriage in the Christian priesthood.[74] After the preaching of the Gospel, the codes of the Old Testament offered no defence of compulsory clerical celibacy.

Citations from the New Testament were not limited to those verses that promised Christian freedom. However, the wealth of material available, and the variety of interpretations offered, ensured that arguments from Scripture all too frequently proved inconclusive. The same biblical verses cited in favour of clerical marriage often featured in defences of clerical celibacy, but commentaries were coloured by different emphases and objectives. This potential for contradiction is demonstrated clearly in the treatment of the seventh chapter of Paul's first letter to the Corinthians, which included one of the lengthiest treatments of marriage in the New Testament, but also one of the most complex. As such, it was exploited by both Catholic and evangelical writers, and a variety of contradictory interpretations were advanced. In evangelical polemic, the most important verse presented marriage as a remedy for fornication: 'if they cannot contain, then they should marry, for it is better to marry than to burn' (1 Corinthians 7:9). Tyndale identified this verse as a valuable argument, and one that could be related to contemporary circumstances. By denying the remedy of marriage to the clergy, he claimed, the Catholic church was inventing sin where there was none, as the behaviour of those clergy who could not keep to their vows revealed. In light of these words of Paul, the disparity between the law of God and the law of the pope was clear. There was no reason why the clergy should be exempt from this remedy, since 'God commandeth all degrees, if they burne, and can not liue chaste, to marry'. In contrast, Tyndale commented, 'the pope saith, if thou burne take a dispensation for a concubine, and put her away when thou art

---

[73] R. Crowley, *A Confutation of xiii articles wherunto Nicholas Shaxton ... subscribed* (1548), RSTC 6083, sigs G7r–8r.

[74] Becon, *Matrimony*, fol. PPp3r–v. Jas. 1:25 refers to the 'perfect law of freedom'.

olde'.[75] The deeds of the clergy were a testimony to the dangers of prohibiting marriage, a remedy without sin, which God had ordained for His children.

Tyndale's argument was echoed by George Joye, who cited the same text in debate with Stephen Gardiner in the 1540s. By this time, the question had acquired a greater significance: Tyndale's attack was a challenge to the interpretations advanced by the Catholic church, but Joye's was as much a criticism of the policy of the Henrician government and the shape of the national church which still prohibited clerical marriage. The persecution of married clergy, Joye argued, contradicted the words of Paul, who had allowed each man to have his own wife, and was testimony to the arrogance of the institutional church.[76] The gift of God should take precedence over the laws of men, especially where the law of man could not remove the need for the remedy ordained by God. Compulsory clerical celibacy, whether enforced by the king or the pope, was a violation of the promise contained in Scripture that men had been given the freedom to marry.

It was precisely this argument, that marriage was a remedy for those who could not contain, which provided the focus for Catholic controversialists seeking a justification for clerical celibacy. Thomas More, Thomas Martin and Richard Smith argued that the fact that marriage was seen as a remedy by Paul revealed that he regarded virginity as more praiseworthy. Thomas More claimed that both Christ and Paul taught that chastity was a holy state, and 'preferred it before wedloke', basing his argument upon Paul's recommendation that it was better for widows and the unmarried to remain as they were.[77] Thomas Martin suggested that marriage was permitted rather than encouraged by Paul. The text of 1 Corinthians 7 was intended as an exhortation to all men to embrace the single life, 'a thing of more higher perfection', but the choice was left free.[78] In fact, Richard Smith argued, clerical celibacy had clear practical advantages. Freedom from the cares of marriage offered greater opportunities for devotion to the Lord's affairs, and Paul had written that it was beneficial for husband and wife to abstain for this purpose.[79] In the minds of Catholic polemicists, the letter to the Corinthians justified abstinence and virginity, but not the marriage of the clergy. The

---

[75] Tyndale, *Obedience*, p. 134.

[76] G. Joye, *The Defence of the Mariage of Preistes* (Antwerp,1541), RSTC 21804, sigs B6v–7r; Becon, *Book of Matrimony*, fol. MMm4v; Bale, *Actes of the Englysh Votaries*, pt II (1551), RSTC 1273.5, fol. 61r; Melanchthon, *Defence*, sig. B4v; H. Bullinger (tr. M. Coverdale), *The Golden Boke of Christen Matrimonye* (1541), RSTC 4045, p. 19v.

[77] More, *Confutation*, p. 306.

[78] Martin, *Pretensed marriage*, sig. Aa1r.

[79] R. Smith, *Defensio*, sig. E5v, 1 Cor. 7:6, sigs A8r–B1r.

fact that evangelical polemicists focused upon the issue of marriage as a remedy for fornication allowed them to comment on the conduct of the contemporary clergy, but it did little to assuage Catholic tendencies to exalt virginity as a state befitting the priests of the new law.[80]

Any assertion that Paul had honoured virginity over marriage, or had recommended that the married abstain from their spouses, was strongly contested by evangelical polemicists. George Joye argued that Paul had, rather, been concerned that the married should not allow themselves to become so preoccupied with one another that they neglected the office of preaching.[81] Thomas Becon admitted that Paul had encouraged abstinence, but temporarily, and only with the consent of both parties. In direct opposition to this, the pope sanctioned the separation of husband and wife on a permanent basis, in order that they might enter religious orders, replacing the law of God with the inventions of men.[82] Becon was equally dismissive of the suggestion that since abstinence aided prayer, perpetual abstinence was required of the clergy. 'All the world knoweth' Becon commented, 'that Priestes do not alwaye praye.'[83] If the clergy did not spend their whole lives in prayer, there was no reason why they should permanently abstain from marriage.

The use of the letter to the Corinthians by both sides in the debate laid bare the tensions which recourse to Scripture alone could create. It was clearly possible that multiple interpretations of biblical verses could be advanced and justified, but it was less clear where the authority and capacity to understand Scripture correctly was located. If the biblical text was indeed perspicuous, and the true meaning was revealed to the reader, as leading evangelical writers argued, it should be possible to reconcile such contradictory readings of key verses. The divergent interpretations of Corinthians could reinforce Catholic arguments for the necessity of external authority, but evangelical writers were forced

---

[80] Accusations of immorality were commonplace in Reformation polemic. Protestant writers made much of the failure of Catholic clergy to keep to their celibate ideal, while Catholic writers, particularly Thomas More and Miles Huggarde, made similar allegations against the reformers in an attempt to discredit their teaching (see Introduction). Peter Marshall has demonstrated that the morality of the clergy was a concern among the laity, especially in the provision for priests to pray for the souls of the dead. Marshall, *Catholic Priesthood and the English Reformation* (Oxford, 1994), pp. 147ff. Simon Fish claimed that the clergy had corrupted some one hundred thousand women in England: *A Supplicacyon for the Beggars*, ed. F.J. Furnivall, EETS, 13 (1871), p. 6. More recently historians have suggested that clerical immorality was far from rife in the pre-Reformation church. J.J. Scarisbrick, *The Reformation and the English People* (Oxford, 1984), p. 50; P. Heath, *English Parish Clergy on the Eve of the Reformation* (London, 1969).

[81] Joye, *Letters*, sigs B7v–B8r, 1 Cor. 7:3.

[82] Becon, *Matrimony*, fol. KKk2v.

[83] Ibid., fol. PPp6v.

simply to denounce the interpretations of their opponents as erroneous and misguided, on their own authority. Points of dispute might also be resolved if the disputed verses were set in context, or compared with other texts which addressed the subject: mistaken interpretations could then be identified by reference to Scripture alone, rather than personal judgement. However, on the subject of clerical marriage, the recommendations of Scripture were not always consistent, with the result that it was possible for either side in the debate to use this approach to turn unfavourable references to their advantage.

The problems of internal reference are demonstrated by the debates that arose around the interpretation of Hebrews 13, which was used in evangelical writing to argue that it was the married who were most fitted to the service of God: 'Marriage is honourable and the bed undefiled, but fornicators and adulterers will God judge.' Alongside 1 Corinthians 7, this verse was frequently cited by evangelical polemicists as a justification for the lifting of the prohibition on clerical marriage. Not only was marriage praised as an honourable estate, but the judgement of God was held over those who were guilty of fornication. It was better, therefore, that the clergy should live virtuously in marriage, than sinfully under the pretence of chastity.[84] In praise of marriage, Paul had not distinguished between priests and other men, therefore the marriage of priests was as honourable before God.[85] Similar references to Hebrews 13 appeared in the works of Joye, Rhegius and Ponet, who warned that if only the celibate were honourable before God, 'then should all the maried people, as well papists as other, as well kings, princes, as other of all sortes / lose the benefet of regeneracion'.[86]

---

[84] Ibid., fols GGg5r cf. title page, GHg4r, HHh6r, HHh5v–6r, PPp3v.

[85] Crowley, *Confutation*, sigs H2v–3r. Thomas Becon, who took the pseudonym Theodore Basil, had been forced to recant in February/March 1541, after preaching reformist sermons in Norwich. There are no extant records of the recantation, although Becon later referred to the incident in his second recantation, where he admitted that he had spoken against clerical celibacy. Becon was forced to recant again, and abjured at Paul's Cross in July 1543, and it is to this incident that Crowley referred. Miles Coverdale produced an English translation of Bullinger's *Der Christliche Ehestand* (*The Golden Boke of Christen Matrimonye*), and Becon provided a preface to the 1543 edition. Becon's original treatise on marriage, *The Book of Matrimony*, first appeared in the folio edition of his works. It is therefore likely that the work to which Crowley referred was the translation of Bullinger's treatise. Further details of the events leading to both recantations may be found in D.S. Bailey, *Thomas Becon and the Reformation of the Church of England* (1952), chs 2–4. The translation of Bullinger's work is discussed in the Introduction; see pp. 16–17 above.

[86] Joye, *Letters*, sig. C2r; Rhegius, *The Olde Learnynge & the Newe*, sig. F1v; J. Ponet, *An Apology fully aunsweringe ... D.Steph Gardiner* (Strasbourg, 1551), RSTC 20175, p. 31. Ponet's work was a reply to Thomas Martin's defence of clerical celibacy, which had

On first examination, the letter to the Hebrews did not offer much comfort to Catholic writers. However, despite the exhortation to marriage in Hebrews 13, Catholic writers were still able to use the text to undermine evangelical claims concerning the unity and perspicuity of Scripture. If Scripture could be exposed as inconsistent, this served to demonstrate both the value of external interpretative authority, and the insufficiency of the written word as a complete and comprehensible source of revelation. Thus Thomas More attempted to turn the text of Hebrews 13 against clerical marriage, criticizing Tyndale's argument that the virtues of God did not contradict one another. By claiming such unity for the written word, More argued, Tyndale had placed himself in the impossible position of either arguing that virginity was not a holy state, contrary to the sentiments of 1 Corinthians 7, or conceding that clerical marriages were neither holy, nor honourable before God, contrary to the sense of Hebrews 13. If Scripture spoke with a consistent voice, Hebrews 13 could not amount to an endorsement of clerical marriage, given the implied contradiction with 1 Corinthians. In admitting this, More triumphantly proclaimed, Tyndale would have confessed that Luther had 'synfully double defyled hym selfe wyth the weddynge of hys nonne'.[87] By diverting attention to Luther's marriage, and playing upon inconsistencies in the writings of Paul, More could at least avoid being drawn into a defence of clerical celibacy based upon the unsupportive text of Hebrews 13.

If divergent opinions within the text of Scripture posed problems for evangelical polemicists, further divisions were opened by the multiplicity of interpretations of key verses. To deny the interpretative authority of the church was to locate correct understanding in the individual conscience, but individual consciences were frequently far from unanimous. In the search for specific references to clerical marriage, evangelical writers turned to the letter to Timothy, and particularly the key verse of 1 Timothy 3:2: 'The Bishop should be the husband of one wife.' This verse appeared to offer the clearest evidence that marriage was not merely tolerated among the clergy of the apostolic church, but actively encouraged, as a state befitting the ministry. William Tyndale noted the importance of the verse in his debate with Thomas More. A priest, he argued, should have a wife for two reasons. First, Tyndale argued, 'He is vnapt for so chargeable an office which had neuer household to rule', and second, since chastity was an 'exceeding seldome

___

been dedicated to the queen in 1554. Ponet had returned to England in 1554 and had been involved in Wyatt's rebellion. The warning that Martin's arguments could be applied to the marriages of Catholics and princes may have been a sharp comment on Mary's marriage to Philip, which had been strongly criticized by the rebels.

[87] More, *Confutation*, p. 306.

gift', it was better for the priest to marry than to live in unchastity.[88]

However, there was a clear difference between a demand that the clergy should be free to choose to marry, and an insistence that the clergy must marry. The recommendation that the bishop should be the husband of one wife could be read as an endorsement of clerical marriage, as an exhortation to the higher clergy to marry, or as an injunction to the Christian community to ensure that its leaders were drawn only from the married. Compulsory clerical celibacy, so vehemently criticized by the reformers, would be replaced by compulsory clerical marriage. The threat of forced clerical marriage was writ large in the works of Catholic polemicists, who feared that unmarried clergy would be persecuted, and argued that to make episcopal office dependent upon marriage threatened the standing of the bishops of the early church. Thomas Martin argued that the claim that all bishops must be married was clearly erroneous, as the example of the early church testified.[89] If only married men could be bishops, then neither John the Evangelist nor Ignatius had been true bishops, since they had remained unmarried. Martin echoed More's warning that the reformers would compel priests to beget children, bishops to marry: 'yea, mu[n]kes & nu[n]nes too, must be married in al the haste, and al religious and professed folkes likewise, leste thei should otherwyse bee found contrary to the aforesaid doctrine'.[90] The Reformation would force marriage upon one and all.

The implication that the acceptance of the Reformation would lead to compulsory marriage for the clergy was something of a misrepresentation, but it did reveal ambiguities within the evangelical position. Many writers simply emphasized the argument that if Paul had allowed bishops to marry, there was no reason for the Catholic church to forbid the practice. This stance was adopted by Philip Melanchthon after the promulgation of the Six Articles in 1539. Those who argued that marriage and holy orders were incompatible, he argued, were implying 'wedlok to be an uncleane state & a viciouse kynde of lyuing', unsuitable for men who aspired to holiness. The letters of Paul to Timothy and Titus proved otherwise, and clearly sanctioned the marriage of bishops, but did not demand it.[91] Ponet argued that the words of Paul confirmed that marriage by bishops was not demanded nor merely tolerated in the church of the Apostles, but rather that it was 'veray conuenient' for bishops and priests to be married.[92]

However, the pressures of polemical debate could encourage or

---

[88] Tyndale, *Obedience*, p. 133.

[89] Martin, *Pretensed marriage*, sig. Y4v.

[90] Ibid., sig. A3r.

[91] Melanchthon, *Defence*, sig. A5v.

[92] J. Ponet, *Defence for the Mariage of Priestes* (1549), RSTC 20176, sig. A8v.

compel writers to adopt a more extreme position, in the effort to put clear water between themselves and their opponents. Both William Tyndale and William Turner came close to making marriage a prerequisite for the clergy, justifying the comments of Thomas More and Thomas Martin. Adherence to the plain word of Scripture could clearly create dilemmas where this plain word appeared to stand in opposition to contemporary evangelical practice. However, to suggest that the recommendations of Scripture could be adapted and reinterpreted by the contemporary church conceded too much ground to Catholicism, and implied that full understanding of the word was only possible through continued divine revelation and external authority. In fact, Tyndale's argument was constructed with the intention of revealing inconsistencies in the writings of Thomas More, rather than with the intention of rejecting the validity of even voluntary clerical celibacy.[93] Turner's demand that the bishop must be the husband of one wife is out of character with much of the rest of evangelical polemic on the issue of marriage and celibacy, where this same element of compulsion was the focus of the attack of vows of celibacy.[94] However, the slightest suggestion that the clergy must be married was clearly grist to the mill of Catholic polemicists, and enabled More and Martin to take the opportunity of defending the voluntary nature of the vow of celibacy, while at the same time reducing the arguments of their opponents to the level of absurdity.

The Bible not only contained recommendations and exhortations, but also provided a record of the actions of the first followers of Christ. The lives of the Apostles were enlisted to support arguments both in favour of clerical marriage and in defence of clerical celibacy. The example of the Apostles, and the conduct of St Paul, were used both as a guide to the interpretation of their work, and as evidence of the practice of the early church. The model of the apostolic church could be exploited and appropriated without detriment to the *sola scriptura* principle. Not only was the period the closest in time to the preaching of Christ, but because the Bible itself documented early Christian practice, the books of the apostolic era were seen as a record of divine revelation rather than human innovation. If the immediate followers of Christ had been married, the reformers argued, future generations of disciples and priests should be under no obligation to forswear marriage. Thomas Becon

---

[93] Tyndale, *Answer*, p. 312.

[94] William Turner, writing in the later years of the reign of Henry VIII, commented on the same passage of Paul, and argued that the text was intended to make marriage a necessary attribute of the bishop, with the result that all candidates for the episcopacy must be married. William Turner, *The Huntyng & fyndyng out of the Romishe fox* (Basle, 1543), RSTC 24354 , sig. E7r–v; cf. *The Rescuynge of the Romishe Fox* (Bonn, 1545), RSTC 24355, sig. L6v.

pointed to the contrast between the first Apostles, who were married men, and the priests of the mediaeval church, monks, friars and 'wyueles hipocrites' who claimed to be the true followers of Christ.[95] Indeed, the text of 1 Corinthians 9 suggested that the Apostles had travelled with their wives, rather than break the bonds of marriage for the sake of a religious calling.[96] Philip the Apostle had four daughters, all of whom were learned in Scripture.[97] Among the other Apostles, Peter was clearly married; a miracle in which Christ had cured Peter's mother-in-law of a fever was recorded in Matthew's Gospel. History also identified St Petronilla as the daughter of St Peter, and Becon added that Peter himself had referred to 'Marcus my son'.[98] Ponet had also cited the healing of Peter's mother-in-law as evidence that the Apostles had been married, and praised them as men who were 'coupled in maryage, and yet not maryed for the fulfyllynge of theyr bodely lustes, but for the mayntenaunce of theyr posterytee and offsprynge'.[99] The fact that Peter, in Catholic eyes the first pope, was married, added further weight to the argument that the subsequent papal prohibition of marriage to the clergy was not founded upon the example of the Apostles. The mediaeval popes were seen to have acted in opposition to the Apostle from whom they claimed their descent.

Catholic polemicists dismissed the claim that the example of the Apostles could be used in the defence of clerical marriage. Thomas Martin denied that many of the Apostles were married, and argued that those who had wives had not remained with them during their minis-try.[100] In contrast, Martin emphasized the virginity of John the Evangelist and James, and suggested that all the Apostles had abstained from 'fleshly felowshippe' with women, including their wives.[101] This example of abstinence had been institutionalized in the vows of celibacy made by the clergy and religious, who renounced everything to devote themselves to the service of God. The women referred to in 1 Corinthians 9 provided companionship, but were not the wives of the Apostles. Again, the debate was fuelled by the development of alternative exegesis and hermeneutic, and to validate claims to correct understanding it was necessary to appeal to past commentators. Martin turned to Augustine for an explanation of the text. The Greeks, he claimed, had one word

---

[95] Becon, *Matrimony*, fol. Iii1v.

[96] Ibid., sigs NNn3r–4r; Ponet, *Defence*, sigs B2v–4v, D2r; Martyr, *Defensio*, sig. B1r–v.

[97] Becon, *Matrimony*, fol. GGg4v. Becon cited Acts 21:10 for the reference to the daughters of Philip, and Luke 1, Matt. 8, Mark 1, Luke 4, and 1 Cor. 9.

[98] Becon, *Matrimony*, fol. KKk5r, Matt. 8, Luke 4, Mark 1, 1 Pet. 2.

[99] Ponet, *Defence*, sig. A6v–7r.

[100] Ibid., sig. Hh2r.

[101] Ibid., sig. Z4r.

that could mean both wife and woman, with the result that Paul's statement that the Apostles were accompanied by women could be misinterpreted as a reference to their having wives. Paul was accompanied by a 'woman of the faith', and not by a wife.[102]

The question of Paul's marriage was certainly the most problematic, and the centrality of the letters of Paul to the debate over clerical marriage added great significance to his statement 'I wish that all men were as I am' (1 Corinthians 7:5).[103] Evangelical writers such as William Turner argued that Paul had been married, and was therefore expressing a wish that all men should also marry. The verse should therefore be understood as an exhortation to men to live in the chastity of marriage, not in perpetual celibacy.[104] However, Catholic polemicists disputed the claim that Paul had married, arguing that the text was an exhortation to chastity.[105] Even if Paul had been married, it was claimed, this would not be a valid argument in favour of marriage for those contemporary clergy who had already made a vow or promise of chastity. Those who contracted marriage after making such a vow placed themselves under the threat of damnation.

The debate over Paul's marriage was complicated by ambiguities in the sources. John Jewel and Thomas Harding both cited Ignatius in their defence of opposing views on the marriage of Paul. Jewel claimed that Paul had married, and supported his assertion with reference to the letter of Ignatius to the Philadelphians. Harding was not impressed by the argument, and accused Jewel of falsifying the evidence, 'for the olde copies have not S Paule's name in the Epistle as Philadelphians, which for that purpose is alleged'. John Booty has demonstrated that it was possible for both writers to be correct in their contradictory assessments of the letter. The passage that related to the marriage of Paul, he suggests, was likely to have been a fourth-century interpolation, which may not have been incorporated into all manuscript copies of the letter. Harding was right to maintain that the early copies of the letter contained no reference to the marriage of Paul, but Jewel's copy of the text, now in Magdalen College Oxford, clearly listed Paul among the married Apostles.[106] The presence of such contradictory evidence justified both the defence of clerical marriage from the example of Paul,

---

[102] Ibid., sig. Gg1r, Gg3r–4r.

[103] Becon, *Matrimony*, fol. KKk5v. Phil. 4, 1 Cor. 9:5.

[104] Turner, *Rescuyng*, sig. M1v; cf. Martyr, *Defensio*, sig. S1r.

[105] Smith, *Defensio*, sigs B3v, G5r–6v.

[106] J. Booty, *John Jewel as Apologist of the Church of England* (1963), pp. 106–8. The existence of different versions of the letter is discussed in M. Parker, ed., *A Defence of Priestes Mariages* (1567), RSTC 17519, sig. S2r; T. James, *A Manvduction or Introdvction unto Divinitie* (Oxford, 1625), RSTC 14460, p. 23.

and the hostility of Martin to Ponet's attempt to make Paul the 'Patrone of maried priestes'.[107]

Both the question of Paul's marriage and the debate on clerical marriage in general, demonstrated the strengths and weaknesses of the appeal to Scripture alone as a source of divine authority. The evangelical assertion of the right and capacity of the individual to read and interpret the Bible allowed reformist writers to present a polemical exegesis of key biblical texts, without the need to refer their interpretations to the authority of the Fathers, or the example of the institutional church. Despite the belief that the Bible would interpret itself, however, it became abundantly clear that one text could support a variety of arguments. The debate on clerical celibacy illustrates the problems that this presented. The fact that both evangelical and Catholic writers could defend opposing opinions from the same books, chapters or even verses of Scripture testified to the dangers and pitfalls of allowing a free interpretation of the Bible. Catholic writers, and particularly Thomas More, defended their use of biblical texts by referring their interpretations to the longstanding tradition of the church, and were quick to point out that where their interpretations brought conflict with Catholic opponents, evangelical writers could only recite the rights of the individual to read and interpret Scripture.

Such claims could have dangerous consequences, however. When evangelical writers asserted their own right to read and interpret Scripture, they opened the way to a multiplicity of individual interpretations, advanced by the newly empowered laity. The threat that this posed to doctrinal uniformity was recognized both by Henry VIII and by Tyndale himself.[108] Such a diversity, in the eyes of More, made the appeal to an outside authority, whether the pope, the Fathers, or the 'common corps of Christendom' all the more essential. In sharp contrast, John Ponet declared that the history of the church and 'al the doctrin of the pope ... is almost nothing els other then a lomp of lerning besids and against the lyuely word of God'.[109] However, the inconclusive nature of the testimony of Scripture, coupled with the defence of the authority of tradition by Catholic writers, encouraged Ponet and his fellow polemicists to give some consideration to this 'lomp of lerning'. The writings of the Fathers, the traditions of the early church, and even the decrees of the mediaeval popes, were not to be the preserve of Catholic apologists alone.

---

[107] Martin, *Pretensed marriage*, sig. Hh1r.

[108] Tyndale, while defending the ability of the individual to interpret Scripture, did offer guidance, in the form of notes and prologues, and in 1543 Henry VIII attempted to restrict access to the Bible.

[109] Ponet, *Apology*, pp. 166–7.

CHAPTER THREE

'Good and Holy Men': Clerical Marriage and the Example of the Early Church

At first sight, the appeal to Scripture alone as the source of all doctrinal authority was an appeal to the written word of God over and above the doctrinal formulations of the church, and a challenge to the unity and integrity of Christian history. With the Bible accepted as the ultimate judge in all areas of dispute, it would seem that the historical faith of the church and the example of its holy men had no role to play in the reformed church of the sixteenth century. However, religious debate during the Reformation did not draw upon the texts of Scripture alone: the traditions and history of the church were not abandoned but rather adapted to fit changing needs and perceptions. The Reformation was not hostile to history, but rather to the normative value which the pre-Reformation church had attached to its past in the development and determination of doctrine. To counteract Catholic claims to institutional and historical continuity, evangelical writers turned to the events of the past, particularly the first centuries of Christianity, in an effort to root the reform movement in events outside the turmoil of the sixteenth century. The purpose was not simply to create a 'reformed' tradition, a chain of true believers stretching from the early days of the church to the present, but also to establish that it was the Catholic church which had betrayed the true Christian heritage, by abandoning the faith of the Fathers and the primitive church in favour of idolatry, innovation and superstition. The history of the early church was to play a crucial role in the definition and identity of the churches in the sixteenth century; as Francis Bacon observed, the controversy with Rome compelled Luther to 'awake all antiquity, and to call former times to his succours, to make a party against the present time; so that the ancient authors, both of divinity and in humanity, which had long slept in libraries began generally to be read and revolved'.[1]

The appeal to the past was an appeal to previous human experience in an attempt to address the burning question of doctrinal authority. The

---

[1] Francis Bacon, *The Advancement of Learning*, quoted in A.B. Ferguson, *Clio Unbound. Perceptions of the Social and Cultural Past in Renaissance England* (Durham, NC, 1979), p. 129.

demands of the Reformation could be provided with a historical context, suggesting that the issues at stake were as much those of renovation and restoration as innovation and novelty. Debates and controversies in the early church were used to shed light upon questions raised by the Reformation, and the recorded faith of the apostolic church was seized upon either to uphold or reject contemporary practice. In the search for authentic documentation which could attest to the antiquity of doctrine, writers on both sides of the religious divide turned to the writings of the Fathers and the declarations of the early councils. For evangelical writers these sources offered an opportunity to undermine the historical and institutional foundations of the mediaeval church, while the defenders of orthodoxy used the materials of the patristic period to underpin claims to doctrinal continuity and rebut accusations of novelty. As early as 1522, a Benedictine monk had warned Pope Adrian VI that the Lutheran challenge was not merely theological but also historical; any successful defence of the Catholic church would therefore have to rebuild these two pillars, and reclaim the past as its own.[2] Therefore, despite the initial promise of the Reformation, the principle of *sola scriptura* was balanced against the stabilizing influence of the appeal to the past. John Jewel's 'Challenge Sermon' of 1559–60 invited his Catholic opponents to defend their church by reference to the first six hundred years of Christianity, but the campaign against radical Protestantism in the Elizabethan church also demanded this same reverence for the practices of centuries past, to the point where the example of the early church seemed to act once more as an objective precedent.[3]

In Catholic polemic, epitomized by the writings of Thomas More, key parts of the authoritative teachings of the church were argued to be contained within its customs, expressed by the faith and practice of the 'common corps of Christendom', a historical consensus among believers across the centuries. It was this continuity of faith, More argued, that both ensured that the church remained true to the Gospel, and testified to the truth of this assertion. In the *Letter to Bugenhagen*, More claimed that the Lutherans were confounded not only by the Scriptures but also by the 'uninterrupted consent of the whole Christian world through so many centuries'. The church enjoyed unity of faith in place and time, and it was this that provided the link between the contemporary faithful and the leaders and members of the apostolic church. Central to this argument, however, was the notion of continuity: it was not simple numerical superiority that legitimated the teaching of the church (as

---

[2] E.W. Cochrane, *Historians and Historiography* (Chicago, 1981), p. 457.

[3] W.M. Southgate, *John Jewel and the Problem of Doctrinal Authority* (Cambridge, Mass., 1962), p. 120.

Tyndale pointed out, this could also be true of Islam), but the ability to trace its doctrines back to the first centuries after the death of Christ.[4] The test of faith, More argued, was the assent and consent of the whole church, including its doctors and saints, a consensus of the living and the dead.[5] Luther's attack upon the Catholic church was therefore an attack upon the public faith by which the church had been known through the ages, an attack on the Fathers and councils which denied evangelicals the right to call upon the primitive church for support.

This unity within the Catholic church was presented in stark contrast to the variety of opinions expressed by its opponents. The common belief of the people of God, More argued, could not be undermined by the fragmented faith of the heretics, either in the past or in the present.[6] Contemporary heresy for More was but one manifestation of an eternal battle between good and evil. Where God had provided for peace and unity, both in the secular world and in the affairs of His church, the devil had sown dissent and discord, undermining the structures of authority and challenging the established doctrinal consensus. The heretics, he claimed, were 'a rabble', a disordered and divided minority, and only in this respect could Lutherans identify themselves with anything in the life of the primitive church. The growing debate over the validity and dissolubility of vows of chastity provided ample demonstration of this point. 'All chrysten people', More argued, had been brought by the grace of God to a unity of belief on the subject, holding that 'the vowe of chastyte may not be by hys pleasure that made it broken and set at nought', and had condemned those who argued to the contrary as heretics.[7] On this point the teaching of the church had been consistent through the centuries, supported by the texts of Scripture and the consent of Christendom. Those who dismissed vows lightly therefore placed themselves not among the intellectual descendants of the Fathers, but in the company of others through history who had opposed the church. 'Than what tyme so euer two or thre begyn vpon theyr own heddys to vary from all the remanaunt, and agaynste the remanaunt do styffely holde the contrary', More noted, 'they holde a playne false heresye.' As had happened in the past, the heretics would leave the church, but the body of the true faithful would long continue, guided by

---

[4] E. Flesseman van Leer, 'The Controversy about Ecclesiology Between Thomas More and William Tyndale', *Nederlands Archiv voor Kerkesgeschiedenis*, 44 (1960), p. 75.

[5] B. Gogan, *The Common Corps of Christendom. Ecclesiological Themes in the Writings of Sir Thomas More* (Leiden, 1982), p. 212, quoting *The Confutation of Tyndale's Answer*, CW, 8, I, 157/12–14; II, 660/1–4.

[6] T. More, *The Confutation of Tyndale's Answer*, ed. L.A. Schuster, R.C. Marius, J.P. Lusardi and R.J. Schoek, (CW 8), p. 1284; pp. 658/36–659/4; 663/12–17.

[7] *Confutation*, 941/32–36.

the Holy Spirit.[8] It was this guidance that ensured unity of faith, a unity that would not be found among those outside the church, in either the past or the present. There were as many sects as there were men, More argued, and this diversity of belief among successive generations of heretics 'of all whych euery one contraryeth his felow in great articles of the faith' was proof enough that they did not enjoy the same divine guarantee of infallibility in matters of faith as the Catholic church.[9]

For Thomas More, and also for John Fisher, this divine protection and sanction was an inviolable defence for tradition.[10] The traditions of the church were defined under the guidance of the Holy Spirit, and therefore must be in accordance with the divine will. The faith of the early church, More argued, had been preserved unspoilt and would endure until the end of time, in stark contrast with the fluctuating fortunes of the heretical groups which had risen and fallen throughout history.[11] The visible and institutional church continued to uphold the faith of the saints and Fathers, and it was possible to trace an identity in doctrine and practice from the sixteenth century to the early years of the church. The church Fathers could be called upon to validate contemporary practice, but also to pass judgement upon contemporary critics of the church, as they had passed judgement upon the heretics of the early church. The role of the Fathers did not have to be that of an independent source of revelation, but rather that of witnesses to the faith of church in the past, and testimony to the crucial unity of belief in time and space which was the mark of the true church. In the works of Thomas More, the Fathers were a vital part of the historical visibility of the church across the centuries, a tangible link to the primitive church which could be used to isolate the evangelical reformers in the sixteenth century by denying them a part of the Christian heritage. If the writings of the Fathers appeared to contradict the teachings and actions of the reformers, any link between the Reformation and the early church could be severed, and evangelical demands dismissed as the resurgence of heresies already condemned. Furthermore, if it could be demonstrated that the church in which the Fathers believed was not substantially different from the church of the sixteenth century, it would be impossible for the reformers to dismiss the Catholic church as the congregation of the devil without also impugning the purity of the early church.[12]

For this reason, Thomas More set patristic writings in opposition to the opinions of evangelical reformers, arguing that the holiness and

---

[8] Ibid., 942/7–20.

[9] Ibid., 772/16; 728/13–22.

[10] Ferguson, *Clio Unbound*, p. 134.

[11] *Confutation*, pp. 669/36–670/23; 679/17–23.

[12] Marius, 'Thomas More and the Early Church Fathers', *Traditio*, 24 (1968), p. 395.

authority of the Fathers could be seen by all to outweigh the character and influence of contemporary heretics.[13] More based his arguments upon the collective weight of the Fathers, pitting the sanctity and intellect of 'on the one syde, saynt Cypryane / saynt Hyerome / saynt Ambrose / saynt Austyne / saynt Basyle / saynt Chrysostem / saynt Gregory & all the vertuous and connyng doctours' against the life and teaching of the 'doctours of this new secte, ... frere Luther & his wyfe / prest Pomerane & his wyfe / frere Huiskyn and his wyfe / prest Carlastadius & his wyfe / don Otho monke & his wife ... & more frantyke Tyndall'.[14] The sheer weight and unanimity of patristic testimony which could be directed against the reformers identified them as a divided and flawed group of individuals, who had dared to set their own opinions above the authoritative pronouncements of the church and its holy men. Far better, More argued, to respect the teaching of the Fathers of the visible Catholic church, than to have faith in the bold pronouncements of those who appropriated for themselves the right of judgement given to that church.[15] The esteem in which the Fathers were held also added weight to More's argument. As men with reputations for holiness, the Fathers gained additional authority, and More took pains to draw contrasts between their celebrated virtue and the conduct of the leaders of the evangelical movement. The issue of clerical marriage loomed large in More's criticisms: patristic exhortations to chastity were set against evangelical demands that the clergy should be allowed to marry, and the reader was offered a choice between the words and example of Augustine, Jerome and Ambrose, and the inchoate thoughts of a married former monk.[16] The Reformation could not be portrayed as the restoration of the ideals of the primitive church if its leaders diverged from these ideals in practice, and argued against them in print. More's argument was echoed some thirty years later by Thomas Harding. Determined to undermine John Jewel's assertion that it was impossible to vindicate the teachings of the Catholic church with reference to the first six hundred years of church history, Harding argued that it was in fact Jewel and his co-religionists who had abandoned the legacy of the Fathers and jettisoned the example of the primitive church, by upholding their own understanding of Scripture against the interpretations advanced by the Fathers.[17]

---

[13] Flesseman van Leer, 'Controversy about Ecclesiology', p. 77.

[14] T. More, *Dialogue Concerning Heresies*, *CW*, 6, p. 434. Bugenhagen (Pomerane) had married in 1522, Oecolampadius (Huiskyn) in 1528, Carlstadt in 1522, Otto Brunfels in 1524. See *Dialogue*, p. 724.

[15] *Confutation*, p. 62/5–14.

[16] Ibid., p. 47/11–26.

[17] Southgate, *Jewel*, p. 177.

The controversy over who had, in Jewel's words, 'forsaken the fellowship of the holy fathers'[18] was made possible by the fact that both sides in the polemical debate held the Fathers in esteem, and were equally determined to appropriate their words and use them against enemies. As expositors of Scripture, the Fathers were attractive to evangelicals because they offered an alternative to mediaeval scholasticism, and also a means by which later interpretations could be tested.[19] The writings of the Fathers were not to be raised above Scripture, but rather tested against Scripture, and exploited as a means of understanding the climate of opinion in the times in which they lived. Both Cranmer and Ridley had turned to the works of the Fathers in the search for a valid witnessing authority in the understanding of Scripture where meaning was not self-evident, although for Cranmer it was the texts of the earliest writers, those whose works illuminated the apostolic church, that were of most value.[20] However, there were clear tensions within the English evangelical position, and particularly between first- and second-generation reformers. William Tyndale had argued that Scripture alone could be trusted as a repository of truth: no two Fathers and Doctors were in full agreement with one another, and even where consensus existed, this did not constitute doctrinal proof.[21] The appeal to Scripture alone was balanced by other writers who were more willing to examine the remains of antiquity, and call upon the Fathers for support where this was possible. Both Barnes and Frith had made considerable use of the history of the church in polemical debate, but it was John Jewel who empowered the Fathers as a positive influence upon the construction of the English church. However, the authority of the Fathers in doctrinal debate was still limited. Opinions advanced in patristic literature were to be tested against Scripture before they were accepted, and the words of the Fathers had no binding authority. This positive endorsement of the value of the history of the early church was to be balanced by the use to which patristic writings were put in religious debate. As Stephen Greenslade has noted, the function of the Fathers was often negative; their works were used to establish which Catholic practices could not be found in the primitive church, rather than to justify the progress of reform or advance any belief or practice as a

---

[18] J. Jewel, *Defence of the Apology of the Church of England*, in J. Ayre, ed., *The Works of John Jewel, Bishop of Salisbury*, 4 vols (Parker Society, Cambridge 1845–50), III, p. 229.

[19] L. Grane, A. Schindler and M. Wriedt, eds, *Auctoritas Patrum. Contributions on the Reception of the Church Fathers in the 15th and 16th Century* (Mainz, 1993), pp. 22–3.

[20] Ferguson, *Clio Unbound*, pp. 178–9.

[21] Flesseman van Leer, 'Controversy about Ecclesiology', p. 75.

positive good.[22] In the context of the debate over clerical celibacy, the example of the Fathers could point to a lack of any binding prohibition of marriage in the early church, but it was the word of God in Scripture that gave the clearest defence of the intrinsic value of marriage. As a locus of *auctoritas*, the Fathers were worthy of esteem, but their works were not to be seen as an absolute standard or normative authority. Differences of opinion expressed in the patristic writings undermined claims of a *consensus patrum*, with the result that the study of the Fathers could be used to undermine notions of unity in faith in past and present. However, if nothing else, the fact that the same authors were held in esteem by both Catholic and evangelical writers ensured that the corpus of existing patristic writings would be all the more relevant in religious controversy. Indeed, the use of such materials served to defend the Reformation from accusations of innovation and individualism, and could provide a historical context and factual foundation for the claim that reformation was in fact the restoration of true Christianity.

The value of patristic materials in debate was further compromised by the limited resources available, and by the unreliability of some texts. It has been suggested that the use of patristic literature in England was largely determined by the resources of the cathedral and monastic libraries, the holdings of which were dominated by Augustine, Jerome, Ambrose, Gregory and Bede.[23] It was only in the fifteenth century that the works of the Greek Fathers were studied in depth in the west, although the spread of the new learning and the Reformation did much to improve the situation, encouraging the production of new editions.[24] The authenticity of texts was frequently called into question; the intrusion of fourth-century interpolations into the text of the letter of Ignatius, for example, was to cause confusion and controversy in the debate over clerical marriage.[25] The use of patristic writings made it possible to condemn the Catholic church in the words of those whom it esteemed most highly, but evangelical writers were still cautious in respect of the influence that they were prepared to accord the Fathers. To grant interpretative authority to the primitive church would be to concede ground to conservative opposition, but to deny any influence to the Fathers would open the door to accusations of innovation and demands for radical reform based upon the free and individual

---

[22] S. Greenslade, *The English Reformers and the Fathers of the Church* (Oxford, 1960), p. 6.

[23] Ibid., p. 9.

[24] Ibid., p. 12. Oecolampadius produced two German translations of Basil, and in the 1520s Latin translations of parts of Gregory Nazianzen, Chrysostom, Theophylact. In 1536 Rhenanus completed Erasmus's edition of the works of Origen.

[25] See above, pp. 19 and 64.

interpretation of Scripture. In fact the unreliability of some texts, coupled with the assertions of the Fathers themselves that they did not possess ultimate authority, enabled evangelical polemicists to place limitations upon the use of such materials. John Jewel warned against building too much upon the words of the Fathers, echoing John Calvin's insistence that the honour accorded them should be no more than was befitting,

> for although we hold that the word of God alone lies beyond the sphere of our judgement, and that fathers and councils are of authority only in so far as they agree with the rule of the Word, we still give to councils and fathers such rank and honour as it is appropriate for them to hold under Christ.[26]

The pronouncements of the Fathers were read and respected in the reformed churches, but their position was one of subservience to Scripture. As the debate over clerical marriage reveals, patristic writings were not abandoned altogether, but rather a process of 'deparentification' evolved, in which their authority in matters of faith was steadily eroded.[27] Where their opinions could be validated by Scripture, the words of the Fathers provided a useful witness to the faith. However, despite their position in the church, the Fathers were human and therefore subject to error; their failings and lack of agreement should therefore be expected and excused.

Where the early church was seen to speak with one voice, in the decrees of the councils, it was more difficult to argue that differences of opinion in the past justified heterodoxy in the present. The councils of the early church, and the extent of their authority were vigorously contested in the sixteenth century, and the debate on the place of clerical celibacy in the history of the church depended heavily upon evidence that could be adduced from conciliar decrees. If the prohibition of marriage to the clergy was to be dismissed as an invention of the Middle Ages, it would be necessary to demonstrate that the early councils had upheld the rights of priests to marry. However, to argue from the evidence of the councils was to imply that their deliberations and conclusions were authoritative and binding: if the decrees of the councils were admitted to have only a temporary relevance, there would be no obstacle to change and development in doctrine and practice. Yet to imbue the councils with any normative authority would be to undermine the place of Scripture as sole arbiter in matters of faith, suggesting that the

---

[26] Quoted in A. McGrath, *Reformation Thought. An Introduction* (Oxford, 1993), p. 104; Ayre, ed., *Works of John Jewel*, IV, p. 1173.

[27] S. Hendrix, 'Deparentifying the Fathers. The Reformers and Patristic Authority', in Grane, Schindler and Wriedt, eds, *Auctoritas Patrum*, p. 57.

interpretations of men were an equally reliable guide to the divine will. For Catholic writers, the defence of the authority of the councils, and the preservation of their decrees, was a central part of the argument for continuity and unity in faith and practice through the centuries. Conciliar pronouncements on celibacy were adduced in support of the claim that clerical marriage was prohibited in the early church, but the study of the decrees on marriage was also part of a wider defence of the role of councils in the life of the church in the past and in the present.

The clergy assembled in a council, Thomas More argued, were the representatives of the body of the faithful in the church, and therefore had the authority to speak as the church of Christ. The council acted as a microcosm of the church, and the attendance of the bishops ensured that the people would be represented in the decisions reached.[28] To deny that this was the case would be tantamount to denying that parliament could act for the people and had the authority to legislate: just as parliament represented the realm, so a council of the church represented the faithful as an equiparation of the general consensus.[29] Indeed, for More the authority of the council was derived from the authority of the general consensus. The role of the common corps of Christendom in the life of the church could be fulfilled by a council called to represent this consensus, and the council could speak for the whole of the community that it claimed to represent.[30] Passage of time created new requirements, but the representative nature of the councils allowed for the continued interpretation of revelation, and for this reason it was possible that the decrees of a council might overturn the decisions of previous meetings. However, the decrees of the council were still binding upon the faithful, because they were promulgated by a body which derived its authority from the consent and the consensus of its constituents.[31] Just as the Holy Spirit worked within the community of the faithful to ensure the integrity of the faith in past and present, so it was also active in the deliberations of a council, guiding participants to uniformity of opinion, or at least to a majority decision.[32] The action of the Spirit in the council, as in the whole ecclesiastical order, lay in the preservation of peace and unity: to attack or disobey the decrees of the councils was to sow seeds of individualism and disorder in the Christian community. If compulsory clerical celibacy could be located among the practices of the early church embodied in the decrees of the councils, the claim that the Reformation sought the restoration of the faith and practice of the primitive church

---

[28] More, *Responsio*, p. 626/21–7 tr. 626/22–35.
[29] More, *Confutation*, p. 146/15–20; *Responsio*, p. 626.
[30] *Confutation*, pp. 940/33–941/8.
[31] Ibid., pp. 922–3.
[32] Ibid., pp. 922/33–923/11.

could be disputed. For evangelical writers to condemn traditions which had been promoted by the early councils amounted to an abnegation of the divine promise of the guidance of the Spirit and a challenge to the representative authority of councils, a challenge that sat uneasily alongside calls for a general council to reform the church.

The treatment of church councils by evangelical polemicists had clear parallels with their approach to the Fathers and their writings. Questions were raised concerning the authority of councils in the determination of doctrine, the constitution of a legitimate council, and the rights of individuals to summon councils. In particular, the role of the popes in the convening of councils was disputed; the incorporation of a council into the structures of authority in the church implied legislative authority and papal control over discussions, and did little to support the claim that decisions were reached under the guidance of the Holy Spirit.[33] Evangelical writers were keen to suggest that the decisions of a council were far from infallible, and could therefore be rejected or modified where mistakes appeared to have been made. Luther had argued that an assembly of bishops was no more than an assembly of private citizens, an assembly which could err like any other, and could therefore have no intrinsic authority over the rest of the Christian community.[34] The ability to legislate in matters of faith was limited to the defence of revelation received in Scripture and the condemnation of innovation, and it was not within the powers of the council to introduce new articles of faith. In the imposition of clerical celibacy in particular, councils had exceeded their authority, had been shown to be unwilling to stand in the way of innovation, and indeed had on occasion advocated and supported the introduction of new practices. Jaroslav Pelikan suggests that it was this attitude to the authority of councils which did more than anything else to distance Luther from Rome.[35] The denial of the binding power of conciliar decrees, coupled with the assertion that councils could and indeed did err in matters of faith, was a dramatic rejection of traditional models of revelation and doctrinal definition.

Luther was not alone among the first generation of evangelical writers in his critical approach to the councils. William Tyndale urged that the decrees of a council should be constrained by the text of Scripture, so that those decrees that were not in accordance with the Gospel could be rejected.[36] Both Tyndale and Becon argued that the people were only to

---

[33] G. Evans, *Problems of Authority in the Reformation Debates* (Cambridge, 1992), p. 245.

[34] Luther, 'Disputatio de Potestate Concilii', quoted in Evans, *Authority*, p. 251.

[35] J. Pelikan, *Obedient Rebels. Catholic Substance and Protestant Principle in Luther's Reformation* (London, 1964), p. 52.

[36] Flesseman van Leer, 'Controversy about Ecclesiology', p. 79.

be bound by decrees which were supported by Scripture, since freedom from error was only guaranteed where there was a clear biblical foundation for decisions.[37] The detailed study of the declarations of faith made by councils revealed disunity and inconsistency, making it impossible to obey all decrees simultaneously. This scepticism over the role of councils and the validity of their decrees as indicators of true faith was to persist throughout the English Reformation, and exerted a powerful influence over polemical debate. The Thirty-Nine Articles of the English church repeated the assertion that councils could err, and that their decisions were frequently contradictory, but did not deny their influence in Christian history altogether. John Jewel conceded that it was possible for the decrees of councils to be useful and beneficial, on the condition that these councils were composed of devout and learned men, and were truly representative of the whole of Christendom – criteria which he claimed the Council of Trent failed to fulfil.[38] In part, the weakness of the Council of Trent lay in its timing. Jewel was insistent that it was only the councils of the first six centuries after Christ which could be claimed to represent the true faith and authority of the primitive church. The Council of Trent did not embody the spirit of the early church, nor did it represent the whole church, with the result that its decrees were of only limited influence. The value of the appeal to the early councils, like the appeal to the Fathers, was that the same materials were used and cited by Catholic polemicists, giving an added impetus to the use of the history of the church to condemn the Catholic church in the sixteenth century. The continued reverence in which the figures and councils of the early church were held allowed Jewel and others to claim that part of Christian history as their own, arguing that the English church had now 'restored again so much as in us lie, the decrees and canons of the ancient councils'.[39] Efforts to identify contemporary reformed practice with the faith of the early church adduced historical witnesses in favour of reform, and could be a persuasive response to accusations that the Reformation had a lackadaisical attitude to the past and its institutions.

There were clear dangers in this approach. Once it had been accepted that councils, traditions and history had a place in the construction of the reformed churches, it became necessary to determine how broad that place should be. The appeal to the example of the primitive church was based upon the assumption that the later history of the institutional

---

[37] W. Tyndale, *An Answer to Sir Thomas More's Dialogue*, ed. H. Walter (Parker Society, Cambridge, 1850), p. 99, J. Ayre, ed., *The Catechism of Thomas Becon* (Parker Society, Cambridge, 1844), pp. 391–2.

[38] Southgate, *Jewel*, p. 129.

[39] Jewel, *Apology*, IV, p. 1054.

church was a history of decline and degeneration. The introduction of seemingly novel doctrines and practices, including clerical celibacy, was seen by evangelical writers as a departure from the purity of the primitive church. For some, this degeneration of faith could be fitted into an apocalyptic interpretation of the past, an interpretation which sought to identify and explain the growing influence of the devil in the world and in the church.[40] Both this understanding of the past and the more general appeal to the early records of the church demanded a degree of consensus over the question of when the history of the church ceased to be a reflection of pure religion, and at which point it became an account of a falling away of faith and the rise of satanic influences. In Catholic polemic there was no such division: history could be treated as a single entity, in which the recurring theme of the struggle on the part of the institutional church to defeat heresy and disorder ebbed and flowed in times of confidence or crisis. In evangelical literature, however, a common line of argument emerged, in which the first six centuries of Christianity were treated as an era of pure faith and practice, and the following thousand years were seen as a period in which the power of Satan was exercised in the institutional church. It was therefore possible to call upon the example of the Fathers and the councils of the early church to validate certain aspects of contemporary belief, while at the same time to dismiss as novelties any practices which could be proved to have their origins in the period after 600.

This was the challenge which John Jewel laid before his opponents in 1559: to produce testimony in defence of Catholic teaching from Scripture or from the first six centuries of patristic writings or conciliar decrees. After this period, he claimed, the church had entered a period of darkness, in which papal claims to supremacy and authority had reached their zenith, and false doctrines such as transubstantiation had been introduced.[41] The authority of the example provided by the early church lay in its adherence to the message of Scripture, against which all practices and customs, past and present, should be tested. To admit such a role for the early church was not to endow the modern institution with a normative role in the formation of doctrine. The difference between Jewel and his opponents lay in the fact that while Jewel claimed that the model of the early church was authoritative, and could indeed be used to condemn later developments, Catholic controversialists argued that it was the contemporary church in any age that spoke with the voice of authority.[42] Thomas Dorman claimed that the primitive church was but

---

[40] See Chapter 5 below.

[41] Jewel, *Sermon Preached at Paul's Cross*, in Ayre, ed., *Works of John Jewel*, I, pp. 1–25.

[42] J. Booty, *John Jewel as Apologist of the Church of England* (London, 1963), p. 134.

an infant, the Christian community in its formative years, and the relative maturity of the church in the sixteenth century meant that it could not be judged against the example of the early years.[43] Jewel's opponents also attempted to undermine his challenge by suggesting that the choice of six hundred years was entirely arbitrary. Rastell claimed that the date was merely convenient for the heretics, since later tradition in the church would prove their beliefs to be misguided. The rejection of a thousand years of history was simply an extension of the rejection of the teaching authority of the church in the recourse to Scripture alone, in order to avoid debate on issues where evangelical ground was weak.[44] In the eyes of Thomas Harding, this refusal to admit the validity of the history of the mediaeval church undermined any efforts which Jewel made to suggest that the Reformation was an act of restoration rather than innovation. By breaking away from recent history, Harding claimed, evangelicals lost any claim to apostolic succession, and thereby continuity with the practice and beliefs of the early church. For Jewel, however, the test of Catholicity and fidelity to the primitive church lay not in the descent through individuals, but in the degree of conformity to the faith of the Apostles.[45] If there was conflict between the Reformation and late mediaeval theology, this was no obstacle to claiming the model of the early church as the ancestry of Protestantism; indeed, in the restoration of the pure faith of the church it would be necessary to break away from mediaeval accretions. The first six Christian centuries were therefore to play a vital role in the formation of Protestant identity, and to exert a powerful influence on the structure and nature of polemical debate in the sixteenth century.

Jewel was not the first writer to turn the early church into a hunting ground for reformation polemicists. Robert Barnes's study of the lives of the popes was the earliest full-length history of the English Reformation, and was written with the aim of proving that key elements of traditional Catholic practice were in fact recent innovations which ran contrary to the faith of the apostolic church.[46] The author of *The Olde Faythe of Greate Brittaynge* (1549) had argued that doctrinal purity had been preserved in the English church for the first six centuries, until the arrival of the Roman mission of Augustine. In the search for historical

---

[43] Dorman, *A Proufe of Certayne Articles in Religion Denied my M.Juell* (Antwerp, 1564), RSTC 7062, p. 108.

[44] Rastell, *Confutation of a sermon pronou[n]ced by M.Juell* (Antwerp, 1564), RSTC 20726, quoted in F.J. Levy, *Tudor Historical Thought* (San Marino, California, 1967), p. 106.

[45] Southgate, *Jewel*, p. 199.

[46] R. Barnes, *Vitae Romanorum Pontificum, quos Papas Uocamus Summa Diligentia ec Fide Collectae* (Basle, 1555).

validation or confirmation of his views on the Eucharist, Thomas Cranmer had also turned to the example of the early church to find supporters for the evangelical position.[47] Indeed, Jewel's Challenge Sermon had a clear precursor in Cranmer's invitation to Stephen Gardiner to find proof that the doctrine of transubstantiation had been the faith of the church in the time of the Apostles.[48] The recourse to Scripture alone provided a useful rallying cry in the early years of the Reformation, but did little to provide a defence against the demands of radical Protestants. However, the example of the apostolic church could be used to sanction practices which were deemed to be a part of the true Christian heritage but were not expressly ordered in Scripture. The appeal to the past also demonstrated that the reformed English church had a firm historical footing as the successor of the Apostles, undermining Catholic claims to fidelity to the faith of the early church. This clear interest of English evangelical writers in the history of the early church has led one writer to argue that the notion of the 'primitive church' emerged as the central historical concept of the English religious struggle.[49] The first Christian centuries, the patristic writings and the decrees of the councils were accepted by many as an objective reality, and a model for the definition of faith and practice in the sixteenth century. Thus John Jewel concluded the *Apology* with the promise:

> we have searched out of the holy Bible, which we are sure cannot deceive us, one sure form of religion, and have returned again unto the primitive church of the auncient fathers and apostles, unto the very headsprings of Christ's Church.[50]

The importance of these 'headsprings of Christ's Church' is well illustrated by the use of such materials in the debate over clerical celibacy and marriage, with both sides in the debate seeking to prove that their position could be vindicated by the example of the first six centuries, the church of the ancient Fathers and Apostles.

'We beleue, as all good men haue euer byleued', Thomas More informed William Tyndale, that the marriage of priests is 'very vnlawful lechery and playne abomynable bychery'. Clerical marriage was a novelty, a departure from the faith of the 'common corps of Christendom' which had been practised since the earliest days of the church.[51] In their discussion of clerical marriage, the appeal to the

---

[47] T. Cranmer, *Defence of the True and Catholike Doctrine of the Sacrament* (1550), RSTC 6000, p. 116.

[48] See S. Gardiner, *Explicatio[n] and Assertion of the True Catholique Fayth* (Rouen, 1551), RSTC 11592.

[49] Ferguson, *Clio Unbound*, p. 179.

[50] Jewel, *Apology*, IV, p. 1084.

[51] More, *Confutation*, p. 646.

example of church history, and that of the early church in particular, was central to the arguments of both Catholic and Protestant polemicists. The writings of the Fathers on virginity and celibacy, the decrees of the councils and the practice of the primitive church were cited by More and other Catholic apologists as evidence of the novelty of Reformation theology. Clerical celibacy, it was argued, had been introduced into the discipline of the church in the early centuries, and the acts of subsequent councils testified to the continuity of the practice. The forbidding of marriage to the clergy was not an innovation of man, but part of the continuing revelation of the divine will. In demanding that the clergy be free to marry, the reformers were setting themselves against fifteen hundred years of tradition.

In evangelical polemic, however, the appeal to the Fathers and the councils of the church was not an appeal to divine revelation, but an appeal to precedent. The fact that compulsory clerical celibacy was not introduced into the church until after the apostolic era confirmed that it was the institution of man and not of God, and therefore at best unnecessary, and at worst iniquitous.[52] God would not lead the Apostles into one belief, and the mediaeval church into another. The history of the early church offered evidence of married priests and bishops who had continued to exercise their function, and the acts of the councils supported the claim that clerical celibacy was introduced into the church at a late date, amid opposition and confusion. The writings of the Fathers, if they were of any value at all, confirmed that it was the prohibition of marriage which had traditionally been associated with heresy, a heresy which had been integrated into the teachings of the institutional church. In the eyes of evangelical writers, the fact that the Fathers were in accordance with Scripture on the issue of clerical celibacy confirmed their place as the Fathers of the reformed church.

As with the argument from Scripture, key texts and personalities became central to Reformation debate over marriage and virginity. The letters of Jerome proved to be a fertile source for arguments in defence of clerical celibacy, and were ruthlessly plundered by Richard Smith, who cited the letters to Jovinianus, Vigilantius, Pammachius, Eustochium, Helvidius and Gerontius.[53] The Catholic church, he

---

[52] Reformation views on the sufficiency of Scripture and the authority of the early church in the determination of doctrine are discussed in Chapter 2 above. See also J.A. Clark, 'The Bible, History, and Authority in Tyndale's *The Practice of Prelates*', *Moreana*, 106 (1991), pp. 105–17; S.L. Greenslade, 'The authority of the tradition of the early church in early Anglican thought', *Oecumenica* (1971–2), pp. 9–33; *idem*, *English Reformers*; Grane, Schindler and Wriedt, eds, *Auctoritas Patrum*.

[53] R. Smith, *Defensio sacri Episcoporu[m] & sacerdotum coelibatus* (Paris, 1550), sigs C4v, E6r, G6r; Martin, *Pretensed marriage*, sigs P1v, C1r.

claimed, did not deny the holiness of marriage, but simply held virginity in higher esteem.[54] Chastity was a virtue honoured in the early church, encouraged by Jerome himself, and therefore appropriate for the priests of the church. Such sentiments had not been shared by all Jerome's contemporaries, however, and Jerome's polemical letters against his opponents offered further ammunition to Catholic controversialists defending clerical celibacy from Protestant attack. The treatises against Vigilantius and Jovinianus were particularly important in this context. Smith referred to the dispute with Vigilantius in his reply to Peter Martyr, and cast himself in the role of a new Jerome, combating a revival of the heresy of Vigilantius. Jerome had claimed of Vigilantius that he 'throws the reins upon the neck of lust, and by his encourage-ment doubles the heat of the flesh'. Smith then elaborated upon the theme, drawing comparisons with the actions of Protestant reformers. It was possible, Smith argued, for the reader to see Luther in Jerome's description of the errors of Vigilantius, and particularly in his rejection of clerical celibacy.[55] The Reformation was the revival of the battle between truth and error in the early church. Both Smith and Gardiner exploited Jerome's letter against Jovinianus for the same purpose.[56] Jovinianus had published a Latin treatise in Rome in which he argued that a virgin was no better than a wife before God, but Jerome's response validated Smith's interpretation of 1 Corinthians 7, and supported the claim that Paul had remained unmarried.[57] The writings of Jerome not only testified to the practice of the early church, but also guided the faithful into the correct interpretation of Scripture.

The evangelical assault on the opinions of Jerome took two distinct forms: a denunciation of his character, intended to discredit his opinions, and a condemnation of the opinions themselves. John Bale, unsur-prisingly, chose to focus upon questions of morality: 'though Hierome was a great prater & boaster of virginite, yet was he no virgine, but may

---

[54] Smith, *Defensio*, sig. E6r–v; Jerome, 'Letter XXII to Eustochium', *The Principal Works of St Jerome*, tr. W.H. Fremantle in H. Wace and P. Schaff, eds, *A Select Library of Nicene and Post Nicene Fathers of the Christian Church*, second series (Oxford and New York, 1893), vol. 6, p. 23. Erasmus referred to the same letter, 'Jerome to Eustochium on Guarding Virginity', in *Patristic Scholarship. The Edition of Jerome*, ed. and tr. J.F. Brady and J.C. Olin, *The Collected Works of Erasmus*, vol. 61 (Toronto, 1992), p. 155.

[55] Smith, *Defensio*, sigs B1v, C3v–4r; 'Against Vigilantius', in *Principal Works of St Jerome*, p. 418.

[56] S. Gardiner, *Exetasis Testimoniorum* (Louvain, 1554), sig. B3r; Smith, *Defensio*, sigs C5r, F8v, G6v; John Angel, *The Agrement of the Holye fathers* (1555), RSTC 634, sig. O8v; 'Against Jovinianus', *Principal Works of St Jerome*, pp. 350–55.

[57] For the exposition of 1 Cor. 7, and the question of the marriage of Paul see Chapter 2, pp. 56–9.

be suspected of yl rule with yonge women'.[58] Other writers questioned
the theological and practical foundation of Jerome's defence of celibacy.
Bucer noted that the rejection of clerical marriage hinged upon the
promise of Christ, 'ask and ye shall receive', which Jerome applied to
celibacy. Celibacy was seen as a gift from God, available to those who
wished it. Bucer argued against this assumption, claiming that the gifts
of God were not available to all equally. Even among the clergy, not all
those who promised celibacy would be able to keep their promise, and
such men should be free to marry.[59] Jerome's letter to Vigilantius was
inadequate as a justification for compulsory clerical celibacy.

Other writers claimed that the theology that underpinned compulsory
clerical celibacy was fatally flawed. Those who condemned clerical
marriage, Ponet argued, were as guilty of perverting the sense of
Scripture as Jerome had been in his condemnation of Jovinianus. Paul
had clearly stated that the bishop was to be the husband of one wife, and
anyone who denied this, from Jerome to Thomas Martin, was in error.[60]
William Turner criticized Jerome's declaration 'So long as I ful fil the
office of a married man / I ful fil not the office of a Christen man.'
Inspired by the devil, Turner claimed, Jerome had laboured to exalt
virginity over marriage, and his writings had been overly influential, at
least until Augustine had defended the honour of marriage and revealed
the faults in Jerome's work.[61] Turner's argument reflected the attitude of
the reformers to the writings of the Fathers in general. Patristic
testimony, as the opinions of Jerome on marriage revealed, should only
be accorded authority if they were consonant with the sense of Scripture.
The Fathers were not infallible, and their authority extended only as far
as they were in agreement with the word of God.

Similar interpretative confusion arose around the letters of St
Cyprian. Both Richard Smith and Thomas Martin drew upon the
writings of Cyprian, who had seemingly criticized those religious who
broke their vows of chastity, and accused them of incest. However, the
letter in question was to become the focus of dispute between Catholic
and Protestant writers. The key passage was taken from the eleventh
letter of Cyprian, and its interpretation was hotly contested.[62] Both

[58] J. Bale, *The Apology of Johan Bale agaynst a Ranke Papyst* (1550), RSTC 1275, fol.
12r.

[59] M. Bucer (tr. T. Hoby), *The Gratulation of the moost famous clerke M. Bucer* (1549),
RSTC 3963, sigs B8v–C1r, 1 Cor. 12. The question of chastity as a gift from God is
discussed in Chapter 6, pp. 144ff.

[60] Ponet, *Defence*, sig. A8r.

[61] W. Turner, *Huntynge & fyndyng out of the Romishe fox* (Basle, 1543), RSTC 24354,
sig. E5v.

[62] The passage reads 'if they were fully sincere in dedicating themselves to Christ, then
they ought to persevere in their modesty and chastity without giving rise to any sort of

Smith and Martin argued that this letter offered confirmation that the Fathers of the early church looked with displeasure upon those who dedicated themselves in chastity to God, only to break such a promise.[63] Indeed, the letter clearly exposed as adultery the marriage of those who had once professed chastity, a condemnation which could be applied readily to those clergy who had married after 1549 and indeed to the married leaders of the Reformation movement. The reformers, Martin protested, had deliberately misinterpreted the passage in an attempt to provide a justification for their own marriages undertaken after vows.[64]

Not surprisingly, evangelical polemicists placed a different interpretation upon Cyprian's letter, arguing that it confirmed that it was permissible to break vows of chastity in order to marry. Such testimony not only confirmed the primacy of the biblical injunction 'it is better to marry than to burn' above the vows and discipline imposed by the Catholic church, but also cast doubt upon the assertion that the breaking of religious vows by marriage had always been forbidden.[65] Thomas Becon argued that Cyprian had simply stated that it would be better for professed virgins to keep their vows, but that they should be permitted to marry for the avoidance of fornication, in order that the faithful should not be offended by impious behaviour. There was a clear contrast between the attitude to vows among the Fathers of the early church and the treatment of married religious in the reign of Mary.[66] The discipline of the early church had allowed marriage to those clergy who could not keep their vows, but the Marian government separated married clergy from their wives, and deprived them of their benefices. John Ponet drew the same contrast, arguing that Gratian had counted as adultery that which Cyprian had termed a valid marriage for the avoidance of fornication.[67] The Catholic church had misrepresented Cyprian to give an illusion of antiquity to a comparatively recent invention. Thomas Becon, referring to Augustine, also argued that the Fathers had accepted that marriage should be permitted to those who were unable to keep their vows of chastity. Those who married were not to be condemned as

---

gossip, and thus with constancy and steadfastness await the reward of their virginity. If on the other hand they are unwilling or unable to persevere, then it is better that they should marry than fall into the fire by their sins', G.W. Clarke, ed., *The Letters of St Cyprian of Carthage*, in J. Quasten, W.J. Burghardt and T.C. Lawler, eds, *The Works of the Fathers in Translation*, 43 (1984), p. 59.

[63] Smith, *Defensio*, sig. D8v.

[64] Martin, *Pretensed marriage*, sigs T2v–3r.

[65] P. Martyr, *Defensio de Petri Martyris* (Basle, 1559), sig. B8r, C1r.

[66] R. Barnes, *That by Gods Worde it is lawfull for Priestes ... to marry wiues*, WW, p. 319; T. Becon, *Booke of Matrimony*, in Becon, *Worckes*, 2 vols (1564), RSTC 1710, I, fols OOo3v–4r; *Relics of Rome*, I, fol. H1v.

[67] J. Ponet, *Defence for the mariage of Priestes* (1549), RSTC 20176, sig. E3v.

adulterers, but rather to be tolerated and permitted to remain with their wives.[68] Against this background, the treatment of married clergy in the sixteenth century revealed how far the church had diverged from the opinions of its Fathers.

Thus evangelical writers argued that the writings of the Fathers demonstrated that it was the Catholic church which had departed from the truth of the Gospel and the practice of the early church. Patristic sources did not suggest that clerical celibacy was either demanded or expected in the early church, but rather confirmed that the stringent ecclesiastical discipline surrounding vows of chastity was a much later invention of man. In this context, the history of the early church and the decrees of the councils were to exert a profound influence on debate. For the defenders of clerical marriage, practice and beliefs in the first Christian centuries could provide valuable evidence of the acceptance of married clergy in the apostolic church. Catholic polemicists, however, argued that respect for chastity, evident in the writings of the Fathers, had remained a common feature of ecclesiastical life throughout the history of the church. Marriage had been prohibited to the clergy from the time of the councils of the early church, in legislation which had been confirmed by subsequent generations.

This continuity of tradition was of central importance to Thomas More in his defence of clerical celibacy. The prohibition of clerical marriage had been received in the form of 'generall custome', with the consent of Christendom, he argued, throughout the history of the church.[69] During these fifteen hundred years, the Holy Spirit had ensured a common belief, in the whole church, that vows of chastity could not be broken. The church taught and believed that the breaking of such vows amounted to a deadly sin and that a marriage entered into after a promise of chastity was to be condemned as incest.[70] Thomas Martin argued that such traditions amounted to a continuity of practice which the reformers could not match; for eight centuries, those clergy who had married had been separated from their wives and punished. The opponents of clerical celibacy were attempting to reverse a tradition of the church that had persisted for centuries, and by allowing their clergy to marry, the reformed churches demonstrated clearly that they had no respect for the practice of the early church.[71]

Evangelical polemicists were equally determined to reclaim the example of the early church, depicting the lifting of the prohibition on clerical marriage as restoration rather than innovation. Becon argued

---

[68] Becon, *Relics*, fol. H1v.
[69] More, *Dialogue*, pp. 311, 376.
[70] More, *Confutation*, p. 109.
[71] Martin, *Pretensed marriage*, sigs J5v, Siv.

that the clergy had been free to marry, 'tyll the Bishop of Rome playd the tyraunt', and prohibited such marriages.[72] Bucer claimed that there had been married priests in the church in the time of Jerome, and that men and women had married in the time of Augustine, even after they had promised chastity.[73] Rather, it was clerical celibacy that was the recent innovation, sanctioned neither in Scripture nor by the Apostles, and a practice foreign to the church of the Fathers. Indeed, there had been many married bishops in the early church, including several who had been succeeded as bishops by their children.[74] Thomas Becon presented a list of married bishops which included Spiridion, bishop of Cyprus, Pelagius, bishop of Syracuse, Philogamus, and others who had succeeded their fathers in their bishoprics, including Gregory Nazianzen, Policrates and Epiphanius, the son of a married priest, who was bishop of Constantinople.[75] Clerical dynasties, he argued, were a common feature of the primitive church. Even these statistics were redundant, when it was noted how many of the popes had been the sons of priests. Becon's list included Boniface I, Felix III (AD 422), Gelasius I (AD 495), Agapetus I (AD 535), Theodorus (AD 615), Hadrian II (AD 640) and John XII (AD 917), who was the son of another pope, Lando II. It would be unjust to regard these children as bastards; rather the marriages of their fathers should be counted as legal, since 'they were all begotten in true wedlocke and borne in holy matrimony according the law of God'.[76] Becon revelled in the irony of the situation. The laws of the Catholic church had prevented these children of clerics from being born in wedlock, and it was the refusal of the church to recognize the marriage of priests as legitimate that tainted these popes with illegitimacy.

On the basis of such evidence, evangelical polemicists denied that there was anything either heretical or novel in the demand that the clergy be free to marry. Rather, it was the Catholic church that had deviated from the truth, and had forced the clergy to accept a discipline which it had once condemned in other sects. John Bale likened compulsory clerical celibacy to the teachings of the Marcionites, Eustachians,

---

[72] Becon, *Relics*, fol. EEEEe3r .

[73] Bucer, *Gratulation*, sigs E3r, F3v.

[74] G. Joye, *Defence of the Mariage of Preistes* (Antwerp, 1541), RSTC 21804, sig. B6r–v; Martyr, *Defensio*, sig. C6v; Ponet, *Defence*, B1v; P. Melanchthon (tr. G. Joye), *A very godly defense ... defending the mariage of preistes* (Antwerp, 1541), RSTC 17798, sig. B3r; Eusebius, *Ecclesiastical History*, tr. A.C. McGiffert, in P. Schaff and H. Wace, eds, *Nicene and Post Nicene Fathers*, 1 (1952), Bk V, ca. 22, p. 240.

[75] Becon, *Matrimony*, fols. GGg4v, IIi1v, KKk5v. Becon referred the reader to the *Ecclesiastical History*, Bk 3, ca. 24, Bk 10, ca. 5 and Bk 9, ca. 30.

[76] Ibid., fol. KKk5v–6r. Barnes provided a similar list in the *Sentenciae ex Doctoribus Collectae* (Wittenberg, 1536), sig. G1r, and the *Supplication* (1534), RSTC 1471, sig. T1r.

Montanists, Priscillianists, Cathars and Jovinianists.[77] Becon compared the Catholic clergy with the Nicolaitans, who, he claimed, preferred the wives of other men to their own.[78] The enforcement of clerical celibacy in Becon's own time was the same heresy as that which had been condemned by the early church. In a play on the name Thomas Martin, Ponet compared his opponent's views on clerical celibacy to the views of earlier heretics on marriage. Martin, he argued, was 'indewed with the very properties of Martion the aunceant Archeheretique and enemy to all Matrimonie'.[79] Catholic doctrine was compared with that of the Pharisees, Eustachians, Manichaeans and others who had attempted to use moral purity to gain respect.[80] The Manichaeans had been condemned by Augustine, but Ponet demanded 'Haue not these popishe heretiques put vpon them this glittering shew and horishe face of the Manicheicall and such like hereticall chastitie?'[81] Indeed, if clerical marriage amounted to heresy, Ponet mocked, then Thomas Martin was accusing St Peter of heresy.[82] Instead, he claimed, the first heretics throughout Europe had been unmarried. Novatian, an unmarried priest, had forbidden marriage to his sect; the first Spanish heretics, the Priscillianists, had forced the separation of husband and wife, in much the same manner as the Marian government in England divided the married clergy from their wives.[83] Such comparisons led Ponet to claim that he and his contemporaries were fighting against the revival of the heresies of the early church. The Catholic church refused to allow the clergy to follow the example of the Apostles and the early church, thus revealing itself as a church in error. The Fathers were the ancestors of the reformed church, united against the revival of the early heresies in the church of Rome. The discipline which the Catholic church promulgated had once been set forth by the very heretics it had condemned.

In reply, Thomas Martin turned the accusation of heresy against Ponet, claiming that there had been no history of clerical marriage in the church apart from the history of heresy. 'Seyng then this doctrine for priestes marriages was first inuented by archeheretikes and practiced also first of their desciples', Martin argued, it should be widely known that

---

[77] J. Bale, *Yet a Course at the Romyshe Foxe* (Antwerp, 1543), RSTC 1309, sig. I7r. Bale's inclusion of Jovianianists is surprising, since Jovinian was opposed to the asceticism of Christian sects.

[78] Becon, *Matrimony*, fols Ili3v, Ili4r; Bucer, *Gratulation*, sig. D4r.

[79] J. Ponet, *An Apology fully aunsweringe ... D. Steph. Gardiner* (Strasbourg, 1555), RSTC 20175, fol. 10, 15.

[80] Ibid., fols 38, 44.

[81] Ibid., fol. 79.

[82] Ponet, *Apology*, fols 50–51, 59–60.

[83] Ibid., fols 125–30.

this 'and all other like new fangled teachynges be now evidently knowen to haue begon with lecherie, to haue continued with couetise, and ended in treason'.[84] The reformers did not seek the restoration of the church to its primitive state, but rather looked to destroy both church and state for their own advantage. Martin provided ample evidence for the association of heresy and clerical marriage. Jovinianus, the 'firste heretike that preached in Rome', had persuaded nuns to marry, as had Vigilantius, and all other heretics from the time of Simon Magus. The first heretics in France and in Italy had been married priests.[85] Martin used the connection between heresy and immorality, established in the opening pages, to condemn the reformers in the same breath as Donatists, Arians and Manichaeans.[86] In fact, each of these groups had urged celibacy upon its members, but Martin was clearly desperate to establish a link between the reformers of the sixteenth century and each and every heretic of the early church. Jerome, he argued, would have condemned Luther in the same manner in which he had condemned the heresy of Jovinianus.[87] Lutheran teaching was no different from that of the heretics who had threatened the early church, which the Fathers had condemned. Martin believed that he acted as the Fathers had done, in extirpating the heresies of the early church which had been revived in the theology of the reformers.

This theme of a genealogy of heresy, stretching from the early church to the sixteenth century, was a common feature of both Protestant and Catholic polemic.[88] Thomas More exploited the image at length, describing the verdict of an imaginary council of the church which had been called to discuss the heresy of Barnes, Tyndale and the Lutherans. On the basis that some of the reformers believed that the church had been in error for eight hundred years, the council was to be held in the pontificate of Gregory I, over nine hundred years previously. The main issue was the defence of clerical marriage set forth by Barnes, Tyndale and Luther, and, in particular, the marriage of Luther to Katherine von Bora. More described the scene in a manner that set the tone of the account in the opening stages. 'Now let vs than suppose', he suggested,

> that there had in the same tyme ben a fonde frantyke frere, and that hys name hadde ben Luther / and that there had than also bene a noughty nonne, and that her name had ben Cate / & that this fonde frantyke frere hadde wedded thys noughty nonne.

---

[84] Martin, *Pretensed marriage*, sig. A3v.

[85] Ibid., sigs A1v–2r.

[86] Ibid., sig. A2v.

[87] Ibid., sig. A3v.

[88] J. Bale, *A Mystery of Iniquity* (Antwerp, 1545), RSTC 1303.

From the beginning, More's sombre and respectful treatment of the Fathers contrasted sharply with his mockery of Luther's marriage. Faced with a 'fonde frantyke frere' and a 'noughty nonne', St Gregory would not have hesitated to condemn the opinions of the reformers. Gregory's defence of the Catholic position was based upon the story of Ananias and Saphyra, an example of the danger which would face those who failed to honour their vows of chastity. Through the medium of Gregory, More defended the authority of this 'generall counsayle of the whole chyrch' to pass judgement upon the heresies of Luther, Tyndale and Barnes. Even the reformers' arguments from Scripture were unacceptable, if judged against 'the writings of the Fathers and the saints who had interpreted Scripture correctly through the centuries'.[89] The Fathers of the early church, St Gregory and the faith of the historic church would all recognize in Luther and his followers the same heresies that they had condemned in their own time.

The decision to try the arguments of the reformers before a council of the church was, in part, motivated by a broader debate over the authority of such councils, both to legislate in matters of religion, and as sources for those seeking to outline the development of religious practice. More's insistence upon the authority of the councils was framed largely as a response to Robert Barnes, who had argued that councils were not the whole body of the church, and therefore lacked the authority to determine the faith of the church. To Barnes and other evangelical writers, the Catholic church had subsequently accorded the councils an unnecessary authority to legislate in matters of doctrine, with the result that opinions that had once been condemned were now incorporated into the corpus of the theology of the church. Some councils had contradicted the decrees of their predecessors, making it impossible to observe the ordinances of all councils simultaneously. Novelty had been condemned as heresy, but the church itself had clearly innovated in matters of religion. However, apparent innovations and inconsistencies allowed both sides in Reformation debates to cite the acts of the councils as support for their position.

History, as far as Luther was concerned, could only confirm the difficulty of establishing unanimity, ensuring that doctrinal proofs based

---

[89] More, *Confutation*, pp. 925–8. The time at which the Catholic church was argued to have fallen victim to error was debated by Protestant polemicists. J.M. Headley, *Luther's View of Church History* (New Haven, 1963), pp. 160ff. Bale dated the corruption of the English church to the arrival of St Augustine. *Actes of the Englysh Votaries*, pt I (Wesel, 1546), RSTC 1270. See Chapter 4 below. The story of Ananias and Sapphira is told in Acts 5, and its implications for the debate on clerical marriage are discussed in Chapter 6, pp. 147–8.

upon the councils were no proofs at all.[90] However, these cautionary remarks on the utility of the councils in Reformation debate do not appear to have been heeded by English polemicists, with both Protestant and Catholic writers drawing heavily upon conciliar decrees. The sources cited on both sides of the debate are almost identical, but were turned to completely different purposes. Catholic polemicists regarded the decrees of the councils and the popes on the issue of clerical celibacy as evidence of both the antiquity and the continuity of the discipline. Clerical celibacy had been established in the early councils, and endorsed by subsequent generations. Protestant writers claimed that there was no scriptural justification for compulsory clerical celibacy, which had been rejected by the early councils until their decrees had been overthrown by subsequent assemblies. The repeated declarations of the councils confirmed the unpopularity and the novelty of the prohibition of marriage, and provided testimony to the gradual corruption of the teaching of the church by the traditions of men.

The most commonly cited decrees from the ante-Nicene period were those of the Council of Ancyra of AD 314. Peter Martyr cited the tenth and nineteenth canons in defence of clerical marriage. The tenth canon, he argued, had permitted the marriage of deacons, allowing those who could not live in chastity to marry, in accordance with the letter of Paul to the Corinthians. The nineteenth canon, rather than prohibiting clerical marriage, condemned those guilty of digamy, who were excluded from holy orders according to the statement of Paul that the bishop should be the husband of one wife.[91] Martyr's account of the Council appears accurate. Roman Cholij's work confirms Martyr's reading of the tenth canon, which allowed marriage to those deacons who could not live in chastity. However, Cholij then notes that if this concession was authentic, it fell into disuse shortly after the Council, and was certainly never referred to in the dispute over clerical marriage between Greece and Rome in the eleventh and twelfth centuries. It is not clear if Peter Martyr was aware that the canon was of no effect, but his interpretation of the original decree is certainly more accurate than that of Richard

---

[90] Pelikan, *Obedient Rebels*, pp. 54ff.

[91] Martyr, *Defensio*, sigs u2r, G5v. H.C. Lea writes that the Council of Ancyra allowed marriage in orders as far as the diaconate, if the postulant claimed that he could not live in chastity. *History of Sacerdotal Celibacy in the Christian Church*, third edition (1907), p. 44. Roman Cholij, on the basis of the decisions of the Council of Trullo, explains that the label of digamist was applied to those involved in a second marriage, after the death of their first spouse. The prohibition of orders to digamists was the practice of the early church, Cholij argues, and provides a list of references to the writings of the Fathers against the ordination of digamists. R. Cholij, *Clerical Celibacy in East and West* (Worcester, 1989), pp. 12–13, 75–8.

Smith, who cited it in defence of the prohibition of marriage to deacons.[92]

The decrees of the Council of Nicaea (AD 325) assumed a dominant role in the Reformation debate over clerical celibacy. The primary purpose of the Council was the condemnation of the Arian heresy, but the issue of clerical marriage was also debated. The key figure in evangelical polemic was that of Paphnutius, who had defended the honour of marriage from Scripture, and prevented the enforcement of celibacy upon the clergy. Becon described the incident in detail, basing his account on the descriptions offered by Sozomen and Socrates, whose histories appear to have been the major source for Reformation polemicists.[93] Paphnutius, 'a blessed and gloryous confessoure, whiche for the true religion sake had suffered greate paynes', Becon claimed, had persuaded the Council that marriage was a form of chastity, on the basis of the text of Hebrews 13. This declaration, Becon argued, should justify the acceptance of clerical marriage, since, if marriage is holy, 'how can the sacraments be prophaned by theym that are chaste and pure ... ?', in other words, the married clergy.[94] Philip Melanchthon also cited the oration of Paphnutius at the Council as confirmation of the assertion that marriage was a form of chastity. Marriage bestowed a higher degree of purity upon the priesthood than vows of chastity that were impossible to keep.[95] The action of Paphnutius at Nicaea not only confirmed that marriage was still honoured in the church in the fourth century, but also revealed that compulsory clerical celibacy was a more recent innovation.

However, the decrees of the Council of Nicaea and the actions of Paphnutius were not passed over in silence by defenders of clerical celibacy. Thomas More mocked the reverence in which Tyndale held 'St. Pannutius', and demanded 'let Tyndale tell vs some of so many sayntes, as synnes the apostles tyme ... that expowned the scrypture in such wyse that yt were by his exposycyon lawefull for a frere to wedde a nunne'.[96] Whatever its foundations, Tyndale's defence of clerical marriage must be erroneous, More argued, because it ran contrary to the determination of

[92] Smith, Defensio, sig. H8v.

[93] The Ecclesiastical History of Socrates Scholasticus, ed. A.C. Zenos, and The Ecclesiastical History of Sozomen comprising a history of the church from A.D. 323 to A.D. 425, ed. C. Hartranft, in A Select Library of Nicene and Post Nicene Fathers of the Christian Church, ed. P. Schaff and H. Wace, second series, II (Edinburgh, 1989). The accounts of the Council of Nicaea are to be found in Socrates, Bk I, ca. 11, and Sozomen, Bk I, ca. 17 and 23; Becon, Matrimony, fols Ili4r, LLl1r; M. Parker, ed., A Defence of Priestes mariages (1567), RSTC 17519, sig. G8r–v.

[94] Becon, Matrimony, fol. Ppp4r; Melanchthon, Defence, sig. G6r; Ponet, Defense, sig. F5v.

[95] Melanchthon, Defence, sig. C2r, D2r.

[96] More, Confutation, pp. 809, 1667.

the church and the faith of the historical common corps of Christendom. Thomas Martin attempted to draw a distinction between the marriages of the laity and those of priests who had promised chastity. In Martin's account of the Council, the underlying theme was remarkably similar to that of Protestant polemicists: that Paphnutius and the other holy men of the early church would condemn contemporary practice. But according to Martin's interpretation, the words of Paphnutius were not intended to be applied to all marriages. The marriage of a man and his lawful wife could be chaste, but the marriage of a priest could never be counted as chastity. In marriage, priestly chastity was replaced by incontinence, and marriage was sacrilege if undertaken in holy orders.[97] In Protestant polemic, it was clerical celibacy that contradicted the councils, but for Martin it was the marriage of the clergy. Whatever the intention of Paphnutius, the fact that the church, even at a later date, had enforced celibacy upon the clergy meant that the words of Hebrews 13 could not be applied to all marriages.[98] The different interpretations of the words of Paphnutius advanced by Catholic and evangelical polemicists provide a clear illustration of the complexities of Reformation debate. Principles of *sola scriptura* were compromised and adapted as the focus of the debate moved into the domain of the post-apostolic church, while assumptions concerning the historical continuity of Catholicism were constantly undermined. However, to appeal to historical precedent was

---

[97] Martin, *Pretensed marriage*, sig. E1r. H.C. Lea argued that from the eleventh century, the account of the Council of Nicaea was altered by those who favoured the introduction of clerical celibacy. In 1076, Bernard of Constance denied that a holy man like Paphnutius would have been guilty of such blasphemy; *Sacerdotal Celibacy*, p. 50.

[98] The debate over the meaning of Hebrews 13 is discussed in Chapter 2, pp. 59–60 above. Other councils and decrees prompted similar debate: e.g. the Council of Gangra (AD 362) cited by Ponet, *Defence*, sig. B5r-v. The decree reads 'If anyone affirms that one should not receive communion during the holy sacrifice celebrated by a married priest, let him be anathema', quoted in Cholij, *East and West*, p. 92. Cholij argues that the canon was not used in a polemical context until AD 867, in correspondence between Pope Nicholas and the patriarch Photius. The fourth canon was never used in the Greek tradition to allow priests to use their marriages, and was only referred to in Latin polemic to illustrate the error of believing that the sacraments could be contaminated by the character of the priest, ibid., pp. 93–6. The Reformation not only rescued the fourth canon from relative obscurity, but also turned it to novel ends. Peter Martyr cited canons 1, 4, 9, 10 and 12. *Defensio*, sig. G6r-v. These canons pronounced condemnations upon those who despised marriage on account of their virginity, or regarded the duties of wedlock as incompatible with salvation. Lea, *Sacerdotal Celibacy*, p. 58; Cholij, *East and West*, p. 96. See also R. Barnes, *Sentenciae ex Doctoribus Collecta* (Wittenberg, 1536), sig. F5r; Becon, *Matrimony*, fols NNn1v, PPp3v; Melanchthon, *Defence*, sig. A6r; E.P., *A Confutatio[n] of Unwritten Verities* (Wesel, 1558), RSTC 5996, sig. G8v. For Catholic use of the decisions at Toledo (411), Carthage (439) and Chalcedon, see Smith, *Defensio*, sigs B7r–8v; Lea, *Sacerdotal Celibacy*, pp. 117–18; Cholij, *East and West*, pp. 35, 60; Martin, *Pretensed marriage*, sigs E4v, R3v, D1r.

to wield a double-edged sword: the records of the conciliar decrees were not always consistent, and their interpretation was often a highly individual matter.

Such conflicts and contradictions were exemplified by the debate over the nature and meaning of the so-called Apostolic Canon. The Canon, a wide-ranging collection of doctrinal and ethical statements, was cited frequently by both Catholic and Protestant polemicists in defence of the claim that their church was the custodian of the apostolic faith.[99] The sixth canon was of the greatest significance to Protestant polemicists. The canon read 'let no bishop, priest, or deacon send his spouse away under the pretext of piety. If he does so, let him be excommunicated, and if he persists, let him be deposed.'[100] It was clearly assumed that the higher clergy were married, and the canon confirmed that such marriages were still binding upon those in holy orders. The fact that the threat of excommunication was applied not to those married clergy who remained with their wives, but to those who put away their wives for the sake of piety, provided Protestant propagandists with a powerful weapon against compulsory clerical celibacy, and, more particularly, against the deprivation of married priests in the reign of Mary. Thomas Becon repeated the arguments in favour of clerical marriage based upon the texts of 1 Corinthians 7 and Hebrews 13, to demonstrate that the canon was in full accordance with the word of God. John Ponet reproduced the canon in full, condemning those clergy who left their wives 'vnder the pretence of holynesse, and colour of religion'.[101] The apostolic church had not only sanctioned clerical marriage, but had actively condemned those clergy who believed that they could attain to greater holiness by separating from their wives.

Yet the argument from the canons was far from conclusive. John Calvin admitted that the collection raised as many difficulties as it resolved. The canons carried the title 'apostolic', he argued, only because of their antiquity, and were of uncertain provenance. Calvin noted one canon which forbade a cleric to put away his wife, but described another of the canons, 'which does not permit clerical persons, except singers and

---

[99] The clearest account of the form of the Apostolic Canons is in Cholij, *East and West*, p. 11. The canons, which numbered 85, were attributed to the Apostle Peter, but, Cholij argues, were in fact the work of a semi-Arian author. The canons were either unknown or widely ignored in the west until the sixteenth century. The first 50 were translated into Latin, but were declared apocryphal by Pope Gelasius. In the eastern church, where the authenticity of the canons was accepted, they were incorporated into other ecclesiastical legislation.

[100] Cholij, *East and West*, p. 97. Cholij notes that in some collections, this canon is numbered as the fifth.

[101] Becon, *Matrimony*, fol. NNn3r; Ponet, *Defence*, sigs B5r, B8v; Martyr, *Defensio*, sig. U6r.

CLERICAL MARRIAGE AND THE EARLY CHURCH

readers, to marry after they have been admitted to office'.[102] The collection of canons appeared to recommend both celibacy and marriage for the clergy. Such ambiguities enabled Catholic polemicists to cite the canons in defence of clerical celibacy. Richard Smith, for example, was clearly aware that there was some doubt over the authenticity of the collection, but argued that the emperor Justinian had accepted their apostolic origin.[103] As the determinations of the Apostles, the canons testified to validity of revelation outside scripture, and confirmed that 'the apostles left to yᵉ churche also by tradition, yᵗ preestes shulde not mary wyues'. Paraphrasing canon 26, Smith admitted that lectors and cantors had been permitted to marry, but argued that marriage had been prohibited to all those in higher orders.[104] Thomas Martin cited the same canon, and added a reference to canon 25, which prohibited marriage to those already in orders.[105] The canon confirmed that compulsory clerical celibacy had its origins in the church of the Apostles. Within the same body of evidence, there was sufficient material for both Catholic and Protestant polemicists to find evidence to support their claims to the legacy of the primitive church. The clearly contradictory nature of the Apostolic Canon led Calvin to conclude 'Hence it appears that there was still in those times considerably more equity than a subsequent age manifested', a comment which could have been applied not only to the Apostolic canon, but to the history of the early church in general.[106]

Writing in 1555, John Angel criticized his opponents for their 'false interpretinge of Scriptures, vtterly denying of yᵉ holy doctours and Fathers of Christes churche, but only such as made for their purpose'.[107] Angel's criticism of the selective use of church history would not have been out of place in Protestant polemic; indeed, Cranmer had made the same point in his assessment of Catholic attitudes to the councils, and

---

[102] J. Calvin, *The Necessity of Reforming the Church* (1541), tr. J.K.S. Reid, Library of Christian Classics, 22 (1954), p. 215. Calvin's reference is to the twenty-sixth canon, which did allow the marriage of lectors and cantors; Cholij, *East and West*, p. 99. Cholij explains the apparent contradiction by arguing that canon 6 was a condemnation of the false piety of the ascetics, who had denounced all legitimate pleasure, threatening the dignity of marriage, and of creation.

[103] Smith, *Brief Treatise*, sig. E1v.

[104] Ibid., sigs O3v–O4r. The second citation by Smith is a correct reading of canon 17/18 which prevented those priests who were digamists, or who kept concubines, from receiving orders; Cholij, *East and West*, p. 15. Cholij argues that the prohibition of orders for those twice married was on the grounds of incontinence, suggesting that the impediment to orders was a defect in the virtue of chastity. The canons could therefore be cited as part of the movement towards a celibate priesthood.

[105] Martin, *Pretensed marriage*, sig. C3r.

[106] Calvin, *Necessity*, p. 215.

[107] Angel, *Agrement*, sig. A2v.

similar allegations were levelled against Thomas Martin.[108] The determination to identify their faith with the faith of the apostolic church led polemicists on both sides of the debate to turn to the Fathers and the councils to support their views. The key question was whether the Fathers and the councils should be treated as a source of divine revelation, or simply as an example of the practice of true religion in the primitive church. John Angel clearly believed the former, claiming of the rites and doctrines of the church 'part therof we haue receaued in writinge, part by the traditions of the Apostles, which both hath like strength vnto vertue'.[109]

In evangelical polemic, however, the Fathers and the early church were not part of a process of divine revelation, but an example of fidelity to the word of God, already given to man in its totality. Patristic sources testified to the purity of the primitive church, and could be used to demonstrate that the faith of the primitive church was in accordance with the tenets of Protestantism. While rejecting More's arguments in defence of continuing revelation, Tyndale still quoted the Fathers where they supported his argument. Augustine was praised because he subordinated his theology to the judgement of Scripture, as was Paphnutius, who had cited biblical texts in defence of clerical marriage.[110] Tyndale was not alone; indeed, S.L. Greenslade argues that 'a concern with the Fathers runs through the history of the church of England', both in works of polemic and in academic treatises.[111] The dispute with Catholic propagandists was not focused upon the question of whether the Fathers were to be respected, but rather the extent to which that respect should be taken. John Jewel expressed a wish that the Fathers be treated with due reverence, but warned 'we may not build upon them: we may not make them the foundation and warrant of our conscience. We may not put our trust in them. Our trust is in the name of the Lord.'[112]

The example of the Fathers, and the presence of married priests and bishops, suggested that the first generations of Christians had interpreted the passages of Scripture which related to marriage and ministry in the same manner as the evangelical reformers of the sixteenth century. It was only later that clerical marriage had been forbidden, in opposition to the revealed will of God in Scripture and the practice of the early Christians.

---

[108] See above, note 70; Parker, *Defence*, sig. C2v.

[109] Angel, *Agrement*, sig. O4v.

[110] Flesseman van Leer, 'Controversy about Ecclesiology', pp. 69, 75; Tyndale, *Answer*, pp. 304, 307.

[111] Greenslade, 'Authority of tradition', p. 9.

[112] J. Jewel, *A Treatise of the Holy Scriptures*, in Ayre, ed., *The Works of John Jewel*, IV, pp. 1173ff.

The history of the church was testimony to a gradual falling away of faith and the assertion of the primacy of the laws of man over the law of God. The apparent persistence of clerical marriage in the early church offered evangelical writers the opportunity to present themselves as the heirs of the Apostles and the Fathers, who were not authorities in their own right, but rather followers of the word of God. If the priests of the apostolic era had been free to marry, the celibate priesthood of the sixteenth century must have its origins in the innovations of the mediaeval church. If, as Ponet had claimed, the history of the church and the decrees of the councils were 'nothing but a lomp of lerning', this lump of learning was of great value to Ponet and his fellow writers.

CHAPTER FOUR

'Disunity and Innovation': The Example of the Mediaeval Church

In the opening pages of the *Actes and Monuments*, John Foxe compared the faith and practice of the primitive church with the state of the Catholic church in the sixteenth century, and presented the reader with a succinct summary of his conclusions. 'The higher thou goest upward to the Apostles time,' Foxe wrote, 'the purer thou shall finde the churche; the lower thou doest descend, euer the more drosse and dregges thou shall perceyue in the bottome, and especiallye within these last 500 yeares.'[1] Foxe was not alone in this belief, but built upon a longstanding tradition in Protestant polemic. In their analysis of the treatment of clerical marriage by the Fathers and the councils of the early church, English Protestant polemicists from Barnes to Foxe wrote with the intention of proving that their position was paralleled in the practice of the primitive church. It was in the early Christian centuries that the pure faith of the Gospel had been practised, a faith that was later corrupted by the addition of traditions and ceremonies, the inventions of men.

Outside the works of the Fathers and the determinations of the councils, there existed another body of material, which demanded a different interpretation. Here the focus of the debate shifted from the claim of antiquity to the issue of continuity and contradiction in mediaeval ecclesiastical legislation and practice. The true church, it was argued, would display uniformity in doctrine and practice in time and in space. Catholic polemicists had drawn upon the traditions of the church to condemn their opponents as innovators, while mocking the divisions among the reformers themselves. In reply, Protestant writers argued that the history of the mediaeval church demonstrated that the church of Rome had itself enjoyed 'litle peace and unitie' in the past.[2] Thus despite the clear importance of the text of Scripture and the testimony of the early church in Reformation debate, an interest in the past, particularly among evangelical writers, did not end with the close of the patristic era. While Reformation polemicists were certainly keen to claim the history of the primitive church as their own, the importance of the mediaeval

---

[1] *AM*, 1563, p. 6.
[2] *AM*, 1570, p. 302.

centuries in religious and secular propaganda and debate should not be underestimated. The religious upheavals of the sixteenth century presented an opportunity to take apart traditional, often monastic models of the past, and piece together new narratives, which reflected changing priorities in the writing of history. Not least, the use of the mediaeval chronicles allowed evangelical writers to claim that the history of the Catholic church could be turned to condemn the contemporary institution, providing evidence of doctrinal decay and the proliferation of works of piety.

The church, it was argued, had been rent by schism, new doctrines had been formulated, and a morass of ceremonies introduced. Chief among these 'unwritten verities'[3] was the prohibition of marriage to the clergy. In Protestant polemic, the councils of the early church spoke with one voice on the subject of clerical marriage, in a unanimity of belief that was only to be shattered by papal pronouncements in subsequent centuries. 'The further we go and nearer to the auncient time of the church,' Foxe argued, 'lesse auncie[n]t we shal finde the depriuacion of lawfull matrimony amongest christen ministers.'[4] The mediaeval past was also replete with models of good and bad kingship and government, precedents for conflict between church and state, and examples of religious conflict and change. The propaganda of the English Reformation made a conscious appeal to history in the effort to legitimate change, and players in the dramas of the mediaeval past came alive on the early modern theatrical and political stage. For those who made and those who experienced the Reformation, history acted as a mirror which reflected past, present and future, offering the opportunity to root the upheavals of the early modern era in events of the past, but also contributing to the formation of communal or national memory. Such developments were not unique to England: in the search for a new understanding of the past, English and continental writers shared material and interpretations, and the reconstruction of the history of the mediaeval church was often an international enterprise.

In the late fourth century, Pope Siricius addressed a series of letters dealing with the issue of clerical celibacy to the bishops of Spain, France and Africa. Siricius argued that celibacy was necessary for priests who officiated at the altar, since their ministry demanded a higher level of purity than that expected of the laity. The letters also implied that papal pronouncements on the subject were being ignored, causing scandal in the church.[5] As one of the earliest papal pronouncements on the subject,

---

[3] E.P., A Confutatio[n] of unwritte[n] verities (Wesel, 1556), RSTC 5996, sig. B6r.

[4] AM, 1563, p. 4.

[5] D. Callum, 'The Origins of Clerical Celibacy', unpublished D.Phil., University of Oxford (1977), pp. 149–171. The letters were written in AD 389.

the letters of Siricius were seized upon by defenders of clerical marriage in the sixteenth century.[6] The argument was two-fold: first, that the prohibition of marriage to the clergy was the doctrine of devils warned against by Paul (1 Timothy 4), and second, that the enforcement of celibacy upon the clergy was an innovation, since the actions of Siricius had no precedent in the early church. John Foxe used the letters to testify to the antiquity of clerical marriage; Siricius would only have issued such instructions if the clergy of France and Spain were actually married.[7] Thomas Becon complained that the papal orders not only prevented men who were married from receiving holy orders, but also sanctioned the deprivation of married clergy, and separation from their wives, in opposition to the decision of the Council of Nicaea.[8] Clerical response to the letters also provided an early example of resistance to the imposition of compulsory celibacy; the opposition of the bishop of Tarragona was confirmation for Melanchthon that the clergy had been free to marry until that date, and that the injunctions were therefore contrary to the established and accepted law of God.[9] For some evangelical writers, therefore, the degeneration of Christianity from the purity of the apostolic church had begun as early as the fourth century. The imposition of clerical celibacy paralleled the growing pretensions of the bishop of Rome, and appeared to offer confirmation that the Catholic church had institutionalized novel teaching and disciplines that were antagonistic to the principles of Scripture and the evidence of the councils.

However, definitions of novelty and innovation were not always consistent. For Bale, Becon and Foxe, the attempted enforcement of clerical celibacy came four hundred years after Christ, and was therefore treated as a new invention of men. For Catholic writers, however, the fact that papal letters had addressed the question in the fourth century confirmed the celibacy of the clergy as a longstanding and valid tradition in the church. The prohibition of marriage to the clergy, it was claimed, had been the affirmed tradition of the church for over one thousand years.[10] The ambiguity of this position could only be resolved by an appeal to the continuing revelation of doctrine within the Catholic church. The fact that the prohibition of marriage dated from the fourth

---

[6] T. Becon, *Booke of Matrimony*, in Becon, *Worckes*, 2 vols (1564), RSTC 1710, I, fol. LLl1r; R. Barnes, *That by God's worde it is lawful for priestes ... to marry wives*, WW, p. 330.

[7] *AM*, 1563, p. 4.

[8] See chapter 3 above, pp. 90ff.

[9] P. Melanchthon (tr. G. Joye), *A very godly defence ... defending the mariage of preistes* (Antwerp, 1541), RSTC 17798, sig. B3r.

[10] R. Smith, *Defensio sacri Episcoporu[m] & sacerdotum coelibatus* (Paris, 1550), sig. K8r.

century certainly confirmed that it was an ancient tradition of the church, but, as Foxe later argued, it also proved that there had been married priests for four hundred years before that date. Both Richard Smith and his opponents recognized that the letters of Siricius were crucial, and were in agreement over their content. However, the assertion that truth would only be revealed over time allowed Smith to count the letters as testimony to the antiquity and continuity of clerical celibacy, while Becon and other Protestant writers regarded them as evidence of the decay and doctrinal innovation in the church.

The letters of Siricius were not the only early papal pronouncements on the subject of clerical celibacy. Indeed, Thomas Martin argued that the sheer weight of papal letters and pronouncements on the subject was evidence enough of continuity and uniformity of practice in the mediaeval church. Martin drew attention to the declarations of Lucius and Calixtus, dating from the early third century, which had prohibited the clergy from marrying, or keeping concubines, and ordered the separation of those priests who had already married from their wives. The guilty clergy would then be subject to penance, which, Calixtus had written, was 'according to the definition of the holy Canons'. To Martin, the fact that the penance enjoined upon married clergy was already defined was conclusive proof that Calixtus was enforcing a received tradition, rather than breaking from the common practice of the church. This decree of Calixtus had been observed in the church for eight centuries, and testified to a unity and continuity of tradition.[11]

The same decrees were reinterpreted in Protestant history. Again, the prohibition of clerical marriage was firmly linked to the growth of Roman primacy and influence in the affairs of national churches. Writing for his queen, whose own attitude to clerical marriage fell short of a positive endorsement, Foxe was able to associate clerical celibacy with a papal challenge to the independence of the English church, a threat that was as real in the present (and meaningful to Elizabeth) as it had been in the past. The image of the adulterous pope, already commonplace in Protestant polemic, was sharpened by Foxe in the light of the decrees of Calixtus to condemn papal involvement in the affairs of churches outside Rome.[12] However, Foxe took his argument further, questioning the validity of the Calixtan epistles themselves. Aware of the value of the sanction of the primitive church, Foxe argued that the letters had been deliberately but erroneously attributed to Calixtus, to preserve an illusion of antiquity.[13] It was clearly essential to prove that these

---

[11] T. Martin, *A Treatise declaryng and plainly provyng that the pretensed marriage of priestes ... is no mariage* (1554), RSTC 17517, sigs J4v–5v.
[12] AM, 1570, p. 84.
[13] Ibid., p. 84.

letters had been wrongly dated; if they were allowed to stand as a reflection of the practice of the church in the early third century, it would be much more difficult to condemn clerical celibacy as a recent innovation.

Protestant polemicists argued that the fact that successive popes, from Siricius onwards, had been forced to legislate on clerical celibacy was confirmation that clergy had continued to marry throughout the early Christian centuries. Any inconsistency in the legislation or opposition to its enforcement was seized upon as evidence of disunity, and any reports of clerical incontinence were cited as proof of the perils of setting laws of men against the law of God. The clearest illustration of this was to be found in the actions of Pope Gregory I. As the pope who had sent Augustine to England, Gregory was of particular interest to English polemicists, but his actions in Rome were also of great significance in the debate over clerical marriage. Gregory had originally intended to legislate against clerical marriage, but, it was claimed, circumstances persuaded him to reverse his decision. John Bale outlined the key events. Gregory, he wrote,

> did firste com[m]aunde priestes to liue single life: but afterwarde when he perceiued that they were giuen secretly to fleshly pleasure, and that here vpon many children were murthered, he disanulled that commaundement, and sayde that it was better to mary the[n] to geue occasion of murther.[14]

After the passing of legislation prohibiting marriage to the clergy, the story ran, the heads of some five thousand children were found in a lake in Rome, supposedly the heads of the illegitimate children of incontinent priests. The discovery persuaded Gregory that the enforcement of clerical celibacy was ill advised, and he returned to the practice of the preceding centuries by allowing the clergy to marry.

Bale was not the only writer to exploit the polemical capital afforded by the story. While it is possible that successive writers borrowed the story from their predecessors, a common source existed for the account of Gregory's decision to reverse the prohibition of clerical marriage. The exploitation of this source by several evangelical writers in the sixteenth century suggests that the rewriting of mediaeval history during the Reformation was frequently collaborative and international in character. The story of Gregory and the attempted imposition of celibacy also raised a variety of questions concerning the relative value of different historical periods in determining or recognizing true doctrine and innovation. Most obviously, the extension of the debate into the history of the mediaeval church demanded some agreement as to the manner in

---

[14] J. Bale (tr. J. Studley), *The Pageant of Popes* (1574), RSTC 1304, sig. E2v.

which Christian history unfolded. For Catholic writers, history deserved
to be treated as a continuous whole, in parallel with the unswerving faith
of the church. Evangelical writers, however, were concerned to shatter
images of institutional continuity, and to deny the existence of a
continuous thread of true faith in the visible church and its history. To
treat the history of the mediaeval church as a history of falling away
from the apostolic faith, it was necessary to determine at which point the
true church and the visible Catholic church ceased to be one and the
same. For many writers, this point was reached in or around the year
600, or during the pontificate of Gregory the Great, bequeathing an
additional significance to his attitudes to clerical marriage.[15]

In 1547, a letter purporting to be written by Ulric of Augsburg to
Pope Nicholas appeared in print, probably from the press of Anthony
Scoloker. The short tract criticized the action of the pope in enforcing
celibacy upon the clergy, and claimed that the dangers in forbidding
marriage to the clergy were illustrated by the events of the pontificate of
Gregory I.[16] Foxe printed the letter of Ulric in the 1570 edition of the
Actes and Monuments. However, despite the clear importance of the
letter, its provenance and authorship were disputed, and Foxe was well
aware of the existence of different theories. The letter, which some 'do
father upon Hulderic, bishop of Augsburg', Foxe claimed, was in fact the
work of Volusianus, 'bishop sometime of Carthage'.[17] The version of the
letter which Foxe claimed to have consulted had been sent by Matthew
Parker to John Bale, and bore the name of Volusianus. Foxe had 'seen
and received of the above-named Matthew' the original manuscript
supplied by Bale, which he took to be 'of an old and ancient writing,
both by the form of the characters, and by the wearing of the
parchment'.[18] Foxe argued that the specific reference in the letter to the
injunction that married priests should not sing Mass could clearly be
dated to the pontificate of Nicholas II, although he conceded that
Bale and Illyricus 'one following the other' could have been easily

---

[15] See for example John Jewel's 'Challenge Sermon', Chapter 3 above, pp. 70, 76–7,
102.

[16] Ulric of Augsburg, *An Epistle of moche learni[n]g sent ... vnto Nicholas, Bysshoppe
of Rome* (1547), RSTC 24514, sig. A7v–8r.

[17] AM, 1570, p. 1320. Those who 'fathered' the work on Ulric included Aeneas Sylvius,
Mathias Flacius and Philip Melanchthon. Illyricus claimed to have seen two copies, both
of which bore the name of Ulric. Ulric was the tenth-century bishop of Augsburg, but
Volusianus appears to have been a figment of Foxe's imagination.

[18] The copy of the letter which was in Parker's possession may be found in CCCC MS
101, fol. 201ff. Foxe admitted that there might be differences between the Latin letter and
its English translation which had appeared earlier in the work, but excused these
discrepancies on the grounds that 'the Latine copie which here we followe came not before
to our handes': AM 1570, p. 1321.

misled.[19] The letter was attributed to Ulric in the *Ecclesiastica Historia*, and Flacius twice referred to Ulric as the author in the *Catalogus*.[20] Bale had attributed the letter to Ulric in his *Catalogus*, and the connection between Flacius and Bale referred to by Foxe is clear from their work and correspondence. Flacius had approached Bale for help in assembling his history in 1554, and in a letter to Parker in 1560, Bale described his *Catalogus* as 'set fourthe by me and Illyricus'.[21] The first of the Latin letters that Foxe printed in the *Acts and Monuments* was the same one as had appeared in the *Catalogus*, although if the letter had been taken from Flacius, it was through the intervention of Bale and Parker. By whatever means Foxe obtained the Latin version of the letter, his indebtedness to both Flacius and Bale is clear.[22]

Despite the debate over its origins and authorship, the letter itself was genuine, although its dating by Bale and Flacius was not accurate. The 'epistle of Ulric' had in fact been written by the eleventh-century clergy of Augsburg, in opposition to the enforcement of clerical celibacy by Gregory VII. The letter was printed by the sixteenth-century German humanist Joannes Nauclerus, and it was this version of the text that was exploited by Barnes, Flacius and later English writers.[23] Catholic writers were not only aware of the existence of the epistle, but were also keen to reveal its flaws as an accurate reflection of mediaeval opinion, and the errors made by evangelical writers who used the material in the sixteenth century. In the *Dialogi Sex* of 1566, Nicholas Harpsfield attacked the authenticity of the letters printed by Foxe in the 1563 edition of the *Actes and Monuments*, drawing attention to the chronological disparity between Ulric and Nicholas II.[24] Harpsfield's criticism appears to have prompted Foxe's defence of the validity of the epistle; no doubt Foxe was aided in his endeavour by the publication of the two letters of Volusianus

---

[19] *AM*, 1570, pp. 1321ff.

[20] M. Judex, and J. Wigand, *Ecclesiastica Historia* (Basle, 1560–74), Cent. IX, cols 540–2, cent. VI col. 388; M. Flacius, *Catalogus Testivm Veritatis, qui Ante Nostram Aetatem Reclamarunt Papae* (Basle, 1566), pp. 92, 99ff.

[21] Bale, *Catalogus*, p. 65; H. McCusker, *John Bale, Dramatist and Antiquary* (Freeport, 1971), pp. 68–70; N. Jones, 'Matthew Parker, John Bale, and the Magdeburg Centuriators', *Sixteenth Century Journal*, 12 (1981), pp. 35–49; J.N. King, *English Reformation Literature. The Tudor Origins of the Protestant Tradition* (Princeton, 1982), pp. 372–4.

[22] For example in the treatment of the pontificates of Silvester II and Gregory VII, and in the detail of the actions of Dunstan and Anselm in England. See pp. 106–12 below.

[23] *Monumenta Germaniae Historica. Libelli de Lite imperatorum et pontificum saeculis XI et XII conscripti* (Hanover, 1891), vol. I, pp. 254–60. I am grateful to Dr Tom Freeman for his invaluable assistance in tracing the origins of the letters. R. Barnes, *Supplication* (1534), RSTC 1471, sig. T3r; *Vitae Romanorum Pontificum* (Basle, 1555), p. 120.

[24] N. Harpsfield, *Dialogi Sex contra svmmi pontificatvs ...* (Antwerp, 1566), sig. K1r ff.

at the instigation of Matthew Parker in 1569.[25] It was Parker's text of the two letters that Foxe printed in the discussion of the Six Articles in the 1570 edition of his work.

The appearance of the letter in the works of Bale, Flacius and Foxe suggests that the writing of Protestant history in the mid-sixteenth century was at times a collaborative process, and these writers were clearly not the only Protestant propagandists who were aware of the text, or who appreciated its value. Thomas Becon drew attention to Gregory's attempt to enforce celibacy upon the clergy, and printed two letters, both attributed to Ulric of Augsburg. The first letter is the same as the first one printed in the 1570 edition of the *Actes and Monuments*, although slight variations in the translation indicate that it was not an exact copy.[26] The second letter was much shorter, but appears to be a paraphrase of a section of the second letter which Foxe had printed in 1570. There are clear similarities in the phrasing of the allegation that the prohibition of marriage would encourage immorality and sodomy among the clergy, and in the claim that all men are 'made of the same Masse', and therefore all bound by the words of Paul in the letter to the Corinthians.[27] Foxe attributed the letter to Volusianus, but Becon declared that the letter was written by Ulric and sent to 'certayne bishoppes'.[28] Becon's *Booke of Matrimony* was first printed in the first volume of the folio edition of his works, which appeared in 1564. These *Whole Worckes* of Becon were printed by John Day, who was also responsible for the 1570 edition of the *Actes and Monuments* in which the two letters of Volusianus were printed. But the variations in the English translation of the first letter of Ulric/Volusianus make it unlikely that Foxe had obtained the letter from Becon, who is certainly not mentioned in Foxe's account of how he obtained the letter. It is more likely that Becon was introduced to the material by John Day, who published Becon's works and the *Actes and Monuments*, or even by John Bale, as both writers enjoyed the patronage of Thomas Lord Wentworth.

Ulric's letter was also cited by John Ponet in the second of his works on clerical marriage. The *Apology* was completed during his period of exile in the reign of Mary, and in a letter to John Bale, Ponet referred to his 'first book' as a 'tryfell', and requested Bale's advice as to how the work could be improved.[29] Baskerville identifies this as the *Apology*, a work which Ponet originally intended to run to two volumes, although

[25] M. Parker, *Epistolae Duae D. Volusiani Episcopi Carthaginensis* (1569).

[26] Becon, *Matrimony*, fol. LLl4rff; *AM*, 1570, pp. 183ff.

[27] Becon, *Matrimony*, fol. MMm1r; *AM*, 1570, pp. 1326 [col. II]; 1327 [col. II].

[28] Becon, *Matrimony*, fol. MMm1r; *AM*, 1570, p. 1325ff.

[29] Ponet noted that Gregory still referred to the women as the wives of the priests, and argued that this confirmed that the clergy would marry legally in the sixth century. BL Add.

the second was not printed in his lifetime. Bale had been chaplain to
Ponet, who would clearly have been aware of Bale's interest in the debate
on clerical celibacy. By virtue of his own marriage, Ponet certainly had a
clear personal interest in the debate, but his knowledge of the history of
clerical celibacy would have been sharpened by contact with Bale, who
may even have drawn his attention to the letter of Ulric. The use of the
letter by Bale, Becon, Ponet and Foxe, and the similarities in their
accounts of the pontificate of Gregory VII,[30] suggests that the scope of
co-operation between Flacius, Bale and Foxe, which Foxe himself
identified, should be broadened to include other English writers of the
mid-sixteenth century.

The fluctuating fortunes of clerical marriage in Rome had repercussions for the church in England. English Protestant writers also turned to
the history of their native church to support the assertion that clerical
celibacy had only been enforced upon the English clergy for the five
hundred years prior to the Reformation. This use of history as a
polemical weapon has been discussed by Rainer Pineas in a number
of articles on key Reformation writers. The central theme of the
polemicists, and indeed of Pineas's account of their work, is that of an
English church gradually corrupted by the introduction of Roman
custom and innovation after the arrival of Augustine.[31] John Bale
provided a detailed account of this process of corruption in the *Actes of
the Englysh Votaries*, which was to influence the writing of subsequent
Protestant historians, particularly Foxe. Pineas suggests that Bale's
primary concern was the illustration of the development of church
ceremony as a political activity,[32] but the history of the early English
church was even more useful to Bale in the cataloguing of innovation in
doctrine and practice. Although Bale, and Tyndale before him, were
highly sceptical of the accuracy of the mediaeval clerical chronicles, both
recognized that their arguments would be all the more powerful if the
Catholic church could be condemned by its own history and historians.[33]
Thus throughout his account of the corruption of English Christianity by

---

MSS 29546 fol. 25; E.J. Baskerville, 'John Ponet in Exile: A Ponet letter to John Bale', *JEH*,
37 (1986), pp. 442–7.
[30] See pp. 110–12 below.
[31] R. Pineas, 'William Tyndale's use of History as a Weapon of Religious Controversy',
Harvard Theological Review, 55 (1962), pp. 121–41; *idem*, 'William Tyndale's Influence
on John Bale's Polemical use of History', *ARG*, 53 (1962), pp. 79–96; *idem*, 'William
Turner's Use of Ecclesiastical History and his Controversy with Stephen Gardiner',
Renaissance Quarterly, 33 (1980), pp. 599–608; *idem*, 'George Joye's Polemical Use of
History in His Controversy with Stephen Gardiner', *Nederlands Archief voor
Kerkgeschiedenis*, 55 (1971), pp. 21–31.
[32] Pineas, 'Tyndale's influence on Bale', p. 85.
[33] Ibid., pp. 79–81.

Rome, Bale was at pains to validate his narrative by references to contemporary chroniclers. The focal point of Bale's history was the assertion that Christianity in England pre-dated the Roman mission. Citing Gildas, Bale argued that the English had been converted in AD 63 by Joseph of Arimathea, who had preached a faith that was more perfect, and less corrupted by human invention, than that introduced by Augustine, 'of the superstycyouse secte of Benet'. Augustine had not introduced Christianity to England, Bale argued, but rather a Roman perversion of it.[34] Joseph had been a married man, and until the fifth century, the priests of the British church had been free to marry. The enforcement of laws of celibacy on the clergy therefore provided one measure of the nature and spread of doctrinal corruption after the arrival of Roman Catholicism in AD 597.

Bale's account of the conversion of the English was taken up by Foxe, who provided a list of citations to confirm that Christianity had reached Britain before the arrival of Augustine. The first signs of involvement with Rome were to be found in the letter of King Lucius to Pope Eleutherius in AD 179, which Foxe argued was proof of the novelty rather than the antiquity of Roman influence in England. The fact that Lucius requested advice from Rome after his baptism, Foxe suggested, indicated that he had been converted to Christianity in Britain before he approached the pope.[35] The use of Gildas to describe the church in England before Augustine may have reflected the influence of Bale, but Foxe's account of the mission of Augustine was more detailed than that provided in the *Votaries*.[36] Foxe reprinted the letter of Gregory which accompanied the mission, and copied from Bede the questions which Augustine sent to Gregory. On the question of whether priests could marry, Gregory replied that clerks who were out of holy orders could marry, drawing the caustic comment from Foxe that the decrees of the popes 'be repugnant to one another'. Foxe noted that clerical marriage had been accepted and tolerated by the early English Christians, and had only been condemned after the Gregorian reform movement of the eleventh century reached the country.[37] Thus the presence of married clergy in the Elizabethan church was confirmation that the Reformation had restored the pure faith practised in the early Christian centuries. The prohibition of clerical marriage was presented as a novelty, and the consequence of foreign, Roman, intervention in the English church.

---

[34] Bale, *The Actes of the Englysh Votaries*, pt I (Antwerp, 1546), RSTC 1270, fol. 23ff.

[35] Ibid., p. 145; *Ecclesiastica Historia*, Cent. II, col. 8–9.

[36] AM, 1570, p. 145.

[37] Ibid., p. 146.

The history of sacerdotal celibacy in the church after the pontificate of Gregory the Great was portrayed as a story of disunity and innovation, as successive popes and prelates attempted without success to enforce celibacy upon their clergy. The death of Gregory was a turning-point for Protestant polemicists. Thomas More had recognized the significance of the date, opting to locate the imaginary council which debated Luther's teachings in the pontificate of Gregory, in an age before doctrinal corruption in the institutional church rendered its history worthless in the eyes of Protestant polemicists.[38] More's assessment of Protestant attitudes to the dating of the subsequent deterioration of the institutional church is confirmed in John Jewel's so-called Challenge Sermon of 1559–60, in which his opponents were invited to confute his arguments either from Scripture or from the example of the primitive church 'for the space of six hundred years after Christ'. Foxe adopted a slightly different position, focusing upon the rapid decay of doctrine in the institutional church in the five centuries before the Reformation. The institutional church had been far from perfect throughout its history, but it was in the 'other latter tymes now following about the thousand yeres after Christ' that the greatest decline had occurred.[39] The forbidding of marriage to the clergy was a clear example of this deterioration. Having established to their satisfaction that the example of these early centuries supported a married priesthood, Protestant polemicists turned to the reform movements of the tenth and eleventh centuries, contrasting the actions of Dunstan, Oswald and Anselm with the practice of the primitive church.

The account of the English tenth-century reform in Protestant polemic was dominated by the actions of Dunstan, described by Bale as the 'holye vycar of Sathan'.[40] As a monk at Glastonbury, Bale claimed, Dunstan was 'very connynge in wanton Musyck, in sorcery, and in image making', and these accusations were to feature heavily in Bale's account of Dunstan's actions as archbishop of Canterbury.[41] His apparent skill in sorcery was displayed in the many miracles attributed to him, not least the circumstances surrounding the prohibition of clerical marriage. Dunstan had ordered the expulsion of the married secular priests and canons from the cathedrals, and replaced them with celibate monks, and his actions were paralleled in the activities of Oswald, the archbishop of York. Oswald, Bale alleged, 'had stodied necromencye wyth other impure scyences at Floryake', and used his authority to replace the

---

[38] See Chapter 3 above, pp. 88ff.
[39] AM, 1570, p. 217. For the significance of the date 1000 see Chapter 5.
[40] Bale, A Mystery of Iniquity (Antwerp, 1543), RSTC 1303, fol. 19v.
[41] Bale, Votaries, pt I, fol. 54v; cf. Catologus, pp. 139–41.

married priests in eight churches in the diocese with monks, likened to the locusts of Revelation 9. The actions of Dunstan and Oswald against married priests were enshrined in statute at the synod of 969, in a decree which Bale referred to as 'an acte for Sodome'.[42] Such was the power of Dunstan over the king that Edgar did nothing to prevent this persecution of married priests, a salutary warning to the English monarchs of the sixteenth century.[43]

The silence of Edgar, the 'dumme image' was in sharp contrast to the events at the Council of Winchester in 975, where, Bale claimed, 'Dunstane maketh an Idoll to speake'.[44] The issue of clerical marriage was raised at the Council, and it appeared that the pro-marriage group would emerge victorious. In an attempt to avoid defeat, Dunstan 'sought out a prectyse of the olde Idolatrouse prestes, which were wont to make their Idolles to speake, by the art of Necromancy'. Dunstan suggested that the assembled clergy should pray before a rood for guidance in their deliberations, and 'In the myddes of their prayer, the roode spake these wordes, or else a knaue monke behynd hym in a truncke throught the wall ... God forbyd (sayth he) ye shuld change this ordre taken.'[45] The prohibition of clerical marriage on the basis of a false miracle and a speaking idol confirmed that clerical celibacy was a symptom of the perversion of true religion by the mediaeval church.

Foxe was also highly critical of church reforms in the tenth century. The actions of Dunstan and Oswald confirmed that the English clergy were still married in the tenth century, and the resistance of the priests of York to the reform did little to support Catholic claims to unity and concord in belief and practice. Both Bale and Foxe described the attempt by the duke of Mercia to restore the deprived priests after the death of Edgar,[46] and Foxe was equally scornful of the miracles associated with Dunstan, not least the miracle of the speaking rood. The account provided by Foxe is strikingly similar to Bale's description in the Votaries. Like Bale, Foxe suggested that the voice might well have been that of 'some blynde monke behynde him in a trunke, through the walle', and also lamented that there had been no Thomas Cromwell at the Council, to test the veracity of the tale.[47] If the tale had any foundation in reality, Foxe argued, it did not confirm that clerical celibacy was

---

[42] Bale, Votaries, pt I, fols 54v–67v.

[43] Ibid., fol. 65r. Pineas, 'Tyndale's Influence on Bale', pp. 87–9.

[44] Bale, Votaries, pt I, fol. 69v.

[45] Ibid.

[46] Bale, Votaries, pt I, fol. 68v; AM, 1570, p. 206.

[47] AM, 1570, p. 207. Cf. Bale, Votaries, fol. 69v. The 'miracle' of the speaking rood was also discussed in the Ecclesiastica Historia, Cent. X, col. 453–4.

sanctioned by miracles, but simply demonstrated Dunstan's proficiency in sorcery.[48]

In criticizing the actions of Dunstan and Oswald against married priests, Thomas Becon drew parallels between the reforms of the tenth century and the events of Mary's reign. Dunstan and his supporters were denounced as hypocrites, who had pretended to act in the name of reform but had instead introduced abuses and immorality into the church. Becon described their expulsion of the married clerks and prebendaries from cathedrals of England, and argued that 'the like thing was practised in the late reigne of queene Mary'.[49] The prohibition of clerical marriage in tenth-century England was an indication that the clergy had been free to marry in past centuries, adding weight to the argument that compulsory clerical celibacy reform ran contrary to the practice of the primitive church. While Mary's action against the married clergy had its roots as late as the tenth century, evangelical polemicists argued that clerical marriage could be justified by an appeal to the primitive church. The implementation of clerical celibacy was a demonstration of the decay of the English church, and the fact that such practice had not been introduced until ten centuries after the birth of Christ confirmed that it was the law of men, and not of God. If the clergy had been celibate from the apostolic era, there would have been no need for action against married priests in tenth-century England. The authority of the past was far from uniform: while the example of the primitive church offered an endorsement of clerical marriage, the history of the mediaeval church lacked this positive normative value. Rather, the history of the church since the sixth century fulfilled a function that was primarily negative, documenting the spread of error in the institutional church. John Bale noted that after the reforms of Dunstan, 'thus bycame the face first of the Brytonysh and then of the Englysh churche sore changed'.[50] Dunstan's actions were testimony to the novelty, and not the antiquity, of clerical celibacy.

The appointment of Anselm as archbishop of Canterbury was a catalyst for further change. The reiteration of the laws of celibacy suggested to Bale and other writers that there were still married clergy in the twelfth century, casting further doubt upon Catholic claims to unity in faith through time. Bale referred to the deprivation of Remigius from

---

[48] *AM*, 1570, p. 207. Foxe made similar accusations of sorcery against Dunstan in his account of another 'miracle'. When the joists of a loft collapsed during a heated debate in a council, Dunstan remained unhurt, supported by the only surviving timber. Thomas Cranmer dismissed the claim that miracles could be taken as a validation of doctrine in *A Confutatio[n] of Vnwritte[n] Verities*, sigs I3rff, N6rff.

[49] Becon, *Matrimony*, fol. MMm5r–v.

[50] Bale, *Votaries*, pt I, fol. 62v.

the bishopric of Dorchester, following confirmation that he was the son of a priest. The revelation was doubly effective, Bale argued, since 'eyther had prestes wyues of their owne in thosse dayes / or els there was some other good workmanshyp a brode'.[51] If his opponents denied that there were married priests in England after Dunstan's reforms, Bale could force an admission that there must at least have been flagrant breaches of vows of chastity by the English clergy. Bale's account of Anselm's actions against married priests drew heavily upon the chronicles of Henry of Huntingdon, which allowed him to gain the polemical advantage by condemning the Catholic church through the words and histories of its own chronicles. This strategy was repeated by Foxe, who also quoted Huntingdon, in his condemnation of Anselm as 'the sore enemy agaynst lawfull mariage'.[52] According to Henry, while some had accepted the prohibition of clerical marriage, there had been vehement opposition, with other participants arguing that it could lead to unnecessary sin by encouraging priests to promise that which was above their strength.[53] Both Bale and Foxe drew attention to the unpopularity of the decree among the clergy in the dioceses of York and Norwich, based upon the complaints made to Anselm by the bishops Herbert and Gerard.[54] The controversies of the twelfth century had a clear relevance to the debate over clerical marriage in the sixteenth.

The opposition of the clergy to these reforms was further evidence of friction within the institutional church, a disunity which was confirmed by both the persistence of clerical marriage and the need for repeated legislation on the matter. Bale recorded the events surrounding the Legatine Council (1125), at which Cardinal John of Cremona presided.

---

[51] Bale, *Mystery*, fol. 21. Bale also alleged that William Rufus had allowed the clergy to keep their wives in return for an annual tribute. *Actes of the Englysh Votaries*, pt II (1551), RSTC 1273.5, fol. 41v. Bale's allegation may have been taken from William Tyndale, *Answer to More's Dialogue*, WW, p. 362: 'the sayde kyng William woulde haue had the tribute that Priestes gaue yearly to theyr Byshopppes for their whores payde to hym'.

[52] *AM*, 1570, p. 246.

[53] Bale, *Votaries*, pt II, fol. 58r–v. Bale's rendering of the acts of the council, and the text of Henry of Huntingdon are both accurate. The acts of the council may be found in D. Whitelock, M. Brett and C.N.L. Brooke, eds, *Councils and Synods with other documents relating to the English church*, 2 vols (Oxford, 1981), I, p. 675. Henry of Huntingdon wrote that 'the prohibition seemed quite proper to some, but dangerous to others; for in their attempt at purity, many might fall into disgusting filth to the great shame of the name of Christendom', quoted in N. Partner, 'Henry of Huntingdon: Clerical Celibacy and the Writing of History', *Church History*, 42 (1973), p. 468. John Ponet referred to the same chronicle to support the claim that there were married priests in England until this time. Ponet, *A Defence for the Mariage of Priestes* (1549), RSTC 20176, sig. C8r; Aelfric (tr. Matthew Parker), *A Testimonie of Antiquitie* (1562), RSTC 159, sigs 2v–3v.

[54] Bale, *Votaries*, pt II, fol. 60r–v; *AM*, 1570, p. 247.

Clerical marriage and clerical concubinage were both discussed, but Bale argued that the effectiveness of the Council's decrees was impaired by the conduct of the cardinal himself, who was found with a prostitute the very night after he had forbidden the clergy to keep company with their wives. Bale was clearly determined that the introduction of clerical celibacy in England should be seen to have been accompanied by an upsurge in clerical immorality, and such allegations carried greater force if levelled against leading churchmen. The accusation against the cardinal was not without foundation, however, and was repeated by later writers. In the *Votaries* and in the *Catalogus*, Bale claimed to have gleaned his account of the actions of the 'luxorissimus cardinalis' from Matthew Paris, who was also cited by Foxe in his attack on John of Cremona.[55] There are some differences in two of the contemporary accounts of the incident – the chronicle of Henry of Huntingdon, and the Annals of Winchester – but the substance of the two chronicles is the same.[56] The story, clearly ideal for the purpose of Bale and other Protestant writers, was not an opportunist fiction. English polemicists exploited rich sources for their histories, and their use of mediaeval clerical chronicles was highly effective. Those passages that did not support the reformers' line of argument could simply be denounced as part of a clerical conspiracy to conceal their misdemeanours, but once again, where the mediaeval chronicles confirmed their allegations, Protestant polemicists were able to condemn their opponents with reference to histories written by their Catholic ancestors.[57]

Anselm's reforms were part of the enactment of papal-led reform throughout Europe in the late eleventh and early twelfth century. Protestant polemicists held Gregory VII responsible for the introduction of compulsory clerical celibacy in the late eleventh century, emphasizing the continuity of clerical marriage in the church until this date, and arguing that the prohibition of such marriages was an unwarranted innovation. Such innovations were regarded as evidence of the rise of the influence of Satan in the institutional church. Robert Barnes claimed that Gregory was 'a great nygroma[n]cer and very familiar with the deuyll', and clearly regarded his opposition to clerical marriage as a consequence

---

[55] Bale, *Catalogus*, p. 175; *AM*, 1570, p. 256; Becon, *Matrimony*, fol. NNn1r–v; Ponet, *Defence*, sig. C8r.

[56] *Councils and Synods*, pp. 732, 740, 747. Huntingdon writes 'for in the council he dealt with the wives of priests very severely, saying that it was the greatest sin to rise from the side of a whore and go to create the body of Christ. Yet having created the body of Christ that same day, he was caught after vespers with a whore.' Quoted in Partner, 'Henry of Huntingdon', p. 472.

[57] Tyndale, *Answer*, pp. 181, 304; Pineas, 'Tyndale's Use of History', pp. 122–3; 'Tyndale's Influence on Bale', pp. 79–80.

of this familiarity.[58] Again, however, opinion was divided, a clear indication that the matter had not yet been settled. Barnes described the opposition of French priests to the prohibition of clerical marriage, citing their declaration that they would rather leave their benefices than their wives. On hearing the suggestion that they should lead the life of angels, the clergy advised the pope that he should summon such angels from heaven to serve their cures. The German clergy also mounted stiff opposition, culminating in violent exchanges at the Council of Erfurt (1075). Barnes repeated these details in the 'life' of Gregory in the *Vitae Romanorum Pontificum*, and this history of Gregory VII was to be the staple of subsequent Protestant histories of his pontificate.[59]

John Bale presented a detailed account of the Gregorian legislation in the *Actes of the Votaries*.[60] The decrees, he claimed, had been resisted by the French and the German clergy, who argued that their marriages were in full agreement with the words of Christ and the example of the Apostles. Their protestations were dismissed by Gregory: 'than made he an other tyrannouse decre, that their wyues shulde be taken for whores, their chyldren for bastardes, & that no man from thens fourth shuld heare the masse of him that kept a concubyne, as he than iudged them'. The enforcement of the legislation, Bale claimed, led many clergy to 'counterfetynge a clennesse for lucre and promocyon only', while others were guilty of 'turnynge marryage into secrete whoredome'. Gregory's action was in direct opposition to the words of the Apostles and the 'olde counsels', which had allowed marriage as a remedy for those who could not contain, and the consequences of the imposition of clerical celibacy confirmed the dangers and errors of such 'profane novelties'.[61]

Just as the accounts of the pontificate of Gregory the Great in Protestant histories were based upon shared information, so the biographies of Gregory VII depended heavily upon several key texts. In the *Pageant of Popes*, Bale followed the example of Barnes and took the letters of Cardinal Benno as his source for the accusation that Gregory was guilty of witchcraft. The same letters of Benno had been cited by Flacius, and were used by Foxe to support accusations of necromancy

---

[58] Barnes, *Supplication*, 1534, sig. U1r–v. For the significance of such allegations of necromancy, and the prominent role played by Gregory in Protestant commentaries on Revelation, see Chapter 5, pp. 126ff. below.

[59] Barnes, *Vitae Romanorum Pontificum*, pp. 196–216.

[60] Bale, *Votaries*, pt II, fol. 32v.

[61] Ibid., fols 33r–v, 34v; *Mystery*, sig. K3r; P. Martyr, *Defensio de Petri Martyris* (Basle, 1559), sig. I7v; Becon, *Reliques of Rome*, in Becon, *Worckes*, I, fol. GGGGg5v; W. Turner, *The Huntyng & Fyndyng out of the Romishe Fox* (Antwerp, 1543), RSTC 24354, fol. 25. For an account of the eleventh-century debates over clerical celibacy see A.L. Barstow, *Married Priests and the Reforming Papacy: The Eleventh Century Debates*, Texts and Studies in Religion, 12 (1982).

against Gregory.[62] The examples of local hostility to the implementation of the Gregorian reforms cited by Barnes and Bale were also common to the works of other Protestant writers. Becon and Foxe described the resistance of the French clergy, who claimed that Gregory's action 'did manifestly repugn against the word of God', thus exposing him as a heretic. Becon, Ponet and Foxe all quoted the suggestion of the clergy to the bishops, that 'if married priests could not please them, they should call down angels from heaven to serve the churches'.[63] The hostility of the clergy in Mainz to the enforcement of clerical celibacy, described by Barnes and Bale, is also treated in an almost identical fashion by Ponet, Becon and Foxe. All three describe the biblical defence of marriage presented by the lower clergy at Erfurt in 1075, and the demand of the archbishop that the clergy accept the laws of the pope even if they appeared contrary to the words of Scripture.[64] John Ponet cited the letter of Gregory to Bishop Otto of Constance, following the refusal of Otto to separate the married clergy of his diocese from their wives.[65] References to the same letter also appeared in Becon and in Foxe, who noted that Otto, 'perceiving the ungodly and unreasonable pretence of Hildebrand would neither separate those who were married from their wives, nor yet forbid those to marry who were unmarried'. Gregory alleged that the bishop was not only flouting the authority of the pope, but was also guilty of disobedience to St Peter.[66] The enforcement of clerical celibacy was seen as part of a programme of doctrinal innovation in the eleventh century, which included the increasingly forceful assertion of papal primacy and apostolic descent.[67] By the death of Gregory VII, it was argued, a chasm had opened between the Roman church and the church of the Apostles which was too wide to bridge.

Despite the vociferous claims by English Protestant writers that the lifting of the prohibition on clerical marriage was an act of restoration

---

[62] Bale, *Acta Romanorum Pontificum*, sig. N4v; Flacius, *Catalogus*, p. 312ff.; *AM*, 1570, p. 228. Both Foxe and Flacius referred to an incident in which Gregory's servants were terrified to discover that they had released a swarm of demons after opening one of Gregory's books. The letters of Benno were printed in T. Swinnerton, *A Mustre of Schismatyke Bysshoppes of Rome* (1534), RSTC 23552.

[63] Becon, *Matrimony*, fol. MMm2v; Ponet, *Defence*, sig. C3r–v; *AM*, 1570, p. 227. Foxe would have had access to the work of Flacius while working in the print shop of Oporinus, who printed the *Catalogus Testium Veritatis*. However, he was clearly not the first writer to refer to the opposition of the French clergy, and would have had a strong English tradition to draw upon in his use of this material.

[64] Becon, *Matrimony*, fol. MMm3r; Ponet, *Defence*, sig. C4v; *AM*, 1570, p. 228. Flacius also provided an account of the council at Mainz, *Catalogus*, p. 324.

[65] Ponet, *Defence*, sig. C2r.

[66] Becon, *Matrimony*, fol. MMm2r; *AM*, 1570, p. 227.

[67] Aelfric, *Testimony*, sig. +2r.

rather than innovation, there remained some who disagreed. Glanmor Williams has argued that the lifting of the prohibition was regarded by the adherents of Catholicism in Wales as the most obvious manifestation of the new and alien Protestant religion, thrust upon them in the mid-sixteenth century. This was despite the fact that the laws of clerical celibacy were an ideal rather than a reality in the mediaeval Welsh church, where married priests had continued to live undisturbed until the dawn of the Reformation. The behaviour of the Welsh clergy had led many in England to believe that clerical marriage was legal in the Welsh church, although Williams argues that this was not the case.[68] After the legalization of clerical marriage in England in 1549, a polemical tract entitled *Ban Wedy I Dynny* (the first printed book to carry parallel Welsh and English texts), was issued as a defence of the antiquity of clerical marriage. The work was an attempt to convince the Welsh, and the English, that clerical marriage had been the practice of both the apostolic church and the early mediaeval Welsh church. The argument hinged upon the discussion of inheritance in the law codes compiled by Hoel da, which included an examination of the legal rights of the sons of clerks. If a married priest had two sons, one of whom was born after he received holy orders, it was asked, did this second son have a right of partible inheritance? The code of Hoel da appeared to give the sons of married priests such rights, and entitled them to a share of their father's land. Drawing upon this ruling, the preamble to the pamphlet declared 'ye maie easely gather that priests at that time had maried wyues, neither was it prohibited or forbidden by the lawe'.[69] The legalization of clerical marriage in 1549 was therefore not an innovation, but a restoration of the traditional law of the Welsh church.

The discussion of the history of the mediaeval church in Protestant

[68] G. Williams, *The Welsh Church from Conquest to Reformation* (Cardiff, 1962), pp. 336–44. Williams suggests that the assertion that the Reformation was neither novel nor English was a key feature of other Welsh texts. 'Some Protestant Views of early British Church History', *Welsh Reformation Essays* (Cardiff, 1967). The title of the work in English is 'A certaine case extracte out of the auncient Law of Hoel da, kyng of Wales ... whereby it maye be gathered that priestes had lawfully maried wyves at that tyme'. Although published anonymously, the work is usually attributed to William Salesbury. C. James, 'Ban Wedy I Dynny: Medieval Welsh Law and Early Protestant Propaganda', *Cambrian Medieval Celtic Studies*, 27 (1994), pp. 61–81. James questions the authenticity of the original manuscript on which the work was based, arguing that some of the law codes were of a later date, and therefore not attributable to Hoel da. Later laws declared the children of priests illegitimate, but Salisbury was either not aware of this, or chose to ignore them.

[69] *Ban Wedy I Dynny*, sig. A3r. The author also noted that Hoel da was the 'eighteenth auncester fro[m] kinge Edwarde the syxth', adding further weight to the claim that the legalization of clerical marriage by Edward was the restoration of the laws of his ancestors.

polemic is dominated by the condemnation of novelty and innovation. The Bible offered confirmation that marriage was compatible with priesthood, and this had been accepted and confirmed by the Fathers and the practice of the early church. The history of the mediaeval church therefore provided Protestant polemicists with the opportunity to identify the point at which key doctrines and practices had been introduced, and to base the appeal for the resoration of the pure faith of the early church upon this evidence of mediaeval innovation. In his consideration of the labours of Dunstan, Bale deliberately couched the demand for the lifting of the prohibition on clerical marriage in terms that would appeal to the king. The image of clerical celibacy as part of a conspiracy to subvert royal authority fulfilled the same purpose as Simon Fish's famous complaint that the power of the clergy prevented the king from exercising authority over his whole realm. If clerical celibacy was a threat to the stability of the kingdom, an example of papal interference in the English church, and a mediaeval innovation which lacked a scriptural mandate, the king was justified in lifting the prohibition.

In their treatment of church history, and particularly the five centuries before the Reformation, Protestant polemicists contrasted the doctrine and practice of the primitive church with the decrees and actions of successive popes and prelates. The simple fact of the continued historical existence of the Roman church did not prove that it was the true church; what mattered was continuity in doctrine. The appeal to the example of the primitive church provided material for Protestant polemicists seeking to defend themselves against allegations of innovation, while the history of the mediaeval church enabled them to turn such accusations against the Roman church. The traditions of the church, which Catholic polemicists claimed as their own, could be adapted to condemn them. At various points in its undeniably long existence, the church of Rome had fallen prey to error, identified by Protestant writers as a proliferation of unwritten verities, including clerical celibacy. The true church adhered to the faith of the Apostles, while the false congregation set the laws of man above the laws of God. The antithesis between the true church and the false was given a simple visual expression on the title page of the *Actes and Monuments*, but this interpretation of the past advanced by writers such as Bale and Foxe had wide-ranging implications. The faith of the apostolic church had not ceased to exist between the sixth and sixteenth centuries, and the separation of the two churches was not simply institutional. Interpreted in the light of Scripture, the whole of human history became the record of the battle between truth and falsehood, the church of Christ and Antichrist, with the result that the history of events and individuals acquired a potent and distinctive significance.

CHAPTER FIVE

Clerical Celibacy as a Mark of the Antichrist in English Reformation Polemic

'Antichrist', wrote William Tyndale in 1528, 'is not an outward thyng, that is to say a man that should sode[n]ly appeare with wonders as our fathers talked of him. No, verely, for Antichrist is a spirituall thing. And this is as much to say as agaynst Christ, ye one that preacheth against Christ.'[1] This description of Antichrist marked a departure from the traditional mediaeval legend, which was based upon the prophecy of a single future figure of evil.[2] The image of Antichrist as a permanent and spiritual presence in the world was to become a central feature of English Protestant polemic, and one that was to exert a powerful influence over the interpretation of the history of the church. Antichrist was not an individual yet to come, but a spiritual force of evil which was already active in the world, and recognizable in the events of the past. In the polemical debate over the authority of Scripture and tradition, both sides were in agreement that truth was to be identified with antiquity, with the result that innovation was by definition error.[3] For Protestant polemicists, however, antiquity was not enough to confirm that the doctrines of the Catholic church were the faith of the true church. Truth and error could be identified only by reference to the Bible, the embodiment of the unchanging divine will. It was not history that engendered right

---

[1] William Tyndale, *Parable of the Wicked Mammon*, WW, p. 60.

[2] The best surveys of English apocalyptic literature in the sixteenth century are to be found in K. Firth, *The Apocalyptic Tradition in Reformation Britain 1530–1645* (Oxford, 1979), and R. Bauckham, *Tudor Apocalypse. Sixteenth Century Apocalypticism, Millenarianism, and the English Reformation from John Bale to John Foxe and Thomas Brightman*, Courtenay Library of Reformation Classics, vol. 8 (Sutton Courtenay, 1978). For the nature of mediaeval prophecies of Antichrist, and the influence of such prophecies, especially that of Joachim of Fiore, on Protestant polemic, see Bauckham, *Tudor Apocalypse*, pp. 10–33; Firth, *Apocalyptic Tradition*, pp. 1–15; M. Reeves, 'History and Eschatology: Mediaeval and Early Protestant Thought in Some English and Scottish Writings', *Medievalia et Humanistica*, new series, 4 (1973), pp. 99–123. The term Antichrist appears only on two occasions in the Bible, although other texts were understood as references to the same figure. 1 John 2:22: 'he is the liar, he is the Antichrist'; 2 John 7: 'they are the deceiver, they are the Antichrist'. cf. Matt. 24:24, 1 Tim. 4:1–3, 2 Tim. 3:1–9, 2 Pet. 2:1–5.

[3] See Chapters 2–4 above.

understanding of Scripture, but Scripture that offered the means of interpreting the past. In the words of John Bale, 'yet is the text a light to ye cronicles & not the cronicles to the texte'.[4]

The key text which was a 'light to the chronicles' was the Book of Revelation. Bale's *The Image of Both Churches* (*c.*1545) was the first full-length English Protestant commentary on Revelation, and offered the clearest demonstration of the application of Scripture to the events of the past. The work was popular, running to four reprints in the reigns of Edward and Elizabeth, and enormously influential. Bale's work was cited by Cranmer, Hooper and other Marian martyrs, provided many of the notes for the Book of Revelation in the Geneva Bible, and exerted a powerful influence on the format and content of Foxe's *Actes and Monuments*. Bale was certainly not the first English writer to make use of historical material, but the vast range of sources utilized in the *Image* sets him apart from his predecessors.[5] Judging by the epigraphs taken from Genesis 19:14, Revelation 18:14, and Jeremiah 50:8, it is clear that Bale regarded himself as an exile from iniquity, in rebellion against the workings of Antichrist in England.[6] The book was written with the aim of providing people with the information with which they could determine the church to which they belonged, since 'eyther we are citize[n]s in the new Hierusale[m] wyth Jesus Christ, or els in the old supersticious Babylon with antichrist the vicar of Satha[n]'.[7]

The two churches, it was argued, had their origins in the time of Cain and Abel, with those who followed the true faith being the descendants of Abel, and the members of the false church the heirs of Cain.[8] For Bale, the true church was the moral and theological embodiment of everything that the false church had suppressed and rejected from its origin.[9] Just as the doctrine and the morality of some Old Testament figures revealed that they had taken the side of the devil in the cosmic battle, so these

---

[4] John Bale, *Image of Both Churches* (1550), RTSC 1298, sig. A4v.

[5] Firth, *Apocalyptic Tradition*, p. 38. Fairfield also draws attention to the novelty of Bale's approach to history and revelation: *John Bale. Mythmaker for the English Reformation* (West Lafayette, 1976), ch. 3, pp. 69ff., ch. 4, pp. 86ff.; Bauckham, *Tudor Apocalypse*, p. 22ff. Bauckham claims that there are marginal references in the *Image* to 115 different authors, particularly German writers. For Bale's influence on Foxe, and his relationship with the Magdeburg Centuriators, see Chapter 4 pp. 100–102 above, and below, pp. 124–6.

[6] Fairfield, *John Bale*, pp. 71–2. Fairfield draws attention to Bale's marriage, and the fact that this would have left him open to persecution under the Act of Six Articles.

[7] Bale, *Image*, sig. A3v.

[8] Tyndale, *Answer to More*, WW, p. 412, 'And as ye see in Cain and his brother Abell, so shall it euer continue betwene the children of God and of the deuill vnto the worldes ende'; Bale, *Image*, sig. K7r; G. Joye, *The Exposicion of Daniel the prophete* (Antwerp, 1545), RSTC 14823, sigs Q3r–vff.

[9] Bale, *Image*, sig. r6.

types could be used to identify the more recent members of the false church. The persecutors, and those guilty of idolatry, placed themselves in the company of this historical type, while the elect were to be identified by the extent to which they embodied certain characteristics which could be seen through history as the marks of the true church. The persecuted, from Abel to the present, were, by virtue of the fact that they were so persecuted, witnesses to the truth and members of the true church. It was therefore possible to argue that the true church had continued, in a variety of mediaeval witnesses, even after the visible church had fallen away from the faith of Christ.[10]

This image of history as the eternal struggle between good and evil dominated Protestant commentaries on Revelation, and coloured their interpretations of events past and present. The history of the church was treated as the manifestation of the continuing battle between Christ and Antichrist and their followers from the time of Adam. Membership of one church or the other was not institutional, but ideological and historical, and the defining characteristics of the two churches were moral and doctrinal. It was continuity of faith, not of the visible edifice, that revealed the origins of a church. As Tyndale wrote in reply to Thomas More, 'not all they that are of Israell are Israelites, neither because they be Abraha[m]s sede, are they all Abrahams childre[n]: but onely that folow the faith of Abraham'.[11] Scripture was the constant that revealed both truth and falsehood, and history was exploited as a repository of moral examples to be used in the identification of manifestations of evil in the church.

If Antichrist did not have to be equated with an individual yet to come, Protestant polemicists were able to apply the term not only to individuals, including the pope, and Mohammed, but also to their followers, the company of the reprobate, throughout history.[12] With the understanding of biblical prophecy as a moral allegory which revealed the true nature of the Antichrist, those historical characters whose behaviour conformed with the established model of Antichrist-inspired degeneracy could be treated as the fulfilment of the prophecies. By fitting the deeds of the popes or their clergy into a model defined by biblical prophecies of Antichrist, the history of the church could acquire a new meaning, and the degeneracy of the visible institution could be explained

---

[10] Ibid., sigs K7r, Aa8v–Bb1r. Marjorie Reeves argues for the emergence of a standard list of mediaeval 'witnesses' in Protestant commentaries on Revelation, including Hildegard of Bingen, Joachim, Robert Grosseteste, Dante, William of Ockham and John Wycliffe. 'History and Eschatology', p. 103; Bauckham, *Tudor Apocalypse*, p. 103.

[11] Tyndale, *Answer*, p. 268.

[12] Bale, *Image*, sig. M3v; J. Old, *A Short Description of Antichrist vnto the Nobilitie of Englande* (Emden, 1555), RSTC 673, fol. 7r; Tyndale, *Wicked Mammon*, p. 60.

by reference to Scripture. The contemporary church clearly differed from that of the Apostles, but to argue this point as a justification for reform depended upon the ability to discern how and when this falling away or degradation had occurred, and where, if anywhere, the true apostolic religion had been practised in the centuries after the Apostles. The identification of the followers of truth and falsehood throughout history was therefore central to the arguments of reformation polemicists.

William Tyndale had already exploited the persuasive possibilities of the comparison of opposites in history: the pope against kings; the practice of prelates as opposed to the law of God; and the corrupt church as compared to the true.[13] The faithful had been deluded, he argued, by corrupt monastic chroniclers, who had attempted to conceal the extent to which the church and clergy had departed from the ideal of the primitive church.[14] Much Protestant apocalyptic literature was directed towards finding evidence to support the equation of the spiritual Antichrist with the institutional papacy on these grounds. The identification of either individual popes or the historical papacy with the workings of Antichrist had important implications for the understanding of the nature of the church, and, more specifically, for the differentiation between the visible and the invisible church. The Protestant search for a historical identity and self-definition depended upon the ability to contrast the reformed faith with another, better-defined entity, which could be exposed in detail in order to justify its destruction.[15] If the pope could be identified as the agent of Antichrist, or the source of evil and false doctrine in the world, Rome could be equated with Babylon, and the Reformation as an act of obedience to the injunction of Revelation 18:4: 'Come my people, away from her, so that you do not share in her crimes and have the same plagues to bear.'[16] Forces of good and evil could be identified in either specific or general terms. Bale asserted that the historical manifestation of the beast of Revelation 11:7 was 'the pope with his bishops, prelates, priests, and religious', but also made more specific identification of individual popes, including Boniface III and

---

[13] Tyndale argued that this information had been concealed by the deliberate falsification of history by monastic chroniclers: *Answer*, p. 304, 'your legends be corrupt wyth lies'.

[14] R. Pineas, 'William Tyndale's use of history as a weapon of religious controversy', *Harvard Theological Review*, 55 (1962), pp. 121, 131–4; 'William Tyndale's Influence on John Bale's Polemical Use of History', *ARG*, 53 (1962), pp. 80–81.

[15] Stephen Greenblatt argues for the presence of a similar theme in the literature of the English Renaissance in *Renaissance Self-Fashioning from More to Shakespeare* (Chicago, 1980), especially pp. 8–9.

[16] W. Turner, *A New booke of spirituall physik* (Emden, 1555), RSTC 24361, sig. L5v.

Silvester II with the Antichrist.[17] The term Antichrist could also refer, in
its broadest context, to all who defended the Roman faith or traditional
doctrine, leading Bale to label Gardiner as the agent of Antichrist, on the
basis that he had obstructed reform.[18]

The identification of Rome with the false church was therefore
accomplished, not through the application of the traditional mediaeval
legend of Antichrist, which Bullinger argued had actually concealed the
real working of evil in the church,[19] but by the definition of the expected
behaviour of Antichrist. These marks, which included immorality,
idolatry, false preaching and contempt for the sacraments, were central
to the condemnation of the papacy as the seat of Antichrist. Tyndale
contrasted the members of the true church, who trusted in their faith in
Christ, and in the word of God for justification,[20] with the adherents of
the false church, who adopted a works-oriented doctrine of salvation,
placing their own merits and human teaching above the word of God.
Other contrasts between the true and the false church were seen in terms
of specific doctrines. Anthony Gilby, in a riposte to Stephen Gardiner,
argued that the doctrine of transubstantiation marked the Roman church
as the false church of the Antichrist, while the faith of the true church of
Christ, the little flock which dated from Abel, was informed by scriptural
knowledge.[21] General concepts of iniquity were applied to the behaviour
of individual historical and contemporary opponents, and to specific
articles of faith in their church, thus defining the nature and origins of
the church to which they belonged.

The issue of clerical celibacy had much to offer Protestant writers in
their efforts to identify the historical Antichrist in terms of morality and
doctrine. The argument that the forbidding of marriage was the mark of
the Antichrist was conducted at two levels. First, the imposition of
clerical celibacy was related to the prophecies of Antichrist as the man of
sin, and the agent of doctrinal innovation. Second, the historical enforcement of celibacy on the priesthood offered reformers the opportunity to
use clerical celibacy to assess the extent of the influence of Antichrist in
the church. Those who prohibited clerical marriage, from popes to
princes, were judged to be members of the false church, and their actions

[17] J. Bale, *Vitae Romanorum Pontificum* (Basle, 1558), sigs k8v, d6r–v, 11v–3v; *Image*,
sigs K8v–L1r; *A Mystery of Iniquity* (Antwerp, 1545), RTSC 1303, fol. 16v, 58r. Bale was
the first English writer to place such emphasis on the pontificate of Silvester II in the
attempt to provide a chronology for the working of the mystery of iniquity in the church.
[18] Bale, *Image*, sig. L5r, r2v.
[19] Bauckham, *Tudor Apocalypse*, p. 99.
[20] Bale, *Image*, sig. Gg3ff.
[21] A. Gilby, *An Answer to the Deuillish Detection of Stephen Gardiner* (1547), RSTC
11884, sigs L5–K2.

were understood as the fulfilment of biblical prophecies. In particular, the interpretation of history as the unfolding conflict between good and evil enabled Protestant writers, most notably John Bale, to depict the Reformation as the latest round in this cosmic battle.

'All that bear the mark of the beast': Clerical Celibacy and the Identification of the Antichrist

This interpretation of the past was highly rigid: there could be no compromise between good and evil, with the result that every historical or contemporary figure was either a member of the true church or a participant in the false religion of Antichrist. For this reason, the debate on clerical marriage and morality featured heavily in commentaries on the prophetic books of the Bible. While ambiguity or uncertainty in Reformation theology could prove difficult to accommodate in this highly polarized form of debate, it seemed that the celibacy or marriage of the clergy could be turned to fit the model perfectly. The conduct of the clergy was highly visible: vows of chastity were either kept or they were not, a priest was either married or he was not, and a church either allowed clerical marriage or it did not. For a scheme of history which demanded that there be no shades of grey in the separation of the two churches, clerical marriage was a clear test of truth and falsehood.

Outside commentaries on the prophetic books of the Bible, the discussion of the place of Antichrist in the Roman church was essentially thematic. Members of the false church were to be identified by their immorality, by their hypocrisy, in their failure to adhere to the ideal of celibacy that they had established, and by their contempt for marriage. The common association of moral degeneracy with theological error in Reformation polemic made clerical celibacy a vital element in the identification of the false church. The argument that the clergy generally failed to keep to their vows, and the equation of such behaviour with that expected of the members of the false church, underpinned the suggestion that the institutional church was the congregation of the Antichrist. References to the Catholic church as the 'whorysh synagoge of Rome', 'the malignaunt madame', 'the mother of myschefe', or the spouse of the devil rather than the bride of Christ abound in Protestant literature.[22] Bale clearly relished the opportunity to vilify the morality of

---

[22] Bale, *Yet a Course at the Romyshe Foxe* (Antwerp, 1543), RSTC 1303, sigs A6v, D6v, D7v, E1v–2r; Olde, *Antichrist*, sig. F2v; J. von Watt (tr. W. Turner), *A Worke entytled of ye Old God and the New* (1534), RSTC 25127, sig. A4r; H. Bullinger (tr. J. Daues), *A hundred Sermons vpo[n] the Apocalips of Jesu Christe* (1561), RSTC 4061, sigs A2v, A4r, B2r, B5v, Hh3r, Ll4v–5r.

the Catholic clergy. Richard Bauckham refers to his 'wellnigh pornographic contempt for popish religious orders', a statement borne out in both the *Image of Both Churches*, and in Bale's other works.[23] Bale described the kingdom of Antichrist as 'a false / fylthye / fleshlye / whoryshe / preposterouse / prostybulouse / promiscuous and abhominable generation',[24] and traced the descent of such behaviour among the members of the false church in a line which could be drawn from the devil, through the Sodomites, Ishmael, Baal, Bel and Judas.[25] Since, Bale argued, 'he that doth synne (sayth the text) is of the deuill',[26] there was little doubt as to the symbiotic relationship between debauchery and the false church.

This theme dominated Bale's *The Actes of the Englysh Votaries*, which was written with the aim of providing as much information regarding the deeds of the English clergy as possible, almost entirely in relation to what he perceived as the consequences of their vows of celibacy. The work is littered with anecdotes describing the 'unchastity' of supposedly celibate priests and religious, coupled with attacks on the morality of Catholic saints and bishops.[27] Bale was not alone. John Ponet used the same argument in his condemnation of monasticism, and Thomas Becon protested that the church of Antichrist did not allow marriage to its clergy, 'rather suffering them to burne and to runne a whoryng'.[28] Anthony Gilby condemned Gardiner's defence of 'sodomiticall chastitie', and George Joye advocated the destruction of false religion, in which licentiousness and debauchery were considered marks of holiness.[29] Deviant behaviour among the clergy not only revealed their moral degeneracy, but also defined the institution which tolerated such conduct as the embodiment of error.

It was not only the conduct of the clergy that was subject to such criticisms: the behaviour of mediaeval popes was also documented in detail and fitted into this scheme. John Frith claimed that the text of 2 Peter 2 'painteth the Popedome', on the basis that the pope 'aboue all

---

[23] Bauckham, *Tudor Apocalypse*, p. 21.

[24] Bale, *Mystery*, fol. 2r.

[25] Ibid., fol. 2v.

[26] Ibid., fol. 10v; R. Gualter (tr. J. Old), *Antichrist: That is to say a true reporte that Antichriste is come* (1556), RSTC 25009, sig. A8r.

[27] J. Bale, *The Actes of the Englyshe Votaries*, pt II (1551), RSTC 1273.5, fols 105v–6v, 114r–114v, 46v (Wulstan), 55r (Anselm).

[28] J. Ponet, *A Defence of the Mariage of Preistes* (1549), RSTC 20176, sig. C7r; T. Becon, *The Actes of Christe & of Antichrist, concerning both their life and their doctrine*, in *Worckes*, 2 vols (1564), RSTC 1710, II, fol. DDDDdd2r.

[29] A. Gilby, *Deuillish Detection*, fol. 20v; G. Joye, *Defence of the Mariage of Preistes* (Antwerp, 1541), RSTC 21804, sigs C8v–D2r.

other walketh after the flesh in the lust of unclenness'.[30] William Tyndale also treated this text as a prediction of papal misconduct, and 'their insatiable couetousnes, pryde, stubbornnes ... with their abhominable whoredome and hypocrisie'.[31] The immorality of individual popes was not only worthy of censure, but also cast the pope as the agent of iniquity, under whom the institutional church had fallen from the truth. John Old argued that the manner of life of the popes proved that they could not be regarded as the successors of the Apostles and the vicar of Christ, but 'rather the deuel's vicar and successoure, or els the deuel himselfe. For by the frute is the tree most certenly knowen'.[32] The popes of the tenth century featured heavily in Bale's exposition of papal immorality, and his narrative of their pontificates exercised a powerful influence over John Foxe. Bale claimed that Pope John X (914–28) was the son of his predecessor Pope Lando and his mistress, who plotted to secure John's election. John was eventually murdered on the instructions of another papal concubine, Marozia, whose son, John XI, had Sergius III as his father.[33] The true church, it was claimed, would not be governed by men of such low moral standing, in either the past or the present. Bale's characterization of Paul III as the head of the false church depended not only upon his dissolute behaviour, but upon the fact that Scripture confirmed that immorality was the mark by which God 'doth detect the man of sinne, suffering him to come to the fulnes of his iniquitye'.[34] The Bible not only contained all true doctrine necessary to salvation, but also provided the means by which error and evil could be identified.

The conduct of the mediaeval popes as described by evangelical polemicists was hardly compatible with the purity expected of the unmarried clergy. Protestant writers argued that priestly chastity, and papal chastity in particular, was little more than a pretence, which fuelled pretensions to spiritual authority. John Frith, referring specifically to the text of 2 Peter 2, alleged that the clergy of the false church 'under the doctrine of godlines (which they shall fain) they shall bringe in ungodlines'.[35] If the false church was identified as the church of the hypocrites, broken vows of celibacy were to become an ideal mark

---

[30] J. Frith, *Pistle to the Christen Reader* (Antwerp, 1529), RSTC 11394, pp. 53v–54r, 67r.

[31] W. Tyndale, *Prologue to 2 Peter*, WW, p. 55.

[32] Old, *Antichrist*, sig. D6r.

[33] Bale, *Actes of the Englysh Votaries*, pt I (Antwerp, 1546), RSTC 1270, fol. 58rff.; *Scriptorum Illustriu[m] Maioris Brytanniae* (Basle, 1557), pp. 122, 129, 121; Foxe, *AM*, 1570, pp. 193–4.

[34] Bale, *Vitae Romanorum Pontificum*, sig. I3vff.

[35] Frith, *Pistle*, fol. 17r.

by which to identify its members. Foxe warned that Antichrist, whom he likened to the pope, cultivated 'a counterfeit sinceritie of unspotted life, yea outward resemblance of true religion, thereby to dazel more easily the eyes and heartes of the unlettered'.[36] Bale made explicit associations between the hypocrisy of the false church and the celibacy of the clergy in the *Actes of the English Votaries*. The gulf between ideal and reality was exemplified in the actions of Johannes Eck, whom Bale accused of fathering three children in the same year as he had condemned those clergy who would have allowed the breaking of vows of celibacy by marriage.[37] Again, the Roman church was mocked as 'the false counterfet churche ... ye insaciable chaos or bottomlesse pyt that S Johan speaketh of ' or the 'holy mother ye churche of Antichrist', and the 'Synagoge of Satan'.[38] The idea that the members of the false church would exalt the ideal of clerical celibacy, and yet fail to keep to that ideal in practice, was a central feature of Protestant polemic.[39]

Although the allegations made against the clergy and papacy had their roots in an attack on vows of chastity, evangelical polemicists claimed that it was not simply the consequences of such vows that identified the church of Rome as the church of Antichrist. The fruits of vows of chastity also revealed that the theology that underpinned them was fatally flawed. There was nothing in Scripture, it was claimed, or in the example of the primitive church, to suggest that the clergy should not be free to marry, making it impossible that compulsory clerical celibacy was the revealed will of God. In the rigid epistemology of the two-church interpretation, if the prohibition of marriage was not the will of God, it could only be the work of the Antichrist. The treatment of marriage in Scripture as a state blessed and willed by God, taken alongside the claim of Paul that the forbidding of marriage was the doctrine of devils, offered further ammunition to reformers in the identification of clerical celibacy as a mark of the false congregation.

The argument that the prohibition of clerical marriage was the doctrine of Antichrist was common in English polemic from the 1520s.

---

[36] J. Foxe (tr. J. Bell), *The Pope Confuted* (1580), RSTC 11241, sig. B3r; Old, *Antichrist*, sig. A5r; J. Ponet, *An Apologie fully aunsweringe ... a blasphemose book gathered by D. Steph. Gardiner* (Strasbourg, 1555), RSTC 20175, p. 41; W. Roy, *Rede me and be nott wroth* (n.p., 1528), RSTC 21427, sig. E7r.

[37] Bale, *Romyshe Foxe*, sig. I6v. The allegations against Eck have strong parallels with the account of the actions of the papal legate John of Cremona. See Chapter 4, pp. 109–10 above.

[38] Bale, *Mystery*, fols 68r, 72v; *idem*, *The Apology of Johan Bale agaynste a ranke Papyst* (1550), RSTC 1275, fol. 65r.

[39] Ponet, *Defence*, sigs C8r–D1r.

John Frith defended clerical marriage in his translation of Luther's *De Antichristo*, and informed the reader that 'Sathan was the author that it was forbede.'[40] The same theme was taken up by later English writers. John Bale argued in 1545 that 'the deuyll loueth wele and first sought out that holye kynde of chastyte for to bewtyfye ther with the Popes holye church / & also to fyll hell', and Robert Crowley made the blunt assertion that 'it is of Antichristes fayeth, to beleue that priestes dedicated vnto God may not marye'.[41] Thomas Becon claimed that those who defended vows of celibacy were the false congregation, on the basis that the church of Christ followed the words of Paul in 1 Corinthians 7. Antichrist, he claimed, despised marriage and prohibited it to his adherents, while the Catholic church and its popes were so hostile to marriage that they preferred to turn a blind eye to clerical immorality.[42] John Ponet used the same image, arguing that those priests who had been persuaded to leave their wives had been tempted from the truth by the Antichrist. The prohibition of clerical marriage was the institution of the devil, invented 'for the maintenaunce of whooredome and all filthye kind of liuing: and it was brought to pass by the deuelles high preest, Antichrist, the byshop of Rome'.[43] No wonder, then, that John Hooper concluded that compulsory celibacy was 'the true mark to know Antichrist by'.[44]

By examining the decrees of the popes on the subject of clerical celibacy, evangelical polemicists could claim to chart the history of the rise of Antichrist in the papacy. As a result of the histories produced by Bale and Foxe, the deeds of two popes in particular dominated this interpretation of the past; Silvester II and Gregory VII. The pontificate of Silvester II spanned the year 1000, which Bale regarded as a crucial date.[45] The Book of Revelation referred to the loosing of Satan after a thousand years, and Bale clearly believed that Silvester was responsible both for the fulfilment of this prophecy and for the prohibition of clerical marriage.[46] The clergy had been free to marry in the primitive church, Bale argued, and had continued to be so, 'tyll Sylvester the .2. ded fatche the deuyll from hell by his nicromancye (where he was a fore tyed vp for

---

[40] Frith, *Pistle*, fol. 71v.

[41] Bale, *Mystery*, fol. 20r; R. Crowley, *The confutatio[n] of xiii articles wherunto Nicholas Shaxton ... subscribed* (1548), RSTC 6083, sig. G8v.

[42] Becon, *Acts of Christe & of Antichrist*, fol. BBBBbb1r.

[43] Ponet, *Defence*, sig. B7r.

[44] Hooper, 'A Brief and Clear Confession of the Christian Faith', in C. Nevinson, ed., *The Later Writings of Bishop Hooper* (Parker Society, Cambridge, 1852), p. 56.

[45] The first part of the *Votaries* concluded with the year 1000. Bale's view is echoed by Foxe, who argued that the decay of the church had been more rapid after this date. See Chapter 4, p. 108 above.

[46] Bale, *Mystery*, fol. 16r; cf. Bale, *Acta Romanorum Pontificum*, sigs k8v, l1v–3v.

a thousande years)'.[47] The allegation that Silvester's witchcraft loosed Satan from the pit was repeated in the *Catalogus*, where Bale provided a summary of other strange occurrences in his pontificate. Having made a pact with the devil to secure the papal throne, Silvester was then assured that he would only lose the papacy if he were to say Mass in Jerusalem. The prophecy was fulfilled when, presumably inadvertently, Silvester said Mass in the temple of Jerusalem in Rome. After his death, his remains were divided, and placed on the back of horses, which were allowed to run free and scatter his body where they wished. However, the horses did not move, with the result that Silvester was buried in the Lateran, where his bones were said to rattle in the tomb to foretell the death of current incumbents of the papal throne.[48] An almost identical account appeared in the *Magdeburg Centuries*, and in Matthias Flacius's *Catalogus Testium Veritatis* in 1566, although the latter made no reference to the rattling bones.[49] John Foxe also repeated the claim that Silvester had obtained the papacy 'through the operation of sathan', and repeated the 'miracles' which surrounded his death.[50] However, the strong association of Silvester's necromancy with the imposition of clerical celibacy came almost entirely from the pen of Bale, reflecting his desire to use this issue to chart the influence of Antichrist in the church.

The fact that Silvester's pontificate spanned the year 1000 clearly suited Bale's purpose in the identification of this period with the loosing of Satan, which was described in the Book of Revelation. Other dates were also important: Bale had argued that true religion had been practised in England until the time of Augustine's mission and the growth of Roman influence, after which time votaries had laboured 'to prepare Antichrist a seate here in England, agaynst the full tyme of his perfight age of .666'.[51] Bale identified this year with the consecration of Theodore of Tarsus, under whom the preparations for the reign of Antichrist were completed, although on this occasion he sacrificed accuracy to the overall scheme of his historical interpretations. Theodore had in fact been consecrated in 668, but the polemical potential of the date 666, when equated with the text of Revelation 13:18, the prophecy of the beast, was too great to miss.[52] The doctrine and the practice of the

---

[47] Bale, *Romyshe Foxe*, sig. I6v.

[48] Bale, *Catalogus*, pp. 142–3.

[49] M. Judex and J. Wigand, *Ecclesiastica Historia* (Basle, 1560–74), Cent. X, col. 547–8, Cent. XI, col. 659; M. Flacius, *Catalogus Testivm Veritatis* (Basle, 1566), pp. 341–2.

[50] *AM*, 1563, p. 11; *AM*, 1570, pp. 217–18.

[51] Bale, *Votaries*, pt I, fol. 26r.

[52] Ibid., fol. 34v. L.P. Fairfield argues that Bale must have known that the date was wrong, since Bede clearly dated Theodore's consecration to 668. Fairfield, *John Bale*, p. 98, n. 46.

English church had continued to deteriorate after that date, it was claimed, especially with the approach of the crucial year of 1000, when the rise of the influence of Antichrist within the English church was made evident by the actions of Dunstan. At this time, Bale claimed, the married clergy had been expelled from the cathedrals, and replaced by the 'layse lean locustes, which not longe afore had leaped out of the bottomlesse pytt'; the locusts were those referred to in Revelation 9:7.[53] Dunstan, already the villain of Bale's history, was given a key role in the apocalyptic interpretation of English history, with the result that his actions were portrayed not only as misguided, but as part of the growing influence of Antichrist in the church. Such persons and events were thus imbued with an eschatological significance, especially given Bale's dependence upon the interpretation of history through the scheme of the Book of Revelation and the emphasis placed upon the importance of the year 1000. The millennium referred to in Revelation 20 appears to have been the determining factor, allowing Bale to exploit the chronology of the institution of clerical celibacy to suggest that it revealed the point at which Antichrist was loosed from the pit.

The pontificate of Gergory VII was more widely accepted as crucial in the enforcement of clerical celibacy and in the identification of the rise of Antichrist in the papacy.[54] Again, allegations of necromancy featured heavily in Protestant accounts of his pontificate. John Bale prefaced his remarks about the reforming decrees of Gregory VII with the accusation 'for holy pope Hylderbra[n]de which was a necromanser made this constitution / that non shuld be admitted to holye orders / vnlesse he foresware marriage for the terme of his lyfe'.[55] Apparently forgetting the earlier accusation made against Silvester II, Bale alleged that Gregory VII had been responsible for this innovation, stating that 'thys tyrannouse coaccyon to fylthynesse came in first of all by pope Hyldebra[n]de, a superstytyouse monke, a nycromanser, a murtherer ...'.[56] Continuing the theme that the moral behaviour of the Roman clergy proved that they were the members of the false church, Bale linked this with allegations of necromancy, castigating the 'pestilent papists' as both 'sorcerers' and 'sodomites'.[57] Similar accusations were levelled at individual popes, including John XIII, Paul III and Benedict IX, the last having allegedly used magical powers to conjure devils and draw women

---

[53] Bale, *Votaries*, pt I, fol. 67v.

[54] The events surrounding the prohibition of clerical marriage by Gregory are examined in Chapter 4 above. It is my concern here to focus upon the importance of Gregory VII in the Protestant identification of the Antichrist.

[55] Bale, *Mystery*, fol. 17v; cf. *Acta Romanorum Pontificum*, sig. N4v.

[56] Bale, *Romyshe Foxe*, sig. K3r.

[57] Bale, *Mystery*, fol. 42r.

to him.[58] Bale's arguments were not unique, and drew heavily upon the letters of Benno, which were known by a number of other writers. Benno's account of the life of Gregory, and the accusation of witchcraft, were cited by Barnes and Swinnerton, and the claim that a host of demons had appeared when Gregory's servants opened one of his books was repeated by Flacius and by Foxe.[59] William Tyndale posited a similar link between necromancy and immorality, depicting the papacy as the whore of Babylon, and commenting 'how shamefull licences doth she geue to them, to vse Nichromancy, to hold whores, to diuorce themselues, to break the fayth'.[60] Clerical celibacy and immorality, coupled with accusations of witchcraft, offered further confirmation that the prohibition of marriage was the institution of the devil.

Even without the allegations of necromancy, Gregory's action against married priests identified him in such polemic as a member of the false church. Robert Barnes noted that, until the pontificate of Gregory, the clergy had been free to marry, and argued that the action taken against married priests revealed Hildebrand as 'Satanae organu[m]'.[61] The same argument was adopted later by Thomas Becon, who claimed that the prohibition of clerical marriage was visible evidence that Antichrist was now established in the see of Rome. The pontificate of Gregory demonstrated how 'in processe of tyme, the Deuyl and the Pope with theyr Antichristian adherents drove away the holy and honourable Matrimony of the mynisters and Priestes', replacing the divine institution of marriage with immorality and tyranny.[62] In the interpretation advanced by Barnes, Bale and Becon, the true congregation could be separated from the false church by their views on marriage, and clerical marriage in particular. The prohibition of clerical marriage thus identified the teachings of Gregory VII with the doctrine of Antichrist, and confirmed that by the turn of the eleventh century the institutional church was no longer cognate to the true church. However, if the two churches could be identified by their attitude to clerical marriage in the eleventh century, there was no reason why the same test should not be applied to the church in the sixteenth century. The word of God was unchanging, with the result that the prohibition of clerical marriage was as much the 'doctrine of devils' in the sixteenth century as it had been in

---

[58] Bale, *Acta Romanorum Pontificum*, sig. i7v–8r, l1v.

[59] R. Barnes, *Vitae Romanorum Pontificum* (Basel, 1555), p. 212; Becon, *Booke of Matrimony, Worckes*, I, fol. MMm1v; T. Swinnerton, *A Mustre of Schismatyke Bysshoppes of Rome* (1534), RSTC 23522, 'The Life of Hildebrand', sig. A6v; Flacius, *Catalogus*, pp. 312ff.; *AM*, 1570, p. 228.

[60] Tyndale, *Obedience*, p. 115.

[61] Barnes, *Vitae Romanorum Pontificum*, pp. 214–18.

[62] Becon, *Matrimony*, fol. MMm3v; Gualter, *Antichrist*, sig. S4r.

the sixth. A church that enforced celibacy upon its clergy in any age was not the church of Christ.

The True Church and the False in the Sixteenth Century

The actions of Gregory VII, and the suggestion that they marked him as an agent of Antichrist, had repercussions for the analysis of contemporary events by evangelical polemicists in the sixteenth century. Philip Melanchthon, while blaming Gregory VII for the introduction of clerical celibacy, was equally critical of current events in England. In a remark obviously directed against Henry VIII in the aftermath of the Act of Six Articles, Melanchthon described how

> the princes & their bisshops stablish many greuouse synnes & mischieifes as long as that defende their wyuelesse chastite / which also thus doing heap the worthy vengea[n]ce of god upo[n] their owne headis shortely to be powered forth. And as lo[n]g as they assent to the deuil the autor of their wycked doctrine / thei do but make municio[n]s & bulwerkis to defende antichristes kyngdo[m] age[n]st god ... yea they confirme al the rest of anticristes idollatrye.[63]

The English Reformation of the 1530s had failed to overturn the innovations of the mediaeval papacy, and by retaining the prohibition on clerical marriage, Henry was acting to secure the dominion of Antichrist in the English church.

Melanchthon was not alone in his dissatisfaction with the state of religion in England. However, on the issue of who was to be blamed for the apparent continuation of the influence of Antichrist in the English church, English polemicists had to show a degree of caution. The Six Articles not only defended key aspects of Catholic orthodoxy; they also expounded and defined the authority of the Supreme Head. The legislation was accompanied by the declaration that disobedience to the king, or, indeed, accusations of heresy or schism, would be regarded as treasonable offences. Any criticism of legislation promulgated under the name of the Supreme Head was therefore highly dangerous. Reformers were reluctant to concede that the royal supremacy alone could justify the apparently unjust and unholy actions of the king, and argued instead that the manner in which the king exercised his authority revealed the origins of such authority itself, either in God or the devil. In theory, the Act of Six Articles placed Henry firmly outside the true church. However, the denunciation of Henry's actions in evangelical literature

---

[63] P. Melanchthon (tr. G. Joye), *A very godly defence, full of lerning, defending the mariage of preistes* (Antwerp, 1541), RSTC 17798, sigs B4v, D1r, D8r.

tended to be concealed behind an attack on those who advised the king. Thus it was the conservative councillors, and Stephen Gardiner in particular, who were blamed for the work of Antichrist, and the restoration of bondage, as 'the other priests of Egypt', who had persuaded Pharaoh to act against God.[64] The image of Pharaoh was hardly a compliment to Henry VIII, but it did absolve Bale, and others, from the guilt of direct, and treasonable, criticism.

Henry Brinklow also held the English bishops responsible for the continued prohibition of marriage to the clergy, and the persecution of those who opposed it.[65] Among the bishops, Brinklow regarded Gardiner as worthy of special censure, attributing to him both the prohibition of clerical marriage in the Six Articles and the imposition of the death penalty on married priests. George Joye, also blaming Gardiner for the Act of Six Articles, claimed that he was the chief agent of Antichrist in England, while William Turner accused Gardiner of necromancy, echoing the association between compulsory clerical celibacy and magic in evangelical history writing.[66] Drawing upon the idea that the devil had always laboured to destroy marriage, Turner claimed that Satan had been disappointed by the original failure of this scheme, and had therefore approached the pope, 'hys vicare in erth the bishop of rom / and hym he styrred & moued to destroy matrimony & to alow comon stewes', promising the pope great riches in return. Yet again, Satan was thwarted, this time by the 'Germans', who recognized compulsory celibacy as the doctrine of devils, and who encouraged Henry VIII to reject the authority of the pope. However, just as Henry moved to destroy the last remnants of papistry in the kingdom, he was persuaded by Satan to maintain the prohibition on the marriage of priests.[67] The influence of the pope in England, and the doctrine and practice of those who adhered to his faith, was a manifestation of the workings of Antichrist. If clerical celibacy was indeed a mark of the Antichrist, the continued prohibition of clerical marriage in England was a sign that the church was as yet unreformed.

The issue of clerical marriage and clerical misconduct had been a central feature of John Bale's *Image of Both Churches* from its opening pages. In the condemnation of clerical celibacy, Bale applied the images

[64] J. Bale, *An Epistle Exhortatory to the English Christian* (1544), RSTC 1291, sig. F2r.

[65] J.S. Cooper, ed., *Henry Brinklow's Complaynt of Roderick Mors and the Lamentatyon of a Christen Agaynst the Cytye of London* (1545), EETS extra series 22 (1874).

[66] W. Turner, *The Rescuyinge of the Romishe Fox, other vvyse called the examination of the hunter* (Bonn, 1545), RSTC 24355, sigs H7–8v.

[67] Turner, *The Huntynge & fyndynge out of the Romishe fox* (Antwerp, 1543), RSTC 24345, sig. E6r–v.

of the Book of Revelation to the history of the church to interpret not only the past but also the present as the fulfilment of the divine plan, which had been revealed to the prophets. In this periodization of history, the Reformation corresponded with the opening of the sixth seal.[68] With the advent of this sixth age, Bale claimed, the working of Antichrist would cease, with the result that the clergy would be required to lay aside 'theyr stynkynge chastyte, (whom God and hys aungels abhorreth and the deuyll most hyghly aloweth)'.[69] The legalization of clerical marriage was therefore an integral part of the reform of the church. Bale's interpretation has parallels in the work of Bullinger, who argued that with the opening of the sixth seal the votaries would flee, aware that 'the monastical life, and their merites, ca[n] not stande before God'.[70] Vows of chastity would be recognized as worthless, as the text of Revelation 6:12 was fulfilled in the events of the sixteenth century.

The prohibition of marriage to the clergy was established in polemical debate as a central part of the cosmic struggle between good and evil. However, the battle was not yet won. Just as the beast of Revelation 13:3 was wounded but not killed, so it appeared that the Roman church had been damaged but not overthrown. The incomplete nature of reform, Bale argued, was revealed in the survival of 'theyr priestybulouse priesthode, their vowynge to haue no wiues, and their Sodomiticall chastitye'.[71] While these remained, the Roman church, identified as the beast, could recover, and continue to spread its blasphemies (Revelation 13:5). In Bale's interpretation, these profanities included both transubstantiation and the continued prohibition of marriage to the clergy, the very doctrines that were set out in the Act of Six Articles, convincing Bale that the reign of Antichrist in England was not yet over. The reformation and the purification of the church could be identified with the symbolism of the opening of the sixth seal, but the images of the Book of Revelation also served to explain the slow pace of reform, and warn of the threat that the wounded beast posed to the nascent church.

The interpretation of contemporary events as part of a historical battle between truth and falsehood was encouraged by reference to the description of the whore of Babylon in Revelation 17. Accusations that the Roman clergy were guilty of both material and spiritual fornication were used to justify the identification of the Catholic church as Babylon. Bullinger pointed to the condemnation of unfaithfulness, impiety, idolatry and fornication in Scripture, and drew the conclusion that

---

[68] Fairfield, *John Bale*, pp. 78–9.

[69] Bale, *Image*, sig. N4v cf. Rev. 7.

[70] H. Bullinger (tr. J. Daues), *A Hvndred Sermons vpo[n] the Apocalips of Jesu Christe* (1561), RSTC 4061, sig. Q2r–v.

[71] Bale, *Image*, sig. g5v–6v.

'Rome therefore was a greate strompet, and is also at this daye a most stynkyng harlot.'[72] Bale was equally direct in his comparisons. Despite its outward appearance of purity and godliness, the Roman church failed to abide by these expectations. In the same manner, broken vows of celibacy, vows which should have indicated the purity and angelic lifestyle of the clergy, reflected this corruption. Rome, like Babylon, was the mother of all actual and spiritual fornication, and the spouse of the devil.[73] The scarlet beast on which the whore was seated, Bale argued, was the body of the clergy and the temporal governors who upheld the church of Rome, and the cup which the whore held was seen as false religion containing the doctrine of devils, lies, sophistry and 'lecherouse liuinge vnder the coloure of chastite'.[74] In a clear reference to the state of religion in England, Bale identified Gardiner, Bonner and Tunstall as those who 'hold vp thys glorious whore in her old estate of romishe religion'.[75]

The overthrow of the whore (Revelation 17:16) would be accomplished by those who had rejected the church of Rome, identified by Bale as Cranmer, Latimer, Luther, Erasmus, Oecolampadius, Zwingli, Pomerane, Bucer, Capito, Melanchthon, Bilney, Tyndale, Frith, Barnes, Coverdale, Cromwell, Joye, Turner and Ridley.[76] The members of the true church in the sixteenth century were the contemporary embodiment of the faithful followers of Christ whose actions were described in the Book of Revelation. The voice from heaven, which had called the people away from the fallen Babylon, Bale argued, summoned them also from the church of Rome, 'hyr false religion and defiled sacramentes'.[77] The simple command to flee in order to avoid the plagues which were to be inflicted on Babylon was developed by Bale into an attack on the doctrine, ceremonies and morality of the Catholic church, for which the Babylon image, and the issue of clerical morality, provided the ideal metaphor. The Book of Revelation, in Bale's understanding at least, had provided a pattern for calibrating both the rise of Antichrist and the institutionalization of error in the Roman church and papacy, exemplified by the growing insistence of the church on a celibate priesthood, and the failure of that priesthood to keep its vows.

The Book of Revelation was the most fertile hunting ground for polemicists in the identification of Antichrist, but their treatment of other, more unusual biblical verses is also highly revealing. The Book of

---

[72] Bullinger, *Hvndred Sermons*, sig. Ll6r.
[73] Bale, *Image*, sig. r4v.
[74] Ibid., sig. r2r–4r.
[75] Ibid., sig. r2v, t1v.
[76] Ibid., sig. s8r.
[77] Ibid., sig. Aa8r; Gualter, *Antichrist*, sig. Z5v.

Daniel, in the eyes of evangelical exegetes, contained one of the clearest accounts of a figure of evil. The images of persecution, the warnings offered to future generations, and the esoteric style of the Book of Daniel allowed reformers to read much of contemporary significance into the prophecies. The most important work in English on the Book of Daniel was George Joye's *The Exposicion of Daniel the Prophet* (1545). Based almost entirely upon the interpretation of Daniel by continental reformers, the work listed as its sources the works of Oecolampadius, Pellican, Melanchthon and John Draconite, and as such is further evidence of the influence of continental writers upon the polemical use of history by English writers. Joye's work was printed by the printer responsible for the publication of Bale's *Mystery of Iniquity* in the same year, and may be seen as part of the developing tradition of English Protestant polemical commentaries on biblical prophecy.

The ideology of the two churches was rehearsed at the beginning of Joye's commentary. The work should enable the reader to 'lerne which is the very chirche of God / & whiche the voice of the gospel of the sone of god soweth / thei might knowe that same to be the chirche which shal fight with the ennemies of cryste'.[78] The study of the monarchies of the Book of Daniel would provide the reader with the means with which to distinguish this true church from the 'Synagog of anticryst', in order that they would not be deceived by a church which openly defended images, superstition and ceremonies.[79] As the wrath of God had fallen upon the idolatrous kings of the Old Testament, Joye warned, so would it descend upon the Roman church, and, by association, England, for the idolatry of the Mass, for superstition in the veneration of relics, and 'for their abhominable horedome / for their forbidding of lawfull matrimony / for separating and violating iustely maryed persones ...'.[80] Such images provided a warning of the power of the devil over princes, 'wherfore very fewe princes in the later dayes shall abolish the pope, retaine and holde trewe worship and religion of god'. Joye's doubts about the ability of the prince to break from the false church and institute true religion undoubtedly referred to the deeds of Henry VIII, whose failure to reject Catholic doctrine when he abolished the authority of the pope in England was the cause of Joye's exile.

The eleventh chapter of the Book of Daniel described the breaking of the land of a mighty king, and warned that the true church would continue to endure suffering at the hands of the Antichrist, who would

---

[78] Joye, *Daniel*, sig. A3v.

[79] Ibid., sig. A7v–8v.

[80] Ibid., sig. J2r.

persecute the faithful.[81] The belief that Antichrist would persecute the innocents was certainly applicable to events in England in the aftermath of the Six Articles; indeed, Joye presumably regarded himself as one such innocent. His later remarks add weight to the argument that his interpretation of the passage was, in reality, an indictment of Henry VIII. Joye argued that the biblical monarchy of Alexander had survived until he had allowed himself to be polluted with lechery, and 'beleued himself to haue a certeyn diuyne prerogatiue and power aboue all men and god', the same accusations that he had levelled against the pope in his identification of the papacy and Antichrist: 'thei wryte themselues the most holy headis and vicares of the catholike chirche of god / but thei be the most profane cheiftaines of sathans synagogue'.[82] However, the pope was not the only individual to have claimed a God-given power over men, and Joye's references could equally well be applied to the situation in England. Not only had Henry VIII claimed divine appointment as head of the church and state, but his marital difficulties in the 1540s had done little to secure the future of his own Tudor dynasty.

According to the prophecy, the agents of Antichrist would not only persecute the innocents, but would also alter the law of God. Of all such innovations, Joye argued, 'their lawe of their preistes chastite / is the moste strong perniciouse perdicion of infinite soules. Nether dothe long custome with their vnlawfull vowes at their vnlawful articles age excuse their dampnable doctrine.' The reference to 'unlawful articles' suggests that Joye had in mind the events of 1539, and particularly the prohibition of clerical marriage. In the enforcement of clerical celibacy, 'now ye se anticristis kingdom & who be the princes therof'.[83] Joye had made it abundantly clear where Henry VIII stood in the struggle between the true church and the false. Far from being the Supreme Head of the church of God, Henry was a prince of the kingdom of Antichrist.

In the commentary on Daniel 11:37, Joye attempted to make an explicit connection between Henry VIII's marital difficulties and his prohibition of clerical marriage. The argument was underpinned by a somewhat flexible transcription of the text. Where it reads 'Neither shall he regard the gods of his fathers, nor the desire of women', Joye makes a key distinction, writing, 'he shall set naught by ye god of his fathers / nether shall he regarde the coniugale loue in wedlocke'. Such emphasis on marriage, rather than women, allowed Joye to assert that it was contempt for marriage, not women generally, that was the mark of the Antichrist. Joye continues:

---

[81] Ibid., sigs Y1v, Z3r–v.
[82] Ibid., sigs Z5r, b2v, c2r.
[83] Ibid., sig. e1r.

> This naturall coniugale loue shall they vtterly destroye forbidding
> the lawfull matrimony of preistis and of all their religious fonde
> vowesses. And they shall set vp therby whoredom aduoutry and all
> prodigiouse lecherie vnder an hypocritish cloke of vnlawfull lawfull
> vowes and sole vnchast chastity.

This was indeed the 'devillish doctrine' warned of by Paul in the letter to
Timothy, to which Joye provided a reference in the margin. Quite whom
Joye held responsible for the prohibition of marriage is not immediately
clear. The clergy were certainly implicated, and Joye argued that the
'authors of this anticrysten act' were 'our bishops and priests'. However,
this remark is prefaced by the warning 'siche forbidders of wedlocke
shall never have good successe and fortune in their own marriages'. Joye
is clearly not referring to the clergy, who had no marriages either to
prosper or to suffer. Placed in the context of contemporary events,
however, this remark has greater significance. Again, Joye's commentary
is focused upon events in England: the Act of Six Articles, English
politics, and the king himself. Henry had married Anne of Cleves in
1540, and the marriage was annulled in July, only a year after the
passing of the Six Articles. The king had then married Katherine
Howard, who was found guilty of adultery in 1541. Henry's marital
difficulties were the judgement of God on his failure to effect a complete
break with the church of Antichrist.

This part of the Book of Daniel was also exploited by several other
polemicists.[84] John Frith, writing in 1529, argued that the vows of
chastity of the religious were not a true godly life, but the fulfilment of
the prophecy of evil contained in Daniel. Rather than abide by the laws
of God, the agent of evil would 'make statutes contrary to god and
matrimony / takinge no thought how impossible it is to beare and suffer
this bourden of matrimony and wedlocke which is denied the[m]'.[85] Frith
was writing over a decade before Joye, and his interpretation obviously

---

[84] Not all Protestant writers were as willing to use the text of Daniel 11:37 in the
identification of the papacy with Antichrist; indeed, John Calvin argued that such
comparisons should not be made. Unlike the works of Old and Joye, Calvin's exposition
was not addressed specifically to an English audience, and was not intended as a popular
commentary on events in England in the 1540s and 1550s. The *Praelectiones in Librum
Danielem* first appeared in 1561, but was not translated into English until 1570, when it
was published by John Day. The vitriolic debate over clerical celibacy in England had
largely subsided by this date, but it is interesting to note that Calvin's work marked a
departure from the common interpretation of this crucial verse of Daniel. Calvin admitted
that some had applied this prophecy to the pope, but claimed that the prophecy in fact
referred only to the period before Christ, and the persecution inflicted by the Romans.
J. Calvin, *A Commentary on Daniel* (Oxford, 1986), II, pp. 345–7.

[85] J. Frith, *A Pistle to the christen reader: The reuelacion of antichrist* (Antwerp, 1529),
RSTC 11394. Frith argued that the passing of such laws revealed that the pope was the
fulfilment of the prophecy of 2 Thess. 2.

would not share the criticisms of Henry VIII which permeated Joye's work. However, Philip Melanchthon, in the aftermath of the Six Articles, did apply the text of Daniel 11:37 to the king. Melanchthon claimed that Paul (2 Thessalonians 2) and Daniel had both prophesied the introduction of clerical celibacy by the Antichrist, 'sayinge / That this wycked kynge shuld raigne as head ouer his chirche / nether God nor wome[n] regarding / but defiling his owne chirche with the most fylthye and incestuouse lecherye'.[86] No names were mentioned, but the description was as fitting to the Henrician church as it was to the church of Antichrist.

The most detailed exposition of the prophecy of Daniel is to be found in the work of Rudolph Gualter, which was translated into English by John Old in 1556. Henry VIII was not the only monarch to find that his place in the cosmic battle was revealed by his attitude to clerical marriage. It could be proved, argued Gualter, that the church of Rome was the church of Antichrist, on the basis that the pope and his clergy had refused to allow marriage to the clergy, and held it to be 'a prophane & an vncleane state'. By the enforcement of clerical celibacy, 'the very propre workemanship of Antichrist', the rise of evil in the church could be measured.[87] Gualter condemned Pharaoh, Ahab and Zedechias, who had rejected the true preachers, behaving as 'shameful hooremo[n]gers, cuckold makers, dycers, dro[n]kerds & ful of al kynde of vices'.[88] In the hands of Old, the commentary had clear contemporary significance. The responsibility for the rejection of true preachers in England lay with the monarch, and the comparisons with Ahab and Zedechias were hardly flattering. The image of Mary as Jezebel was already well established in Protestant polemic, and since Ahab, guilty of idolatry, and responsible for provoking the wrath of God upon the people (1 Kings 16:29–34) was the husband of Jezebel, there can be little doubt that the image was intended to represent Philip II. Philip and Mary shared the faith of Jezebel and Ahab, and therefore shared in the same authority of Antichrist. This interpretation of the text offered hope to Protestant exiles, however, in the promise of God to strike down the descendants of Ahab, and 'avenge the blood of my servants the prophets' (2 Kings 9:7).

With the identification of the congregation of Antichrist in terms of morality and doctrine, the issue of clerical celibacy became central to the identification of the members of the false church. Protestant writers were able to identify the false congregation in the past and the present on the basis of the scriptural warning that the condemnation of marriage was

---

[86] Melanchthon, *Defence*, sig. B2v.
[87] Gualter, *Antichrist*, sigs R5v–S3v.
[88] Ibid., sigs S4v–T2v, X6r.

the doctrine of the Antichrist. To relate accusations of clerical debauchery to key biblical prophecies altered the level of the debate, with the result that allegations of immorality became more than merely arbitrary abuse. Rather such accusations could be related to the expectation that the source of evil in the church and the world would be identified by such behaviour. Clerical concubinage did not prove merely that the clergy could not live in chastity; it proved that they were the congregation of Antichrist. The relationship between sexual licence and doctrinal error was defined in Scripture, especially in the later chapters of Revelation. If the prophecy of John was to be fulfilled in the course of human history, retribution would be heaped upon those who were guilty of the crimes of Babylon. The failed celibacy of the clergy marked them out for such punishment. Broken vows of chastity were evidence of clerical hypocrisy, which was not only the means by which the clergy deceived the people into thinking that they were holy, but also a mark of Antichrist. To call the pope, or his clergy, hypocritical was to place them in the company of all such followers of Antichrist through history, as members of the false church. By conflating the prophecies of Antichrist in the Bible, commentators produced an image of Antichrist as one who would despise the word and sacraments of God, make additions to the law of the Gospel, and eventually be destroyed by the breath of the mouth of God. The fact that clerical celibacy, in its acceptance and transgression, could be identified with any one, or all of these characteristics, made it an ideal weapon in Protestant condemnation of the Roman church as the church of Antichrist.

The prohibition of clerical marriage justified the identification of the pope as Antichrist, but Protestant writers did not stop short of suggesting that a failure on the part of a monarch to reform also placed him in the company of the false church. In their assessment of the history of the English church before the Reformation, Protestant polemicists were able to draw sharp distinctions between the two churches, and separate the godly from the false. After 1530, however, and particularly after the Six Articles of 1539, the situation was more complex. If there could be no compromise between good and evil, Protestant writers were faced with the problem of accommodating the Henrician church into the dualistic model of human history. The papal Antichrist had been banished from the realm in name, but certain features of the Henrician church, including the celibate priesthood, suggested that the national church was not part of the true congregation. The prohibition of clerical marriage, and its consequences, may have been central to the identification of the papal Antichrist, but such arguments created clear problems for English Protestant writers, struggling to find a place for Henry VIII in the two-fold historical scheme. In the interpretation of contemporary events through the medium of Scripture, several polemicists were willing to identify themselves as the persecuted true church, and to cast their king, who prohibited clerical marriage and persecuted the faithful, as the agent of Antichrist. However, others were less direct in their criticism of the king, concealing their comments beneath a cloak of the typology of Old Testament kings who failed to purge the church of false doctrine and idolatry. Clerical celibacy was to be an important feature of such arguments, and the ultimate conclusion was the same: princes who acted against God were members of the false church. The key issue was the vow of chastity. Were such vows commanded by God and efficacious in salvation, or were they the work of Antichrist, an idol erected in the hearts of men, and a sign of a church unreformed?

CHAPTER SIX

A Compulsion From Which They Should Be Set Free: Vows of Celibacy and the English Reformation

The question of the nature and validity of the vow of chastity itself was central to the sixteenth-century debate on the necessity and value of clerical celibacy. Catholic writers before and during the Reformation defended both the validity of monastic vows in general, and that of chastity in particular. The issue at stake was not only whether vows should be kept, but whether it was possible for man to merit his salvation by making such promises. It was not denied that chastity was a difficult state to maintain; rather the emphasis was placed upon its efficacy in the salvation of the individual, and the promise of God that He would provide for those who called upon Him. The promise of celibacy demanded of the clergy fitted them for their priestly and sacrificial function. Since priests were expected to live a life that approached the heavenly, it could not be argued that this manner of life was readily obtainable by all. To achieve such perfection was regarded as a sign of the divine favour that separated the priest from the laity.

Peter Marshall has argued that, by the sixteenth century, it was the call to celibacy, more than anything else, that defined the status of the priest.[1] In part, this argument is supported by the works of traditional Catholic writers cited by Marshall, including Dionysius the Carthusian, Richard Whitford and Henry Parker. Celibacy offered a level of perfection to which the married laity could not attain, and suggested a proximity to God which was denied to others.[2] As may be seen from literature discussing the Eucharist, the ideal of purity was also firmly linked to the function of the priest.[3] If the laity were to abstain from sexual relations for three days before they received communion, a much higher degree of purity was to be expected from the priest, who would

---

[1] P. Marshall, *The Catholic Priesthood and the Reformation* (Oxford, 1994), p. 142.

[2] H. Parker, *Dives and Pauper* (1536), RSTC 19214, p. 225; Dionysius the Carthusian, *The lyfe of Prestes* (1533), RSTC 6894, sig. H3v; W. Lyndwood, *Provinciale seu Co[n]stitutiones Anglie, cu[m] sumariis atque annotationibus* (Paris, 1505), quoted in Marshall, *Attitudes of the English People*, p. 195.

[3] This is discussed at greater length in Chapter 7.

consecrate the elements and touch the body of Christ. In their discussion of the celibate ideal, traditional Catholic writers did much to emphasize the unique status of the priest, and his 'angelic' lifestyle. However, the extent to which it was the celibacy of the clergy alone which separated them from the laity should not be exaggerated. Indeed, it would be more accurate to suggest that the celibacy of the clergy was the outward sign of that which actually distinguished them from the laity, their ability to effect the eucharistic miracle. The arguments in favour of the making and keeping of such promises were more complex than Marshall's statement suggests, and encompassed issues beyond the separation of priest and layman.

The idea that vows should be made voluntarily was a central feature of the pre-Reformation literature on the subject.[4] If vows were to be treated as meritorious, and effective in salvation, it was essential that they should be seen as a positive and voluntary commitment on the part of the individual. The voluntary nature of vows was also vital to the argument that once such promises were made, they should not be broken. Reason, if nothing else, dictated that a promise made voluntarily should be kept. The claim that celibacy was entered into willingly became increasingly important after the Protestant condemnation of celibacy as a state enforced upon an unwilling clergy which ran contrary to the freedom promised in the Gospel.[5] While the defence of the voluntary nature of the vow was not merely a response to the challenge of the Reformation, it was articulated with greater force when such vows came under attack. Richard Whitford discussed the matter at length in his *Pype or Tonne of the lyfe of Perfection* in 1532.[6] Whitford claimed that he had written the work years before its publication, but had felt the need to print the tract to defend the religious life in the face of Lutheran criticism. He urged the reader to respect the free choice of those who had vowed to follow a monastic rule, and argued that the vow of chastity was 'a counsayle' and not a 'com[m]au[n]dement or bou[n]de therunto'.[7] For this reason, the vow of chastity, or indeed any other vow, could not be regarded as a bond upon the individual. Freedom was attained by adherence to the law of Christ, in contrast to the liberty of Whitford's

---

[4] Although it was the regular clergy who made vows of poverty, chastity and obedience, such a distinction was rarely made in the polemical literature. This appears to have been deliberate, certainly among Protestant writers. By failing to distinguish between secular and regular clergy, the focus of the debate was broadened beyond the narrow issue of whether monks and nuns could leave their monasteries.

[5] See below, pp. 141ff.

[6] R. Whitford, *Here begynneth the boke called the Pype / or Tonne / of the lyfe of perfection. The reason or cause wherof dothe playnely appere in the processe* (1532), RSTC 25421.

[7] Ibid., fols 20r, 22v, 204v; cf. Matt. 19, Luke 12.

opponents, which was the liberty of the flesh, the 'very bondage and thraldome of synne'.[8]

Similar themes were taken up by Catholic apologists who were more directly involved in Reformation controversies. Thomas More, in the *Responsio ad Lutherum* (1523), argued that because the church did not compel any man to become a priest, it could not be accused of forcing men to live as celibates. Rather, a man would decide to become a priest, knowing what was expected of him:

> But nowe whan euery man is at his lyberte not to be preste but at his pleasure / how can any man say that the chyrche layeth a bonde of chastyte in any mannys necke agaynst his wyll? The chyrche dothe in effecte no further but prouyde / that where as men wyll of theyr owne myndys some lyue chast and some wyll not / the mynysters of the sacrament shall be taken of that sorte only / that wyll be contente to professe chastyte.[9]

More repeated the same argument in the *Confutation of Tyndale's Answer* in 1532.[10] The issue at stake, at least in this passage, was not whether the forbidding of marriage to the clergy was justified, but rather whether they had rejected marriage voluntarily, and not under papal or ecclesiastical coercion.

More and Whitford had written in defence of the voluntary nature of vows long before the legalization of clerical marriage in the reign of Edward VI. However, with the restoration of Catholicism under Mary, the issue of the validity of such vows once again featured prominently in Catholic polemic. In this context, it was the actions of those clergy and religious who had married after 1549 that motivated the defence of vows. The claim that such vows had been entered into freely remained important as a basis for the discussion. Richard Smith argued that to perform that which Christ had counselled, but not commanded, was a work of perfection.[11] The free nature of the vow was central to Smith's argument, since if the promise were to be extorted rather than offered, none of the assured benefits would be received. St Paul might have received no command regarding virgins, but, Smith argued, this did not mean that vows of chastity were erroneous, 'because that thing which is not required of vs by compulsion, and yet it is geuen, is of a greater rewarde'.[12] Thomas Martin, writing against the marriage of priests, used

---

[8] Whitford, *Pype or Tonne*, fols 12r, 14v, 17r–v.

[9] T. More, *Responsio ad Lutherum*, CW, 5, pp. 310, 311. Peter Marshall notes that More's Utopians 'possessed a profound reverence for consecrated virginity', but neglects to mention that Utopian priests were married. Marshall, *Catholic Priesthood*, p. 143.

[10] T. More, *The Confutation of Tyndale's Answer*, CW, 8, pp. 585–6.

[11] R. Smith, *A bouclier of the catholike fayth of Christes church* (1554–5), RSTC 22816–7, sig. B5v–6r.

[12] Ibid., sig. C1r.

the same argument. Paul had recommended the single life, but had left the individual free to decide whether to make such a commitment.[13] Martin echoed Thomas More's argument that although celibacy was compulsory among the priesthood, there was no compulsion for the individual to become a priest. A man must decide whether he had the ability to live in celibacy before deciding to enter the priesthood, and those who could not fulfil this condition would not be forced to become priests.[14] There should be no suggestion that those who had broken their promises of celibacy could be excused on the grounds that they had entered into them unwillingly.

Despite the insistence of Catholic writers that vows were voluntary, Protestant polemicists often chose to focus upon what they perceived as an element of compulsion. In the early stages of the continental Reformation, the debate on monastic vows focused heavily upon the vow of chastity. David Bagchi suggests that this followed from Luther's conviction that it was the vow of chastity that was most likely to produce a crisis of conscience among the religious.[15] However, despite his hostility to what appeared an infringement of Christian freedom, Luther was reluctant to suggest that a monastic vow could be broken merely because an individual could no longer keep it. He was critical of the arguments advanced by Andreas Karlstadt in Wittenberg, who had encouraged the clergy to marry, and focused instead upon the theological error inherent in the making of such vows. To enter into monastic vows was to reject saving faith, and implied that chastity, a gift from God, was available or attainable by all.[16] It was this argument that governed the content of Luther's 1522 work, *The judgement of Martin Luther on Monastic Vows*, which focused upon the apparent contradiction between faith, Christian freedom and works. The Gospel should be allowed its true authority, even if this threatened the existence of the monasteries, but Luther did not call for an immediate exodus from the cloister.[17]

This emphasis upon the theological and moral justifications for the breaking of vows was also common to the works of English Protestant writers. William Tyndale, in the *Obedience of a Christian Man* (1528), condemned vows as a burden, commenting on the canon lawyers 'what

---

[13] T. Martin, *A Treatise declaryng and plainly provying that the pretensed marriage of priestes ... is no mariage* (1554), RSTC 17517, sig. Aa1r.

[14] Ibid., sig. O2r–v.

[15] D. Bagchi, *Luther's Earliest Opponents. Catholic Controversialists 1518–1525* (Minneapolis, 1991), p. 150.

[16] Luther, 'Letter to Melancthon, Wartburg, August 3rd 1521', *LW*, 48, pp. 283, 293.

[17] For more discusion of this theme, see Martin Brecht (tr. J.R. Schaaf), *Martin Luther*, 2 vols (Philadelphia, 1993), 2, pp. 21–3, 83ff.

an unbearable burden of chastitie do they so violently thrust on other me[n]s backes'.[18] Robert Barnes claimed that where God had allowed marriage, the pope demanded celibacy from a man who wished to enter the priesthood just as a thief would take money from a traveller before allowing him to cross a bridge. This was no voluntary promise, but rather an attempt to compel men to observe a papal decree.[19] Later writers drew the same conclusions. John Bale argued that vows of chastity merely served to promote immorality if they could not be broken by those who wished to marry to avoid fornication. To demand that the clergy should lead the lives of angels, Bale argued, was a form of tyranny, a 'cruel constitution'.[20] Writing during the Marian restoration of Catholicism, John Old complained that although the whole world cried out against clerical immorality, priests were still compelled to make promises that they could not keep.[21] The issue at stake was the element of compulsion, as much as the fruits of the vow. Just as Catholic insistence upon the voluntary nature of vows remained consistent throughout the Reformation, so the Protestant response to it remained equally dismissive. If the voluntary nature of vows was central to their defence, so was the contention that vows of chastity were compelled central to any justification for the breaking of a vow which involved more than the fact that some clergy could not keep it.

The evangelical cause could be irreparably damaged by the implica-tion that gospel freedom included the right to neglect or relinquish all social obligations, either religious or secular. Vows of chastity could be broken, it was argued, only because they were forced upon individuals, or because they were founded upon theological premises that were fatally flawed. An individual's failure to keep a vow did not in itself justify the breaking of that vow: to argue that it did would be to undermine all vows, oaths and obligations by suggesting that they were a matter for the individual's conscience. The defence of good order hinged upon a common understanding that *bona fide* laws were to be respected and obeyed, with the result that the law of celibacy (albeit the law of the pope) could only be disregarded if it could be proved erroneous. For this reason, the evangelical attack upon vows focused primarily upon their doctrinal acceptability, rather than the more pertinent question, at least in practical terms, of whether they could be

---

[18] W. Tyndale, *The Obedience of a Christian Man*, WW, p. 140.

[19] R. Barnes, *That by Gods laws it is lawfull for Priestes that hath not the gift of chastite to marry wiues*, WW, p. 319, 328.

[20] J. Bale, *Yet a Course at the Romyshe Foxe* (Antwerp, 1543), RSTC 1309, sig. K2r; *Apology of John Bale Agaynste a Ranke Papyst* (1550), RSTC 1275, fol. 4r; *Actes of the Englysh Votaries*, pt. II (1551), RSTC 1273.5, fol. 34v.

[21] J. Old, *A Short Description of Antichrist* (Emden, 1555/1557?), RSTC 673, sig. B4v.

broken by those who found them problematic. To discuss valid grounds for the breaking of vows could precipitate an avalanche of demands that other material or social controls be abandoned, but to focus upon theological acceptability limited the scope and impact of the debate.

At the centre of the theological debate lay the issue of whether man had the ability to effect, or participate in, his own salvation through his works. Richard Whitford argued that the monastic life was a life of perfection, and one that carried the promise of eternal reward. Good works were proof of a stronger love for Christ, who had urged men to do more than merely keep the commandments in order to attain perfection and enter the kingdom of heaven.[22] Vows in general, and the promise of chastity in particular, were held to be particularly pleasing to God. Dionysius argued that the clergy should be celibate 'forbycause they may please god reconsyle other vnto god / and clence the[m] that be vncleane / therfore they are bound to please god with chastyte and clennes ... they that be in the fleshe (that is to say) they that lyue carnally can not please god'.[23] The author of the *Doctrinal of Sapience* argued that those who promised celibacy would receive a greater spiritual reward than the married. Chastity was both more pleasing to God than marriage, and more profitable.[24] John Angel, writing in 1555, drew the same conclusions,[25] and his contemporary, Thomas Martin, used similar arguments in his controversy with John Ponet. Martin argued for the value of celibacy in particular, since, he claimed, all who could subdue the desires of the flesh 'shall obteine a more ample rewarde of grace in heaven'.[26] The correlation between celibacy and works righteousness could hardly have been more clearly stated.

As early as 1521, Luther had argued that vows of chastity were in opposition to the Pauline concept of freedom, and claimed that all vows that had been made with the purpose of meriting salvation were contrary to the word of God. The pope, he argued, taught that monks and celibate priests lived in the holiest state, and established celibacy as 'the kind of life that would open heaven'. This, Luther claimed, implied that celibacy was a means of earning grace, salvation and the promise of eternal life, with the result that true faith – a faith in Christ – would be lost.[27] The

---

[22] Whitford, *Pype or Tonne*, fol. 24v, 18r–19.

[23] Dionysius, *Lyfe of Prestes*, sig. G3v.

[24] *The Doctrinal of Sapience*, ed. J. Gallagher, Middle English Texts, 26 (Heidelberg, 1993), pp. 188, 173.

[25] J. Angel, *The Agrement of the holye fathers and Doctors of the church upon the chiefest articles of Christian Religion* (1555), RSTC 634, sig. O6v.

[26] T. Martin, *A Treatise*, sig. Y1v.

[27] Luther, *I.Timothy 4:3*, *LW*, 28, p. 312; R. Kyle, 'John Knox and the Purification of religion: the intellectual aspects of his crusade against idolatry', in *ARG*, 77 (1986), pp. 265–80.

same view was expressed in the works of English reformers. Barnes argued that despite the promises attached to a vow of perpetual virginity, it would achieve nothing since, by the ordinance of God, virginity was a thing indifferent, and could therefore be either kept or rejected without sin.[28] However, it was William Tyndale who explored the issue of vows and works at the greatest length, largely in the *Answer to More*, and the *Obedience of a Christian Man*. Faith, Tyndale argued, provided the only route to God, and all who attempted to gain salvation or forgiveness by other means were heretics, and outside the church of Christ.[29] For Tyndale, chastity, whether vowed or not, was in itself no more pleasing to God; and trust in works would benefit nobody, whether married, widowed or celibate. Rather, the individual should live in the manner in which he would be best able to keep the commandments of God.[30] Subsequent writers echoed these established themes. John Bale not only argued that vows should not be counted as efficacious in salvation, but also claimed that, by offering such impure works to God, the monks actually defiled themselves.[31] William Turner, arguing that monastic vows revealed the extent to which the Roman church had invented a new religion, contrasted the belief in the merits of vows with the 'old learning' which taught that works did not justify man before God.[32] John Foxe rejected the idea that celibacy offered the clergy any form of superiority, and mocked the labours of the monks who attempted to attain a level of 'Angelical purity' by fasting, chastity and charity.[33] Monastic vows, because of the perfection which they appeared to promise, were the ideal target for the Protestant attack on a works-oriented soteriology.

The argument that vows of chastity offered access to a state of perfection raised the question of whether men were able to keep such promises. Richard Whitford argued that baptism itself made it possible to keep a vow and claimed that the graces afforded by baptism could be strengthened in a variety of ways.[34] Whitford argued that the first aid to chastity was prayer, and Thomas Martin claimed that all who called on God by prayer would receive the gift of chastity: the nature of man was such that meritorious works and promises were hard to maintain, Martin argued, 'but in respecte of the ayde of Goddes grace, there is

[28] Barnes, *That by Gods law*, p. 313.
[29] W. Tyndale, *Answer*, WW, p. 257.
[30] Ibid., pp. 313–4, 316.
[31] J. Bale, *The Image of Both Churches* (1550), RSTC 1298, sig. K3r–v.
[32] U. Rhegius (tr. W. Turner), *A co[m]parison betwene the Olde learnynge & the Newe* (Southwark, 1537), RSTC 20840, sig. E6r–7r.
[33] J. Foxe (tr. J. Bell), *The Pope Confuted* (1580), RSTC 1124, sig. B3r.
[34] Whitford, *Pype or Tonne*, fol. 28r.

nothinge at all impossible'. Christ had promised that all who asked would receive, and God would not allow men to be tempted beyond their capacity.[35] The fact that God had made the gift of chastity readily available to those who called upon Him made resistance sinful. If God had given grace through Christ to the church that all men could live in 'perfect continencie', Martin demanded, 'Howe then can ye pretend it either to be a thinge impossible to liue chaste, or els, if it be a thinge possible, howe greuously haue ye offended which haue not performed unto God your vowe solemly professed ...?'.[36] Vows of chastity were not only voluntary, but those who made such promises, protected and guided by God, should have no cause to break them.

The claim that the nature of man could accommodate a life of perpetual chastity was vehemently rejected by Protestant writers. The argument that vows of chastity were impossible to fulfil underpinned the attack on their theological validity, and was often supported by accounts of the misdemeanours of the clergy who had made them.[37] George Joye claimed that those who had promised chastity had vowed something that was not within their power to attain, and recommended 'therfore let them loke before they leape'. Joye could find no precedent that God would even accept those vows that were impossible to keep, since a vow should be 'a free promyse / of that thi[n]g which is in our power to performe'.[38] It was not within the ability of an individual to promise to attain what was, by its very nature, an ideal of perfection. Protestant writers also questioned the assumption that God would automatically offer the gift of chastity to all who appealed to Him. Tyndale argued that it would be unwise to promise chastity, a gift that was not given to all, and concluded that it would be even more unwise to promise perpetual chastity, because the ability to keep to such a vow would not remain constant over time. Without a gift of chastity, such a vow should not be made, because it was only possible to offer to God that which was within the power of the individual.[39] Developing the argument further, William Turner conceded that 'what soeuer a man asketh of God which is

---

[35] Ibid., fol. 207v; Martin, *Pretensed marriage*, sigs X4r, Z4v, referring to Matt. 7, Luke 6, sig. Dd2v.

[36] Martin, *Pretensed marriage*, sigs Cc2r, Cc1v, Mm2v. As a final retort to Ponet, a married bishop, Martin argued that since Ponet had kept his vow of celibacy before his marriage, God must have given him the gift of chastity. It would therefore be possible, Martin claimed, for a priest to live without his wife were they to be separated, without the need to marry again. Ibid., sig. Ee4r.

[37] J. Bale, *Votaries*, pt I (Antwerp, 1546), RSTC 1270.

[38] G. Joye, *The letters whych Johan Ashwell ... where the sayde pryour accuseth George Joye ...'* (Antwerp 1531), RSTC 845, sig. C1r; idem, *Defence of the Mariage of Preistes* (Antwerp, 1541), RSTC 21804, sig. C3v, C7v–8r.

[39] Tyndale, *Obedience*, p. 175.

necessary unto saluation that he wil grant hym the same', but argued that God would not grant the gift of chastity to all who asked, because chastity was not necessary to salvation.[40] The flawed theology of such vows demonstrated that such promises should not be made, were not part of divine law, and could therefore be broken.

The issue of conditions under which vows could be broken was discussed both by pre-Reformation writers, and those who took to the defence of the indissolubility of vows after the clergy and religious had begun to marry. Dionysius the Carthusian argued that the celibacy of the priesthood was unbreakable. Nobody should be promoted to clerical office, he argued, unless he had first promised celibacy, and this promise was permanently binding. A vow of chastity not only broke the bonds of any previous marriage, but also invalidated any future marriage. Priests were dedicated to the service of God alone. Dionysius concluded that just as taking the goods of another person was theft, so the abuse of the holy, including the breaking of a vow by those consecrated to God, was sacrilege.[41] Richard Whitford argued that a vow should always be fulfilled, and suggested that it would be better not to make the vow at all than to make and then break it, which, as Scripture demonstrated, was a grievous sin (Ecclesiastes 5:3).[42] Not even the pope, he claimed, had the power to dissolve a vow once made, and those who did not keep their vows were to be held accursed. 'For as chastite duely kepte: is of hyghe merite and glorious rewarde', Whitford wrote, 'so broke: is it of most horrible and depe dampnacion.'[43]

Thomas More echoed the argument that promises of celibacy were indissoluble, and claimed that marriages contracted after such declarations had been made were therefore invalid. More cited 1 Timothy 5:11–12 against the breaking of vows, and claimed that, by teaching otherwise, Tyndale had disregarded the testimony of the Bible, the church and the saints.[44] Those monks who had married were guilty of adultery and sacrilege.[45] The idea that vows invalidated future

---

[40] W. Turner, *Huntyng & fynding out of the Romishe fox* (Antwerp, 1543), RSTC 24354, sig. B3r ff.; *The Rescuynge of the Romishe Fox* (Bonn, 1545), RSTC 24355, sig. L7r–v; M. Bucer (tr. T. Hoby), *The gratulation of the moost famous Clerke Martin Bucer* (1549), RSTC 3963, sig. C2v–C7r.

[41] Dionysius Carthusianus, *Lyfe of Prestes*, G2r–v; Parker, *Dives and Pauper*, fol. 225v.

[42] Whitford, *Pype or Tonne*, fol. 30v; 'If you make a vow to God, discharge it without delay, for God has no love for fools. Discharge your vow. Better a vow unmade than made and not discharged.'

[43] Ibid., fols 205v–206v.

[44] More, *Confutation*, pp. 646, 262; *Dialogue*, pp. 304, 434. 1 Tim. 5:11–12 carried a warning against allowing the remarriage of young widows, even if 'their natural desires get stronger than their dedication to Christ'.

[45] More, *Confutation*, p. 109.

marriages was More's most powerful weapon. The argument that marriage betweeen a monk and a nun was incest was well grounded in canon law, and More exploited its potential to the full.[46] For a priest to contract an unlawful marriage was to shame both the sacrament of orders and that of matrimony. More denounced Tyndale, Joye, Bainham and Frith as 'heretics', and called upon his readers to avoid the works of the reformers until they 'fyrste forswere & abiure the defence and mayntenaunce of that incestuouse sacrylege and very bestely bychery'.[47] The assertion that to break a vow of chastity and marry was to commit fornication provided a useful riposte to Protestant accusations of immorality among the Catholic clergy. Drawing upon the traditional representation of broken vows of chastity as adultery, incest and sacrilege, More advanced the argument further by applying such ideas to the clergy who had actually married. The claim that vows could not be broken remained a central feature of Catholic polemic during the Reformation, but it was the implication which this held for the validity of clerical marriages which was to become increasingly important, especially during the period of the Marian deprivations.

Pointing to the example of Ananias and Sapphira, Richard Smith claimed that if God had struck down those whose greed had led them to break a vow, then the prosecution of the married Edwardian clergy was clearly justified.[48] Smith argued from Numbers 30 that those who failed to perform their vows would be damned, and used the example of Solomon to demonstrate that an unfaithful promise was displeasing to God.[49] Having established that there was no precedent for the lawful breaking of vows, Smith then turned his attention to the married clergy around him. Their marriages, he claimed, were nothing more than 'pretensed marriages', taken after vows which invalidated them. The fact that Luther, Bucer, Ridley and others had married proved to Smith that they had rejected the testimony of the Fathers and placed themselves outside the church.[50] The debate hinged upon the the question of whether the breaking of a vow of chastity constituted a breach of 'first faith', as outlined by Paul (1 Timothy 5:8). Richard Smith drew the

---

[46] *Corpus Iuris Canonici editio lipsiensis secunda post Aemili Ludovici Richteri curas ad librorum manu Scriptorum et Editionis Romanae Fidem Recognovit ed Adnotatione Critics Instruxit Aemilius Friedberg* (Leipzig, 1879), pars prior, Dist. XXVIII c.9, col. 103; Stephen Sipos, *Enchiridion Iuris Canonici as usum scholarum et Privatorum Concinnavit* (Rome 1954), p. 102.

[47] More, *Apology*, CW 9, pp. 28, 30.

[48] Smith, *Bouclier*, sig. B4v–5r. see Acts 5:1–11, cf. Martin *Pretensed marriage*, sig. P1v.

[49] Ibid., sig. G2r, Luke 9, 17:32; sig. G8r–v, Eccles 5.

[50] Ibid., sigs I4r , I6v, K1r, K5r–6r, I. Pet. 3.

attention of Peter Martyr to this verse of Paul, noting in the margin, 'Miseritaque est Petrus Martyr'.[51] The same reference was repeated later in the text, Smith claiming that the verse referred specifically to those who had made a vow of celibacy and had then married, condemning Luther, and other reformers, who broke this 'first faith' by marrying, contrary to their monastic vows.[52] Miles Huggarde claimed that the prohibition of clerical marriage was an act of benevolence on the part of the church, which still commended marriage to those for whom it was lawful. The church merely prohibited marriage to those who had already promised celibacy, in order that they 'might not incurre into the lapse of da[m]pnation as Paule reporteth'.[53] The fact that Paul had condemned this breaking of the first faith offered further confirmation that the text of 1 Corinthians 7:9 could not be used in defence of those clergy who had broken their vows and married.

This interpretation of 1 Timothy 5 was disputed by Protestant polemicists. Peter Martyr questioned the identification of vows with the 'first faith', and criticized those who used the verse against married clergy. Martyr argued that lasciviousness was widely denounced, whereas Christian marriage did not condemn anyone to damnation. More importantly, vows of chastity were not pleasing to God, and therefore could not be counted as an integral part of this so-called first faith.[54] Martyr offered further justification for his argument in his interpretation of Acts 5, the account of Ananias and Sapphira cited by Smith. Against the interpretation advanced by his opponents, Martyr denied that the story had any bearing upon the issue of vows of chastity. The sin of Ananias and his wife was not the breaking of a promise, but the simple failure to contribute in full to the communal living of the early Christians.[55] The text could certainly not be applied to the married clergy who were acting out of obedience to the will of God, and who should therefore not be punished. Luther argued that even the Roman church permitted the rejection of erroneous laws, and used this himself to encourage the clergy to relinquish their vow of chastity.[56] Any vow or promise which was not demanded by God, or which was contrary to the law of God, was an institution of the devil. Since God did not demand vows of chastity, there was no reason why they should be either made or

---

[51] R. Smith, *Defensio sacri episcoporu[m] & sacerdotum coelibatus* (Paris, 1550), sig. B5r.

[52] Ibid., sig. B8r–v.

[53] M. Huggarde, *The displaying of the Protestantes* (1556), RSTC 13558, sigs B7r–v, C1v.

[54] P. Martyr, *Defensio de Petri martyris* (Basle, 1559), sigs C3v, C6r.

[55] Ibid., sig. B4v–5v.

[56] Luther, *Answer to the Hyperchristian Book*, LW, 39, p. 210.

kept.[57] Tyndale shared Luther's belief that unlawful vows could be and should be cast aside: 'Whosoeuer voweth an vnlawful vow promiseth an vnlawfull promise, sweareth an vnlawful oth, sinneth against God and ought therfore to breake it.'[58] There was a danger in creating a sin where none existed, in binding an individual under pain of damnation to something unattainable for which God had provided a remedy.[59]

Further conflict arose over the question of dispensations. Tyndale questioned whether even the pope viewed vows as binding, given that dispensations were available for regular clergy who wished to leave the cloister and serve as priests.[60] John Bale repeated Tyndale's argument that there was no reason why dispensation should not be offered to priests who wished to marry, claiming that the pope had offered such dispensations from vows in the past when it had profited him. Scripture testified that ill-advised vows which were subsequently broken had not been punished; Peter had denied Christ despite his promise, and David had failed to perform his vow to destroy Nabal.[61] Indeed, priests who had made vows which they could not or did not perform had placed themselves in peril.[62] Crowley expanded the argument, referring to the vows of the Jews who had declared that they would not eat until they had killed Paul. Had the Jews kept the vow, he continued, they would have lost rather than gained the favour of God, because they would have been guilty of a greater crime – murder. Yet had they not fulfilled the vow, they would have died themselves, and sinned again. The only conclusion, therefore, was that erroneous vows should not be kept, and that those who had made them should disregard the vow and call upon the mercy of God. If there was no reason why a misguided vow should be binding, there was no justification for disputing the validity of clerical marriages undertaken after such vows were made.

The issue of the validity of clerical marriages was addressed at length by Thomas Martin in *A treatise declaryng and plainly provyng that the pretensed marriage of priestes ... is no mariage* (1554). The tract was written in reply to Ponet's *A defence for the mariage of priestes* (1549), and was the first vernacular work by a Catholic writer to address the problem of the Edwardian married clergy. Martin argued from the collection of the Apostolic Canons that vows of chastity had long been regarded as an impediment to marriage, thus making the marriages of the clergy invalid. Priests, as well as the religious, Martin argued, were

---

[57] Luther, *Genesis, LW* 1, pp. 106, 135; *LW*, 2, p. 274; *Exhortation, LW*, 45, p. 148.
[58] Tyndale, *Answer*, pp. 124, 326, 327; p. 328.
[59] Tyndale, *Numbers, WW*, p. 20.
[60] Tyndale, *Obedience, WW*, p. 108.
[61] Bale, *Romyshe Foxe*, sigs I8r–K2r; 1 Sam. 25.
[62] R. Crowley, *Confutation of xiii articles* (1548), RSTC 6093, sig. H1r.

votaries, and were therefore bound not to marry.[63] Having established
that a vow of chastity rendered any subsequent marriage invalid, Martin
reiterated the argument that to attempt to break such a vow by
marriage, was to commit incest and adultery. The fact that a priest's
marriage was undertaken after a vow meant that it was 'not iust
matrimonie, but incest, and worse than adouutrie', and a deadly sin.
If Paul had condemned widows who had vowed chastity and then
married, how much more severe would God be on virgins, 'which after
their consecration to God & profession of continencie, haue geuen
themselues to mariage'.[64] Martin was approaching a justification for
action against Edwardian married clergy on the basis that their
previous promise of celibacy rendered their marriages invalid. Under
these conditions, it was questionable whether the married clergy
who had disregarded their promise of celibacy could still exercise the
priestly function, and retain their benefices or their 'pretensed' wives.
The first consideration was whether the married priests were actually
priests. Those priests who had married had shunned chastity, which
had been proved to be annexed to the priesthood and unbreakable. If,
as Martin argued, the clergy could not perform their priestly function
without this promise of celibacy, it was arguable that a married priest
should not be allowed to remain in his benefice.[65] Martin devoted the
ninth chapter of his work to a discussion of the correct punishment of
the married clergy of England. The sin of Adam, he argued, had left
man facing sin, death, a loss of liberty, and the burden of laws and
commandments which must be obeyed. Deviance was to be punished
by both civil and ecclesiastical authority, and it was this public authority
which had been brought to bear upon the English clergy who had
disregarded their vows and married.[66] Both secular and ecclesiastical
authorities had the necessary jurisdiction to enforce the deprivation of
married clergy, and to separate them from their wives. To do otherwise was to condone a couple living in deadly sin. The sin of
adultery was committed by the coupling together, as much as the actual
marriage, making it imperative that the married priest be separated
from the woman he had married, even if their marriage was not valid.
There was no pardon available for incest, such as that committed by
a married cleric, unless the couple separated and amended their

---

[63] Martin, *Pretensed marriage*, sig. C2v–3r. Canon 25 forbade marriage to those in holy
orders; sig. N2v. For vows as an impediment to valid marriage, see also W. Harrington,
Commendacions of matrymony (1528), RSTC 12799, sig. B1r ff.; Angel, *Agrement*, sig.
O7v. For a discussion of the Apostolic Canon, see Chapter 3, pp. 92–3 above.
[64] Ibid., sigs E2r, P1r, R3v, Bb2r, Dd1v.
[65] Ibid., sig. P3r.
[66] Ibid.

ways.[67] The whole argument depended upon the nature of the vow of chastity, which Martin held to be permanently binding. Church and state were justified in their actions against married clergy, in depriving them of their benefices and separating from their wives.[68]

It was thus essential that Protestant writers should establish a defence of the validity of clerical marriages in the face of the Catholic contention that such marriages were invalid if undertaken after the profession of chastity. Rather than attempt to justify the discarding of vows on the basis that they were hard to fulfil, Protestant polemicists directed their attack at the central issue of the nature of the vow itself. The objective was to prove that there were sound, and positive, reasons for disregarding vows of celibacy, by suggesting that such a vow was ill advised, if not unlawful, and that God did not demand that such vows be fulfilled. If it could be established that a vow of chastity could be broken, Protestant writers would not be forced into the defensive position of justifying clerical marriages which were in breach of valid and binding vows. The argument put forward by Martin and others was undermined, rather than disputed, by a concentration on the theological validity of the vow rather than an attempt to justify the breaking of *bona fide* vows. If there was no binding vow, there was no impediment to marriage.

'A monk is an idolater': Clerical Celibacy, Idolatry, and the Duty of the King

Much of the reformers' hostility to monastic vows as good works remained on the fairly basic level that faith in Christ, rather than promises of chastity, justified the individual before God. However, in the writings of both English and continental writers from the 1520s, another, more complex, argument against such vows was introduced. From the premise that man should trust in the merits of Christ alone for salvation, it was claimed that vows made in the hope of earning grace

---

[67] Ibid., sigs R3v–S1r.

[68] E. Messenger states that under canon law, the position of the married clergy left them incapable of exercising the orders that they held, or of receiving further orders; in effect the clergy were irregular. Irregularity was incurred by bigamy, which Lyndwood defined both as true bigamy, that of a person married twice, and 'interpretative bigamy', that of a man who had married a widow, or who had attempted marriage while in orders. Those clergy who had married faced excommunication *ipso facto*, and would become irregular if they continued to exercise their function. Both deprivation and separation were justified on these grounds. Canon law held that no man could occupy a benefice unless he were admitted to the clerical estate, and stipulated that no married man could hold a benefice. From this it followed that a cleric who had married would be obliged to give up his

were blasphemous and idolatrous.[69] This principle could be readily applied to the promise of celibacy, in its keeping and breaking, given the multitude of examples in the Old Testament in which idolatry was associated with immorality. Heiko Oberman briefly touches upon this theme, suggesting that Luther's marriage amounted to an act of open iconoclasm. Indeed, the marriage of a monk, it is argued, was all the more striking than the theological objection to images, precisely because it was directed against the false saintliness in the hearts of the living, rather than against the images of dead saints.[70]

Reformation iconoclasm, and the treatment of idolatry in Protestant polemic, have featured highly in recent histories of the Reformation period.[71] In England, images and cults were attacked in the Injunctions of 1536, and the 1538 Articles declared that such practices would incur 'great threats and maledictions of God, as things tending to idolatry and superstition, which of all other offences God almighty doth most detest and abhor'. At the start of Edward's reign, the hostility of the government to idols and images was made abundantly clear. Eamon Duffy argues that 'at the heart of the Edwardine reform was the necessity of destroying, of cutting, hammering, scraping, or melting into deserved oblivion the monuments of popery, so that the doctrines they embodied might be forgotten'. Iconoclasm, he suggests, was the central sacrament of the reform, and radical Protestants enforced this so-called sacrament of forgetfulness in every parish of the land.[72] The presence of images was a constant reminder of the doctrines that they embodied, and as such presented a threat to the reformation of the religion of the people. The

---

benefice. The question of higher and sacred orders did not arise, Messenger argues, because the prohibition applied to all tonsured clerics. If the cleric performed penance satisfactorily, and promised future chastity, he could be relieved of censure, and be appointed to a benefice elsewhere, in accordance with the *Decretals* of Gregory IX. When Cardinal Pole received his first faculties, they included the power to absolve those guilty of heresy and apostasy if they repented, and to remove the censure of irregularity, and 'also for dispensing concerning bigamy by the same clerics, whether it be true or fictive bigamy, and even arising from the fact that the same clerics, being in sacred orders, have contracted matrimony de facto with widows or other corrupt persons, provided they first put away and expel their wives to whom they have been de facto joined in this way'. E.C. Messenger, *The Reformation, The Mass, and the Priesthood*, 2 vols (1936), II, pp. 10–14, 27–9.

[69] Luther, *Commentary on Isaiah 27:10*, *LW*, 16, pp. 216, 107, 108, 110–11.

[70] H. Oberman, *Luther. Man Between God and the Devil* (1993), p. 282.

[71] E. Duffy, *The Stripping of the Altars. Traditional Religion in England 1400–1580* (1992), esp. ch. 13; S. Brigden, *London and the Reformation* (Oxford, 1989); C. Haigh, *English Reformations. Religion, Politics, and Society under the Tudors* (Oxford, 1993), esp. ch. 10; R. Whiting, *The Blind Devotion of the People. Popular Religion and the English Reformation* (Cambridge, 1989), esp. ch. 4; M. Aston, *England's Iconoclasts: Laws Against Images* (Oxford, 1988).

[72] Duffy, *Stripping of the Altars*, pp. 406ff., 480ff.

Articles of 1547 recognized this threat, demanding that shrines, images and 'all other monuments of feigned miracles' should be removed 'so that there remain no memory of the same'. In the last years of the reign of Henry VIII, the polemicist John Bale wrote from exile that 'had there been no ceremonyes neuer had there bene superstitions ... yt wyll be easye ynough to bringe in them ageyne yf the other remayne'.[73] If true religion was to be practised in England, the realm must first be purged of idols and superstitious practices that kept their memory alive.

However, images and shrines were not the only casualty of this assault. If people believed that their own works were efficacious in the process of salvation, then these works were no less idols than the statues of the saints. Idols did not have to be seen to be believed. In her discussion of Reformation attitudes to idolatry, Margaret Aston draws attention to the existence of these 'idols of the mind', and the demand that they should be purged from the hearts of the individual believers, just as the churches were cleansed of images. However, Aston identifies this as a phenomenon of the later Reformation in England, in the closing years of the sixteenth century and beyond.[74] The Protestant denunciation of vows as a form of idolatry is not discussed; neither is it suggested that there was anything other than material iconoclasm in the first decades of reform. Yet the debate over clerical celibacy reveals that the iconoclasm of the early English reformers was not limited to material objects, and that evangelical polemicists measured the progress of the Reformation not only in terms of the breaking of statues, but also in terms of the destruction of other idolatrous doctrines and practices. Demands that the realm be purged of idols, both material and spiritual, featured heavily in the discussion of key issues, including clerical marriage, in Reformation polemic. In the same manner in which the presence of images encouraged trust in the saints, the presence of a celibate priesthood pointed to the sacrificial function of the priest, the theology of the Mass, and, in the eyes of evangelical writers, the persistence of superstition, idolatry and incomplete reform.

In 1522, Luther protested that in monasticism, 'a new god is invented by Satan for men without their even being aware of it'.[75] Describing the practices of the ungodly, he argued that, by making vows and trusting in works, they had made the living God into a calf, 'an idol of the

---

[73] Bale, *Romyshe Foxe*, sig. A5r.

[74] Aston, *England's Iconoclasts*, pp. 220, 2.

[75] Luther, *Genesis 3:1*, *LW*, 1, p. 148. Luther continued 'a monk is an idolater', in believing that he would enter the kingdom of heaven if he lived according to a monastic rule; ibid., p. 149.

heart'.[76] The issue was not whether vows were worshipped as gods, but whether people worshipped God in them, and hoped to attain divine favour through them. Specific comparisons were drawn between the behaviour of the Roman clergy and the priests of Baal. Luther cited 1 Kings 15:13, the account of the deeds of King Asa, who 'drove out of the country the men who had made sacred prostitutes and cleared away all the idols that his ancestors had made'. If the reforms of the godly king Asa were to be repeated in sixteenth-century Germany, it would be necessary not only to remove images, but also 'the men who had made sacred prostitutes', a thinly veiled reference to the Roman clergy and their concubines. The priests of Baal, Luther suggested, had laboured to excel each other in piety and sanctity, claiming a special union with God. They had chosen far stricter observances than Mosaic law demanded, exactly as the monks, and 'especially the Carthusians, whom one would have every right to call Baalites, do today'.[77] Monks were the living embodiment of the idolaters of the Old Testament, and the action taken against them should be the same. As the heirs of the heathen, Luther claimed, the Carthusian sought justification by means of his monastic lifestyle and show of righteousness. Thus both appeared to be engaged in the same false religion, although the material of the idolatry was not the same. Luther elaborated, explaining that while it was not an act of idolatry to wear the cowl (although even that was offensive), 'to attach the name and form of justification to that cowl, this is an idol'. While the heathen did not adore the wood of the image, they worshipped the image of God that they had made from it. Similarly, the monk did not worship his vow, but still adored his work as a god formed in the name of God. A good work would be a sin if the individual placed his hope of salvation in it.[78] In terms of the intrinsic danger of idolatry, there was no difference between a graven image and a monastic vow.

English evangelical polemicists also exploited the identification of celibacy with idolatry to condemn both vows and works righteousness. As had been the case in the more general attack on vows as meritorious works, it was William Tyndale who first made the comparison explicit. Tyndale condemned trust in works as a form of idolatry which was worse than the worship of graven images, because it was an 'inward Idolatrie of a false faith and trust in their own deeds'. To believe that

---

[76] Luther, *Genesis 11*, *LW*, 2, p. 214. The tract *The interpretation of the two horrible figures: the Papal Ass in Rome and the Monk's Calf found in Freiburg in Meissen*, composed by Luther and Melanchthon in September 1523 and illustrated by Cranach, depended on the association of monasticism and idolatry. The Monk was represented as a calf, the traditional Old Testament image of idolatry.

[77] Luther, *Genesis 43*, *LW*, 7, p. 344.

[78] Luther, *Isaiah 40*, *LW*, 17, pp. 22–3; *LW*, 17, p. 135; Bale, *Votaries*, pt I, p. 37r.

God was honoured in the tonsure and other works of men was to 'serue God with bodely seruice as they did in tymes past their idols'.[79] When parents were beguiled into compelling their children to vow chastity, they had 'no other mynde then those old Idolaters sacrificed their children vnto the false God Moloch: so that they thinke, by the merites of their childrens burning, after the Popes false doctrine, to please God and to get heauen'.[80] Such vows were still a false sacrifice, a contemporary manifestation of the idolatry of the Old Testament.[81]

Tyndale's example was followed by other writers, with two lines of argument developing: one in which the vow of celibacy itself was treated as a form of idolatry, and a second, not as obvious in Tyndale, in which precise parallels were drawn between the Old Testament and the contemporary church. In *Yet a Course at the Romyshe Foxe* (1543), John Bale used the association of monasticism with idolatry to make thinly veiled criticisms of the slow progress of reform under Henry VIII. In his condemnation of the Six Articles, Bale opted for concealment, blaming Gardiner in the text, but making pointed allusions to idolatrous kings in the margins. The first reference, to David, was complimentary to the king, and a standard image for the defeat of the pope by Henry VIII.[82] However, other citations, including a reference to the cursing of David in 2 Samuel 16, were more critical. 'Soche vyllenouse contempt of matrimonye spryngynge now of late ...' Bale complained, 'hath brought vpon David for all hys wonderfull vyctorye ... the plage promysed of the lorde for soche vngodlynesse.'[83] The warning is clear – that Henry VIII has incurred the wrath of God, both by his own personal conduct, and perhaps also by his continued efforts to enforce clerical celibacy, embodied in the Six Articles. Despite the attention given to Stephen Gardiner in the body of the text, the extent to which the passage is directed as much at Henry as at Gardiner is clear from the reference to 2 Samuel 12 in which David is punished for his sin by the death of his child, a barely disguised comment upon Henry VIII and the English succession.[84] Bale's demand was that Henry VIII should use the

---

[79] Tyndale, *Answer*, pp. 263, 291; Tyndale argued that 'thou maiest commit as great Idolatrie to God, and yet before none outward Image, but before the image which thou hast fained of God', *Exposition of John*, WW, p. 424.

[80] Tyndale, *Answer*, pp. 315–16. Moloch was a Phoenician deity to whom living children were sacrificed. Cf. Lev. 18:21, 20:2, Jer. 32:35, 1 Kings 11:7.

[81] Ibid., pp. 317, 319, 328, 395, 398, 415.

[82] J.N. King, *English Reformation Literature. The Tudor Origins of the Protestant Tradition* (Princeton, 1982), pp. 161, 166, 176–7.

[83] Bale, *Romyshe Foxe*, sig. K2v–3r.

[84] Bale was not the only writer to make such comments. See Chapter 5, pp. 129ff. above.

supremacy to set forth the laws of God and not the laws of men, even royal men. Only with the restoration of the law of God, and the lifting of the prohibition on clerical marriage, could Henry VIII redeem himself.

Compulsory clerical celibacy became the issue by which the progress of reform, identified with the destruction of idolatry, could be measured. Anthony Gilby, writing against Gardiner, used the example of Saul to make the same point. Saul, he claimed, had attempted to offer a false sacrifice to God, while Stephen Gardiner was guilty of failing to see the wickedness of the same idolatry, practised in his own age, in the 'sodomatrie, babilonical bondage, supersticiouse blindnesse of the Abbaies'.[85] Only that which was contained in Scripture, Gilby claimed, was necessary to salvation, and to deny the sufficiency of Scripture in matters of faith was in itself an act of idolatry. From this standpoint, Gilby launched an attack on the English bishops, arguing that their promises of celibacy were not listed by Paul among the requirements for episcopal office, and were therefore 'nothings, that make the Idol bishops, thinges of no value'.[86] The fate of Saul should serve as a warning to the bishops, to Gardiner, and even to the king himself. Vows were idols, the precepts of men, and while they remained, reform could never be complete, and the stability of the realm was threatened.

Writing in 1555, William Turner used the promotion of idolatry in England in an attempt to rouse the nobility to act in defence of the true religion. Turner praised Edward VI as the second Josiah, the reforming king, describing how God had shown favour to Asa, who had fulfilled the duty of the king to destroy idolatry, but punished Uzziah (2 Chronicles 26), who had effected only incomplete reform. Although he behaved in a manner which was pleasing to Yahweh, the people had continued to offer sacrifices, and the king had been struck down. However, Turner presents a less critical picture of royal reformations than Bale. For Bale, the blame for incomplete reform rested with the king, but in the eyes of Turner, even a godly king could fail when confronted by the superstition of his people. The nobility also had an obligation to set forth the word of God, to effect the destruction of false doctrines themselves, and fulfil the commandment of God to 'ouerthrowe ... the aultares of the heathen, breke in peces their images and cut down their graves', a paraphrase of the account of the deeds of

---

[85] Gilby, *Deuillish Detection*, fols 4r, 8v, 12r. See 1 Chron. 10:13, 1 Sam. 15; J. Frith, *Pistle to the Christen Reader: The Reuelation of Antichrist* (Antwerp, 1529), RSTC 11394, fol. 10r.

[86] Gilby, *Deuillish Detection*, fols 193v, 210r; 1 Tim. 3.

Josiah, and the renewal of the covenant in 2 Kings 23.[87] Turner had identified the dilemma that faced English evangelical writers, both in the reign of Henry VIII and that of his daughter Mary. In the eyes of such writers, the word of God in Scripture held a position of authority over and above that of a king, even if that king was the Supreme Head of the church. Ideally the law of God and the law of the king would be the same, but this was not always the case, as the prohibition of clerical marriage demonstrated. The possibility that an ungodly monarch could exercise authority over the church was not completely discounted; by 1543, Bale was protesting 'alack that the prince's authority should ever be used to the blasphemy of God'.[88] Henry was not named, but the object of the reference was clear. Even if it was enforced by royal rather than papal authority, error could not become truth. Clerical vows of celibacy, idols introduced by the pope, were still idols when enforced by the king.

Vows of celibacy, and the supposed failure of the clergy to keep them, were also used to draw associations between the contemporary clergy and the Old Testament accounts of sacrifices made to idols to justify reform.[89] It was John Bale who exploited the comparison to the greatest effect. Bale claimed that the clergy, the 'shorne smered Sodomites', offered sacrifice to Baal rather than to Christ by their deeds. The clergy were not only guilty of fornication, but each, by their vow, made themself a 'holye, spirituall, anoynted, shauen, shorne, priestly and mytered whoremo[n]ger'.[90] Bale manufactured a connection between the immorality of the clergy and the idolatry of image worship, based upon the image of spiritual fornication. In describing the sacrifices made to Baal-peor, Bale cited Baruch 6, a letter from the prophet Jeremiah to those who were about to be taken in captivity to Babylon. From the epigraphs on the title page of the *Image of Both Churches*, it is clear that Bale regarded himself as just such a prophet in exile from the English Babylon. Thus the priests of Babylon, of whom Jeremiah had warned, became types for the English clergy, and references to prostitutes a thinly veiled attack on clerical concubines. Jeremiah had condemned the priests of Babylon, who 'filch gold and silver from their gods to spend on

---

[87] W. Turner, *A New Booke of Spirituall Physik* (Emden, 1555), RSTC 24361, sigs C3v, C2v.

[88] Bale, *Romyshe Foxe*, sig. C3.

[89] G. Joye, *Exposicion of the prophete Daniel* (Antwerp, 1545), RSTC 18423, sig. d6v; W. Roy and J. Barlow, *Rede me and be nott wrothe* (n.p., 1528), RSTC 24127, sig. G3v, also referring to Daniel and the priests of Babylon. William Turner depicted Edward VI as the destroyer of the idol Baal: *A New Booke of Spirituall Physik* (Emden, 1555), RSTC 24361, sig. C6r.

[90] Bale, *Image*, sigs p2v, Qq5v–6r.

themselves, even using it on presents for the temple prostitutes'.[91] The possibilities afforded by comparison with the contemporary situation were not lost on Bale, or indeed on one of Foxe's martyrs.[92] Just as the priests of Babylon used the silver from their idols to finance prostitution, so the contemporary clergy used the money that they accumulated from offerings to images to pay their concubines. A direct link was established between immorality, idolatry and clerical vows of celibacy. The clergy were seen to finance their immoral activity with the proceeds of superstition, false religion and image worship.

The debate on religious vows in Reformation polemic was complex, and focused upon issues beyond the relatively simple question of clerical immorality. While the fact that there were clergy who did breach their vows of celibacy did not escape the attention of either Catholic or Protestant polemicists, it was far from being the dominant argument for the rejection of vows. Later Catholic writers were not so inflexible as to ignore the questions raised by contemporary developments. Condemnation of breaches of vows of celibacy was applied to the clergy who had married, and the issue of clerical marriage, not only clerical fornication, was discussed at length. Arguments which had been used against clergy who had failed in their obligation to celibacy were applied in a similar form to married priests. Catholic controversialists saw no need to distinguish between clerical concubinage and clerical marriage. What was at stake was less the extent to which marriage could be regarded as a lesser state than celibacy than the fact that a promise had been disregarded. Priests who had taken wives had not contracted valid marriages, and such 'pretensed marriages' could be treated in the same manner as the relationship between a priest and a woman who was not his wife. By defending celibacy and chastity as efficacious of salvation, arguing that God would assist the keeping of such vows, and denying that the vow could be broken under any circumstance, writers such as More and Martin could prove clerical marriages to be null and void. Justification for the deprivation of married priests, both in religious polemic and in ecclesiastical law, came from the fact that they had broken their word. The important issue was the nature of this promise, which determined the validity of all future action.

For evangelical writers, the defence of the legality of clerical marriage

---

[91] Bale, *Romyshe Foxe*, sigs E1v, K2v; 1 Kings 15 (Asa drove the prostitutes from the country, and destroyed the idols), Num. 25 (the account of the idolatry and debauchery at Peor), Baruch 6.

[92] *AM*, 1570, p. 1187. Philip Brasier drew the same parallel between the income gleaned from idolatry and priestly concubines, claiming that priests deluded the people into making offerings to images 'and with the offerynges the Priestes fynde their harlots'.

rested upon the extent to which the whole concept of compulsory celibacy could be shown to be erroneous. Clerical marriages could be shown to be valid only if it could be proved that no sin had been committed in the breaking of promises of celibacy. The claim that no divine ordinance suggested that vows should be either made or kept was central to Protestant arguments in favour of clerical marriage. Thus in order to defend its validity, Protestant writers turned to arguments that challenged the purpose of the vows themselves, and focused on issues of soteriology, Christian freedom, and the idolatry of works to destroy the foundations on which vows rested. If vows could not be kept, they should not be made, and if the conditions of a vow could be readily fulfilled, there was nothing to be gained from making such promises. If a vow fulfilled no function, and had no divine warrant, it was not binding on the individual.

In the Old Testament the mark of the reforming king had been the destruction of idolatry. The representation of clerical celibacy as a form of idolatry made the issue one by which the progress of reform in the sixteenth century could be measured, and the history of England could be narrated as the history of Israel. The association of idolatry with particular Old Testament kings ensured that the English king could be identified with a particular type, by examining the extent to which he cleansed the realm of idolatry. Margaret Aston provides references to the works and letters of Hooper, Foxe, Bale and Calvin, in the identification of Edward VI with Josiah, and J.N. King has argued at length for the existence of a consistent policy in the promotion of this image of the young king.[93] John Bale's *Apology*, dedicated to Edward VI as the new Josiah, identified the duty of the Christian king to reform the realm completely, by the destruction of all that could be associated with false worship. The same argument featured in the *Expostulation*, written in 1551. Bale described Edward as 'our new Josiah, which hath already overthrown the hill altars, broken in pieces the idols, destroyed the religious buggary, restored the book of the Lord'.[94] The reform of the laws on clerical marriage was treated as an integral part of the ideology of Edwardian Protestantism, as part of the purging of idols and the re-establishment of the primacy of the word of God. If idolatry were the outward manifestation of theological error – in the case of celibacy a false belief in works righteousness – it would be incumbent upon a reforming king to allow marriage to the clergy. Within this scheme, to

---

[93] Aston, *England's Iconoclasts*, pp. 219, 222, 249, 271–2; King, *English Reformation Literature*, pp. 161–2.

[94] Bale, *Apology*, 'an offyce in ydolatrye is the priesthode, and the vowe y^t they cal of theyr chastyte a seruyce of prodigiouse buggery', fols 4v, 12r, 133r; *An Expostulation or Complaynte agaynste ... a franticke papyst* (1551), RSTC 1294, sig. B7v.

treat the celibacy of the clergy as a form of idolatry was to pass critical, but covert, judgement on a king such as Henry VIII, who refused to allow that vows might be broken. The discussion of vows of chastity in Reformation polemic clearly stretched far beyond the assumption that they divided the laity from the priesthood, but rather determined the validity of the proceedings against married clergy, and became, to Protestant writers, the measure of the character of the king and the success of reform.

CHAPTER SEVEN

'Massinge and that cannot agre together': Clerical Marriage and the Eucharist in English Reformation Polemic

The theology of the Eucharist was central to the understanding of the functions and attributes of the priesthood in the sixteenth century. The role of the priesthood, and indeed the theological justification for its existence as a caste apart, exercised the minds of controversialists on both sides of the emerging religious divide. The cult of chastity, which had its roots in the asceticism of the early church, had been vital in defining the character of the ministry, and was to remain so during the Reformation. Clerical celibacy and eucharistic doctrine were closely linked in Reformation polemic; the fact that arguments in favour of the celibacy of the clergy were focused heavily on the necessity for purity in the priesthood placed the issue at the centre of theological debate and understanding. For the laity also, the moral purity of the priesthood was a matter of practical and soteriological importance. While the notion that supposedly celibate priests preyed upon the women of their parish appears to have been grounded in fiction rather than fact, even isolated incidences of clerical misconduct could generate widespread concern. The role of the priest in the consecration of the eucharistic elements contributed not only to the status of the priesthood, but also to growing expectations of high standards in clerical conduct. As the other-worldly image of the celibate priest was promoted in print and in sermons, so the extraordinary qualities demanded of the priest threw into relief the ordinary character of the clergy as a whole.

The priests of the Old Testament had shared in the sacred from which the majority were excluded (Exodus 29:33), and as such were expected to maintain a ritual cleanness, bridging the gap between the sacred and the profane (Leviticus 22:4–7). Catholic propagandists argued that the same level of purity was required of the priests of the New Testament, who, in the celebration of Mass, acted as intercessors on earth between God and the laity. The priest alone had the ability to effect the eucharistic miracle, and administer the sacraments necessary to salvation; the possibility that he could influence the fate of the laity after death was linked, almost inextricably, with the cultic purity expected and demanded of those called to the priesthood (1 Samuel 21:2–8). That the unchaste priest could celebrate Mass, touching the body of Christ with unclean hands, was, in theory at least, almost inconceivable. The theology of the Mass was central in the definition of the Catholic priesthood. Emphasis was placed upon not only the real objective presence of Christ in the elements, but also the role of the priest in the invocation of the divine power that effected the eucharistic miracle.[1] However, the priest offered the eucharistic sacrifice not only to the faithful, but also for the sake of the faithful, for the remission of sins, in life and after death. Lay dependence upon the priestly function meant that the ability of the priest to offer an efficacious propitiatory sacrifice was a vital issue to the whole church. A broken promise of celibacy was not only a matter for the conscience of the individual priest, but also a cause of concern for the laity, who believed that their salvation rested upon the efficacy of the sacraments administered by that priest. The image of the priest who came to the altar from the bed of a prostitute was a common topos in the polemic of the Reformation, and its meaning came not from the comic nature of the imagery, but from its resonance with the very real fears of the faithful. Modern historiography has done much to rebuild the moral reputation of the late mediaeval priesthood, but even in isolated instances, the unchaste priest could still become a catalyst for social tension and doctrinal uncertainty within the community in which he lived.[2] Any dichotomy between the ideal and the reality of priestly conduct, on whatever scale, required a means of providing assurance that the eucharistic miracle could be effected by a priest who was far removed from the ideal of perfection so often expressed.[3]

Although high moral standards were expected of the clergy, it had been argued throughout the history of the church that the validity of the sacrifice was independent of the qualities of the priest. Clerical celibacy was still defended on the basis of the holy function of the priest, but it was argued that lapses on the part of individual clergy did not threaten either the nature of the sacrament or the salvation of the faithful. In the later Middle Ages, however, increased devotional emphasis upon the moment of the consecration of the elements during the Mass[4] gave added

---

[1] E. Messenger, *The Reformation, the Mass, and the Priesthood. A documented history with special reference to the question of Anglican Orders* (London, 1936), p. 11; C.W. Dugmore, *The Mass and the English Reformers* (London/New York, 1958), p. 5.

[2] P. Marshall, *The Catholic Priesthood and the English Reformation* (Oxford, 1994); J. Thomson, *The Early Tudor Church and Society 1485–1529* (1993), p. 169; J.J. Scarisbrick, *The Reformation and the English People* (Oxford, 1994).

[3] Marshall, *Catholic Priesthood*, pp. 46–7.

[4] See for example, *The Lay Folks Mass Book*, ed. T.F. Simmons, EETS, 71 (1879), p. 38, quoted in E. Duffy, *The Stripping of the Altars. Traditional Religion in England*

importance to the sacrificial act of the priest, fuelling expectations of
higher moral standards among the clergy. Fourteenth-century preachers
such as William Staunton and Nicholas Phillips encouraged further
debate on the consequences of priestly immorality, and there is evidence
that the issue was also of concern to the laity. Peter Marshall has
demonstrated that bequests for masses in lay wills often included the
proviso that the celebrant should be of high moral character. Lay
demands that the priest should be an 'honest' man, Marshall argues, may
be seen as an accepted shorthand for a priest known to be continent.[5]
While concern that the moral standards of the clergy should be
exemplary was common among Catholic writers, it was also a feature of
heterodox criticism of the Catholic church and clergy. A further
challenge was posed by the Wycliffite doctrine of election, which argued
for a clear link between the moral standards of the clergy and the efficacy
of their sacraments.[6] The suggestion that the power of the clergy, from
the pope to the parish priest, was not in itself absolute, but was rather
determined by their conduct, presented a clear challenge to Catholic
teaching that the perfection of the sacrament was independent of the
character of the priest.

The suggestion that there was a correlation between priestly morality
and the efficacy of the sacrament was widely condemned. In Mirc's
sermon for the feast of Corpus Christi, it was stated that Christ had
given to His disciples, and to every priest, the ability to effect the miracle
of transubstantiation, 'be he bett[y]r, be he wors'. The sacrament itself
was so holy that no good man could improve it, and no evil man could
impair it.[7] The suggestion that the impure priest did not offer a valid
sacrifice had its roots in Donatist beliefs, and was continually proscribed
by the church. The Lollard claim that a priest in mortal sin did not
properly baptize or consecrate was condemned as heretical at the
Blackfriars Council of 1382, but such pronouncements did little to allay
popular fears. In 1547, the seventh session of the Council of Trent
pronounced anathema upon those who denied that a priest in mortal sin
effected and conferred the sacrament even if he observed that which was
essential to its execution, yet, as Marshall notes, a separate strand in
devotional literature advised the laity to absent themselves from the
Mass of an unchaste priest. The priest alone could consecrate and touch

---

1400–1580 (New Haven, 1993), p. 91. Duffy goes on to discuss the bequests in wills that
lights should be burned at the time of the sacring, and the fact that the moment of the
elevation dominated artistic representations of the Mass.

[5] Marshall, *Catholic Priesthood*, pp. 51–3, 161–2.

[6] Dugmore, *Mass and the English Reformers*, p. 55.

[7] John Mirc, *Mirk's Festial. A Collection of Homilies by Johannes Mirkus*, ed. T. Erbe,
EETS, 96 (1905), p. 169.

the host, and the purity expected of the priest was central to his function. For a priest to fall into incontinence was to introduce a pollutant into that which should be the most sacred.[8] Despite the correlation drawn in evangelical polemic between the behaviour of the Catholic clergy and the veracity of the theology of their sacraments, the suggestion that the sacrament was dependent upon the character of the priest was also condemned in reformed articles of faith.[9] However, concern still remained that the clergy should lead lives of virtue and purity. The sacrament was not rendered invalid by priestly immorality, but the possibility of such a correlation continued to arouse concern, and featured heavily in the religious literature of the sixteenth century.

Rather than suggest that the actions of the clergy could be detrimental to the faithful, writers chose to focus instead upon the consequences for the unchaste priest. The author of *The Doctrinal of Sapience* warned that 'the preste that lyueth in dedely synne, specialy in sinne of lecherie' administered the sacraments under pain of damnation.[10] The same sentiment was echoed in the *Orchard of Syon*, where it was suggested that the holiness of the sacrament was not dependent upon the purity of the priest, and that an unchaste priest who celebrated Mass harmed himself but not the sacrament.[11] The efficacy of the sacraments of the unchaste priest was also discussed at length in *Dives and Pauper*. Where Pauper suggested that immoral clergy should be forbidden to play any role in the ministration of the sacraments, Dives stated plainly that, even

> though a priest be a shrewe, the sacraments that he ministreth be not the worse. For the goodnes of the priest amendeth not the

---

[8] Mary Douglas suggests that the idea that the holy could be in some way threatened by contact with the profane is common to many religions and societies: *Purity and Danger. An Analysis of Concepts of Pollution and Taboo* (London, 1966). However, such a broad model cannot be readily applied to the ideas discussed in Reformation polemic. The insistence on the part of orthodox writers that the efficacy of the sacrament was not impaired by the moral standing of the priest challenges Douglas's assumption that impurity implies danger. There was no suggestion, in either Catholic or Protestant literature on the Eucharist, that the actual holiness of God was diminished by the ministrations of the profligate priest. John Foxe addressed the issue of pollution in much the same terms as Douglas, quoting the epistle of Volusianus. With regard to the sacraments, he questioned whether 'the polluted life of others did any thing pertain thereto to pollute the same', but concluded that this could not be the case, since Christ would not have sent Judas to preach, or allowed him to work miracles, or share in the Last Supper, if there was a chance that his treachery could 'infect' the other disciples. *AM*, 1570, pp. 1321ff.

[9] Marshall, *Catholic Priesthood*, p. 48.

[10] *The Doctrinal of Sapience*, ed. J. Gallagher, *Middle English Texts* 26 (Heidelberg, 1993), p. 173.

[11] Catherine of Siena, *The Orchard of Syon* (1519), RSTC 4815, sig. R1r; Mirc, *Festial*, p. 169.

sacrament: ne his wyckednes appeyreth them not as the law sheweth well.[12]

The same claim was made by Thomas More. Although God would not be pleased by the behaviour of such priests, the fact that the Mass was offered for the faithful meant that it would be accepted by God for the sake of these people.[13] In particular, the laity would not be harmed if they were not aware of the behaviour of the priest: however, implicit in this was the suggestion that the sacraments of known concubinary priests should be avoided, which did little to inspire confidence in the official orthodox position.

The traditional argument that the Mass celebrated by a priest in a state of sin was still acceptable to God did not lessen the force of the demand that the clergy live in a state of higher purity than the laity. The demand that the clergy be celibate was almost entirely founded upon their role in the Mass, but this purity was also the mark of the holy in general. Dionysius the Carthusian laid down the qualities demanded of the clergy, the only group who could enjoy such proximity to the most sacred. Purity was to be expected of all who would devote themselves to the service of God, but the true servants of Christ were those who 'ponyshed theyr fleshe with abstinence from vice and concupiscence'.[14] Such perfection was to be expected of those in holy orders, whose duty and vocation it was to serve God with a pure heart and a chaste body. For the laity, but more particularly for the clergy, unchastity was a grievous sin, 'for in the synne of the fleshe is the moste great & manifest turpitude bestlynes / dishonestie / and fylthynes', vices that distracted men from the holy.[15] 'Wanton prestes', who continued in their living, the author suggested, presented a poor example to the laity, and[16]

> In so much as that that holy ministerye of the altare is most pure / and the sacramentes of the churche be most clene and ghostly (especially the sacrament of the blessyd body of our lord) it is most vicyous and inconuenie[n]t that the minystres of the church and altare / should so precyous sacramentes defyle and corrupt / with the most fowle of fylthye and abhominable synne of the flesh and bestly concupiscence / ye and to presume to serue.[17]

---

[12] H. Parker, *Dives and Pauper* (1536), RSTC 19214, fol. 224v.

[13] T. More, *Dialogue Concerning Heresies*, CW, 6, p. 299.

[14] Dionysius Carthusianus, *The Lyfe of Prestes* (1533), RSTC 6894, sig. B5r–v.

[15] Ibid., sig. C4v–5r.

[16] Ibid., sig. C8r–v This allegation was repeated later in the same text, in the ninth reason offered for the celibacy of the priesthood, 'bycause the carnalyte of them is so abundau[n]t / to the great iniurye / and conte[m]pt of almyghty god / and geueth so euyll occasyon vnto the people', sig. G4v.

[17] Ibid., sig. C5r.

An unchaste priest brought the profane into the world of the sacred, the flesh into the realm of the spirit. In contrast, the obligation to celibacy had been fuelled by the expectation that the purity of the priest would enable him to stand astride the gulf in the celestial hierarchy, leading a life which approximated to that of the angels. In the *Lyfe of Prestes*, it was argued that the lowest of the heavenly hierarchy and the highest of the earthly hierarchy should approximate to one another. 'The lowest of the hygh hyerarchy or ordre is the company of holy aungeles', he explained, 'and the hyghest in the lower ordre of the church mylytaunt is the ordre of prestes and clerkes wherfore the prophet Malochie callyth a preste by the name of aungell.'[18] The celibate priest was the intermediary between the sacred and the profane, the church militant on earth and the heavenly church triumphant.

The application of the image of the 'life of angels' to the priesthood was a common theme in pre-Reformation literature, and in the writings of Catholic opponents of the Reformation. In the *Doctrinal of Sapience*, priests were described as 'the lyght of the world', and it was suggested that their office and sanctity made them deserving of the title 'the angellis of our Lord'.[19] The state of virginity could never be praised too highly, 'for it is the lyf of angellis celestyall'.[20] Richard Whitford argued that even without the making of a formal vow, chastity was still a noble virtue for all, 'For it doth make a man : familiar w[i]t[h] god as Angell.'[21] Thomas Martin used the same analogy in 1554, arguing that in the promise of chastity, 'a man is ones iogned in feloweshippe with the Angels'.[22] Priests were to lead the life of angels, but their power was greater than that of the angels, because the priest alone had the privilege of celebrating Mass. In the same Corpus Christi sermon in which it had been argued that the character of the priest had no influence upon the efficacy of the sacraments, the virtuous priest was still extolled, because he had a gift from God, 'þat he gaf neuer to no angele in Heuen: þat is forto make Godis body'.[23] Luther expressed the same view in a sermon of 1541, albeit in a different context, complaining that reverence for the mass was so great that the priestly state and office was ranked above

---

[18] Ibid., sig. G3r The text referred to is Malachi 2:7–8.

[19] *The Doctrinal of Sapience*, pp. 172–3: 'And as touchyng to absoyllyng or to gyue absolucyon, they doo that the angelles may not do ...'.

[20] Ibid., p. 188.

[21] Richard Whitford, *The Pype / or Tonne / of the lyfe of perfection* (1532), RSTC 25421, fol. 7r, cf. fols. 22r, 206r. For the Protestant rejection of the idea of the life of angels, see A. Marcort, *A Declaration of the Masse* (Wittenberg, 1548), RSTC 17314, sig. A7v; J. Ponet, *A Defence for the Mariage of Priestes* (1549), RSTC 20176, sig. C3v.

[22] T. Martin, *A Treatise declaryng and plainly provyng that the pretensed marriage of priestes ... is no mariage* (1554) RTSC 17517, sig. Ff2r.

[23] Mirc, *Festial*, p. 169.

Mary and the angels.[24] The role of priests exceeded that of both men and of angels, and their chastity placed them in proximity to the heavenly, giving them alone the privilege of approaching the sacred.

The expectation that those in proximity to the sacred would themselves be pure was grounded in the nature of the Old Testament priesthood. God had demanded of the priests of the Old Law 'be you holy for I am holy',[25] and many defenders of clerical celibacy argued that this text should be held as an example to the priests of the New Testament. Dionysius claimed that the injunction should be applied to the sacrifice of the Mass, and urged priests to 'be ware of all unlawful actes / that we may lyft by clene handes unto almyghty god (which sayth) be you holy for I am holy'.[26] The same passage was exploited by Thomas Martin in the fourteenth chapter of his attack on clerical marriage. He urged married clergy to repent of their error, and contrasted their conduct with that of the priests of the old law.[27] If the priests of the Old Testament abstained from their wives, the priests of the new law were under an even greater obligation to chastity. Under the law of Moses, animals had been sacrificed, but the sacrifice of the Mass was Christ himself. In these circumstances, Thomas Martin argued, it was only right that 'Christian priestes which muste offer a more worthy, a more noble, a more divine sacrifice, then all the priestes of the olde lawe shoulde liue in perpetual chastitye.'[28] The call to greater holiness was embodied in a pure life, and expressed in the promise of celibacy made by the priesthood.

Despite the insistence that the validity of the sacraments was not impaired by the imperfections of the clergy, condemnation of the failure of the clergy to keep to their vows of chastity was frequently couched in terms of the dishonour that it caused to the sacrament, and to God. Priests who were guilty of breaching their vows were accused of committing sacrilege, as the author of *The Lyfe of Prestes* explained: 'It is callyd sacrylege / for that it corruptyth holy ordre / by unworthy handelynge and myscheuous abusyng that thyng that to god is consecrate.'[29] Priests, whose bodies should have been the temples of God,

---

[24] Luther, 'Ein predig D. Martin Luther das man Kinder zur Schulen halten solle' (Wittenberg, 1541), quoted in F. Clark, *Eucharistic Sacrifice and the Reformation*, second edition (Oxford, 1967), p. 113.

[25] Leviticus 21:6; cf. the rejection of this argument in Robert Barnes, *That by God's worde it is lawfull for priestes that hath not the gift of chastitie to marry wiues*, WW, p. 332.

[26] Dionysius Carthusianus, *Lyfe of Prestes*, sig. F8r.

[27] Martin, *Pretensed marriage*, sigs Ll4v, Mm1r.

[28] Ibid., sig. B4v; cf. Bb2v.

[29] Dionysius Carthusianus, *Lyfe of Prestes*, sigs D1r, G2v.

had become instead the temples of the devil.[30] This common charge of profanation had parallels in the work *Dives and Pauper*. The character Pauper explained that while there were many different degrees of lechery, clerical immorality was particularly worthy of opprobrium, since those who broke their chastity were guilty not only of adultery, but also of sacrilege and treachery.[31] Thomas More made a similar complaint, although in the more positive context of encouraging prayer for the sinful priest. More complained that 'Christ is betrayed into the hands of sinners when His most holy body in the sacrament is consecrated and handled by unchaste, profligate and sacriligious priests', and argued that the example of such priests allowed vice to contaminate the people.[32] The fact that Christ was still present in the elements consecrated by such priests did not lessen the serious nature of their transgression; indeed, the sin was worsened by the fact that Christ was present, and thus dishonoured.

The image of the concubinary priest who touched the consecrated elements with 'unclean' hands was a common theme in both Catholic and, later, evangelical literature. Thomas Brunton, the bishop of Rochester, commended a priest who had refused to celebrate Mass because he had slept with a concubine the previous night, and the Franciscan preacher William Staunton denounced the behaviour of unchaste priests who had 'become most fowl in the Devil's service'.[33] A priest who engaged in such conduct before the celebration of Mass defiled himself at the time when he should be most pure, and introduced the profane into the realm of the most sacred. The author of *The Lyfe of Prestes* bemoaned such behaviour, and John Colet condemned the 'abhominable impiety' of the multitude of the clergy, 'who fear not to rush from the bosom of some foul harlot into the temple of the church, to the altar of Christ, to the mysteries of God'.[34] In pre-Reformation literature, the object of derision was the concubinary priest, but the image was later applied by Catholic polemicists to contact between married priests and their wives. Thomas Martin protested that the sacraments were treated with disrespect in England in the 1550s, and had few doubts as to why this situation had arisen. 'The cause of the which contempt', he argued, 'issued forth partly of the unreuerent and

---

[30] Ibid., sig. H2r; cf. St Bernard had condemned the priest who should have been the 'sepulture of the blessyd body of Chryst', but had fallen from purity; ibid., sig. G7r.

[31] *Dives and Pauper*, fol. 226r.

[32] T. More, *De Tristitia*, CW, 14, pp. 351–3.

[33] G.R. Owst, *Literature and Pulpit in Mediaeval England. A Neglected Chapter in the History of English Letters & of the English People* (Oxford, 1961), pp. 247, 267.

[34] Dionysuis Carthusianus, *Lyfe of Prestes*, sig. G7v; T. More, *The Debellation of Salem and Bizance*, CW, p. 379; Marshall, *English Priesthood*, p. 46.

vncleane handling of the holy sacramentes by the old priestes, partlye also, & that most especially by the unlawful and most wicked marriages of the new ministers ...'.[35] The dishonour done to the sacraments by impure priests was exceeded by that inflicted by the married clergy. The fact that married priests were berated for the same reason as unchaste priests reveals the extent to which writers such as Martin equated purity with celibacy alone, and celibacy with the function and nature of the priesthood.

The obligation to celibacy placed upon the Catholic clergy was a concomitant of their function and role in handling the body of Christ, effecting the eucharistic miracle and dispensing the fruits of the sacrifice. Evangelical rejection of any or all of these functions presented a threat to this sacrificial priesthood, and indeed to the necessity of celibacy. The attack on traditional eucharistic doctrine during the Reformation challenged not only the theology of the Mass, but also the nature of the priesthood. Where the Catholic priest was empowered to mediate between God and man, the Lutheran concept of the priesthood of all believers offered the privilege of access to God to all. The theology of the Mass, which gave priests alone the ability to effect a daily miracle, had exalted them above the laity, and clerical celibacy was the outward sign of this separation. Evangelical eucharistic theology undermined notions of material sacrifice in the Mass and thus encouraged a redefinition of the nature and function of the priesthood. If eucharistic theology was the major determinant in the Catholic understanding of the priesthood, so the rejection of the real physical presence appeared to negate the necessity for celibacy, if not purity, on the part of the clergy. As Tyndale reminded Thomas More, if Christ was not physically present in the Eucharist, then His body could not be defiled if the eucharistic elements were handled by married, or even unchaste, priests. With the rejection of the doctrine of transubstantiation and the bodily presence of Christ in the elements, there was no reason why the clergy should be enjoined to chastity.[36] It was the rejection of the theology of the Mass, as much as the doctrine formulated in its place, that had the greatest impact upon attitudes to clerical celibacy. While the debate continued over the exact nature of the presence of Christ at the Eucharist,[37] the rejection of the sacrificial function of the priesthood was common to all reformers. The true priesthood was not a separate and celibate priestly caste.

---

[35] Martin, *Pretensed marriage*, sig. A4v.

[36] W. Tyndale, *Answer to More*, WW, p. 316.

[37] D. Daniell, *William Tyndale. A Biography* (New Haven, 1994), p. 218; Messenger, *The Reformation, The Mass, and the Priesthood*; Dugmore, *Mass and the English Reformers*; P.N. Brooks, *Thomas Cranmer's Doctrine of the Eucharist* (Basingstoke, 1992).

The issue of eucharistic theology dominated evangelical polemic in the first years of the reign of Edward VI, encouraged by the patronage and protection of Protector Somerset, and the initial lifting of restrictions on printing.[38] Over forty works devoted to the Mass and the Eucharist were produced, and 31 were printed in 1548 alone. All rejected the theology of transubstantiation, and the majority were written by the more radical among the English reformers, including Robert Crowley and Luke Shepherd. The views expressed in the anti-Mass polemic are exemplified in the 1548 tract entitled *The v. abhominable Blasphemies conteined in the Masse*. To assert that the Mass was a true sacrifice and oblation, by which the priest and the participants could obtain forgiveness for their sin *ex opere operato*, the author argued, was blasphemy, because it denied the merits of the sacrifice of Christ. The sacrificing priesthood detracted from the eternal priesthood of Christ, and encouraged the laity to believe that the death of Christ was not sufficient atonement, but one which it was necessary to repeat daily.[39] There should be no room for repetitions of Calvary, and nothing for the priest and people to offer other than praise and thanksgiving. The priests of the Old Testament had retained their ritual purity in order that they might offer pure sacrifices; with no material sacrifice to offer, and the abrogation of the Old Law and ministry by the priesthood of Christ, there was no need for such ritual cleanness. Indeed, where Catholic writers had argued that priestly incontinence profaned the sacred, evangelical authors regarded the doctrine of transubstantiation as a similar pollutant, a doctrinal error that defiled the holy.[40] This was the central argument of such polemical literature: the assertion of the unique and perfect immolation of Christ, which removed the necessity for further expiation, transubstantiation and a celibate, sacrificing, priesthood.

The rejection of the physical and local presence of Christ in the elements did not alter the requirement that the clergy should lead morally pure lives, and the belief in a sacrifice of thanksgiving rather than a physical sacrifice did not mean that the minister had no moral obligations. Instead, it was the idea of what exactly constituted sufficient

---

[38] This issue is discussed at greater length in J.N. King, 'Freedom of the Press, Protestant Propaganda, and Protector Somerset', *Huntingdon Library Quarterly*, 40 (1976–7), pp. 1–10.

[39] *The v. abhominable blasphemies conteined in the Masse* (1548), sigs A2ff, A5–B7, quoted in N. Pocock, 'The Condition of Morals and Religious Belief in the reign of Edward VI', *EHR*, 10 (1895), pp. 419–21.

[40] Gilby, *Deuillish Detection*, fol. 115v: 'this is not consecration or holy makynge, but thys is contamination, poluting, and defiling of the name of God wyth intollerable blasphemies'.

purity to administer the sacraments that was modified. John Jewel mocked those who would distinguish between the sacraments of celibate and married clergy, believing that one was more holy than the other. 'These men put such a difference between them, that they straightway think all their holy service to be defiled', Jewel protested, 'if it be done by a good and honest man that hath a wife.'[41] The sacraments administered by the married clergy were as valid as those of priests who had vowed celibacy. In evangelical works of controversy, clerical marriage was justified more by the value and virtue of marriage itself than by developments in eucharistic doctrine. However, the established link between clerical celibacy and the theology of the Mass, and the polemical capital afforded by this association, was not wasted by evangelical writers. The emphasis was not upon the extent to which clerical celibacy was no longer necessary in the light of doctrinal change, but rather the extent to which the theology of the Mass could be discredited by the failure of the clergy to keep their vows. Evangelical writers commonly treated theological and moral corruption as coterminous, but it was in the discussion of the Eucharist that the link was most clearly defined, precisely because the demand for clerical celibacy had its genesis in the theology of the Mass.

At the most basic level, the failure of priests to live according to the celibate ideal cast doubt upon their role as mediators between man and God. Evangelical writers were unwilling to suggest that the morality of the clergy could invalidate their ministry, but still argued that it was unlikely that the sacrifices of profligate priests would be the only means of securing salvation. Pre-Reformation writers had discussed the extent to which the qualities of the priest affected the efficacy of his sacraments, but the veracity of the theology of the Mass had never been called into question by clerical immorality. The focus in evangelical polemic was different. A relationship was posited between the morality of the priest and the actual theology of the Eucharist: the unchaste priest did not impair the efficacy of the sacrament, but rather indicated the extent to which the theology of the sacrament was flawed. The language of purity and morality traditionally associated with clerical celibacy was turned to attack Catholic eucharistic theology. Luke Shepherd used the name 'Philogamus', 'lover of women', to set the tone of *Pathose*, in which the base language, and the supposed lascivious thoughts of the priest, contributed to the mockery of both the Mass and the celibate ideal. Idolatry and failed chastity were linked, with the allegation 'Quod non estis Nupti / Eo plus Corrupti / Castum profitentes / Non custodientes /

---

[41] J. Jewel, 'Defence of the Apology of the Church of England', in J. Ayre, ed., *The Works of John Jewel*, 4 vols, Parker Society (Cambridge, 1849), IV, p. 413.

... Incestui cedentes / Lupi Existentes / Priapo servientes / In Deum statuentes ...'.[42]

Shepherd's contemporary John Bale applied such arguments not only to the priesthood in general, but also to those theologians who had formulated Catholic eucharistic doctrine. The formulation of the theology of the Mass was attributed to Peter Lombard who, according to Bale, was the son of a nun. Lombard's doctrine was corrupt because he was living testimony to the breaking of vows of celibacy. 'Peter the Lombarde, or the Master of their Sentences', Bale wrote, 'was begotten / bredde / and borne of an holy whore / a nonne I shulde say / vndre the sacred vowe of chastyte / and he gaue vnto y^t transubstanciacyon.'[43] The accusation was repeated later in the same work, with Bale alleging that the morality of contemporary clergy was no better than that of their predecessors: 'your wayes are all after the Master of your sente[n]ces / which was in an whoryshe nonne a fylthy frute of your vowed chastyte'.[44] Lombard was not the only figure ridiculed in an attempt to discredit Catholic teaching. Other examples of the unchaste living of the clergy were offered; Bale drew particular attention to Lombard, Peter Comestor, the historian, and Gratian, the compiler of the *Decretum*, concluding that 'with the doctrine of these .3. frutes of one fornycacyon, hath both churche and the scriptures bene corrupted these .4. hondreth years'.[45] The Mass could be discounted as at best erroneous, and at worst the institution of the devil, by the argument that those responsible for setting forth the doctrine of transubstantiation were either themselves guilty of fornication, or were the illegitimate offspring of priests and votaries.

The alleged immorality of contemporary priests provided further opportunity to discredit the doctrine of transubstantiation. Anthony Gilby rejected the theology of the Mass on the premise that immoral priests could not be agents of the miraculous. God, Gilby argued, although omnipotent, 'wyll not be chaunged into any newe formes, by the mu[m]bling and breathing of an whoremo[n]ger or sodomiticall priest'.[46] The fact that the papists expected God to work a new miracle every day was proof enough that they were misguided. The conduct of

---

[42] Luke Shepherd, *Pathose, or an Inward Passion of the Pope* (c. 1548), sig. B1r–v; J.N. King, *English Reformation Literature. The Tudor Origins of the Protestant Tradition* (Princeton, 1989), pp. 269–70 (because you are not married / because you are more corrupt / professing chastity / without keeping it / ... giving into incest / living as wolves / serving Priapus / setting up God ...).

[43] Bale, *Mystery*, fol. 33v.

[44] Ibid., fol. 39v.

[45] J. Bale, *Yet a Course at the Romyshe Foxe* (Antwerp, 1543), RSTC 1309, sig. I4r.

[46] Gilby, *Deuillish Detection*, fols 56v–57r.

the clergy made their belief more improbable still, with Gilby challenging the assumption that 'euerie whoremoungar, drunckarde and Idiot shal haue a god of his owne makinge, so sone as he mumbled vp .iiii. Latine wordes'.[47] John Ramsey demanded that his Catholic opponents justify their claims that 'horemasters prestes, by their ministracio[n] so com / to alure Christ out of heaue[n] as me[n] do byrdes to twigges'.[48] The same imagery was employed by Anthony Marcort, who argued that it was impossible to defend the belief that any priest, 'all be it y^t he is infecte and a harlot full of fylthynesse' could take a piece of bread, and 'at his onely worde there to cause the sonne of God to come and descend in bodye and in soule all a lyue'.[49] St Paul had encouraged the people to refuse the company of those who were guilty of fornication, and Marcort argued that this proved that the laity should absent themselves from the sacraments of unchaste priests.[50] The perceived immorality of individual priests offered the reformers tangible proof that the miracle of transubstantiation was impossible. By its very nature, the doctrine of transubstantiation demanded a belief in a miracle which could not be seen. To suggest that God would deny such a miracle to the undeserving clergy was a more potent and convincing argument than the claim that transubstantiation was in itself outwith the competence of God.

Evangelical polemicists made use of the image of the concubinary priest to discredit the ministry of these priests, and every priest of the Catholic church. While the church prohibited clerical marriage, priests who were compelled to remain celibate in order to devote themselves to the service of God were instead distracted, even governed, by their concubines. Hurlestone argued that the clergy devoted their attention to the 'apparell of their concubynes', and 'trimme the[m] and haue them in no lesse estimacion the[n] theyr aulters, for I dare not say they take the[m] for saintes'.[51] Tyndale condemned what he believed to be an absurd situation whereby a married priest would face immediate punishment, yet if a priest 'keep a whore, then is he a good chaste child of their holy father the pope whose example they follow; and I warrant him sing mass on the next day after, as well as he did before, without either persecution or excommunication'.[52] Melanchthon lamented that even though God had sanctified marriage, those who argued for celibacy did so on the grounds that 'their sacrame[n]ts may not be handled of

---

[47] Ibid., fol. 89v, cf. 123r, 138r.

[48] J. Ramsey, *A Plaister for a galled horse* (1548), RSTC 20662, unpaginated.

[49] Marcort, *Declaration*, sigs A7v, B6v.

[50] Ibid., sig. G1r.

[51] R. Hurlestone, *Newes from Rome* (Canterbury, c. 1550), RSTC 14006, sig. D3r; H. Hilarie, *The Resurreccion of the Masse* (Wesel, 1554), RSTC 13457, sig. A6r.

[52] W. Tyndale, *Exposition of Matthew*, WW, p. 242.

maryed men for that they be vnclene / but of whore handlers they may be handled'.[53] Such arguments served to defend marriage as a state sufficiently favoured by God to allow married priests to continue in their ministry. Again, however, the issue was not just the defence of marriage, or indeed the rejection of compulsory clerical celibacy. The failure of the clergy to keep to the ideal of purity was so important to evangelical polemicists precisely because of the close relationship between celibacy and eucharistic theology. An unchaste priest not only proved that the ideal to which he had aspired was wrong, but also that the theology which both supported and depended upon that ideal was fatally flawed. The image of the concubinary priest was much more than a justification for clerical marriage, it was a justification for doctrinal reform.

This association between moral and theological corruption was not applied to the clergy alone. The character of 'Mistress Missa' was a common feature in evangelical polemic – a personification of the Mass, frequently as a debauched woman, who condemned herself by her words and actions. The unchaste priest was the refraction of the pure and celibate priest, and the figure of Mistress Missa was the antithesis of the reformed communion service. Just as the priests were alleged to have used their feigned chastity to enhance their worth and power, so it was argued that the Mass had been instituted 'vnder shadow and colour of holynesse, the more easely to seduce & deceyue the worlde'.[54] In Hugh Hilarie's work, the figure of the Mass compared herself with the reformed communion service, and admitted that 'I haue no grounde at all' in God's word. Despite the conduct of her clergy, the figure of the Mass expressed indignation when the 'simple maid communion' denounced her as 'a thefe and a God robber, An harlot and a spirituall whore'. The attempts by the Mass to defend herself were unconvincing, however, in light of her almost boastful admission that she was 'as common as the Barbours chayre'.[55] Shepherd, too, allowed the Mass to condemn herself, with the lament, 'Wo worth my lyuynge dampnable and vicious / Wo worth my dygnyte crept out of the dust / Wo worth my thyrstye and my bloody lust.'[56] The moral conduct of the figure of the Mass paralleled that of her clergy.

John Bradford described the Mass as 'This dancing damsel, the darling of her mother, the fair garland of her fathers (for she hath many

---

[53] P. Melanchthon (tr. G. Joye), *A Godly defence ... defending the mariage of preistes* (Antwerp, 1541), RSTC 17798, sig. C5v.

[54] Marcort, *Declaration*, sig. A6v–7r.

[55] Hilarie, *Resurreccion of the Masse*, sigs B3r, A3v, B4v. The authorship of this work has been disputed, and the piece attributed to Bale. C. Garrett, '"The Resurreccion of the Masse". By Hugh Hilarie or John Bale?', *The Library*, 4th series, 21 (1940), pp. 143–59.

[56] L. Shepherd, *The Vpcheringe of the Messe* (1547), RSTC 17630, sig. A4r.

fathers), the gaudy gallant of her grandsire, is trimmed and tricked on the best and most holy manner or wise that can be', decked in the finest jewels, velvets and vestments.[57] Such references to the parentage of the Mass were not unusual. In what J.N. King has argued to be a parody of the inflated genealogical praise of rhetoric, the Mass was depicted as the fruit of the union between successive popes, bishops, descendants of Mohammed, and as the personification of other sins.[58] In Shepherd's *Pathose*, the Mass was first the grand-daughter of Pluto, then an illegitimate daughter of the pope, and the niece of Mohammed.[59] There was no clear agreement as to which pope was in fact the father of the Mass; indeed, the fact that she was the 'child' of various 'unions' added further weight to the polemicists' cause, by offering further associations between the Mass and immorality. Hilarie's personification of the Mass admitted herself that her own roots were somewhat confused:

> From Rome I came / I can not it denye
> A Citie in tymes paste most florishyng
> Of the famous Goddes Idolatrie
> Had I without fayle my fyrst beginning
> Popes many were my fathers / as stories tell
> Eyghte hundred yeares they were in begetting me ...
> My mother Idolatrie was common
> To many a Pope in the meane whyle.[60]

Turner, repeating the argument that the pope was the father of the Mass, replaced Idolatry with 'dame Avaritia' as the figure of the mother of the Mass, and suggested that the pope and the Mass had then begotten several children, including 'missa de pro defunctis, missa pro pluuia, masse de nomine Jesu ...',[61] and a multitude of others. The sins of which the clergy were accused – avarice, idolatry and concupiscence – were thus seen to be present at the inception of the Mass, and were depicted both as the cause and the fruit of its theological error.

The extent to which evangelical polemicists believed that clerical misconduct cast doubt upon the veracity of the theology of the Mass is clear. The figure of the Mass, as represented in evangelical polemic, was a woman of low moral standing, the archetypal biblical image of the whore of Babylon.[62] This image was expanded in the tract *Wonderfull*

---

[57] J. Bradford, 'Confutation of Four Romish Doctrines', in A. Townsend, ed., *The Writings of John Bradford*, Parker Society (Cambridge, 1853), p. 288.

[58] King, *English Reformation Literature*, p. 265.

[59] Shepherd, *Pathose*, sigs A3v, B6r.

[60] Hilarie, *Resurreccion*, sigs A2r, A5v.

[61] W. Turner, *A Breife Recantacion of maystres Missa* (1548), RSTC 17137, sig. A3r.

[62] Anon, *A New Dialogue called the endightment agaynste mother Messe* (1548), RSTC 20499, sig. C3r.

newes at the death of Paul.iii., in which the Mass was compared to the woman seated on the beast of Revelation 17, who carried 'a golden cup lyke unto these which the priestes lyft vp at the altare'.[63] Clerical fornication fuelled speculation on the divine origins of the Mass, and the veracity of the miracle of transubstantiation. However, evangelical writers also used the image of the Mass as a debauched woman to treat the Mass itself as the root cause of the immorality of the clergy. Such arguments were the inverse of the Catholic assertion that the holiness of the Mass required that the clergy be pure. Rather, it was suggested that the Mass encouraged, or even demanded, that clergy reject marriage in favour of adultery and depravity. In Hilarie's tract, the Mass openly admitted that although she had the power to make people marry, and 'gyue you housebands and wyues at my pleasure', she preferred the clergy, her 'smered shauelynges', to remain unmarried.[64] Rather than being dishonoured by unchaste clergy, as Catholic authors suggested, the figure of the Mass claimed that 'Nothyng defyleth me / but honest marryage', and admitted that she took delight in the number of idle and immoral clergy that were raised 'to be makers of christes'.[65]

The role of the Mass in promoting immoral behaviour had been a feature of English Reformation polemic since the 1520s, and was highlighted in the debate on clerical marriage in the middle decades of the century. In 1528, the clergy had been depicted lamenting the fall of the Mass in Strasbourg, where it had been 'The chief vpholder of our liberte / whereby our whores a[n]d harlots euerychone / Were maytayned in ryche felicite',[66] an allegation echoed in the work of Hilarie, who stated that the Mass wished her clergy to make 'theyr children to syt by other mens fyres'.[67] After recounting her exile during the reign of Edward VI, and bemoaning the lifting of the prohibition on clerical marriage, the figure of the Mass then celebrated the accession of Mary, and expressed her wish for the future, that 'priestes from their wyues shal be separate', because 'Massinge / and that can not agre together'.[68] The fortunes of the Mass and clerical celibacy had been closely

---

[63] P. Equillus (tr. William Baldwin), *Wonderfull newes at the death of Paul .iii. last bishop of Rome* (1551), RSTC 10532, sig. A7r.

[64] Hilarie, *Resurreccion*, sigs A3r–v; cf. Old, *Short description of Antichrist*, sig. C3v; Marcort, *Declaration*, sig. E7r; cf. G4r.

[65] Hilarie, *Resurreccion*, sigs A3r, A8r.

[66] W. Roy, *Rede me and be nott Wroth* (1528), RSTC 21427, sig. A7r. The text continued, 'Our bauds a[n]d brothels have lost their siding / Our bastardes compelled to go astraye / Oure wynni[n]ge mill hath lost her gryndi[n]ge / which we supposed never to decay.' Where once the clergy had been able to clothe their concubines with the money that they received for saying Mass, the death of the Mass made this impossible; sig. A8v.

[67] Hilarie, *Resurreccion*, sigs A8v, A3r; Shepherd, *A Pore helpe*, sig. A3r.

[68] Hilarie, *Resurreccion*, sigs C1r, B8v.

intertwined from the outset. Bale argued that the doctrinal definition of the Mass dated from the papacy of Agathon, and the Council of Constantinople of 677, the same time at which 'marryage was fyrst forbidde[n] to prestes a[n]d whordome admytted'.[69] The Mass was central in the creation of an unmarried priesthood, but while for Catholic writers the expectation was that this would necessitate a celibate clergy, evangelical polemicists suggested that the Mass required a corrupt clergy, threatened by the purity of marriage. Clerical immorality could be attributed directly to the Catholic theology of the Eucharist, not only by the suggestion that it was the prohibition of clerical marriage which led priests to keep concubines, but in the argument that the Mass positively demanded that priests behave in this manner. From this point, it was argued that the Mass should be abolished, because God would not have instituted such a corrupt sacrament as a vehicle of salvation.

Such arguments depended upon the possibility of drawing clear connections between the Mass and the demand that the clergy be celibate. Sixteenth-century Catholic writers benefited from a strong literary foundation on which they could construct arguments both in favour of clerical celibacy and against clerical marriage. The idea that celibacy was a higher state than matrimony, and the belief that the celebration of the Mass and other sacraments necessitated such purity, permeated the work of Catholic writers throughout the period of Reformation. After the prohibition of clerical marriage was lifted in 1549, the attack on the mediaeval concubinary priest was redirected against the married clergy, with the rejection of the validity of such 'pretensed' marriages.[70] If their marriages were invalid, the married clergy were no better than concubinary priests. Throughout such works, however, the idea that the sacraments of the unchaste priest were invalid was always condemned. Arguments in favour of celibacy were instead constructed around the assumption that because God demanded purity in the presence of the holy, priestly immorality dishonoured God, was a further betrayal of Christ, and offered a poor example to the laity. The clergy were marked as a caste apart by their function, and accordingly their lifestyle should be above that of the rest of the church militant on earth.

Evangelical polemicists repeated and re-emphasized this link between clerical celibacy and eucharistic theology. The link between the holiness of the Eucharist and compulsory clerical celibacy was spurned, but the determination of Catholic apologists to argue for the existence of such

---

[69] Bale, *Romyshe Foxe*, sig. C8r ; *Mystery*, fol. 4r–4v.

[70] Martin, *Pretensed marriage*.

an association was exploited to the full. While it was argued that if Christ was not bodily present in the elements, He could not be dishonoured by the ministry of an unchaste priest, this was not the most important issue. Indeed, it was rarely suggested that evangelical eucharistic theology alone was a justification for the lifting of the prohibition on clerical marriage. Since marriage was ordained by God, it defiled neither the priest nor the sacraments which he offered, whatever their nature. More important was the possibility of using the failure of the clergy to keep their vows of celibacy to discredit the theology that supported such vows. Evangelical writers built upon the traditional link between celibacy and the Eucharist and the debate on the extent to which the impurity of the priest threatened the efficacy of his ministry, but they also offered a new perspective. The unchaste priest did not celebrate a sacrament of less intrinsic value than a celibate priest; rather he revealed the extent to which the whole theology of the Mass was erroneous. God would not allow the words spoken by such a priest to effect a miracle which was necessary to salvation. In the eyes of reformers, the degeneracy of the clergy not only proved the improbability of transubstantiation, but also confirmed that the theology of the Mass was false, and instituted by Satan to deceive the people. Evangelical polemic on the relationship between clerical conduct and the Eucharist reveals the extent to which vows of celibacy, and the breaking of such vows, were not only moral issues, but also issues of doctrine. The kernel of such arguments was the connection between the Mass and the unmarried priesthood. The very strength of the link between Catholic eucharistic theology and clerical celibacy allowed evangelical writers to turn the depravity of the clergy into a justification for doctrinal change. It was not the change in eucharistic theology which argued for the freedom of the clergy to marry, but rather the perceived consequence of the limitation of that freedom, clerical debauchery, which, at the level of polemical debate, justified theological reform.

Outside the pages of the printed book, such arguments could be digested, adapted or rejected altogether. The efforts of pre-Reformation writers to allay fears that there was a connection between the efficacy of the sacrament and the morality of the priest appear to have failed to calm the fears of the laity, many of whom sought to secure the services of so-called 'honest' priests to safeguard their souls after death. The turmoil of the Reformation and the demands of its propagandists encouraged a new approach, which implied a much clearer correlation between theological error in general and moral dereliction. But new questions were also raised. Would married clergy be treated any differently from unchaste or concubinary priests? Would clerical marriage prove to be either a cause or a consequence of shifting doctrinal allegiances? What influence did the polemic of the 1530s and 1540s have on the behaviour and decisions of the parish clergy, and to what extent did they conform to the rigid patterns of conduct and belief outlined in such works? Evangelical writers had attempted to establish clerical celibacy as a feature of the false church, encouraging a strong association between clerical marriage and true religion. In the parishes, however, lay attitudes to marriage clergy, and indeed the motivations of those priests who chose to marry, were often less than perspicuous or predictable.

CHAPTER EIGHT

'That they might better attend to the ministration of the gospel': Clerical Marriage in England, 1549–70

The Reign of Edward VI

The polemical works of English and continental reformers had established the lifting of the prohibition on clerical marriage as a central feature of a reformed religious settlement. Compulsory clerical celibacy had been condemned as the mark of the Antichrist, an idol to be purged from the church, a discipline which opposed the word of God in Scripture and ran contrary to the practice of the early church. English clergy, including Thomas Cranmer and Matthew Parker, had already married, and it was essential that the position of the Edwardian church on the issue should be clarified.[1] The repeal of the Act of Six Articles, the most recent affirmation of clerical celibacy, created further ambiguity about the legality of clerical marriage in the Edwardian church. Eric Carlson has argued that 'the passage of some sort of act legalising clerical marriage was perhaps the single greatest certainty of the new reign',[2] and the speed with which moves were initiated to lift the prohibition demonstrates that the issue of clerical marriage was a matter of importance to both the clergy and the laity. The legalization of clerical marriage was discussed in Convocation in November 1547, and debated in the first parliament of the reign.

The passage of the legislation which lifted the prohibition of clerical marriage was far from easy, and both parliament and Convocation were deeply divided on the issue. In the first session of parliament, the House of Commons accepted a proposal that married men might be admitted to the ministry. However, by the time parliament was prorogued, the bill had received only one reading in the House of Lords. In the second session, another bill was debated in the Commons, where it was

---

[1] H.C. Lea, *A History of Sacerdotal Celibacy in the Christian Church*, third edition, 2 vols (1907), II, p. 117.

[2] CCCC MSS 113; E. Carlson, *Marriage and the English Reformation* (Oxford, 1994), p. 51; M. Prior 'Reviled and Crucified Marriages. The Position of Tudor Bishops' Wives', in M. Prior, ed., *Women in English Society 1500–1800* (London, 1985), p. 123.

amended to allow all priests to marry, and this more radical proposal was passed on 20 December. The tenor of this bill was similar to the motion passed in Convocation in 1547, which would have removed all canons and statutes that made clerical marriages illegal, enabling those who had already received orders to marry. Strype records that this motion was passed by 53 votes to 22, after the intervention of John Redman, himself unmarried, on the side of the pro-marriage group.[3] The details of the 1549 vote in Convocation, preserved in Parker's manuscripts, record a vote in favour by 32 to 14.[4] Despite opposition from the conservative bishops in the House of Lords, the bill finally became law in February 1549. Eight bishops voted against the measure, and were joined by four of the secular lords.[5]

In discussing the events of 1547–49, William Jordan, Anne Barstow and Eric Carlson have emphasized the essentially apologetic nature of the legislation on clerical marriage.[6] The Act declared that it was

> better for the estimation of priests and other ministers in the church of God to live chaste, sole, and separate from the company of women and the bond of marriage, that they might better attend to the ministration of the gospel, and be less intricated and troubled with the charge of household.[7]

Since it was clear that many of the clergy could not keep to this 'chaste and sole life', however, the Act declared that it would be better for the commonwealth if those who could not contain were permitted to marry. At first glance, the vehement opposition of evangelical polemicists to clerical celibacy appeared to be at odds with the attitudes of government and parliament, and this is certainly the view advanced by Carlson and Jordan. However, the wording of the Act did reflect many of the views expressed by such writers. The Act declared that it was better that the clergy remained unmarried, on the condition that such a life was entered into 'willingly and of theirselves'. Nowhere was it suggested that promises of celibacy were to be extracted from unwilling clergy, that such promises were unbreakable, or that they were a means by which the individual obtained grace and the promise of eternal life. Such sentiments

---

[3] J. Strype, *Ecclesiastical Memorials Relating Chiefly to Religion and the Reformation of It*, 3 vols (Oxford, 1822), II pt. I, p. 209; W.K. Jordan, *Edward VI. The Young King. The Protectorship of the Duke of Somerset* (London, 1968), p. 309.

[4] CCCC MS 113, fol. 170; Carlson, *Marriage and the English Reformation*, pp. 51ff.

[5] Jordan, *Edward VI. The Young King*, p. 309. The votes against were those of Bonner, Tunstall, Rugg, Aldrich, Heath, Bush, Day and Kitchin, and Lords Morley, Dacre, Windsor and Wharton.

[6] Ibid., p. 309; A.L. Barstow, 'The First Generation of Anglican Clergy Wives: Heroines or Whores?', *The Historical Magazine of the Protestant Episcopal Church*, 52 (1983), pp. 3–16, 6–7; Carlson, *Marriage and the English Reformation*, pp. 51–2.

[7] 2&3 Edward VI c. 21.

appear to be in accordance with the views of writers such as Bale, for whom vows of celibacy, not celibacy itself, were abhorrent.[8] This was a vital distinction: an unmarried man was not by default an idolater, but he who placed hope of salvation in an unbreakable vow of chastity had created an idol in his heart. The 1549 legislation claimed that the 'uncleanness of living and other inconveniences' had resulted from 'compelled chastity' which again echoed the sentiments of those who had written against compulsory clerical celibacy in the preceding decade. Although John Redman argued that the Bible counselled chastity, he conceded that 'the bond of containing from marriage doth only lie upon priests in this realm by reason of the laws and constitutions of the church, and not by any precept of God's word'.[9] Such laws were neither universal nor of everlasting effect, 'therefore the king's majesty and the higher power of the church may upon such reason as shall take them take away the clog of perpetual continence from the priests and grant that it may be lawful that such as cannot or will not contain to marry one wife'. Redman's speech, and the final wording of the Act, followed the recommendation of St Paul in 1 Corinthians 7 in commending those who were unmarried, but permitting marriage to those who could not contain, thus giving primacy to the word of God over the law of Rome, or the law of man. Those who had attacked clerical celibacy in the 1530s and 1540s, arguing for the supremacy of Scripture and the rejection of idolatrous vows, could be well satisfied by the 1549 Act.

The lifting of the prohibition on clerical marriage was not without its problems. The Visitation Articles produced by Cranmer for his diocese in 1549 asked whether 'any do contemn married priests, and, for that they be married, will not receive the Communion or other sacraments at their hands'. The Visitation Articles for Gloucester and Worcester displayed similar fears in 1551–52. Hooper's articles declared that the forbidding of marriage was the doctrine of devils, and argued that the marriage of priests and bishops was 'holy agreeable to God's word'. Further articles asked whether midwives refused to attend to the wives of married clergy, and whether 'any man raileth, speaketh uncharitably, or calleth any ministers wife whore, or destest and abhor their company'.[10] It is unlikely that such questions were asked if they had no foundation in reality. Mary Prior suggests that the laity were concerned that the sacraments would be improperly administered, if not polluted, by married clergy. As a result of such fears, she argues, clerical wives

---

[8] See Chapter 6 above.

[9] CCCC MS 113, fol. 174.

[10] W.H. Frere, *Visitation Articles and Injunctions for the period of the Reformation*, 3 vols, Alcuin Club (1910), II, pp. 274, 292, 189.

faced abuse on an almost daily basis, and were indeed often refused the services of midwives.[11] Such hostility was a natural development from lay attitudes to concubinary priests. Demands that those with care for souls should be morally pure and 'honest' men had featured strongly in lay will bequests on the eve of the Reformation, and such opinions and prejudices were hard to overthrow.[12] Writers such as Bale and Turner laboured to establish an unmarried priesthood as a sign of a church unreformed, but for those for whom the main point of contact with that church was a celibate priest, a married minister was perhaps an all too visible and unsettling sign of the rapid pace of change. Robert Horne, the dean of Durham, was accused of polluting the cathedral precincts by living with his wife, and in Oxford, Peter Martyr's house was pelted with stones, and his wife became an object of derision.[13] Eric Carlson records incidences of hostility to clerical wives in the diocese of Ely in the aftermath of the legalization of clerical marriage, and David Peet has identified similar cases in the diocese of Norwich.[14] The women who were separated from their clerical husbands after 1553 were abused as whores and harlots, no better than priests' concubines.[15]

Such attitudes were reinforced by the written word. Robert Parkyn, curate of Adwick-le-Street, was distinctly unflattering in his description of married clergy as men 'whiche had ledde ther lyffes in fornication with ther whores & harlotts'.[16] One of the few Catholic controversialists active in the mid-sixteenth century, Miles Huggarde, was equally disparaging. Huggarde claimed to have read defences of clerical marriage in the works of several Protestant writers, but was not persuaded by their arguments. 'A lust plague of God vpon such dissolute preistes' Huggarde railed,

> who cared not what wemen they married, common or other, so they might gette them wyues. For true are S Paules wordes: they enter into houses bringing into bondage women laden with synne. The wemen of these married preistes were such for the most part that

---

[11] Prior, 'Reviled and Crucified Marriages', p. 125; P. Marshall, *The Catholic Priesthood and the English Reformation* (Oxford, 1994), pp. 51–3.

[12] See Chapter 7 above.

[13] Barstow, 'Heroines or Whores?', pp. 9–10; J. Loach, 'Reformation Controversies', in J. McConica, ed., *The History of the University of Oxford* (Oxford, 1986), III, p. 374.

[14] Carlson, 'Clerical Marriage and the English Reformation', Journal of British Studies, 31 (1992), p. 7; D. Peet, 'The Mid Sixteenth Century Parish Clergy, with particular consideration of the dioceses of York and Norwich', unpublished Ph.D., University of Cambridge (1980), pp. 309–10.

[15] A.G. Dickens, *Lollards and Protestants in the Diocese of York 1509–1558* (London, 1959), pp. 190–91.

[16] A.G. Dickens, 'Robert Parkyn's Narrative of the Reformation' in Dickens, *Reformation Studies* (London, 1982), p. 310.

either they were kept of other before, or els as com[m]en as the
cartway & so bound them to incestuous lechery.[17]

However, other criticism came from more surprising sources. Despite his
role in the promotion of reform, Northumberland commented to Cecil
that married clergy tended to neglect their cures, being 'so sotted with
their wives and children that they forget both their poor neighbours and
all other things which to their calling appertaineth'.[18] The Protestant
polemicist Robert Crowley complained about the behaviour of clerical
wives, and claimed that clergy families were often far from models of the
godly household. Assuring the clergy that he did not wish them to be
separated from their wives, he appealed to married priests to 'let your
wives therefore put off their fine frocks and French hoods, and furnish
themselves with all points of honest housewifery' and aid rather than
hinder the work of their husbands.[19] Anthony Gilby, who had defended
clerical marriage against Stephen Gardiner, claimed that the bishops and
priests regarded England 'as the devil doth look over Lincoln (as is the
common proverb of that country) or else durst they never practice for
purchasing other men's lands and houses to make their wives ladies and
their sons lords'.[20] The ideological justifications for clerical marriage
could be less attractive when confronted with the practical realities of a
married ministry.

Hostility to clerical wives may have necessitated the passing of a
second Act of Parliament in 1552, which reaffirmed the legality of
clerical marriages and established that children born in such unions were
legitimate. The fact that such an Act was required, three years after the
lifting of the prohibition, suggests that some were still uncertain that
priests were indeed permitted to marry. George Grayme, a clerk, had
married Anne James in accordance with the Edwardian legislation, but
found that he was unable to recover the debts of her previous husband,
because the mayor and bailiffs of Carlisle had alleged that, as a priest in
holy orders, he could not marry. Anne was prevented from trading from
her shop while the bailiffs sought confirmation that clerical marriage was
no longer prohibited. The dispute was initiated by Alexander Stagg, a
curate in the cathedral, who had already declared that he believed that
clerical marriage was against the law of God, although Grayme blamed
his predicament upon the general failure of the king and government to

---

[17] M. Huggarde, *The Displaying of the Protestantes* (1556), RSTC 13558, sigs O6r–v,
I1v–2r. Huggarde listed Bale, Turner, Ponet and Knox as the authors of defences of clerical
marriage; T. Martin, *A Treastise declaryng and plainly provyng that the pretensed
marriage of priestes is no mariage* (1554), RSTC 17517, sig. D1v.

[18] T.M. Parker, *The English Reformation to 1558* (Oxford 1956), p. 138.

[19] R. Crowley, *The Way to Wealth* (1550), RSTC 6096, sig. A8v.

[20] A. Gilby, *On the Prophet Mycha* (1550), RSTC 11889, sigs C8v–D1r.

spread the word of God in the North.[21] The bailiffs of Carlisle were not the only people who regarded clerical marriage as a recent innovation. In 1549, Hugh Bunbury asked Anne Andrew of Chester to marry him, but she asked 'that the said Hugh would tarry, and not to marry her until there were some other priests married'.[22] Anne presumably feared the reaction of those around her while clerical marriage remained such a novelty.

The marriage of two Edwardian bishops did little to improve public estimation of clerical marriage. Both Robert Holgate, the archbishop of York, and John Ponet, bishop of Winchester, became involved in legal disputes as a consequence of their marriages, providing further ammunition for those who remained opposed to clerical marriage in general.[23] Ponet had written A defence for the mariage of Priestes in 1549, but his own marital career was hardly a model of propriety. After attempting to enter into marriage with a woman already married to a butcher from Nottingham, Ponet was forced to pay damages to the man concerned, and was divorced from his 'wife' in July 1551. In October of the same year, however, he was married again, this time to Maria Hayman, in a ceremony in Croydon attended by Thomas Cranmer. The fact that the archbishop attended the wedding implies that he did not believe that Ponet had been discredited by the first marriage, but the damage to public perception of clerical marriage may well have been more severe.[24] The author of the Greyfriars chronicle recorded that the bishop had been 'devorsyd from hys wyffe', and ordered to pay 'a sartyne mony a yere' to the butcher, and the London diarist Henry Machyn noted that 'the xxvii day of July was the new bishoppe of W. was devorsyd from the bucher wyff with shame enogh'.[25] Miles Huggarde used the failed marriage of Ponet to discredit clerical marriage in general, and to show that the arguments contained in the Defence for the mariage of Priestes were worthless. Ponet, he claimed, had disregarded the very biblical text on which he had constructed his defence of clerical marriage. Instead, Ponet,

[21] Marshall, Catholic Priesthood, p. 170-71.

[22] C. Haigh, English Reformations. Religion, Politics, and Society under the Tudors (Oxford, 1993), pp. 226-7.

[23] For Holgate's marriage see A.G. Dickens, 'Robert Holgate, Archbishop of York and President of the King's Council in the North', in Dickens, ed., Reformation Studies, pp. 323-51; 'Archbishop Holgate's Apology', idem, pp. 353-362; 'Two Marian Petitions', idem, pp. 83-91; 'Robert Parkyn's Narrative of the Reformation', idem, pp. 293-312.

[24] DNB, vol. XVI, p. 79; Prior, 'Reviled and Crucified Marriages', p. 125; D. MacCulloch, Thomas Cranmer. A Life (1996), pp. 492-3 suggests that Cranmer arranged the second marriage.

[25] J.G. Nichols, ed., Chronicle of the Grey Friars of London, Camden Society, 53 (1852), p. 70; The Diary of Henry Machyn, Citizen and Merchant Taylor of London From AD 1550 to AD 1563, Camden Society, 42 (1848), p. 8.

'with his double mariage two wyues at a clappe maketh S Paule to correct that whiche fyrst so earnestly he taught, and will haue wydowes to vow chastitie no more'.[26] Albeit in a somewhat subjective history of the Reformation, Nicholas Sanders cited Stephen Gardiner on the subject of his successor's failed marriage. Asked if he believed that he would be restored to his bishopric, Gardiner apparently replied 'Why not? The butcher has recovered his wife.'[27] Ponet's very public difficulties did little to inspire confidence in a married priesthood and episcopacy. Dogmatic certainties were few and far between in the middle decades of the century, and the married ministry was far from being an established feature of the institutional church.

The Reign of Mary

With the death of Edward VI the situation of married priests and bishops altered dramatically. Holgate was imprisoned, and deprived of his archbishopric, 'for divers his offences' on 16 March 1554.[28] Ponet, Bush, Bird, Harley, Scory, Coverdale, Ferrar, Hooper, Barlow and Cranmer all faced the same penalty. Strype notes that many of the bishops were deprived 'upon pretence of treason, heresy, or marriage or the like', but the majority were married men.[29] There were some protestations of innocence. Dr Rudd preached at Paul's Cross and 'repented that he ever was married', and Bishop Bird of Chester attempted to explain his actions by confessing 'the woman beguiled me', before accepting a benefice in the diocese of London, and joining the drive against heresy in Essex.[30] Bush's wife died within days of his deprivation, and he not only conformed with the Marian religious settlement, but actively took to its defence, publishing *A Brefe Exhortation Set Fourthe* in defence of the Real Presence in 1556.[31] Some bishops had embraced clerical marriage as part of their broader acceptance of evangelical principles. William Barlow had married his wife, Agatha Wellesbourne, before the legalization of clerical marriage, in a union which was to establish the kind of

---

[26] Huggarde, *Displaying*, sig. C1r.

[27] N. Sanders, *The Rise and Growth of the Anglican Schism*, tr. D. Lewis (1877), p. 209; J.A. Muller, *Stephen Gardiner and the Tudor Reaction* (1926), pp. 202–3.

[28] *Diary of Henry Machyn*, p. 58.

[29] Harley was Bishop of Hereford, Scory Bishop of Chichester, and Ferrar the Bishop of St David's. *DNB* VIII, p. 1281; XVII, pp. 946–7; pp. 1244–6; J. Strype, *Memorials of the Most Reverend Father in God Thomas Cranmer* (Oxford, 1812), vol. I, bk III, p. 442.

[30] Baskerville, 'Suppression', p. 249; Haigh, *English Reformations*, p. 227; *Diary of Henry Machyn*, pp. 69, 48.

[31] Prior, 'Reviled and Crucified Marriages', p. 125; Haigh, *English Reformations*, p. 227.

clerical dynasty which had been so feared in 1539. William, his son, was later to become bishop of Lincoln, and each of the daughters married future bishops.[32] Others had married relatives of continental reformers, and were well aware of the doctrinal foundation which underpinned their actions. Cranmer married the niece of Osiander's wife, John Hooper married the sister-in-law of Vallerand Poullain, who succeeded Calvin at Strasbourg, and Miles Coverdale's wife was the sister-in-law of the chaplain to the king of Denmark, John Maccabeus.[33] The continental influence on clerical marriage in England was not limited to the polemical debate alone.

Action against the married clergy was one of the priorities of the Marian regime. In the first parliament of the reign, all Edwardian religious legislation was repealed, including the legislation which had lifted the prohibition on clerical marriage, and the 1552 Act which had legitimized the children of such unions.[34] The disciplinary process which originated in the first Act of Repeal was outlined in the queen's injunctions of March 1553/54. In articles addressed to Bonner, bishop of London, and sent to the other bishops on 4 March, Mary ordained that bishops and ecclesiastical judges

> with all celerity and speed, may and shall deprive, or declare deprived, and amove according to their learning and discretion all such persons from their benefices and ecclesiastical promotions, who, contrary to the state of their orders and the laudable custom of the church, have married and used women as their wives.

The fruits of the benefices of married clergy were to be sequestrated, but clemency was to be shown to those whose wives had died, or 'such priests, as with the consent of their wives, or women, openly in the presence of the bishop, do profess to abstain'. The bishop could, in the case of these clergy, readmit them to their administration, although they were not to be returned to the same benefice of which they had been deprived. The former religious, who, unlike the secular clergy, had made a vow of chastity, were to be deprived of any benefice that they held, and 'be also divorced every one from his said woman'.[35]

---

[32] E. Marshall, 'Bishop William Barlow', in *Notes and Queries*, sixth series, 8 (1883), pp. 33–4; A. Wood, *Athenae Oxonienses. An exact history of all the writers and bishops who have had their education in the University of Oxford*, 5 vols (1813–20), I, pp. 364–6; R. Manning, *Religion and Society in Elizabethan Sussex: A Study of the Enforcement of the Settlement of Religion 1558–1603* (Leicester, 1969), p. 52; Prior, 'Reviled and Crucified Marriages', p. 125.

[33] Prior, 'Reviled and Crucified Marriages', p. 125.

[34] I Mary c. 2.

[35] E. Cardwell, *Documentary Annals of the Reformed Church of England* (Oxford, 1839) I, pp. 109–13.

The injunction had an immediate effect. In London nine clergy were deprived of their benefices within three days, and by 12 March the first clergy to be cited appeared before the commission in York.[36] Ernst Messenger argues that the clergy who had married after receiving orders were guilty of 'interpretative bigamy', and therefore unable to exercise ecclesiastical functions. It was the marriage of priests, and not the orders which they had received, that required them to forfeit their benefices.[37] The Bull of Julius III of 8 March 1554, which defined the legatine powers of Cardinal Pole, authorized the excommunication, deprivation and separation of married clerks. Pole's own Legatine Constitutions of 1555 declared that the marriages of those within prohibited orders were null and void, and ordered that those who remained in such marriages or otherwise defended them should be punished according to the 'ancient canons'.[38]

The only statistical evidence for clerical marriage in the period 1549–53 is to be found in the records of the Marian deprivations of married priests, and for the majority of dioceses, the only evidence that a priest was deprived of his benefice is the subsequent institution of another cleric to the benefice 'vacante per deprivationem'. Any attempt at quantification is therefore difficult. Lists of benefices vacant through deprivation offer no insights into the fate of the married unbeneficed clergy, and episcopal registers do not always state the cause of deprivation, or the name of the last incumbent.[39] However, these difficulties are not insurmountable. The name of the previous incumbent can usually be traced with a degree of accuracy by reference to the last institution to the benefice, and the possibility that clergy were deprived of their cures for any reason other than marriage is remote.[40]

The level of deprivations for marriage in the reign of Mary varied greatly across the country, affecting one third of the clergy in London,

---

[36] W.H. Frere, *The Marian Reaction in its Relation to the English Clergy* (London, 1896), p. 64.

[37] E. Messenger, *The Reformation, the Mass, and the Priesthood. A documented history with special reference to the question of Anglican Orders*, 2 vols (London, 1936), II, pp. 10–14. The passage cited from the decretals is Lib.III tit.iii, 'de clericis conjugatis' cap. 1, cap. 4.

[38] Cardwell, *Documentary Annals*, I, p. 153.

[39] Margaret Bowker draws attention to such problems: *The Henrician Reformation. The Diocese of Lincoln under John Longland 1521–1547* (Cambridge, 1981), p. 173, and Christopher Haigh makes a similar point in *Reformation and Resistance in Tudor Lancashire* (Cambridge, 1975), p. 181.

[40] Richard Spielman notes that the only other justification for deprivation would be homicide. R. Spielman, 'The beginning of Clerical Marriage in the English Reformation. The Reigns of Edward and Mary', *Anglican and Episcopal History*, 56 (1987), p. 259. A similar argument is advanced by Michael Zell, 'The Personnel of the Clergy in Kent in the Reformation Period', *EHR*, 84 (1994), p. 530.

yet barely one tenth in the diocese of York.[41] The ramifications could be severe: in early 1554 it was reported that 'the vicars and curates in Sandwich being all married men, there are no ministers to perform divine service'.[42] In the diocese of Norwich, where a separate book of deprivations was kept, Baskerville has calculated that there were some three hundred and sixty married clergy, occupying at least a quarter of the benefices in Suffolk and Norfolk.[43] Hilda Grieve, in an examination of the Essex deprivations, counted some 93 institutions to vacant benefices, suggesting that one third of the Essex clergy had married.[44] Further away from London, the number of married clergy was much smaller. In Lancashire, only seven of the 257 beneficed clergy appear to have married, and in the dioceses of Exeter and Coventry and Lichfield barely 10 per cent of the clergy were deprived.[45] In Lincoln, a diocese of over one thousand parishes, there were some 111 deprivations,[46] and in Winchester, again approximately 10 per cent of the clergy had married. Despite the relatively small numbers of clergy involved, it cannot be denied that the Marian deprivations had a significant impact. Few areas experienced the problems of Sandwich, but even if new clergy were instituted promptly to vacant benefices, the impact of the deprivations, in terms of dislocation, discontinuity and damage to public perceptions of the priesthood, would have been powerful.

Such perceptions would not have been improved by the prosecution of married priests in the church courts. The proceedings against individual clergy could often take several weeks, especially if the case was contested. After he had promised to separate from his 'wife', a public penance was often enjoined upon the priest before he could seek appointment to another benefice.[47] The priest was asked whether he had been a member of a religious order, when he had received sacred orders,

---

[41] Barstow, 'Heroines or Whores?', p. 8; Carlson, 'Clerical Marriage', p. 6; Haigh, *English Reformations*, p. 220. In the city of York itself, only four priests, including three vicars choral, can be identified as married. Claire Cross, 'Priests into Ministers: The Establishment of Protestant Practice in the city of York', in P.N. Brooks, ed., *Reformation Principle and Practice. Essays in Honour of Arthur Geoffrey Dickens* (London, 1980), p. 216.

[42] Zell, 'Kent', p. 530.

[43] R. Baskerville, 'Married Clergy and Pensioned Religious in the Norwich Diocese', *EHR*, 48 (1933), p. 45. In the diocese of Ely, the proportion of married clergy was slightly higher, at approximately one third. F. Heal, 'The Parish Clergy and the Reformation in the diocese of Ely', *Proceedings of the Cambridge Antiquarian Society*, 66 (1976), p. 155.

[44] H. Grieve, 'The Deprived Married Clergy in Essex 1553–1561', *TRHS* 4th series, 22 (1940), pp. 141–2.

[45] Carlson, 'Clerical Marriage', p. 6; Haigh, *English Reformations*, p. 220.

[46] Bowker, *Longland*, p. 173.

[47] Strype, *Memorials of Thomas Cranmer*, pp. 469–70.

whom he had married and where, whether he lived with his wife 'ut vir cum uxore', and whether he still administered the sacrament of the altar. John Turner, the deprived priest of Eastcheap in London, was ordered to return to that church on 14 May 1554, to perform penance for his sin. Holding a wax taper, he confessed before his former parishioners that 'being a priest, I have presumed to marry one Amy German, widow, and [lived] under the pretence of that matrimony, contrary to the canons and ordinances of the church, and to the evil example of good christen people'. Declaring himself to be 'ashamed of my former wicked living here', Turner asked God, the whole church, and those whom he had offended by his marriage for forgiveness.[48] Such public penances for priests or for their wives certainly did little to improve the standing of married clergy in the community. Indeed, Robert Parkyn noted that while most welcomed the accession of Mary, the married clergy 'dyd nothinge reiouce, butt began to be asshamyde of tham selffes, for the common people wolde pontt tham withe fyngers in places when thay saw tham'.[49]

Clergy who were prepared to leave their wives and perform penance were at liberty to seek appointment to another benefice.[50] Baskerville argues that nearly all the deprived Norwich clergy were almost immediately instituted to other benefices, although filling the vacant livings took most of 1554.[51] For some, the process of reappointment took longer, and the disruption to parish life was prolonged. Nicholas Appleby, the married vicar of Gately, was appointed to the rectory of Bereford in 1555, and the married vicar of West Rudham, Peter Stancliff, was instituted to the rectory of Burnham Thorpe in 1556.[52] Hilda Grieve identified a similar pattern in Essex. John Draper, formerly rector of Rayleigh, divorced his wife, and was appointed to the rectory of St Michael Paternoster Royal on 7 April 1556, and William Rowbottom, deprived of the vicarage of North Shoebury, was instituted as vicar of Tolleshunt Major in August 1556.[53] In one case, two married clergy appear to have exchanged benefices. Anthony Redfern, deprived of the rectory of Little Chesterford, was admitted as rector of Panfield in January 1554/55, left vacant by the deprivation of Adam Richardson. Richardson was appointed to

---

[48] Ibid., pp. 470–71; cf. J.F. Williams, 'The Married Clergy of the Marian Period', *Norfolk Archaeology*, 32 (1961), p. 93.

[49] Parkyn, *Narrative*, p. 308.

[50] Wilkins, *Concilia Magnae Britanniae et Hiberniae*, 4 vols (1737), IV, p. 104.

[51] Baskerville, 'Married Clergy and Pensioned Religious', pt I, 45.

[52] Baskerville, 'Married Clergy and Pensioned Religious', pt II, *EHR*, 48 (1933), pp. 50, 55.

[53] Grieve, 'Essex', pp. 142–3.

Little Chesterford, although both men were restored to their original benefices after the accession of Elizabeth.[54] However, the impact of the Marian deprivations in other areas of the country has not been studied in detail, and the extent to which these patterns identified by Grieve and Baskerville are applicable across the country remains unclear.

Married Priests and the Reformation in England

Since the pioneering work of Hilda Grieve on the Marian deprivations in Essex, the experiences of married clergy in England have been examined in a series of local studies. Most have focused upon the eastern and south-eastern dioceses, covering Yorkshire, Norfolk, Suffolk, Cambridgeshire, London and Kent.[55] These investigations have discussed the careers of married clergy after the loss of their benefices, and the prosecution in the ecclesiastical courts of those who did not conform. Some effort has been made to establish motivations for marriage among the clergy, particularly the extent to which clerical marriage may be taken as an indication of evangelical sympathy. Yet this concentration of effort in the areas of the country which were more susceptible to evangelical influences raises questions about the typicality of any patterns that emerge. In parts of the country where the Reformation was at times slow to take hold, married clergy may well have been one of the earliest and most visible signs of religious change, and the decision of a priest to marry appeared even more radical in the eyes of the laity. The actions of clergy in dioceses farther away from the main political and ecclesiastical centres offer insights into the dissemination and reception of reforming impulses in these areas, and in particular any correlation that might have existed between clerical marriage and clerical Protestantism. Taken together, the dioceses which form the basis of this study – Chichester, Winchester, Salisbury and Lincoln – cover a swathe of territory from the south coast to the archdiocese of York. They include both pockets of religious radicalism and centres of conservatism, and were governed by bishops who often held strong views on the Reformation, and indeed on clerical marriage.

The diocese of Lincoln was the largest in England, accounting for 21.5 per cent of the parishes in the country, bordering the diocese of York in

---

[54] Ibid., p. 156.

[55] Cross, 'Priests into Ministers'; Baskerville, 'Married Clergy and Pensioned Religious'; J.F. Williams, 'The married Clergy of the Marian Period'; Peet, 'Sixteenth Century Parish Clergy'; Heal, 'Ely'; Brigden, *London*; Zell, 'Kent'.

the north, and Salisbury and Winchester in the south.[56] Between 1521 and 1547 it was governed by Bishop John Longland, described by Foxe as 'a fierce and cruel vexer of the faithful poor servants of Christ'.[57] Margaret Bowker concedes that while the diocese could have been the springboard for a Protestant Reformation, Longland was well aware of the threat posed both by indigenous Lollardy, and by the circulation of heretical literature, and made concerted efforts to control preaching in the diocese.[58] Longland's successor, Henry Holbeach, was more favourable toward doctrinal change, and supportive of the Edwardian Reformation. He denied the corporeal presence in the debate on the Eucharist in the House of Lords in 1548, and was married, probably in violation of the Six Articles of 1539.[59] Some concerted efforts were made at evangelism in the diocese in Edward's reign. John Taylor, who succeeded Holbeach in 1552, had presided over the destruction of images in the cathedral in the aftermath of the 1548 Injunctions, and Catherine, duchess of Suffolk, provided patronage on a local level for those with reformist sympathies, including Hugh Latimer, who preached in the diocese in 1550.[60] With the accession of Mary, however, Taylor was deprived, and the restoration of Catholicism in Lincoln was overseen by John White (1554–56) and Thomas Watson (1557–59), an active propagandist in defence of Catholicism.[61] Although White enforced the deprivation and separation of the married clergy, there is no

---

[56] M. Bowker, 'The Henrician Reformation and the Parish Clergy', *BIHR*, 50 (1977), p. 32. After the foundation of the new sees of Peterborough and Oxford in 1541 the diocese of Lincoln was reduced in size, but still numbered some 1135 parishes in the reign of Mary. Bowker, *Longland*, p. 173.

[57] Ibid., p. 58.

[58] Ibid., pp. 60–64. By the end of the 1520s, the problem of heresy appeared confined to the Chilterns and the University of Oxford; ibid., pp. 143–5. *LP*, X, 891, E. Duffy, *The Stripping of the Altars. Traditional Religion in England 1400–1580* (1992), pp. 388–9. Duffy argues that the Lincolnshire rising of 1536 confirmed Longland's assessment that such preaching was unpopular. Ibid., p. 399; Bowker, *Longland*, pp. 164–8.

[59] R.B. Walker, 'Reformation and reaction in the county of Lincoln', *Lincolnshire Architectural and Archaeological Society Reports and Papers*, 9 (1962), p. 49.

[60] Walker, 'Reformation and reaction', p. 59; Latimer, 'A Sermon preached by M. Hugh Latimer at Stamford, November 9th Anno 1550', in G.E. Corrie, ed., *Sermons of Hugh Latimer sometime Bishop of Worcester*, Parker Society (Cambridge, 1844), p. 293. Latimer used the sermon to complain that while many opposed the truth, 'they may rail upon it, as in many places lewd fellows do against priests marriages: "that dame, his wife, his whore &c." but they cannot deny it by any scripture, but that the marriage of a priest is as good and godly, as the marriage of any other man ...', taking the text of Hebrews 13 as his defence.

[61] White produced two works in defence of the Mass: *Two Notable Sermons* (1554), and an exposition of Catholic doctrine in 1558, *Holsome and Catholyke Doctrine*. L.E.C. Wooding, 'From Humanists to Heretics', unpublished D.Phil., University of Oxford (1995), pp. 80, 107. Bale described White as 'Saltans asinus'. *DNB* XXI, pp. 52–4.

evidence of wide-scale persecution of heresy during his episcopate. The diocese produced only two martyrs, and there was little overt resistance to the restoration of Catholicism. Those who were apprehended for heterodoxy generally submitted to authority, in what has been described as a decidedly 'unFoxeian manner'.[62] R.B. Walker's conclusion that the Edwardian Reformation in Lincolnshire was imposed from above upon an unchanging clergy appears to be supported by the apparently low levels of resistance to the Marian restoration.

The diocese of Winchester was the wealthiest in the country, and the jurisdiction of the bishop included 180 parishes in Hampshire, Surrey and the Isle of Wight.[63] The Henrician bishop of Winchester, Stephen Gardiner, and his Edwardian successor John Ponet were active participants in Reformation politics and polemic.[64] J.E. Paul argues that 'in the first half of the sixteenth century few counties were more fundamentally Catholic in culture than Hampshire',[65] and this view appears to have been shared by the proponents of reform. John Bale, beneficed in the diocese, published a tract in 1551 entitled *An Expostulation or Complaynte agaynste the blasphemyes of a franticke papyst of Hamshyre*, suggesting that in the eyes of one Edwardian Protestant, Hampshire was still opposed to the message of the Gospel.[66] There is nothing to suggest that there was a strong tradition of Lollard heterodoxy in the diocese, and there were very few prosecutions for heresy in the reign of Henry VIII.[67] However, an outbreak of iconoclasm in Portsmouth early in Edward's reign was a greater cause for alarm, and this was not the only evidence of reformist sympathies in the diocese. Later the same month, Gardiner urged Somerset to take steps to regulate the book trade, and complained that a seditious ballad was being sold openly in Winchester, along with copies of Bale's work on Askew, which

[62] R.E.G. Cole, ed., *Chapter Acts of the Cathedral Church of St Mary in Lincoln. AD 1547–1559*, Lincoln Record Society, 15 (1920), pp. xiv, xxvi. Walker, 'Reformation and reaction', pp. 58–9.

[63] J.A. Muller, *Stephen Gardiner and the Tudor Reaction* (1926), pp. 42, 250.

[64] Both had strong views on clerical marriage, and the circumstances of Ponet's marriage were infamous. The best biographies of Gardiner are Muller, *Stephen Gardiner and the Tudor Reaction*, and Glyn Redworth, *In Defence of the Church Catholic. The life of Stephen Gardiner* (Oxford 1990); C. Garrett, *The Marian Exiles* (Cambridge, 1938), pp. 253–4; J. Ponet, *Apology Fully Aunsweringe ... a blasphemouse book gathered by D. Steph. Gardiner* (1555), RSTC 20175; *Short Treatise of Politike Power* (Strasbourg, 1556), RSTC 20178.

[65] J.E. Paul, 'Hampshire Recusants in the Time of Elizabeth I with special reference to Winchester', in *Proceedings of the Hampshire Field Club*, 21 pt. II (1959), p. 63.

[66] J. Bale, *An Expostulation or Complaynte agaynste the blasphemyes of a franticke papyst of Hamshyre* (1551), RSTC 1294, sig. A2v, C1r.

[67] Muller, *Stephen Gardiner*, pp. 388, 90, 355, n. 47.

had been brought from London.[68] Despite Gardiner's concern, these events do not seem to have been the symptom of a rapid growth in popular Protestantism in the diocese. In fact the climate appeared to remain largely conservative. Several clergy were called before the episcopal court in the 1560s for upholding Catholic practice, and in 1570 alone some 245 individuals were cited as recusants.[69] Nearly forty clergy in the Winchester diocese were deprived in the reign of Mary, but it seems unlikely that they were all acting under the influence of a powerful or widespread reformist sentiment.

The diocese of Salisbury bordered the diocese of Winchester in the south, and the newly formed dioceses of Gloucester and Oxford in the north. In a recent study of the mediaeval diocese, Andrew Brown has drawn attention to the difficulties faced by the bishops in imposing discipline in the remote areas of the diocese, and argues that the cloth-producing regions around Hungerford, Devizes and Marlborough acted as breeding grounds for Lollard heresy. Foxe described the 'glorious and sweet society of faithful followers of the Gospel' at Newbury, and there were executions for heresy at Devizes, Bradford and Salisbury in the reign of Henry VIII.[70] In the 1530s, however, there was little sign of sympathy for the Reformation. The appointment of the reformer Nicholas Shaxton as bishop after the deprivation of the absentee Campeggio did little to improve the fortunes of evangelicals in the diocese. In 1537 Shaxton complained to Cromwell that the people of Salisbury called him a heretic and would have him hanged, and his chaplain informed Cromwell that people had torn down the proclamation which relaxed fasting in Lent, and neglected to remove the name of the pope from the service books.[71] Writing in 1539, Miles Coverdale reported to Cromwell that there were innumerable papist books in circulation which kept the people in error, and a marked lack of hostility to the pope, or to the cult of Becket despite the Injunctions of 1538.[72] John Goodale, the vice-bailiff, stood accused as a heretic in 1539 after ordering the removal of an image which was venerated in St Martin's

---

[68] Ibid., pp. 149–51; Redworth, *Gardiner*, pp. 256–7; J.A. Muller, *Letters of Stephen Gardiner* (Cambridge, 1933), no. 120; Bale, *The first examinacyon of Anne Askewe* (Wesel, 1546), RSTC 848; *The lattre examinacyon of Anne Askewe* (Wesel, 1547), RSTC 850.
[69] E.g. HRO, 21 M 65 C1 / 7, fol. 95r–v; C1 / 8, fol. 4v, 8v; C1 / 9/ 1, fol. 58r, 73v; Paul, 'Hampshire Recusants', p. 67.
[70] A. Brown, *Popular Piety in Late Medieval England. The diocese of Salisbury 1250–1550* (Oxford, 1995), pp. 219–22; AM, 1570, pp. 2073ff.
[71] LP, XII, i, 1114; Brown, *Popular Piety*, p. 238.
[72] LP, XIV, i, 245, 253, 444.

church.[73] Shaxton's opposition to the Act of Six Articles was to cost him his bishopric, and his later inconstancy, particularly his separation from his wife, was attacked in print by Robert Crowley.[74]

Shaxton's successor was John Capon, who retained the see until his death in 1557; indeed, his apparent willingness to comply with successive alterations in religion has led to his condemnation as 'an able and discerning and unscrupulous trimmer'.[75] The diocese produced six martyrs between 1553 and 1558: John Maundrel, William Coberly and John Spicer in Salisbury, and Julins Palmer, Thomas Robyns and John Gwyn in Newbury.[76] Capon's sympathies were almost certainly conservative. He was aged nearly eighty by the death of Henry VIII, and in the discussion of the Six Articles he opposed clerical marriage, communion in both kinds, and defended auricular confession.[77] The majority of the clergy appear to have followed Capon's lead and conformed with both the Edwardian and Marian religious settlements, although several parishes were slow to adapt to change. There is no evidence of vocal opposition to the Edwardian Reformation, and nothing to suggest that the imposition of the 1549 Prayer Book was widely resisted. However, the slow pace at which the Reformation proceeded in the diocese cannot be taken to mean that every aspect of Edwardian reform was unpopular. The lifting of the prohibition on clerical marriage found favour with a significant number of the diocesan clergy, and over seventy were deprived of their benefices for marriage between 1554 and 1556. The changes wrought in the previous reign had been influential in at least one respect.

The diocese of Chichester lay to the south of Winchester, and bordered upon Rochester and Canterbury in the east. Despite its proximity to London, large parts of the diocese were clearly conservative in matters of religion. M.J. Kitch argues that both the cathedral and the parish clergy were firmly attached to the old religion, and Stephen Lander has emphasized the general lack of an evangelical reforming impulse in the diocese.[78] In 1538, the chancellor of the diocese admitted

---

[73] LP, XIV, i, 777. In fact the image contained a consecrated host. Brown, Popular Piety, p. 238 corrects Duffy who described the incident as taking place in the cathedral. Duffy, Stripping of the Altars, p. 421. Duffy provides further evidence of conservatism in the city of Salisbury itself. Ibid., p. 406.

[74] R. Crowley, The Confutation of xiii Articles wherunto Nicholas Shaxton, late byshop of Salisbury, subscribed (1548), RSTC 6083.

[75] I.T. Shield, 'The Reformation in the Diocese of Salisbury', unpublished B.Litt., University of Oxford (1960), p. 19.

[76] AM, 1570, pp. 2073–4, 2117ff.

[77] LP, XIV, i, 1065 (3).

[78] M.J. Kitch, 'The Reformation in Sussex', in Kitch, ed., Studies in Sussex Church History (1981), p. 80; S.J. Lander, 'The diocese of Chichester 1508–1558. Episcopal

that his religious beliefs had not altered in the last 20 years, and in the visitation of 1535, Layton vigourously condemned the 'papisticall clergy' of the diocese.[79] The vernacular New Testament, the banner of the Reformation, was not always well received. William Howe, the vicar of Eastbourne, argued that those who possessed copies of the New Testament were the preachers of the devil, and the rector of Brede imprisoned Thomas Netter in the stocks for possession of an English psalter in 1535.[80] In general, the eastern part of the diocese was more sympathetic to reform, and was the only area which had any form of contact with the continental Reformation.[81] The Henrician and Marian martyrdoms were all in the Lewes archdeaconry, in Rye, Lewes, Hastings, Brighton, Eastbourne, and the surrounding area.[82]

The Reformation in Chichester lacked firm leadership in the reign of Edward VI. George Day, the bishop of Chichester at the accession of Edward VI, was hardly favourable to reform, and the Privy Council were sufficiently alarmed by the situation in the diocese to send Cox to preach against the bishop in his own diocese.[83] Day was eventually deprived of his office after voting against the Act of Uniformity in 1549, and refusing to comply with orders to remove altars in November 1550. His successor, John Scory, bishop from 1552, was the first enthusiast for reform to govern the diocese, but his influence was short-lived.[84] Scory was deprived on the accession of Mary, to allow the restoration of Day, who preached both at the funeral of Edward VI and at the coronation of the new queen. His successor in 1557, John Christopherson, was an active proponent of the Marian restoration, and was blamed by Foxe for the vigorous persecution of heresy in the diocese. Christopherson was chaplain to the queen, and the author of An Exhortation to all menne to take hede and beware of rebellion, in 1554.[85] By 1553 some seventy clergy had married, and although the majority of the clergy acquiesced in the Marian restoration, there were 41 executions for heresy in Sussex, suggesting that the Reformation had at least begun to take hold, if only

---

Reform under Robert Sherbourne and its Aftermath', unpublished Ph.D., University of Cambridge (1974), p. 208.

[79] LP, XIII, ii, 829 (3); LP, IX, 509; LP, XIII, ii, 1062.

[80] LP, XI, 300; LP, IX, 1130.

[81] Lander, 'Diocese of Chichester', p. 239.

[82] Kitch, 'Reformation in Sussex', p. 96; C.E. Welch, 'Three Sussex Heresy Trials', Sussex Archaeological Collections, 95 (1957), pp. 59–72.

[83] APC, III, 137, 154.

[84] APC, IV, 339; III, 368–9, 396. After the accession of Mary, Scory submitted to Bonner, and renounced his wife. After his recantation, however, he spent the rest of the reign abroad, as superintendent of the exile church in Emden, and from 1556 in Geneva. See DNB, XVII, pp. 946–7.

[85] DNB, IV, pp. 293–5; RSTC 5207.

in the east.[86] However, in the diocese as a whole, the situation that greeted Barlow, the first Elizabethan bishop, was unfavourable to reform. Barlow could report few reliable clergy in the diocese in 1564, and the situation had improved little by the visitation of 1569, with clear evidence of the survival of Catholic practice in Arundel, Findon and Racton.[87] Battle, the family seat of Anthony Browne, Viscount Montague, remained a centre of Catholic loyalism, and at least seven Marian priests who had opposed the 1559 settlement were still beneficed in the diocese ten years later.[88] In 1571, five parishes were still lacking a copy of the Book of Homilies, sixteen had failed to purchase a copy of Erasmus's *Paraphrases*, and four were without a copy of the Bible.[89] Reactions in the diocese to official pronouncements on religion clearly varied considerably, but the conduct of those clergy who chose to marry after 1549 offers insights into the attitude of this small but influential group to religious change in the middle decades of the sixteenth century.

The four dioceses under consideration cover a significant proportion of southern and central England. Despite large variations in size and wealth, there are clear similarities between the dioceses. While none of the four embraced the Reformation wholeheartedly in the first half of the sixteenth century, doctrinal and practical reform under Henry VIII and Edward had exerted considerable influence on the clergy. The proportion of clergy who married after 1549 certainly does not approach the high levels of clerical marriage in the dioceses of London and Norwich, but taken in conjunction with other local studies, the four dioceses constitute a large sample of married clergy in England in the middle decades of the sixteenth century. The number of clergy involved is sufficiently high to allow tentative conclusions to be drawn concerning the factors that influenced the decision of a priest to marry, and the attitude of these clergy to doctrinal change.

From the actions of the married clergy in the dioceses of Chichester, Winchester, Salisbury and Lincoln, it is possible to suggest four factors which may have influenced the decision of clergy to abandon their promises of celibacy. Given the prominent place accorded to clerical celibacy in evangelical polemic against Rome, the possibility that clerical marriage reflected clerical Protestantism is certainly worthy of

---

[86] Kitch, 'Reformation in Sussex', p. 94.

[87] Lander, 'Diocese of Chichester', p. 244; R.B. Manning, *Religion and Society in Elizabethan Sussex*, pp. 51ff.; E.G. Rupp, 'The early career of Bishop Barlow', in Rupp, ed., *Studies in the Making of the English Protestant Tradition* (Cambridge, 1966), pp. 62–72.

[88] Kitch, 'Reformation in Sussex', pp. 79, 81; Manning, *Religion and Society*, p. 43.

[89] Lander, 'Diocese of Chichester', p. 246.

consideration. However, a number of clergy had also demonstrated a willingness to conform with the full panoply of religious change between 1530 and 1553, including the Marian deprivations and the restoration of Catholicism. Such behaviour suggests that their marriages should not necessarily be taken as a sign that they had strong sympathies with other aspects of the Edwardian Reformation. The records of diocesan visitations and proceedings in the ecclesiastical courts do offer some insights into the attitude and conduct of individual clerics, and the wills of married clergy and those of their successors have been used to formulate tentative conclusions about the beliefs of these priests. Second, the examination of the geographical distribution of married clergy within each of the four dioceses raises the possibility that the decision of a priest to marry was influenced by the actions of clergy in the surrounding area. In all four dioceses under consideration, clusters of benefices were left vacant by deprivation, suggesting that local influences could be as powerful as national changes in religion in influencing the actions of the clergy. The possibility that a low income acted as a disincentive to marriage has been considered, in an analysis of the value of the benefices from which clergy were deprived, based upon the *Valor Ecclesiasticus*. Finally, in considering whether educated clergy were more likely to understand the doctrinal implications of their marriages, the possibility of a correlation between clerical marriage and clerical education has been examined, based upon a comparison of the proportion of married and unmarried clergy who were graduates.

'Turning head to tayle': Clerical Marriage and Clerical Protestantism

A.G. Dickens argues that the typical married priest in the diocese of York was 'a clergyman first, an Edwardian second, a martyr not at all, and, as a champion of clerical marriage, far from convinced or convincing'. Dickens's analysis echoes Hilda Grieve's conclusion that in 1553 the married clergy were prepared to jettison both the wives and the beliefs that they had acquired in the reign of Edward.[90] However, the actions of clergy who left their wives was widely condemned by both Catholic and Protestant propagandists. John Foxe believed that some had simply married without due consideration, and were merely demonstrating their inconstancy by forsaking their wives in the reign of Mary.[91] Thomas Becon was distinctly less complimentary. The married

---

[90] A.G. Dickens, 'The Marian Reaction in the Diocese of York', in *Reformation Studies*, pp. 93–158, 109; Grieve, 'Essex', p. 153.

[91] *AM*, 1570, p. 1591.

clergy who had separated from their wives in order to secure appointment to new benefices were 'tymelynges', he argued, who admitted
before the people that their marriages had merely been a pretence. He
derided the priests who had pleaded for the forgiveness of their flock,
who 'most wretchedly crouche and knele downe before the people, and
desyre them to forgeue them, and promyse that they will neuermore com
in their wiues company'. The godly had returned to immorality; such
men may have promised to abstain from wedlock, but they instead
defiled themselves with fornication.[92] The Catholic polemicist Miles
Huggarde capitalized upon the capricious character of the priests who
were deprived. The married clergy had broken their 'first fayth', the
promise of chastity, and 'pretended godlynes, and vnder the hypocrisie
of marrying deceived the simple & begyled their owne selues. For when
they thought themselues surest of their fained wyues, they did the
soner forgo them.'[93] If the married clergy were not prepared to defend
their own marriages, then there could be little justification for such
unions.

The reluctance of the great majority of the deprived clergy to cling fast
to their marriages and leave the priesthood suggests that there was little
correlation between clerical marriage and commitment to the
Reformation.[94] This question of the relationship between evangelical
belief and marriage has been hotly debated by historians. A priest who
married in 1550 had demonstrated a rejection of ecclesiastical tradition
in at least one sphere, and, Dickens claims, 'truly, clerical marriage and
Protestant doctrine show strong historical links'. However, Dickens
argues that clerical marriage provides a poor index to Protestant belief
among the clergy, especially given the numbers who conformed to the
restoration of Catholicism. He concludes that 'the assumption that
married priests necessarily held "advanced" doctrinal opinions would
carry us far beyond the evidence and beyond common sense itself'.[95]
Such sentiments are echoed by Christopher Haigh and Margaret
Bowker, who suggests that for the majority of clergy, the decision to
marry was certainly not a matter of doctrine.[96] Peter Marshall, however,
assumes a rather more positive link between clerical marriage and
Protestantism, arguing that the spread of marriage paralleled the spread
of the Reformation, especially among the clergy who married before the
1549 legislation. A married priest, he argues, was making a statement,

---

[92] T. Becon, *An Humble Supplication vnto God*, in *Worckes*, II, fol. EEEEE3r.
[93] Huggarde, *Displaying*, sig. I2r.
[94] See for example Barstow, 'Heroines or Whores?', pp. 8–9.
[95] Dickens, *Marian Reaction*, pp. 105–6; *English Reformation*, pp. 275, 308.
[96] Haigh, *English Reformations*, p. 227; Bowker, *Longland*, pp. 173–4.

even if it was directed only against the oppressive discipline and authority of the Catholic church.[97]

Historians whose research is based upon the experience of married clergy in southern dioceses have identified a clearer relationship between clerical marriage and clerical Protestantism.[98] Susan Brigden, studying the married clergy of London, argues that 'Whenever a priest married he declared implicitly his allegiance to reform', and claims that married priests were deprived of their benefices and replaced by priests who were 'staunch in their popery'.[99] Such perceptions are indicative of a close correlation between polemical principle and local practice, but there are clear dangers in assuming that the black and white of controversy either reflected or informed personal choices in all cases. David Peet suggests that for the clergy in the diocese of Norwich, marriage 'became an outward sign of acceptance of Protestant beliefs', an implicit denial of the eucharistic sacrifice and the spiritual power of the priest.[100] Whereas much of the historiographical debate on clerical marriage and Protestantism hinges upon the assumption that, unless proved otherwise, married clergy should be regarded as essentially conservative, Peet argues that the reverse should hold. Without positive evidence of conservatism among the married clergy, he claims, the historian should take seriously the possibility that such clergy also held reformist views on other points of doctrine.[101] It is arguable, however, that neither approach to the problem is correct. Without any indication of the religious persuasions of individual clergy, it is unwise to assume that they were either sympathetic or hostile to reform, or that their response to theological controversy was rigidly defined and static. The fact that there is no immediate evidence that an individual priest favoured reform does not automatically make him a doctrinal conservative, but the example of one Protestant married priest cannot be taken as an index of the beliefs of all married clergy.

At least one contemporary chronicler was convinced that the clergy who married were in sympathy with other aspects of the Reformation. Robert Parkyn noted that the married clergy 'when thai dyd celebraitt wolde mayke no elevation at masse after the consecration', and claimed that at the accession of Mary the people rejoiced, with the exception of those who were 'of hereticall opinions, withe bischopps and preastes havinge wiffes'.[102] The adherence of the married clergy to the Edwardian

[97] Marshall, *Catholic Priesthood*, p. 167.
[98] E.g. Heal, 'Ely', pp. 154–5.
[99] Brigden, *London*, pp. 399–400, 570.
[100] Peet, 'Mid Sixteenth Century Parish Clergy', pp. 272–3.
[101] Ibid., p. 348.
[102] Parkyn, *Narrative*, pp. 297, 308.

Prayer Books was in sharp contrast to the reactions to accession of Mary, when 'preastes unmariede was veray glade to celebratt & say masse in Lattin'.[103] Robert Holgate, the deprived archbishop of York, also implied that others who had married had done so in sympathy with other aspects of the Edwardian Reformation, 'beinge moche further gone amysse in religion then he was and with obstynacie'.[104] In the eyes of some observers, the decision of a priest to marry was an outward sign that he endorsed the tenor if not the totality of the Reformation of the 1540s.

As might be expected, hostility to clerical celibacy was usually part of a wider rejection of Catholic theology and practice among the Lollard and Protestant martyrs of Foxe's *Actes and Monuments*.[105] Foxe recorded an incident which took place at the church of St Pancras in Cheap, London, at Easter 1555. The crucifix and pix were found to have been removed from the church, and suspicion fell upon the previous incumbent, George Marsh, who had been deprived for marriage, but continued to live with his wife. Indeed, in his defence, Marsh declared that he thought that 'the queen had done him wrong, to take away his living and his wife', suggesting a dissatisfaction with at least part of the Catholic restoration.[106] There is nothing in Foxe's account to suggest that Marsh was found guilty of removing the pix, but his former parishioners were clearly prepared to associate clerical marriage with other less than orthodox behaviour. Bonner, restored as bishop of London, was equally concerned that clerical marriage might be encouraged by other vestiges of the Edwardian Reformation. In his 1554 Articles, later reproduced and criticized by John Bale,[107] Bonner condemned the practice of writing verses of Scripture upon the walls of the churches. Some 'children of iniquity' had used these passages falsely as a 'stay to their heresies', to 'uphold the liberty of the flesh, and the marriage of priests'.[108] Bonner's concern that heresy would survive if Scripture remained on the walls of churches echoes the fears of evangelical polemicists of the 1540s and 1550s, that Catholic doctrine

---

[103] Ibid., p. 309.

[104] Dickens, 'Holgate's Apology', p. 357.

[105] E.g., Roger Dods, AM, 1570, p. 959; Friar Ward, ibid., p. 1379; Thomas Benet, ibid., pp. 1180ff.; Thomas Patmore, ibid., pp. 1188ff.; T. Freeman, 'Research, Rumour, and Propaganda: Anne Boleyn in Foxe's "Book of Martyrs"', *Historical Journal*, 38 (1995), pp. 797–819.

[106] AM, 1570, p. 1639.

[107] John Bale, *A Declaration of Edmonde Bonner's Articles* (1561), RSTC 1289.

[108] AM, 1570, p. 1646. Bonner's view has parallels with Duffy's description of the 'sacrament of forgetfulness' in the Edwardian Reformation – the belief that the destruction of images would destroy the theology which supported them. *The Stripping of the Altars*, pp. 480–83. See Chapter 6 above, pp. 151–60.

would endure if images remained in churches, and, indeed, if the clergy remained unmarried. Church and state were clearly prepared to regard clerical marriage as a barometer of broader theological opinion.

Married priests in his own diocese would have made Bonner all the more aware of the potential link between clerical marriage and heterodoxy. John Cardmaker had been an Observant Friar until the dissolution, vicar of St Bride's in Fleet Street, and a prebendary of Wells in the reign of Edward, but was burned at Smithfield in May 1555. At his examination, Cardmaker declared that he had once believed in the Real Presence, but confessed that he now believed Christ to be present in the sacrament only spiritually.[109] Other married priests, including William Flower, Thomas Whittle, Robert Drakes and Thomas Rose, were also apprehended for heterodox beliefs.[110] Parkyn's contention that the married clergy could be identified by their failure to elevate the host at the consecration was certainly borne out by the conduct and opinions of at least some of the London married clergy.

Other married priests were less willing to suffer persecution for the theology which had allowed them to marry, and many secured appointment to new benefices after their deprivation. In the diocese of Lincoln, William Todd was appointed rector of Stilton in April 1558, after being deprived of the rectory of Hougham for marriage.[111] William Downham, deprived of Datchworth, replaced John Gale, himself a married priest, in the vicarage of Edlesborough.[112] John Morgan was deprived of the rectory of Newdigate in the diocese of Winchester by May 1554, but was appointed rector of Ockely in September 1556.[113] Among the married clergy in the diocese of Salisbury, several had found new benefices by 1558, including John Roberts, the deprived rector of Fovant, instituted to the rectory of Brixton in July 1555.[114] In the diocese of Chichester, John Arnold, deprived of Horsted Parva in

---

[109] AM, 1570, pp. 1749ff. Cardmaker had already come to the attention of the authorities in 1546, and had preached against the Mass with Rowland Taylor in 1548; Brigden, London, pp. 401, 435.

[110] AM, 1570, p. 1746ff., 2018–22; Grieve, 'Essex', pp. 142, 150.

[111] 'Institutions to Benefices in the Diocese of Lincoln in the Sixteenth Century', in Lincolnshire Notes and Queries, 5 (1896–8), p. 134; LAO, Reg. 28, fol. 46r.

[112] LNQ, 5, pp. 228, 174; LNQ, 5, p. 136 (William Cautrell); LNQ, 5, pp. 175, 144; LAO, Reg. 28, fol. 33v (Thomas Clayton).

[113] H. Chitty, ed., Registra Stephani Gardiner et Johannes Poynet Episcoporum Wintoniensium, Canterbury and York Society, 37, (1930), fol. 8v; CCCC MS 122, fol. 128, 139, printed in G. Baskerville and A.W. Goodman, eds, 'Surrey Incumbents in 1562', Surrey Archaeological Collections, 45 (1937), pp. 97–115.

[114] WRO, Reg. Capon, fol. 60r, 67r; Robert Stevenson, fols 54v (Avebury V), 68v (Wotton R); Robert Fyggion, fol. 59v (Winterbourne Stoke V); T. Phillips, Institutiones Clericorum in Comitatu Wiltoniae ab anno 1297 ad annum 1810 (1825), p. 219 (St Edmunds V, Salisbury).

1554, was appointed rector of Boxgrove in 1556, and later rector of Coombes and rector of Wiston.[115] Some married clergy secured appointments in other dioceses. Lambert Pechey, the married vicar of Eartham in Sussex, was presented to the rectory of Helmingham in the diocese of Norwich in April 1558, and the rectory of Tilbury juxta Clare in Essex, after producing letters granted by the bishop of Chichester in 1554.[116]

Many of these clergy, and others who married, had witnessed a wide range of religious change under Henry VIII and Edward VI, while many were to enjoy long careers despite their troubles in the reign of Mary. However, marriage was not the preserve of secular clergy alone, and a number of former religious were willing to abandon their vows; indeed, it has been estimated that some one hundred of the former religious had married in the diocese of Norwich.[117] Several former religious in the Winchester diocese chose to marry, including William Paynter, who was deprived of his cure at Leigh in Kent, and John Saling, a chantry priest of Oxford, later deprived of the rectory of Polstead in Suffolk.[118] The vicar of Dorrington in Lincolnshire in 1553 was Christopher Cartwright, formerly of the Gilbertine Priory of Catley. He married Joan Astely, a former nun of Sempringham, and was deprived of his benefice for marriage, although he was restored after the death of Mary.[119] Christopher Lancaster, deprived of the rectory of Birdham in Sussex by May 1554, had been a monk in the monastery of Michelham,[120] and another Chichester priest, John Cartwright, the married rector of Ore, had formerly been a monk of Robertsbridge.[121] Augustine Curtis had been a canon at Dunstable in Bedfordshire until the surrender of the house in December 1539.[122] In January 1543/4 he was instituted to the vicarage of Framfield in the diocese of Chichester, but had been deprived for marriage by August 1554. At least two other canons of Dunstable were to lose their benefices in the reign of

---

[115] *WSRO*, Ep. 1/1/6, fol. 95v; Ep. 1/1/7, fol. 11v; BL Add. MSS 39326 III, fol. 686; *WSRO*, Ep. 1/1/6, fol. 98r, Ep. 1/1/7, fol. 4v; *WSRO*, Ep. 1/1/6, fols 96v, 93v, 99r; *WSRO*, Ep. 1/1/6, fols 96v, 93v, 99r.

[116] *WSRO*, Ep. 1/1/6, fol. 95v; Grieve, 'Essex', p. 154; *CPR Philip and Mary*, IV, 1557–58 p. 356. 4&5 P&M pt. xv m. 29. Pechey was appointed to a prebend in Chichester cathedral after the death of Mary. *CPR Elizabeth*, I, 1558–60, p. 125 I Eliz. pt. x m. 4.

[117] Ibid., p. 264.

[118] Baskerville, 'The dispossessed religious in Surrey', *Surrey Archaeological Society*, 47 (1941), pp. 17, 22.

[119] Baskerville, *Suppression*, p. 256.

[120] PRO, E164/31 (1556 Pension List of Cardinal Pole), fol. 25r; *WSRO*, Ep. 1/1/6, fol. 94v.

[121] *WSRO*, Ep. 1/1/6, fol. 97r; L.F. Salzman, 'Sussex Religious at the Dissolution', *Sussex Archaeological Collections*, 92 (1954), p. 345.

[122] Baskerville, *Suppression*, p. 256.

Mary.[123] Sixty-eight ex-religious in the diocese of Lincoln had married, accounting for 17 per cent of the monastics, 13 per cent of the collegiate clergy, 19 per cent of the nuns, and nearly 10 per cent of the chantry priests.[124] Significant numbers of former religious appear to have been prepared to relinquish their orders, and the vows which they had made.

A handful of the married secular clergy in the Chichester diocese had held their benefices since the 1530s, and had acquiesced in successive changes before 1553, apparently peaceably. John Biston had been vicar of Rogate in 1535, but was deprived of this benefice before June 1554.[125] John Parke, the married rector of Singleton, had been the incumbent there since 1535 and Matthew Ryle had held the vicarage of Lyminster for twenty years before his deprivation.[126] Other married clergy, including Francis Hiberden, John Dale, John Gregory, Thomas Parker and Richard Darell, had held benefices in the diocese at the time of the *Valor Ecclesiasticus*.[127] In the diocese of Lincoln, Thomas Clayton had been rector of Wadingham St Peter since 1535, and continued to hold the benefice until his deprivation, and Roger Killingbecke, listed as the incumbent of the rectory of Irnham in the *Valor*, was deprived of the same benefice in 1554.[128] John Dewe, John Onley and John More had also held their benefices for at least twenty years.[129] Several Winchester married clergy, including John Alen, John Lynde and John Warner, had been beneficed in the diocese since 1535.[130] Two married priests in the diocese of Salisbury had held their benefices since at least 1535, while others had held benefices elsewhere in the diocese.[131] The careers of such clergy both suggest that marriage was not the preserve of younger clerics alone, and indicate a willingness on the part of many clergy to accommodate successive doctrinal change. Michael Zell has suggested that if Mary and her bishops had not been so determined to eradicate clerical marriage, 'a majority of those incumbents who were deprived

---

[123] Ibid., pp. 295–6; G.A. Hodgett, 'The State of the ex-religious and former chantry priests in the diocese of Lincoln 1547–1574. From returns in the exchequer', *Lincoln Record Society*, 53 (1959), p. 98. The two men involved were John Wyxe and Robert Somar.

[124] Hodgett, 'Ex-religious', p. xix.

[125] *Valor Ecclesiasticus temp. Hen. VIII*, ed. J. Caley and J. Hunter, 6 vols (1810), I, p. 325; WSRO, Ep. 1/1/6, fol. 95r.

[126] *Valor*, I, pp. 309, 316; WSRO, Ep. 1/10/10, fol. 15v.

[127] *Valor*, I, pp. 343, 338, 317, 302, 341.

[128] *Valor*, IV, pp. 133, 99; LNQ, 5, p. 175; LAO, Reg. 28 fol. 98r.

[129] *Valor*, IV, pp. 191, 154, 231.

[130] *Valor*, II, pp. 32, 28, 40.

[131] *Valor*, II, p. 146 (Philip Stanlacke and Nicholas Hobbes); Phillips, *Institutiones Clericorum*, e.g. Richard Arche (pp. 193, 195); Robert Gerrish (p. 201); Adam Rosewell (p. 202).

would have remained in their benefices and conformed to the theology of the day', an argument supported by the careers of those married clergy who had held their benefices through a variety of doctrinal changes since the 1530s.[132] Few, if any, such clergy were likely to regard marriage as a binding declaration of allegiance to a permanent religious settlement.

The issue of compliance with the deprivation procedure was of great importance to the ecclesiastical authorities. Brook's articles for the diocese of Gloucester in 1556 asked whether any of the priests 'that were under the pretense of lawful matrimony married and now reconciled do privily resort to their pretensed wives or suffer the same to resort unto them', and the same fear is echoed in Pole's injunctions for Canterbury in 1556 and 1557.[133] After the visitation of 1556, two Norwich priests were accused of consorting with their wives,[134] and two priests in the diocese of Chichester, Peter Stede and Thomas Parker, were accused of keeping company with their wives. However, the great majority of the deprived clergy in the diocese appear to have accepted separation from their wives, and continued in their ministry.[135] In the diocese of Lincoln, only a handful of married clergy were apprehended after remaining in contact with their wives, including William Watkyns, the former rector of Kibworth, Richard Wynne, deprived of the rectory of Bever, and Thomas Ancocke, the married priest of Willoughby.[136] The careers of the married clergy, and their apparent willingness to conform with the Marian restoration of Catholicism, suggest that whatever enthusiasm they might have felt for other aspects of the Edwardian Reformation was short-lived.

Of course a minority of married clergy did display a clear commitment to their marriages, and to the religious settlement which allowed them to marry. Edmund Scambler, appointed vicar of Rye in 1547, and described as 'a sufferer for the gospel in ye reign of Queen Mary', was deprived of his benefice in 1554, two years after his marriage.[137] He acted as pastor to the underground Protestant congregation in London in the reign of Mary, and enjoyed a distinguished career in the Elizabethan church.[138] Scambler was not the only Protestant cleric in the

---

[132] Zell, 'Kent', p. 530; Heal, 'Ely', p. 141.

[133] Frere, *Visitation Articles*, II, pp. 403, 386, 422.

[134] Williams, 'Norwich', p. 94.

[135] WSRO, Ep. 1/10/10.

[136] *LAO*, Vj, 13, fol. 154r, 197v.

[137] BL Lansdowne MS 982, fol. 57; Strype, *Memorials of Thomas Cranmer*, appendix, p. 261.

[138] *CPR Edward VI*, I, 1547–48, I Edward VI pt IX m. 23; WSRO, Ep. 1/1/6, fol. 96r. Scambler was chaplain to Matthew Parker, and held a York prebend and Westminster

diocese. Gregory Dods, also a married priest, was deprived of the rectory of Nuthurst, which he had held since 1552.[139] In a chancery suit which followed the deprivation, it was alleged that Dods had leased the parsonage to John Wood and William Coleman, in an attempt to avoid the transfer of the house and revenues to his successor. Outlining the case against Dods, Bernard Mason argued that Dods had been deprived of his benefice not only because he was married, but also 'for diuers other hereticall opinions by hym sett forthe and obstinately stande in'.[140] Dods's opposition to the Marian restoration of Catholicism extended beyond his marriage into an attempt to subvert the process of deprivation, and the dangerous territory of doctrinal heterodoxy. Another Chichester priest, Alexander Wymshurst, had been deprived of his rectory of Tillington for marriage by April 1554, but continued to protest that he had broken no law in marrying, which suggests an irreverence if not total disregard for the traditions and canons of the pre-Reformation church.[141] Continued resistance led to imprisonment, but Wymshurst escaped, and presumably welcomed the accession of Elizabeth, securing appointment to All Hallows Breadstreet in 1559, and restitution as rector of Tillington by 1560.

Further evidence of the link between clerical marriage and hetero-doxy is to be found in the location of the parishes of which clergy were deprived. The geographical spread of heresy in the diocese of Chichester, described above, has clear parallels with the distribution of married clergy. There are clusters of parishes left vacant by deprivation in East Sussex, where Protestant influence was strongest, especially in the areas around Eastbourne, Mayfield, Rotherfield and Buxted. The vicar of Willingdon, Andrew James, was married, as were the vicar of Westham, the rector of Folkington and the rector of Hailsham; all these parishes were close to Eastbourne.[142] Further north, in the area around Rotherfield and Buxted, several clergy had married, including William Levet, the rector of Buxted, and Richard

canonry before his appointment as bishop of Peterborough. BL Add. MSS 39344, fol. 164; CPR Elizabeth, I, 1558–60, 24 November 1559 2 Eliz. pt I m. 27; 24 May 1560 2 Eliz. pt XI m. 15; 4 Feb. 1561 3 Eliz. pt IX m. 3. Other Chichester married clergy were promoted after 1559, including Laurence Nowell and John Warner; DNB, XX, p. 851; J. Foster, Alumni Oxonienses, the matriculation registers of the University, 4 vols (Oxford, 1887–88), IV, p. 1574.

[139] WSRO, Ep. 1/1/6, fol. 99v.

[140] PRO, C1/1454/41. For further cases of this kind see PRO, C1/134/14; C1/1336/25; C1/1336/26; C1/1340/11; C1/1358/10; C1/1342/7; C1/1459/72, in which the priest was described as married and as a heretic.

[141] WSRO, Ep. 1/1/6, fol. 94r; AM, 1570, p. 2276; WSRO, Ep. 1/18/10, fol. 10.

[142] WSRO, Ep. 1/1/6, fol. 95v, 109v, 96r. For the concentration of heterodoxy in East Sussex see p. 196 above.

Collier, the rector of Rotherfield. Married priests were also deprived of benefices in the neighbouring parishes of Mayfield, Framfield, Waldron, Isfield, Little Horsted and Barcombe.[143] In certain parts of the diocese, therefore, clerical marriage may indeed have been tolerated or even encouraged by a general climate of heterodoxy and a tradition of dissent.

The Henrician bishop of Lincoln, John Longland, had been active in the persecution of heresy in the diocese, and Margaret Bowker concludes that, at his death, 'his clergy and laity were far from having embraced the tenets of Protestantism'.[144] Even in comparison with the conservative diocese of Chichester, the proportion of the Lincoln clergy who took advantage of the lifting of the prohibition on clerical marriage is small. Approximately 10 per cent of the clergy had married by the death of Edward, but there are wide variations across the diocese. In the archdeaconry of Leicestershire, less than 5 per cent had married, but in the archdeaconry of Bedford, 13 per cent of the clergy were deprived of their benefices. In Buckinghamshire, which was both a centre of Lollard heterodoxy and closer to the reformist influences of London, a lower proportion of clergy had married than in the diocese of York. Such figures have led Margaret Bowker to conclude that the example of the Lincoln clergy does not support the hypothesis that clerical marriage was an indication of Protestant belief.[145]

However, some of the Lincoln clergy had clearly departed from both the discipline and the doctrine of the Catholic church. John Man, the deprived prebendary of Biggleswade, had already displayed his less than orthodox opinions and, 'being detected of heresy was expelled from New College, Oxford'. After the death of Mary, he was appointed to a canonry in the diocese of Lincoln, and was later dean of Gloucester, and ambassador to Spain.[146] John Hardyman, vicar of Sutterton in Lincolnshire, and of Colsterworth, had been prosecuted under the Act of Six Articles, having alleged that confession was merely 'confusion and defamation', denouncing the ceremonies of the church and declaring that faith in Christ, even without the sacraments of the church, was sufficient for salvation.[147] As the Edwardian 'reforming rector' of St Martin's Ironmonger Lane in London, Hardyman and his churchwardens had removed the images from the church rather too quickly for the liking of

---

[143] WSRO, Ep. 1/1/6, fol. 95v, 96r.

[144] Bowker, Longland, p. 184.

[145] Ibid., p. 174.

[146] DNB, XII, p. 897.

[147] J. Venn and J.A. Venn, Alumni Cantabrigienses. A Biographical List of all known students, graduates, and holders of office at the University of Cambridge, 6 vols (Cambridge, 1922–54), II, p. 304; Brigden, London, p. 400.

the parishioners.[148] Another Lincoln priest, John Carter, the married vicar of Streatley in Bedfordshire, had faced accusations of heresy in the reign of Henry VIII.[149] Carter had first appeared before the episcopal court on 4 May 1545, when it was alleged that he had declared in his church that 'ther is noo true booke in the church than the bible Ffor ther are manye lyes in the masse booke'.[150] On 25 May he was back in court, accused of denying the existence of purgatory, and claiming that the laity were entitled to withhold tithes if the parson failed to fulfil his duties, a charge which he denied. Carter had apparently mocked the practice of veiling the rood and images in Holy Week, 'except it shoulde be for wanton children to playe pype bo'. The laity gained nothing by hearing Mass, he claimed, because they could not understand Latin; there was no advantage in attending an early morning Mass, and those who did so 'have done nothinge butt disqyted yor selves, and hurted your bodyes with erly rysinge'. Finally, Carter confessed that he had taught his parishioners that 'the goode workes that one dothe, dothe nott profitte from them butt for the faithe he doth them on'.[151] The decisions of Hardyman and Carter to marry deserve to be seen as another illustration of their clear sympathy with the Reformation.

It is evident that other married clergy were far less committed to the Reformation. The vicar of Whaplode in the diocese of Lincoln had made a highly personal interpretation of the Edwardian legislation on clerical marriage. At the visitation of 1552, the churchwardens complained that the vicar had for three years kept a woman in his house 'under colour of his wyff, but not maryed, to the evyll example of others'. When questioned, the vicar had declared that 'yf my woman was in bedde w[i]t[h] me what then is she my laufull wyffe'. However, the church-wardens also complained that he spoke inaudibly at the communion service, failed to examine the children of the parish on the catechism, and did not possess a copy of the Paraphrases or the New Testament.[152] The vicar had taken advantage of the lifting of the prohibition on clerical marriage, but seemed reluctant to accept other aspects of the Edwardian Reformation.

George Fairbank, the married incumbent of Tarring Neville in the diocese of Chichester, was denounced by Richard Woodman, an

---

[148] Brigden, London, p. 424.

[149] Margaret Bowker states that Carter had been removed from his cure as a consequence, but he was evidently restored at a later date as his name appears in the Liber Cleri of 1551 as vicar of Streatley. Bowker, Longland, p. 169; LAO, Vj 13, fol. 82r.

[150] LAO, Cj 3, fol. 70r.

[151] LAO, Cj 3, fol. 73v–74v.

[152] LAO, Vj 13, fol. 102r–105v.

ironmaker in the parish of Warbleton.[153] Woodman admonished him for his inconstancy, and protested that he

> often perswaded the people not to credite any other doctrine but that which he then preached, taught and set forth in K. Edwardes dayes: and afterwardes, in the beginning of Q. Maryes raygne, the sayd Fayrebanke, turning head to tayle, preached clean contrary to that which he had before taught.

Under examination, Woodman defended clerical marriage from Scripture, but admitted that he no longer believed in transubstantiation, and rejected the teaching of the church on original sin. In the fourth examination, Woodman justified his actions in interrupting a preacher by claiming that Fairbank had not been authorized to preach, 'nor had put away his wife'. It was not Fairbank's marriage that Woodman objected to, but the fact that 'he taught false doctrine ... because he had been a fervent preacher against the Mass, and all the idolatry thereof, seven years before, and then came and held with it again'.[154] There is no way of knowing whether Fairbank's conformity with both Edwardian Protestantism and Marian Catholicism reflected his own changing theological opinions, or merely a desire to retain ecclesiastical office. However, his example illustrates well the situation of many married priests, and the confusion that the Marian deprivations could cause.

Edwardian visitations in the diocese of Salisbury revealed that several of the married clergy were somewhat ambivalent towards other aspects of the Protestant Reformation. John Roberts was deprived of the rectory of Fovant in 1554, but this was not his first encounter with ecclesiastical discipline. At the visitation of 1553, there were complaints that there was no preaching in the parish, and that the church lacked a carpet for the communion table.[155] Robert Fyggion, the married vicar of Winterbourne Stoke, did not fulfil the requirement to preach, and the churchwardens complained that there had been no sermons for seven years.[156] At Little Cheverell, little had changed since the death of Henry. The incumbent, Philip Stanlacke, had held the benefice for two decades, and marriage appears to have been the only aspect of the Edwardian Reformation that he embraced. The church lacked a copy of the Paraphrases, there had only been one sermon preached in the last year,

---

[153] WSRO, Ep. 1/1/6, fol. 96v.

[154] AM, 1570, pp. 2171–95.

[155] WRO, D1/43/1, fol. 106v. One unfortunate priest experienced the same difficulties as Bishop Ponet after his marriage; the churchwardens reported in 1553 that William Nanseglose, the vicar of Bremhill, 'maried a wo[m]an whose husband is yet lyving'; ibid., fol. 144v.

[156] Ibid., fol. 117r.

and 'the highe alter is not defaced'.[157] It seems unlikely that the marriage of these clergy was motivated by a more general or enthusiastic commitment to the Edwardian Reformation.

The marriage of the Winchester priest, Henry Hays, vicar of Godshill on the Isle of Wight, was certainly not an expression of sympathy with the Reformation. In 1570 a variety of articles was alleged against him. Hays was 'suspected of papistrie', because he 'stayed in p[er]a[m]bulations at crosses', neglected to preach against the pope, and because 'he put away his wiff from him in Quene Mareyes dayes'.[158] Judging by his behaviour, Hays would have welcomed the restoration of Catholicism in 1553, and his decision to marry appears to have been motivated by opportunism rather than Protestantism. Fifteen years later, the fact that he had agreed to separate from his wife in the reign of Mary was taken as a sign of doctrinal conservatism: the perceived connection between celibacy and Catholicism remained strong long after the collapse of the Marian restoration.

The wills of clergy offer some of the clearest insights into their reactions to the religious changes of the sixteenth century. However, the material contained in wills needs to be handled carefully, and the statistical analysis of the wills of married priests presents several problems. The most obvious indication of the nature of the faith of the individual lies in the preamble to the will, but there can be no absolute guarantee that this was written by the testator, or that it is an accurate reflection of his religious persuasions. Eamon Duffy argues that even before the Reformation, individuals modified the provisions in their wills to take into account changes in the law, and Tudor testators avoided making bequests which could inconvenience their heirs, or complicate probate.[159] The value of wills as evidence of personal belief has been debated at length in recent years.[160] A.G. Dickens warns against 'statistical pedantry' in the use of wills as evidence, and Rosemary O'Day is even more dismissive of their value, claiming that 'far from revealing the religious beliefs of the average testator, wills and their preambles

---

[157] Ibid., fol. 122v; cf. fols 124r, 129r, 136v, .

[158] HRO, Act Book 21 M 65 C1/14/ 2, inserted between fols 78 and 79.

[159] Duffy, *Stripping of the Altars*, pp. 510–11.

[160] M.L. Zell, 'The use of religious preambles as a measure of religious belief in the sixteenth century', *BIHR*, I (1977), pp. 246–9; C. Cross, 'Wills as evidence of popular piety in the Reformation period: Leeds and Hull 1540–1640', in D. Loades, ed., *The End of Strife. Papers Collected from the Proceedings of the Colloquium of the Commission Internationale d'histoire ecclésiastique* (Edinburgh,1984), pp. 44–51; C. Marsh, 'In the name of God? Will making and faith in early Modern England', in G.H. Martin and P. Spufford, eds, *The Records of the Nation*, British Record Society (1990), pp. 215–49; J.D. Alsop, 'Religious Preambles in Early Modern England. Wills as Formulae', *JEH*, 40 (1989), pp. 19–27.

hide them from the historian's gaze'.[161] Christopher Marsh is more positive, arguing that the 'worldly bequests' of testators, if not the preambles to their wills, can be highly revealing of their beliefs.[162] In the case of clergy wills, it is perhaps more likely that the preamble reflected the belief of the testator, given that they were written by individuals who had at least a measure of theological knowledge, and who were more likely to have views on how their faith should be expressed. If the tone of the preamble is supported by the bequests made in the will, it seems reasonable to consider the preambles as an accurate reflection of the beliefs of the priest.

For the purposes of this discussion, a preamble to a will has been counted as Catholic if the testator bequeaths his soul not only to God, but also to 'the whole company of heaven', 'the virgin Mary', or individual saints. In those which are described as 'evangelical', the individual bequeaths his soul to God, but includes a clause suggesting that he trusted to be saved by the merits of Christ alone. Other wills, in which the preambles make no reference either to the saints or to salvation through Christ alone, have been bracketed in the 'unclear' group. Bequests for the adorning of churches and the commemoration of anniversaries in the body of the will offer further insights into the faith of the testator, and these have been considered alongside the preambles. The tone of preambles clearly changed over time, with the wills of those clergy who died between 1553 and 1558 displaying a stronger 'Catholic' influence simply by virtue of their date. Given the fact that many of the clergy appeared to have conformed with a variety of religious changes in the mid-sixteenth century, an 'evangelical' preamble in a will from the 1560s may not present an accurate picture of the religious persuasions of the priest when he married ten or more years previously.

The small number of clergy wills surviving from the dioceses of Chichester, Winchester, Salisbury and Lincoln do not constitute a representative sample of the beliefs of all married clergy nationwide, and any conclusions based upon them can only be tentative. Taken as a whole, however, the surviving wills of the married clergy suggest a predisposition to Protestantism, or at least a rejection of the traditional Catholic form of dedication. Of the twenty surviving wills of married Chichester clergy, eleven have a clearly evangelical dedication, three priests bequeath their soul to God and to the saints, and in six, there is no clear evidence of doctrinal belief in the preamble. However, the latest

---

[161] A.G. Dickens, *Lollards and Protestants in the Diocese of York* (Oxford, 1959), p. 171; R. O'Day, *The Debate On the English Reformation* (1986), p. 157.

[162] Marsh, 'In the name of God', p. 225.

of the Catholic wills dates from 1558, and the earliest of the 'evangelical' wills is that of Augustine Curtis, dated September 1559, suggesting that the date at which a priest died exerted a strong influence on the tone of the preamble. Of the six wills in the 'unclear' grouping, three date from the reign of Mary, and the remaining three date from between 1559 and 1579. Henry Thorneton, who had been deprived of the vicarage of South Bersted, wrote his will while vicar of Yapton, in November 1557.[163] The will opens with the statement 'I bequeth my soule unto almyghtie gode and to our blessed lady sancte marie, and to all the holy companye of heaven to praye for me.' The tone of his will, taken alongside his appointment to a new benefice, suggests that Thorneton had complied with the letter and the spirit of the Marian reaction. However, after bequests to the church of Chichester, and the altar in the church of Yapton, Thorneton left the rest of his goods 'unto John Thorneton my childe', perhaps an indication that the family had remained in contact despite their separation. Richard Brisely, whose will was proved in the prerogative court of Canterbury in April 1558, had been deprived of Bracklesham by 1556, but died as rector of Stoke.[164] In the preamble to his will he beseeched 'the holly virgyn Marye and all the blessed company of heaven to praye for me', and he ordered that his executors should ensure that two books were produced after his death. The first, for the benefit of the choristers, was to include the anthems, verses and responses for all the feasts of the year, and the second 'all manner of gratias, Alleluyas, and all suche thinges as the children must singe at Masse'. Marriage appears to be the only aspect of the Edwardian Reformation that Brisely had embraced wholeheartedly.

As might be expected, the wills of Edmund Scambler, John Warner and Laurence Nowell are distinctly evangelical in their tone.[165] Another Sussex priest, William Walter, who was deprived of the vicarage of Mountfield, left a will dated August 1554, in which he bequeathed his collection of books to the vicar of Salehurst.[166] The preamble to the will would place it in the 'unclear' grouping, but the gift to William Blacknall of 'a Testame[n]t in Englysh' is more interesting, suggesting a possible sympathy with reform, and demonstrating the importance of interpreting the preamble in the context of the rest of the will. Alexander Wymshurst, deprived of the rectory of Tillington, had openly defended

---

[163] WSRO, STC I/9, fol. 13r.

[164] PCC 15 Chaynay, BL Add. MSS 39353.

[165] PCC 50 Dixon 1594; PCC 11 Morrison 1565; PCC 33 Doughtry 1577. Lawrence Nowell was the Elizabethan dean of Lichfield, John Warner has been described as a 'friend to the Reformation', *DNB* XX, p. 851, Edmund Scambler was minister to the Marian underground Protestant congregation, and Bishop of Peterborough from 1561.

[166] ESRO, ACL III, fol. 137r.

his marriage in 1557, and both the preamble to the will and the bequests display strong evangelical sympathies.[167] Two sermons were to be preached in the church of St Michael, Bassinghurst, and two in All Hallows, Breadstreet, on baptism, the Eucharist, the creed, and the ten commandments. A sermon was also to be preached in Goodchurch and in Tillington in Sussex, for which each preacher would be paid five shillings. His wife was to choose five or six of his English books for her use, his daughters could also make their selection, and the other books, 'whether they be englysshe or latten', were to be given to John Wymshurst. Among the other 'evangelical' clergy wills, there are many references to the families of the priests. Richard Browne, in a will dated October 1580 left bequests to his wife Pauline, and his children Robert and Elizabeth; the will of John Slutter, the deprived rector of Bramber, included bequests to his wife, daughter and grandson.[168] Francis Hiberden left provision for his wife in his will in 1567, and Thomas Stunt, who described himself as parson of Northiam in 1574, appointed his wife, Margaret, as the sole executrix.[169] The evidence of the wills of married clergy deprived of Chichester benefices in the reign of Mary suggests that many of them did carry their support for clerical marriage into the 1560s.

In an analysis of wills in Lewes and Battle, C.A. Mayhew has identified a high proportion of 'traditional' preambles until the mid-1540s, and concludes that this may be taken as an indication that the Reformation was slow to arrive in Sussex.[170] However, the Edwardian Reformation appears to have exerted a powerful influence on the beliefs of testators, with the proportion of traditional preambles contained in wills in the county falling to below 10 per cent by 1552–53. The changing directions of the official Reformation were important: under Mary, the proportion of wills with a traditional formula rose to 30 per cent, but by 1559 this had fallen by a third. The greatest swing towards evangelical preambles was to be found in the coastal Marshland areas, around Rye, Winchelsea and Hastings, an area traditionally associated with heterodoxy, and one in which several married priests were deprived of their benefices under Mary (see Appendix).[171] The views of the clergy could be reflected in the wills of their flock: John Cartwright, the

---

[167] PCC 1 Sheffield, 23 July 1568, proved 13 January 1568/9.

[168] *WSRO*, STC I/13, fol. 146v; *WSRO*, STC I/13, fol. 38v.

[169] *ESRO*, ACL V, fol. 476r–v, 6 November 1567; *ESRO*, ACL VII, fol. 29r, 6 December 1574.

[170] C.A. Mayhew, 'The Progress of the Reformation in East Sussex 1530–1559: The evidence from wills', *Southern History*, 5 (1983), pp. 38–67. Mayhew claims that there were only three wills with 'Protestant' preambles in the county in the reign of Henry VIII.

[171] Ibid., pp. 48–9.

deprived rector of Ore and Hastings St Clements, appears to have been the influence behind an increase in 'evangelical' preambles in his new benefice in Brighton after 1558.[172] Mayhew's work suggests that the increased proportion of reformist preambles in the wills of married clergy by 1560 has parallels with broader changes in will formulas across the county, but it also offers a further indication of the correlation between clerical marriage and sympathy with the Reformation at a local level.

The number of wills of married clergy which survive for the dioceses of Winchester, Salisbury and Lincoln is much smaller. Of the five Winchester wills, four have a clearly evangelical preamble, and the other is ambiguous, making no reference to the saints, or to salvation through the merits of Christ. All five wills were written after 1560, and it is not surprising, therefore, that they display a predisposition to Protestantism. In a will dated 24 September 1561, Edward Mothe, who had been restored as parson of the church of St John, Sherbourne, bequeathed his soul to Christ, 'by whose precious blood shedyng I faythfully trust and beleue to haue remyssio[n] of all my sinnes'.[173] He left most of his belongings to Margery, his wife, allowing her to distribute them as she thought best among his children, William, John and Susan. The will was witnessed by William Grete, 'clerk', himself a married Edwardian priest who had been deprived of the vicarage of Heckfield by August 1554. The inventory that accompanied the will included a variety of household goods, but also a collection of books valued at five shillings, including a copy of 'the new testament in Englyshe'.[174] Mothe's will suggests a longstanding commitment to clerical marriage, and perhaps to the Reformation, although it is clearly impossible to determine whether his apparent sympathy with reform dated from the reign of Edward or from 1559.

The wills of six married clergy from the diocese of Lincoln survive. Four, the earliest of which is dated 1567, fall into the 'unclear' category, one dated 1557 is clearly Protestant, and the other, also dated 1557, has a traditional preamble.[175] John Jameson, deprived of Witham on the Hill, and vicar of Corbie at his death, bequeathed his soul to 'gode, owre leady Saynt Marie & to all the blessed company of heven'.[176] The one 'evangelical' will is that of John Barnardiston, deprived of Great Coates in Lincolnshire.[177] Barnardiston placed his soul in the hands of 'my

---

172 Ibid., p. 51.
173 *HRO*, B 1561 [2], 133.
174 *HRO*, B 1561 [2], 134.
175 John Jameson, *LAO*, 1557 Book I, fol. 372.
176 *LAO*, LCC Book I, fol. 372.
177 *LAO*, Act Book III, fol. 167.

savior and redeamer Jesus Christ through whose most panefull deathe and bitter passion of all my synnes I trust to have free p[ar]done'. The will also included a bequest to one Agnes Hogge:

> otherwise called Agnes Barnardiston if she bee a live at my decesse in consideracon recompense and respecte of all suche pretensed right or claim w[hi]ch she can or maye hereafter challenge to have of or into any p[ar]te of my goodes and catalls the whole and full somme of £xx...

Barnardiston appeared to have been unsure of the legal position of his wife and family after his death, but opted to make adequate provision for them in his will. Thomas Sewen, in the diocese of Salisbury, made an equally vague reference to Jane Sewen, 'a singlewoman', and his three children in his will, which suggests that he had not broken off contact with his family after his deprivation.[178]

John Strype alleged that the Marian deprivations provided a 'harvest for popish curates', who secured appointment to benefices left vacant by married priests.[179] However, if the aim was to replace 'Protestant' married clergy with Catholic priests favourable to the Marian restoration, it is unlikely that married clergy who separated from their wives would have been instituted to other benefices within a matter of months. Yet despite this apparent contradiction, the wills of the clergy who were appointed to benefices vacant by deprivation do display a greater commitment to traditional religion. The same caveats must be applied to the interpretation of these wills as those of the married clergy, but the statistics are highly suggestive. In the diocese of Chichester, only one of the replacement clergy left a will that is clearly evangelical, but five retained the traditional Catholic formula. The Catholic wills cover the period 1557–59, and include that of Leonard Ostler, who replaced the married John Kitchin as vicar of Wartling in June 1554.[180] Ostler placed his soul in the hands of God, 'oure blessed ladye saynt Marye & to all the holie companye of heaven', and requested that 'as many prestes as may be gotten' should officiate at his funeral. The preambles to the wills of Laurence Cox, John Andrew, Bernard Mason and Dominic Legar took a similar form.[181]

In Winchester, the contrast between the wills of the married clergy and their replacements is just as striking. Of the five wills of replacement clergy surviving, four have clearly Catholic preambles. The will of

---

[178] WRO, Sarum Archdeaconry bk III, fol. 152r.

[179] Strype, *Ecclesiastical Memorials*, III.i. p. 171, Brigden, *London*, p. 570, see above p. 200.

[180] WSRO, Ep. 1/1/6, fol. 95r; ESRO, ACL IV, fol. 283v.

[181] WSRO, STC I/9, fols 29v, 173v, 178r–v; ESRO, ACL IV, fol. 46v.

Thomas Wade, in which he bequeathed his soul to God 'and to our lady sancte mary & to all the holly cumpeny of hevyn', was dated October 1558, and proved the following month. Wade had replaced John Kirkham, the married rector of Deane, and described himself as the parson there in his will. He left six shillings and eight pence to the church of Deane, and requested that 'at my buryall & my mu[n]ths mynde & yeres mynde at every tyme 6s 8d' should be distributed to the poor.[182] The wills of Thomas Unton, Resse David and Thomas White all contained similar preambles.[183] Among the four wills of Salisbury clergy who profited from the Marian deprivations, only one has a Catholic preamble.[184] This is the only will surviving from before 1559, and the presence of evangelical and 'unclear' preambles in the other three wills, which date from the period 1569–80, cannot provide conclusive evidence of Edwardian Protestantism. It does appear that many of the clergy who were instituted to benefices which were vacant by deprivation were more conservative in their beliefs than their married predecessors. However, the majority of the 'evangelical' wills of married clergy date from the period after 1558, and to compare these with wills written in the period of the Marian restoration is dangerous. While Strype and Brigden may be correct in arguing that the intention was to replace Protestant clergy with doctrinal conservatives, the evidence of two sets of chronologically disparate wills alone cannot confirm that this was in fact the case.

It would certainly be unwise to suggest that in all cases clerical marriage may be taken as an indication of clerical Protestantism. The lifting of the prohibition on clerical marriage was clearly a key objective of evangelical reformers and propagandists, and deserves to be considered as a central feature of the Edwardian Reformation. Many clergy who married appear to have taken on board other aspects of the new religion, but others managed to combine marriage with doctrinal conservatism, and for the great majority, there is no evidence of their religious persuasion. Of the clergy whose marriage was clearly the concomitant of their reformist sympathies, several were to enjoy distinguished careers after the accession of Elizabeth, and their beliefs are perhaps not an accurate representation of the faith of the majority of the clergy. Many of the deprived married priests were prepared to forsake their wives and serve as priests in the Marian church, but some were sufficiently committed to their marriages and the religion which allowed them to marry to face persecution, exile and martyrdom. In the light of

---

182 *HRO*, B 1558, 708–9.

183 *HRO*, A 1563 [6], 140; B 1558 [8], 183; B 1568, 229.

184 *WRO*, Sarum Archdeaconry Wills Bk III fol. 58v (Philip Vicount).

the behaviour of the English married clergy, and especially those in the dioceses of Chichester, Salisbury, Lincoln and Winchester, it is safer to suggest that many evangelical clergy chose to marry, rather than to claim that married clergy as a group were more sympathetic to the Reformation.

'Giving lewd example' : The Geographical Distribution of Clerical Marriage

Reformation ideology was not the only factor that might have influenced the decision of a priest to marry. The proportion of clergy who married varies widely across the country, but the distribution of married clergy within regions deserves further examination. Robert Parkyn believed that Holgate had given 'lewd exemple' to the clergy of his diocese, and the archbishop himself confessed that by his marriage he might have given 'evell example' to others.[185] The fear that the marriage of one priest might encourage others to follow their example was expressed in the royal proclamation of 1538, and echoes the complaints against the vicar of Mendlesham.[186] The argument that some clergy were following the example of their neighbours in marrying is supported by the presence of several 'clusters' of parishes left vacant after the deprivation of married clergy. It has already been demonstrated that in the diocese of Chichester, clergy in neighbouring parishes which had other associations with heterodoxy had married, but there are other clusters of married clerics spread throughout the diocese[187] (see Appendix). Married clergy were deprived of their benefices in the neighbouring parishes of Ewhurst, Mountfield, Bodiam, Northiam and Whatlington in East Sussex. The incumbents of Rye, Pett, Icklesham, Guestling, Fairlight, Ore and Hastings were also deprived of their benefices. Further west, there were married clergy in the adjacent parishes of Ditchling, Streat and Westmeston. In the western half of Sussex, there was a concentration of married clergy in the area around West Dean, including the parishes of Cocking, East Dean, Singleton, Eartham, Aldingbourne, Barlavington, North Marden and West Dean itself.

Similar groupings of married clergy may be identified in the diocese of Winchester (Appendix). Four clergy from the Isle of Wight had married, in Shorwell, Wellow, Gatcombe and Calbourne. The incumbents of Whitchurch, Laverstoke, Ashe and Deane had all married, and at the

---

[185] Dickens, 'Holgate Apology', p. 357; Parkyn, *Narrative*, p. 298.

[186] *BL* Cotton MS Cleo E v fol. 381; *LP*, XII, ii, 81.

[187] See pp. 206–7 above.

start of Mary's reign there were vacancies caused by deprivation in Winchester and the surrounding parishes of Weeke and Winnall (Appendix). In Surrey, such groupings are less pronounced. Clergy had married in the neighbouring parishes of Sutton and Banstead, and in Send and Merrow, but there are no clusters of married clergy as large as those in Chichester. In Lincoln, the married clergy were not evenly distributed across the thousand benefices in the diocese (Appendix). A group of parishes near the Bedfordshire–Hertfordshire border were vacant after the deprivation of married incumbents (Appendix). Richard Wilson was deprived of the vicarage of Flitton, John Fish lost his benefice of Toddington, the vicar of Flitwick was similarly deprived, and the vicarage of Streatley was vacant after the deprivation of John Carter. Elsewhere in Bedfordshire, clergy were deprived for marriage in the neighbouring parishes of Kempston and Wootton, and Biggleswade and Edworth. In Hertfordshire, five clergy in the vicinity of Welwyn had married, and their deprivations left benefices vacant at Hatfield, Digswell, Datchworth, Knebworth and Ayot St Lawrence (Appendix). The incumbents of Pickworth, Welby, Ropsley and Haseby in Lincolnshire were deprived of their benefices, and other clergy in neighbouring parishes had also married (Appendix). The incumbents of Colsterworth and Stainby were deprived; the Edwardian incumbent at Pinchbeck was married, and William Stafford lost the neighbouring parish of Dowsby. The Marian deprivations left clusters of benefices vacant in the diocese of Salisbury. In Wiltshire, William Davis, the vicar of Minety, had married, along with clergy in the neighbouring parishes of Kemble, Crudwell, Oaksey, Charleton and Garsdon (Appendix). To the south, married priests were deprived of their benefices in a group of five parishes around Melksham, and in the neighbouring parishes of Winterbourne Stoke, Berwick St James and Stapleford. In Berkshire, priests in the neighbouring parishes of Winkfield, New Windsor and Clewes were deprived of their benefices, and another cluster of parishes around Bradfield and Basildon were vacant (Appendix).

On a national scale, the proportion of clergy who chose to marry after 1549 varied widely, with clerical marriage appearing to be most popular in London and the south-east. However, even in counties and dioceses where marriage and deprivations affected only a small proportion of beneficed clergy, clear patterns can be identified, with married clergy often concentrated in clusters of neighbouring parishes. The marriage of one priest may have served to confirm the legality of clerical marriage in the eyes of neighbouring clergy, and may even have persuaded them that married life had advantages. In areas where the Reformation was slow to take hold among clergy and laity, the example of other priests could be a powerful indication of the realities of doctrinal change, and perhaps bolster the confidence of individual clergy in the face of hostility or scepticism on the part of the laity. Given the penalties for deviation from official religion in the middle decades of the sixteenth century, only those with firm doctrinal allegiances may have had the courage of their convictions in 1549: for clergy who were inclined to accommodate and adapt, the example of their fellow priests could be a more powerful argument for and legitimation of clerical marriage than an Act of Parliament. The distribution of clerical marriage within the four dioceses suggests that the fears of Sir Thomas Tyrell that one married priest would set an example for others were justified. Local influences could be powerful in determining reactions to religious change on a national scale.

Clerical Marriage and Clerical Wealth

The decision of an individual priest to marry may also have been influenced by more practical considerations, including the wealth of the cure. Peter Heath and J.J. Scarisbrick have outlined the financial demands faced by the clergy, and identified the limited resources available to them. The incumbent of a benefice was responsible for keeping the parochial house in a state of good repair, and was also expected to contribute in taxes to Rome, or, by the mid-sixteenth century, the crown. The Act in Restraint of Annates promised relief from what Scarisbrick describes as 'intolerable and importable' fiscalism, but the new burden of taxation placed upon the clergy, including first fruits and tenths was, if anything, more severe. By 1540, Scarisbrick argues, clerical taxation was ten times higher than the levies paid to Rome, despite the fact that the taxable wealth of the church had decreased.[188] Rectors depended upon income from tithes, fees, oblations and the yield of the glebe lands, and vicars received only part of the original rectorial income.[189] Bearing in mind these considerations, it has been suggested that on a national scale, an income of fifteen pounds per year would have been 'desirable and reasonable', but Heath argues that in reality only a small percentage of the clergy were this affluent. In the *Valor Ecclesiasticus* of 1535, three quarters of the livings were valued at less than fifteen

---

[188] J.J. Scarisbrick, 'Clerical Taxation in England 1485–1547', *JEH*, 11 (1960), pp. 41–54; F. Heal, 'Clerical Tax Collection under the Tudors: The Influence of the Reformation', in R. O'Day and F. Heal, eds, *Continuity and Change. Personnel and Administration of the Church of England 1500–1642* (Leicester, 1976), pp. 97–122; P. Carter, 'Royal Taxation of the English Parish Clergy 1535–1558' (University of Cambridge Ph.D., 1994).

[189] P. Heath, *The English Parish Clergy on the Eve of the Reformation* (1969), pp. 138–48.

pounds, half were worth less than ten pounds, and many clerics had an income of less than seven pounds per annum.[190] These figures are borne out in a recent assessment of the wealth of the clergy in the diocese of Lincoln, where the average income for a rector was £11 12s., and for a vicar £8 3s., although many were considerably worse off.[191] In the diocese of Chichester, six livings were too poor to attract clergy at all.[192]

However, it appears that the wealth of his cure had little bearing upon the decision of a priest to marry (Figure 8.1). A wife and family may have been attractive to a poorer cleric looking for help in farming the glebe, but a priest in a rich benefice may have felt better able to support his future wife and children. Many married clergy had an income below that deemed reasonable by Heath, but as a whole they do not seem to have been much better or worse off than their unmarried counterparts. In all four dioceses, the majority of married clergy held livings valued at less than fifteen pounds; indeed, in the diocese of Lincoln nearly half the married clergy were in benefices valued at less than ten pounds. From the *Valor Ecclesiasticus*, the average income of a married priest in the diocese of Winchester was £16 3s. 4d, and in Salisbury £14 3s. In Lincoln, the figure was lower, at £13 17s. 7d, and in the diocese of Chichester the income of a married priest averaged £11 13s. 10d. Marriage was not the prerogative of the wealthier clergy alone.

The bequests contained in the wills of married clergy suggest that many were unable to make adequate provision for their wives and families, particularly in the reign of Mary when the legal standing of the women involved was poor. In part, these difficulties may be attributed to the inadequate attention paid to such questions in the Edwardian legislation on clerical marriage. The 1549 Act made no reference to the material and economic problems raised by the arrival of a married priesthood, failed to address the issue of the legitimacy of the offspring of such unions, and made no provision for widows' rights to dower. After the passing of the legislation, Cranmer and Holgate attempted to guarantee security for their own wives and households through the purchase of land, but this option was not open to the majority of the parish clergy. Indeed, any transfer of revenue to support clergy wives and families could be met with allegations of greed and covetousness, further undermining the standing of married priests and their wives in the community. The legislation which authorized the deprivation of married priests made no positive contribution to the women involved, and urged that those priests who were prepared to leave their wives, or those who

---

[190] Ibid., p. 173.
[191] Bowker, *Longland*, p. 134.
[192] Kitch, *Reformation in Sussex*, p. 6.

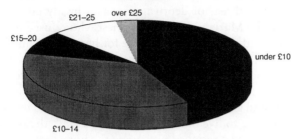

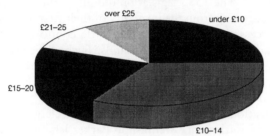

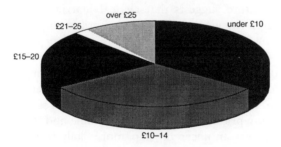

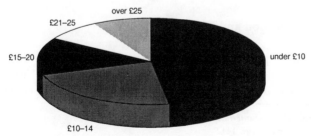

8.1 The value of benefices held by married clergy, taken from the *Valor Ecclesiasticus*, 1535

had been predeceased by their spouses, should be treated with greater leniency.[193] The threat of deprivation was a highly effective weapon in the hands of the Marian hierarchy: a priest who refused to separate from his wife forfeited the means to provide for her and for his children, while those who did accept separation were prohibited from further contact with their spouse. Some enterprising clergy attempted to circumvent at least the practical and material consequences of deprivation by leasing the vicarage and glebe to supportive parishioners, who might then permit them to continue to live on the land. Thomas Hall, the married rector of Ashen in Essex, even resigned his cure in the hope that a successor would be found who would be prepared to care for him and his wife in the months to come.[194] The 1553 legislation did allow the women involved to marry again, arguing from the invalidity of their first marriage that no divorce was necessary, but this provided little comfort for those who wished to stand by their clerical husbands. Such difficulties were not limited to the incumbents of poorer benefices, and even among the higher clergy, and often wives were abandoned in haste, with no guarantee of safety or security.[195]

The legal position of the wives and families of clergy was improved little by the 1559 settlement. Archbishop Parker legitimated his son by Act of Parliament to guarantee his position in law, and allegations that the wives of Worcester canons melted down the organ to make domestic utensils and furniture suggests that clerical marriages were far from financially secure. The women who married priests and even bishops in 1549 rarely came from wealthy backgrounds, and their reputations were blackened by Catholic controversialists such as Miles Huggarde who argued that only women of dubious moral character would marry priests.[196] Throughout the middle decades of the sixteenth century the future of clerical marriage was uncertain, and material security proved to be elusive. For any priest, regardless of his income and the wealth of his parish, marriage was an uncertain step, more likely to impoverish than enrich.

Clerical Education and Clerical Marriage

Reformation polemicists and propagandists, official and unofficial, wrote with the intention and aspiration that their words should influence those who read them, from the king to the ploughboy. The printed word

---

[193] Cardwell, *Documentary Annals*, vol. I, pp. 112–13.
[194] Grieve, 'Essex', p. 146.
[195] Prior, 'Reviled and Crucified Marriages', p. 127.
[196] Huggarde, *Displaying*, pp. 73–5.

became a vital medium of communication, as religious battles were for the first time fought out not only among the clerical hierarchy, but in cheap, mass-produced, vernacular literature. The ideals of the reformers, the arguments of polemicists, then, it might be argued, were most likely to fall on fertile ground where they could be read, understood and absorbed: among the educated and the literate – those for whom the book was a part of daily life. Certainly the first stirrings of English evangelicalism have traditionally been located in the universities, and among those involved in the book trade, both local and international. If the visual image were to be replaced with the written word, the evangelical movement would have to capture the hearts and minds of those who could read and absorb the intricacies or even the banalities of polemic and propaganda. In assessing factors which may have influenced the decision of a priest to marry, the educational background of individual clergy is worthy of consideration. Arguments in favour of clerical marriage which were founded in Scripture, church tradition and historical interpretation were more likely to be found persuasive and convincing by those individuals who understood them, and could read for themselves the references provided to biblical or patristic passages. In a climate of material uncertainty, clergy who chose to marry were perhaps more likely to risk their livelihood if they were firmly convinced of the legal and theological acceptability of marriage, and the doctrinal implications of marriage would certainly have been more obvious to those clergy who were capable of comprehending theological change.

Clergy with a university education, especially those who had attended the universities during the early years of the Reformation, might have been more susceptible to reformist ideas in general, and to the arguments in favour of clerical marriage in particular. Augustine Curteis, who was instituted to the vicarage of Framfield in 1543, was deprived for marriage in 1554. Curteis had gained a BA from Oxford in 1540, and proceeded to an MA in the same year.[197] Other Chichester-married clergy were also Oxford graduates, including Richard Darell, who was a fellow of All Souls, Andrew Davison, Nicholas Kemys and Henry Marshall.[198] Both Darell and Marshall were Bachelors of Canon Law, and it is unlikely that the implications of their marriages had passed them by. However, the educational standards of the married clergy must be compared with those of the diocesan clergy in general, and the evidence of the diocese of Chichester suggests that there was no strong link between clerical education and clerical marriage. In the mid-sixteenth century, approximately one quarter of the clergy in the diocese

---

[197] *Alumni Oxonienses*, I, p. 363.
[198] Ibid., pp. 373, 385; II, p. 842; III, p. 974.

had received a university education,[199] compared with only 18.3 per cent of the married clergy. The same pattern is repeated in other dioceses: at least eighteen married clergy in the diocese of Salisbury were Oxford graduates, including Richard Arch, Thomas Cradock, Thomas Davis, Nicholas Hobbes and John Leke, but an equal number of unmarried clergy shared the same university background.[200] Margaret Bowker has estimated that in the diocese of Lincoln under Bishop Longland, one quarter of the resident clergy were graduates.[201] Among the married clergy of the mid-sixteenth century, the percentage of graduates is almost identical, at 26.01 per cent. Some were Oxford graduates, including William Downham, Oliver Chip, John Onley, William Tode and John Lowth, while others, including John Aylmer, Nicholas Bullingham and John Hardyman, had been educated at Cambridge. While the latter group clearly had reformist sympathies, there is no evidence that a university education was a factor that encouraged clergy to marry. The debate on clerical marriage generated a vast volume of literature, which may have served to create a climate of opinion more favourable to such unions. However, if the polemical debate had any impact upon the decision of a priest to marry, the extent of this influence was not determined by the educational background of the individual.

Indeed, it may be argued that the married priests of the mid-sixteenth century are highly representative of the clergy as a whole. Some held wealthy benefices, others had an income of less than £8 per annum; some were graduates, but three quarters were not. A number clearly had reformist sympathies, but others were unwilling to embrace other aspects of the Reformation, and even more were willing to conform to the demands of successive monarchs and their religious settlements. The precise reason why each and every individual priest chose to marry is impossible to determine. The behaviour of married clergy in the four dioceses under consideration suggests that those clergy who took advantage of the lifting of the prohibition on clerical marriage in 1549 appear to have done so for their own reasons, influenced by a sympathy with Protestantism, the behaviour of their neighbours, a genuine desire to marry, or a combination of all of these.

The Reign of Elizabeth

Whatever factors influenced the decision of a priest to marry, the decade between 1549 and 1559 was a period of disruption, dislocation and

---

[199] Kitch, 'Reformation in Sussex', p. 82.

[200] *Alumni Oxonienses*, I, pp. 29, 344, 383; II, p. 721; III, p. 895.

[201] Bowker, *Longland*, p. 127.

discontinuity for the personnel of the English church. Within these ten years, the centuries-old prohibition on clerical marriage had been lifted and reimposed, marriages entered into in accordance with the law of the time had been declared invalid, wives were reduced to the status of concubines, and significant numbers of clergy were uprooted from their benefices or threatened with the loss of their livelihood. Doctrinal change could have profound practical consequences, and it was not only the married clergy who were affected by changes in the law of celibacy. The accession of Elizabeth created further problems for the clergy who had been instituted to benefices left vacant by the deprivation of the married clergy in the previous reign. In 1559, the queen issued a warrant for the court of High Commission in Courts Ecclesiastical, which gave those named the authority to determine

> according to your discretions and by the laws of the realm, all causes and complaints of all them, which in respect of religion, or for lawful matrimony contracted and allowed by the same, were injuriously deprived, defrauded, or spoiled of their lands, goods, possessions, rights, dignities, livings, offices, spiritual or temporal: and them so deprived, as before, to restore into their said livings, and to put them in possession, amoving the usurpers.

The Edwardian married clergy who had been deprived of their benefices in the first years of the reign of Mary were to be restored, and the clergy who had replaced them removed. The injunction was effective. In Chichester, at least thirteen clergy were expelled from their benefices, and their married counterparts restored. Ralph Post had been instituted to the rectory of Burton and Coates in April 1555, on the deprivation of the married Richard Browne. By 1560, Browne had been restored, and was to remain in Burton until his death.[202] John Slutter was returned as rector of Bramber, where he remained until his death in 1582, and Robert Best was restored to the vicarage of East Grinstead, which he held until his resignation in 1563.[203] Andrew James had been deprived of the vicarage of Willingdon for marriage before June 1554, and after separating from his wife, he was instituted to the vicarage of Eartham, vacant by the deprivation of Lambert Pechey.[204] However, in the *Liber Cleri* for the visitation of the Chichester diocese in May 1560, James was listed as the incumbent of Eartham, 'who put away his wife and so caused her to commit adultery'.[205] The

---

[202] T. McCann 'The Clergy and the Elizabethan Settlement in the Diocese of Chichester', in Kitch, ed., *Studies in Sussex Church History*, p. 110.

[203] Ibid., p. 110. For Best see WSRO, Ep. 1/1/7, fol. 22v; cf. WSRO, Ep. 1/1/7, fol. 23v; Ep. 1/18/18, fol. 10.

[204] WSRO, Ep. 1/1/6, fol. 95v.

[205] WSRO, Ep. 1/18/10, fol. 3v.

226 CLERICAL MARRIAGE AND THE ENGLISH REFORMATION

clock could be turned back in practical matters, but deeply rooted memories were more difficult to dispel, and the events of the previous reign were not easily forgotten.

In the dioceses of Winchester, Salisbury and Lincoln, the task of tracing the later careers of the deprived clergy is facilitated by the surviving diocesan returns ordered by Archbishop Parker for 1561.[206] Among the Winchester clergy, Ralph Kirkham, who had been deprived of Ashstead had been restored to his benefice, and was described as 'married' in the 1561 returns.[207] George Stoughton had been restored as rector of Ashe by May 1568, and Anthony Cawse had also regained his benefice at Compton.[208] Robert Fyggyn, deprived of the rectory of Winterbourne Stoke in the diocese of Salisbury, had been restored by 1561, and described himself as married.[209] Thirteen other Edwardian married priests were described as married in Salisbury returns for 1561, including Humphrey Galymore, John Leke and Robert Gerrish, all of whom had been restored to the benefices which they had held in 1553.[210] A number of Lincoln clergy who were deprived of their benefices in the reign of Mary had also been restored by 1561. John Fox, deprived of the vicarage of Stewkley in Buckinghamshire, was again listed as vicar there, and William Moone had been returned to his rectory in Welby.[211] Richard Gill had been reappointed as prebendary of Leighton, and Thomas Larke, the Edwardian prebendary of Norton, was listed as the incumbent in 1561.[212] However, other married clergy remained in their new benefices. William Cautrell, who had been deprived of the vicarage of Crosberton by December 1554, was the incumbent at Evedon in 1561, and Thomas Simpson, the Edwardian vicar of Skillington, had secured appointment to the vicarage of Newton.[213] In the 1561 return, Fox, Moone, Gill, Larke, Cautrell and Simpson all described themselves as married, suggesting that the events of the previous reign had done little to alter their opinions.

Suits for the restoration of married clergy deprived by Mary were initiated across the country. During the Royal Visitation of the Northern Province in 1559, 21 incumbents who had committed no other offence were removed from their benefices simply to allow the restitution of the

---

[206] CCCC MS 97 (Lincoln), and MS 122 (Winchester).
[207] CCCC MS 122, fol. 143, ed. G. Baskerville and A.W. Woodman, *Surrey Archaeological Collection*, 45 (1937), p. 112.
[208] HRO, 21 M 65 B1/9 fol. 63r, 147r.
[209] CCCC MSS 97, fol. 188r.
[210] Ibid., fol. 191r, 197r, 192v.
[211] Ibid., fol. 62r, 77r.
[212] Ibid., fol. 94r, 94v.
[213] Ibid., fol. 75r, 65r.

Edwardian married clergy.[214] In August 1559, Christopher Sugden, formerly vicar of Newark, brought a case against the current incumbent John Tavernham, whom he described as 'vicarium pretensum ibidem', and Anthony Blake was restored as vicar of Doncaster after the removal of the previous incumbent, John Hudson.[215] In the diocese of London, John Spendlowe, who had been deprived of the rectory of Finchley by June 1554, brought a case against Edward Turner, the Marian incumbent of the benefice, and John Robson, the Edwardian incumbent of St Clement in Eastcheap, sought restitution at the expense of John Coles, who had been instituted to the benefice on 16 April 1555.[216] Henry Parry, who had been deprived of his benefice in the diocese of Salisbury, pleaded for restitution in August 1559. Parry argued that Richard Akers, who had replaced him in Burscot, occupied the benefice unlawfully, and claimed that the Marian deprivations were contrary to the laws of England and to the laws of the church. The visitors restored Parry to the living, and the judges at Westminster recorded that he had held the living continuously, ignoring Akers's tenure.[217] The Marian deprivations were dismissed as unfounded in law, and the clergy who filled the vacancies caused by them were argued to have no legal right to the benefices to which they had been appointed.

Despite this insistence that the Marian deprivations were unjust, the attitude of Elizabeth herself to clerical marriage and married clergy was ambiguous. Anne Barstow has argued that the queen clearly disapproved of clerical marriage, was rude to the wives of her clergy, and sought to have them expelled from the cathedral precincts.[218] Eric Carlson emphasizes the hostile tone of the Elizabethan legislation on clerical marriage, and suggests that the queen was determined to avoid scandalous episcopal marriages in particular, which might threaten the credibility of the church.[219] His argument is supported by the passage cited from article 29 of the 1559 Injunctions, which stated that although many of the clergy had married, 'there hath grown offence, and some slander to the church, by lack of discreet and sober behaviour in many ministers of the church, both in the choosing of their wives and indiscreet

---

[214] 'The Royal Visitation of 1559. Act Book for the Northern Province', transcribed and ed. C.J. Kitching, *Surtees Society*, 187 (1975), pp. xxiv–xxv; cf. Robert Wisdom and George Monsume, ibid., pp. xxv, 42.

[215] Ibid., pp. 42, 43.

[216] Bonner Register, fol. 453r; *PRO*, Prob 34/1 fol. 8v. Spendlowe was also restored as rector of Hackney, which had been left vacant by his deprivation in May 1554. Bonner Reg., fol. 452r, 462r; *PRO*, Prob 34/1, fol. 14v.

[217] C.G. Bayne, 'The Visitation of the Province of Canterbury, 1559', in *EHR*, 28 (1913), pp. 644–5.

[218] Barstow, 'Heroines or Whores?', p. 11.

[219] Carlson, *Marriage and the English Reformation*, pp. 58–9.

living with them'. It was therefore ordained that no priest should marry, unless testimony to the character of his wife had been provided by two justices of the peace and was confirmed by the bishop of the diocese.[220] However, the tone of the rest of the article was more positive. The opening lines stated that there was no reason why clerical marriage should be prohibited 'by the word of God, nor any example of the primitive church', and confirmed that it was lawful for clergy to marry 'for the avoiding of fornication'. Clerical marriage, it was stated, had been legal in the English church 'in the time of our dear brother king Edward the Sixth', suggesting that there would be no prohibition of such marriages by the new queen.

Carlson argues that the appointment of married bishops early in the reign supports the assertion that Elizabeth was hostile to clerical scandal rather than clerical marriage *per se*: over three quarters of episcopal appointments between 1559 and 1603 went to married men.[221] In the early months of the reign, however, the choice of bishops was made with care. MacCulloch suggests that Elizabeth had intended to balance more radical evangelicals with conservative appointments, a plan thwarted by the refusal of all but one of the Marian bishops to cooperate with the 1559 settlement. The choice of Parker as archbishop of Canterbury was not so much a reflection of the queen's support for his marriage, and clerical marriage in general, as of Elizabeth's decision to appoint 'a distinguished former Cambridge academic who had not fled to the continent'.[222] The majority of the leaders of the exiled English church were also married men, further limiting the options available to Elizabeth, even if she had hoped to appoint a celibate episcopal bench.[223]

The strong associations of the prohibition of clerical marriage with papistry made compulsory clerical celibacy doctrinally insupportable in the eyes of the reform-minded bishops. However, this did not mean that Elizabeth herself welcomed a married priesthood with enthusiasm; indeed, an article which would straightforwardly have lifted the prohibition on clerical marriage was removed from the Supremacy Bill by the queen. Archbishop Parker believed that her attitude was overwhelmingly negative, and Sandys complained that 'the queen's majesty will wink at [marriage] but not stablish it by law, which is

---

[220] Cardwell, *Documentary Annals*, vol. I, p. 192.

[221] Prior, 'Reviled and Crucified', p. 129; Carlson, *Marriage and the English Reformation*, pp. 60–61.

[222] D. MacCulloch, *The Later Reformation in England 1547–1603* (Basingstoke, 1990), p. 31.

[223] For example Barlow (Chichester), Allen (Rochester), Pilkington (Winchester), Berkely (Bath and Wells), Sandys (Worcester), Young (St David's), Bullingham (Lincoln).

nothing else but to bastard our children'.[224] In August 1561, Elizabeth issued injunctions from Ipswich 'for the better government of Cathedrals' in which it was stated that prebendaries, students and members of colleges had married 'whereof no small offence groweth to the intent of the founders, and to the quiet and orderly profession of study and learning within the same'. Marriage was not to be prohibited to such men, but they were forbidden to bring their wives and children to live within the precincts of the colleges, under threat of deprivation.[225] On 12 August Cecil wrote to Parker, describing the conduct and opinions of the queen, and it is this letter that Carlson sees as confirmation that Elizabeth's apparent hostility to clerical marriage was based upon the fear of scandal alone.

If the letter is placed in context, however, it is clear that Elizabeth was not only hostile to clerical scandals, but to clerical marriage itself. The tone of the letter, and of Parker's reply to it, suggests that both men knew the strength of the queen's feelings. Cecil wrote that 'Her majesty continueth very ill-affected to the state of matrimony in the clergy. And if I were not therein very stiff, her majesty would utterly and openly condemn and forbid it.' The Ipswich Injunctions, he claimed, had been devised 'for her satisfaction', presumably to prevent harsher measures being taken.[226] Parker declared that he was 'in horror to hear such words to come from her mild nature, and christianly learned conscience, as she spake concerning God's holy ordinances and the institution of matrimony'. He was astounded that his marriage was not pleasing to the queen, not doubting that it would please 'God's sacred majesty', and believing that he could stand before God with a clear conscience, 'for all that glorious shine of counterfeited chastity'. The Marian clergy, he claimed, would 'laugh prettily' to see how Elizabeth behaved towards the married clergy.[227] Such sentiments are echoed in the correspondence of English churchmen with continental observers. Bullinger noted that clerical marriage was treated as a 'thing impure, just as was formerly the practice among the priests of antichrist'.[228] This was no prejudice built upon fear of scandal alone. Strype claimed that when Parker appeared before the queen, she not only spoke against the state of matrimony, but even repented that she had ever appointed married men as bishops.[229]

---

[224] *The Correspondence of Matthew Parker DD Archbishop of Canterbury*, ed. J. Bruce and T. Perowne, Parker Society (Cambridge, 1853), pp. 66, 156–8.

[225] Cardwell, *Documentary Annals*, pp. 273–4.

[226] *Parker Correspondence*, p. 148.

[227] Ibid., p. 157.

[228] Letter to Grindal and Horn, September 1566, in H. Robinson, ed., *Original Letters Relative to the English Reformation*, Parker Society, 2 vols (Cambridge, 1847–8), II, p. 338; cf. pp. 129, 164, 359–60.

[229] Strype, *The Life and Acts of Matthew Parker* (Oxford, 1821), I, p. 217.

In 1562, John Veron published *A stronge defence of the maryage of pryestes*, complaining that there were many who still 'kycke against the lawful maryage of the faythful ministers of the church'.[230] Some protests were motivated by fear of clerical avarice, he claimed, the consequence of warnings that the clergy would be preoccupied with their families, and would neglect their flock. Veron responded to such allegations by claiming that there had been more 'godly sermons' preached in the year since the accession of Elizabeth than 'were made in all Queene Maryes time by theyr wyfelesse and virgyne Pryestes'.[231] Clerical celibacy was a poor measure of clerical competence, and the married ministry deserved to be seen as an asset and not a liability. The question of the legality of clerical marriage also aroused Parker's interest and concern. In 1567 he provided a preface to *A Defence of Priestes mariages, stablysshed by the imperiall lawes of the Realme of Englande*, noting, perhaps in light of the opinions of Elizabeth, that the tract was a work 'at these dayes not unprofitable to be read for this controuersie'.[232] The polemical debate which had surrounded the legislation on clerical marriage in the 1530s and 1540s had all but evaporated by 1570, but a collection of theological and historical justifications for a married priesthood survives among Parker's papers, presumably compiled to persuade those, like his queen, who remained unconvinced.[233] There is nothing in this collection, or indeed in Veron's work, that even approaches the vitriolic and highly critical tone of the polemical defences of clerical marriage composed in the 1530s. In contrast to the rhetoric of the 1540s, the possibility that Elizabeth's attitude to clerical marriage placed her in the congregation of Antichrist is not raised. However, the fears of Elizabeth's archbishop of Canterbury and secretary offer little support for Carlson's assertion that the queen was not hostile to clerical marriage in principle.

The 1559 Injunctions had demanded that clergy who intended to marry provide testimony to the character of their wives from two local justices of the peace, and in the diocese of Lincoln, 50 of these 'letters testimonnial' have survived.[234] From the content of these letters, it is clear that ten clergy had married widows, of whom at least two had been married to other clerics. Anne Warren, the widow of Richard Warren, clerk, was examined in 1593 before her marriage to Richard More, and an undated letter of testimony to the character of

---

[230] J. Veron, *A stronge defence of the maryage of pryestes* (1562), RSTC 24687, sig. A2r.

[231] Ibid., sig. B5v.

[232] M. Parker, *A Defence of Priestes marriages agaynst T. Martin* (1567), unpaginated preface.

[233] CCCC MS 109.

[234] LAO, Lic/Cler/W.

Elizabeth Vaughan referred to her as the widow of Francis Vaughan, clerk.[235] Alice Notte, the intended wife of John Gill, was described as 'bothe an honeste maide and also of good fame and name', and those who testified to the character of Elizabeth Harris claimed that she 'is both and hath been ever accompted a modeste maide sober and discrete of her behaviour, descended of honest parents & brought up by them in the feare of God & trewe religion'.[236] None of the letters suggest that the woman concerned would be inappropriate, and most of the diocesan clergy appear to have complied with the 1559 legislation. The few who did not were prosecuted in the diocesan courts; on 7 March 1602 Thomas Banckes, the vicar of Southelkington, appeared, charged with entering into marriage with one Katherine Racke of Louth, without seeking episcopal sanction.[237] In 1599, George Merton, clerk, confessed before the archdeacon's commissary at Lincoln

> that he had procured matrimony to be celebrated in the face of the church between himself and Mary Randes ... within the archdeaconry of Lincoln, without having observed all things prescribed in the twenty ninth injunction of the year 1559, and submitted himself to the correction of the said master Thomas.[238]

Merton's actions seem particularly ill advised, as the commissary, Thomas Randes, was his father-in-law. The Lincoln records are a unique collection of such material, yet are highly revealing of attitudes to clerical marriage, and of perceptions of the clerical estate. The fact that such letters were required at all suggests that the Catholic polemic of previous decades had struck a chord: allegations that the wives of clergy were women of low standing and dubious moral character might be stemmed if the background of the women involved were subject to thorough investigation. The need to seek episcopal approval before marriage was deemed valid might also have served to ensure that the manse acted as a model of godly family life, or as an inspiration to others. However, these legal requirements could equally be detrimental to the standing of the clergy and to the public perception of their wives. The requirement that letters testimonial be provided was an additional obstacle which suggested that church and state still feared the implications of the lifting of the discipline of celibacy. Any action which appeared less than a wholehearted endorsement of clerical marriage would clearly encourage those individuals identified by Jewel who viewed the sacraments and

[235] LAO, Lic/Cler/W, fols 2, 74.
[236] Ibid., fols 1, 4.
[237] LAO, Additional Register I, fols 181; 145v.
[238] C.W. Foster, 'The State of the Church in the Reigns of Elizabeth and James I as illustrated by documents relating to the diocese of Lincoln' (vol.1) Lincoln Record Society, 23 (1926), xxii.

ministry of married clergy as inferior to those of their celibate colleagues.[239] Even after 1559, the life of married clergy was far from secure.

Despite the upheavals of the previous decade, and the ambivalent attitude of the queen, many diocesan clergy married in the decade after 1559. In the Winchester diocese, one third of the clergy in the archdeaconry of Surrey, and one quarter of the clergy in the Winchester archdeaconry were described as married in the 1561 returns. On the Isle of Wight, married clergy were in the majority.[240] In Worcester, 28 of the 165 clergy were married, and in the dioceses of Rochester and Canterbury, half the clergy had married.[241] Eighty-three of the clergy in the diocese of Salisbury were described as married in 1561.[242] In the diocese of Lincoln, 13 of the 61 Cathedral clergy had definitely married by 1561, and in the archdeaconry of Lincoln 64 of the 317 priests were described as married in the 1561 returns. In the other archdeaconries, a smaller proportion of the clergy had married by 1561. Thirty-one of the 194 clergy in Buckingham were described as married, but only 9 of the 129 priests in the archdeaconry of Leicester. In the diocese as a whole, 17.2 per cent of the clergy were described as married in the returns of 1561.[243] For the diocese of Lincoln, further details are available in *Libri Cleri* for Leicester, Lincoln and Stow in 1576, and for Stow in 1598. In Lincoln and Stow, 229 (57.25 per cent) priests were described as married in 1576, and in Leicester 64 (43 per cent) clergy had married. By 1598, in the archdeaconry of Stow, three quarters of the 80 clergy were described as married.[244]

On 12 January 1571, the Winchester priest Hugh Tunckes declared that he had married because 'I am called a papist and so hooted at.'[245] By 1571, it appeared that the clergy in the diocese of Winchester were expected to marry, and that their marriages were taken as a sign of their acceptance of the reformed church. The manner in which Tunckes justified his marriage is reminiscent of the attempts of Archbishop Holgate to defend his own marriage to Barbara Wentworth, but the circumstances demonstrate how much had changed in the intervening decades. Holgate had married, he claimed, in accordance with the wishes

---

[239] See p. 171 above.

[240] CCCC MS 122.

[241] D.M. Barratt, 'The Condition of the Parish Clergy between the Reformation and 1660, with special reference to the dioceses of Oxford, Worcester, and Gloucester', unpublished D.Phil., University of Oxford (1949), p. 346.

[242] CCCC MS 97.

[243] CCCC MS 97; Foster, 'The State of the Church', p. 455.

[244] Foster, 'The State of the Church', p. 455.

[245] A.J. Willis, *Winchester Consistory Court Depositions 1561–1602* (Winchester, 1960), pp. 4–8.

of Northumberland, but, if Parkyn is to be believed, without the support of the majority of the laity. Tunckes's marriage may have proved his doctrinal credentials to the people, but was certainly not in accordance with the express wishes of the queen. Overall, the accession of Elizabeth renewed enthusiasm for marriage among the English clergy, and the fate of the Edwardian married clergy does not appear to have created widespread clerical antipathy to marriage in the first decade of the new reign. Even without specific legislation in favour of such unions, more clergy in the diocese of Lincoln married between 1559 and 1561 than in the four years of Edward's reign in which such marriages were legal.

The incidence of clerical marriage in the diocese of Lincoln by 1576 supports the general tone of Carlson's argument that clerical marriage was soon to become a secure feature of the Elizabethan church.[246] However, a degree of caution should be exercised. Carlson argues that clerical marriage was secure by 1563, only two years after the Statute of Ipswich, and the assessment of the opinions of the queen by Parker and Cecil. The legality of clerical marriage may have been established in the dioceses by 1563, but there is nothing to suggest that Elizabeth regarded a married priesthood as a necessary feature of her church. Yet the fact that clerical marriage was still legally insecure in the first years of Elizabeth's reign does not appear to have been a powerful disincentive to marry. In other areas, the Elizabethan Reformation was slow to advance, and many clergy were reluctant to commit themselves to the latest changes in religion. Christopher Haigh cites the testimony of Thomas Bentham in October 1560 that in Shropshire 'the most part of the churches ... hath not only yet their altars standing but also their images reserved and conveyed away'.[247] The High Commission at York issued repeated orders for the removal of images, and many churches retained their rood lofts until the 1570s.[248] Eamon Duffy argues that 'the confusion evident in the minds of the clergy and laity about the likely direction of religious policy in the regime is understandable even as late as 1560'.[249] It might be expected, then, that this confusion among the clergy would be expressed in a reluctance to enter into marriages in the first months of the reign, especially given the reactions of the laity to married clergy after 1549. Even if, as Collinson argues, the reign of Elizabeth was indeed 'the end of the beginning'[250] of the English Reformation, this does not explain the confident decision of so many

---

[246] Carlson, *Marriage and the English Reformation*, p. 64.

[247] Haigh, *English Reformations*, p. 245; Duffy, *Stripping of the Altars*, pp. 572ff.

[248] Haigh, *English Reformations*, p. 245-6.

[249] Duffy, *Stripping of the Altars*, p. 567.

[250] P. Collinson, 'The Elizabethan Church and the New Religion', in C. Haigh ed., *The Reign of Elizabeth* (Basingstoke, 1988), p. 194.

clergy to marry in the first years after the accession of the new queen.

The memory of the action against married priests in 1554–55 certainly did not dissuade clergy from marrying after 1559. Indeed, as Parker's survey of the church demonstrates, several deprived Marian priests described themselves as married in 1561, suggesting that the events of the previous reign had not persuaded even this group that marriage was too much of a risk in unstable times.[251] It seems more likely that the restitution of the deprived Marian clergy after 1559 gave a clear indication of the attitude of the new regime to married priests. Those clergy who had married after 1549 had done so with little promise of security, given the legal position of married priests in the aftermath of the Act of Six Articles, and their Elizabethan counterparts appear to have followed their example. Clergy had accommodated themselves to doctrinal change throughout the middle decades of the sixteenth century, and welcomed the opportunity to marry on the two occasions that it arose. In the first years of Elizabeth's reign, the presence of married bishops in the Elizabethan church was an encouraging sign that the personal views of the queen would not present a threat to a married priesthood. Local influences had played an important role in the decision of the clergy to marry after 1549; for the majority of those who married after 1559 it is likely that these influences were stronger than the reported ambivalence of the queen. As with other aspects of the Reformation, the importance of habit in inculcating acceptance of a married priesthood should not be underestimated. The Edwardian legislation on clerical marriage stood for only four years, with the result that the Marian deprivations affected only a minority of the clergy. If sympathy with reform, coupled with the example of other priests, influenced the decision of Edwardian clergy to marry, the effect in Elizabeth's reign would be all the more dramatic. The longer that the clergy were able to exert their freedom to marry, the deeper the roots of the married priesthood would become. Elizabeth's attitude to clerical marriage may have been far from positive, but in the absence of any general prohibition of such marriages, time alone would secure the future of the married priesthood.

---

[251] For example, Thomas Cradocke and Thomas Arnolde (Salisbury); CCCC MS 97, fols 194v, 192v; William Wakelin, Henry Bissel (Winchester), CCCC MS 122, fols 117r, 126r.

Conclusion

In 1567, Matthew Parker summarized the problem which had exercised the minds and pens of Reformation polemicists for half a century. 'The question is', Parker wrote, 'whether to them that cannot containe, mariage were not more meete to be graunted. And whether a priest in chaste matrimonie maie not do the office of a prieste, as the scripture requireth of hym.'[1] The question was far from new in the sixteenth century, but was approached with new urgency after Luther's protest.[2] Parker's summary is concise if simplistic. The Reformation debate was not limited to the narrow question of whether married priests could exercise their office, but touched upon the most central issues of theology and ecclesiology, and contributed to the formation of confessional identity. The celibacy of the clergy was discussed in debates on the theology of the Eucharist and the nature of doctrinal authority, and proved to be central to the identification of orthodoxy and error, the true church and the false in the past and the present.

In all these aspects, the discussion of clerical celibacy in the works of English Protestant polemicists reveals the centrality of the Bible to their ideology. Scripture was not merely a vast source text which could be ransacked to find support for theological opinions; it was the key to the understanding of the events of past and present. The importance of the issue of clerical celibacy to such an understanding is clear from the works of English writers in exile in the 1540s. Clerical celibacy was identified as an innovation, a departure from the law of God. The prohibition of clerical marriage was the mark of the false church, and the English church, which upheld the celibate priesthood, was therefore a church as yet unreformed. The argument was sharpened by the application of Old Testament models to the religious situation in England. Richard Rex has argued that Henry VIII's kingship 'was recast by the supremacy propaganda into the image of the Old Testament monarchs', with the result that Henry then began to 'play the part'.[3] Whatever the intention of Henry VIII and his propagandists, however, the use of such images by

---

[1] M. Parker, ed., *A Defence of Priestes mariages agaynst T. Martin* (1567), RSTC 17519, sig. C3r.

[2] For the mediaeval debate see A.L. Barstow, 'Married Priests and the Reforming Papacy: The eleventh century debates', *Texts and Studies in Religion*, 12 (1982); J. Stecher, *Oeuvres de Jean Lemaire de Belges*, 3 vols (Louvain, 1885), III, 'De La Difference des schismes et des Conciles', pp. 245, 358–9; P. Vergil, *De Inventoribus Rerum*, bk. V, ca. 4.

[3] R. Rex, *Henry VIII and the English Reformation* (Basingstoke, 1993), p. 173; J.N. King, *English Reformation Literature. The Tudor Origins of the Protestant Tradition* (Princeton, 1982), ch. 4; C.J. Bradshaw, 'David or Josiah? Old Testament Kings as

Protestant polemicists in the 1540s was far removed from the representation of Henry VIII as the godly reforming king. Clerical celibacy was central to their identification of the king as a member of the historical false church. Just as the clergy were either married or they were not, an individual was either a member (or Supreme Head) of the false church, or he was not. Modern historians have argued that the Reformation had not been embraced by the English people by 1547; in the eyes of the Protestant writers of the 1540s, it had not been yet embraced by the national church.[4] The affairs of secular princes were inseparable from issues of doctrine.

The debate over clerical marriage, and indeed Reformation polemic in general, testifies to the importance of theology to the history of the sixteenth century. In the view of Dickens and Tonkin, 'Historians who exclude theology from their enquiries are usually committing a supreme act of folly.' The Protestant Reformation was a 'conscious, essentially religious, mission', with the aim of restoring Christianity to a state untouched by the inventions and manipulations of men.[5] The debate over clerical marriage in the sixteenth century supports such a claim. The lifting of the prohibition on clerical marriage in 1549 was fundamentally a religious piece of legislation; it was an act of doctrinal iconoclasm which upheld the supremacy of the word of God over the laws of men. In the campaign for the legalization of clerical marriage, Protestant polemicists wrote with the same motives as those who called for the destruction of images – the restoration of true, biblical religion in a church purged of idolatry.

For Protestant writers in exile during the reigns of Henry VIII and Mary, there could be no compromise with the religion of Antichrist which was enforced at home. Such dogmatic certainties were beyond the reach of the majority. For those who remained in England, with the exception of the martyrs of Foxe's history, accommodation was more viable than resistance. The experience of the Edwardian married clergy is a clear demonstration of the chasm that could exist between ideology and reality. The married priesthood might have been the mark of the true church, but in the eyes of the deprived married priests in Mary's reign, it was also the road to poverty and insecurity. Those clergy who had

Exemplars in Edwardian Religious Polemic', in B. Gordon, ed., *Protestant History and Identity in Sixteenth-Century Europe. vol. II. The Later Reformation* (Aldershot, 1996), pp. 77–91.

[4] C. Haigh, *English Reformations. Religion, Politics and Society under the Tudors* (Oxford, 1993), chs 6–9; E. Duffy, *The Stripping of the Altars. Traditional Religion in England 1400–1580* (New Haven, 1992), ch. 14.

[5] A.G. Dickens and J. Tonkin, *The Reformation in Historical Thought* (Oxford, 1985), pp. 1, 327.

married after 1549 voluntarily embraced one aspect of Edwardian Protestantism, but many had also fulfilled the requirements of pre-Reformation Catholicism and the Henrician Reformation, and were to acquiesce in the restoration of Catholicism under Mary. However, the fact that some married clergy were clearly sympathetic to Protestantism should act as a caveat to the condemnation of all married priests as opportunistic time-servers practising a degree of theological eclecticism; even the Marian exiles recognized that there could be sound practical considerations behind the decision to conform.[6]

The behaviour of married clergy in England in the middle decades of the sixteenth century is a clear demonstration of the impact of local, and no doubt personal, influences upon the reactions of an individual to national religious change. The willingness of the clergy to acquiesce in religious change does not mean that they had no opinions on such matters; Robert Parkyn held his cure in the reigns of three Tudor monarchs, but clearly had strong views on the content of the religious settlements that they promulgated. However, the conduct of the married Edwardian clergy reveals some of the problems faced by the Marian church, and indeed the sixteenth-century English church as a whole. Creating a committed ministry, equipped for the reformation of the English church, would not be an easy task, given the propensity of the clergy to accommodate rather than agitate in defence of their beliefs. The Protestant message, even if it was preached by a minister with reformist sympathies, was likely to be treated with scepticism by those who had seen the same minister married in 1549, but separated from his wife and celebrating Mass in 1554.

The changing fortunes of clerical marriage and married clergy are incomprehensible outside the context of the doctrinal considerations which dominated the polemical debate over clerical celibacy in the sixteenth century. Even where the conduct of the married clergy did not live up to the expectations of the reformers, the fact that such marriages were legal at all was testimony to the labours of those who had defended the right of priests to marry. Whatever their views on clerical marriage, successive monarchs from Henry VIII to Elizabeth recognized that the issue was one that demanded consideration. At times, the English debate on clerical marriage was influenced by events in England: the Six Articles of 1539, the legalization of clerical marriage in 1549, and the deprivation of married priests after 1553 prompted a variety of reactions from Catholic and Protestant polemicists. However, the debate between English writers was not conducted in isolation. The marriage of Luther

---

[6] A. Pettegree, *Marian Protestantism. Six Studies* (Aldershot, 1996), p. 26 and more generally, ch. 4.

and other German reformers dominated discussions in the 1520s, the Act of Six Articles attracted comment from foreign reformers, the 1540s and 1550s witnessed literary exchanges between English and continental writers, and the experience of exile shaped the ideology of English Protestant writers in the mid-sixteenth century. The Protestant interpretation of history by Barnes and Bale owed much to the labours of German scholars, and Matthias Flacius and the Magdeburg Centuriators exercised a powerful influence on the composition of Foxe's *Actes and Monuments*. The debate on clerical celibacy testifies to the power of continental influences in the early English Reformation, and the content of the *Actes and Monuments* confirms Diarmaid MacCulloch's contention that the accession of Elizabeth did not deserve the headline '1559 Settlement passed by parliament: Continent cut off'.[7] The question of whether the clergy should be allowed to marry had no conclusive answer by 1559, but time was on the side of the married ministry. Writing in 1546, John Bale mocked the claim of his opponents that marriage was 'a most co[n]tagyouse poyson to holye orders'; the persistence and virulence of the debate on clerical marriage in the sixteenth century suggests that it was a poison which many had drunk.[8]

---

[7] D. MacCulloch, *The Later Reformation in England 1547–1603* (Basingstoke, 1990), p. 7.

[8] J. Bale, *The First Examinacyon of Anne Askewe, lately martyred in Smythfelde* (Wesel, 1546), RSTC 848, sig. A7v.

Appendix

Diocesan Maps

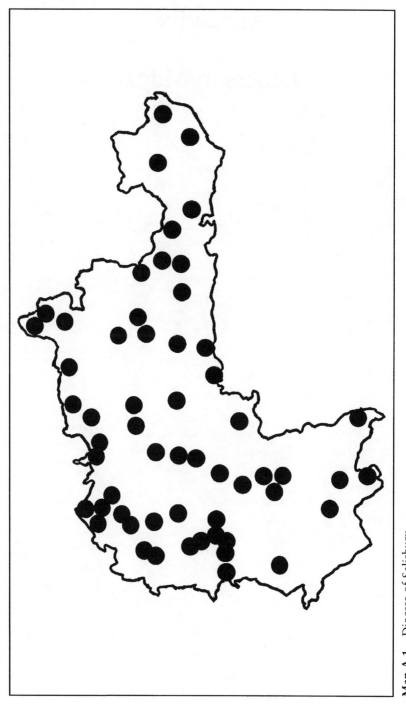

Map A.1   Diocese of Salisbury

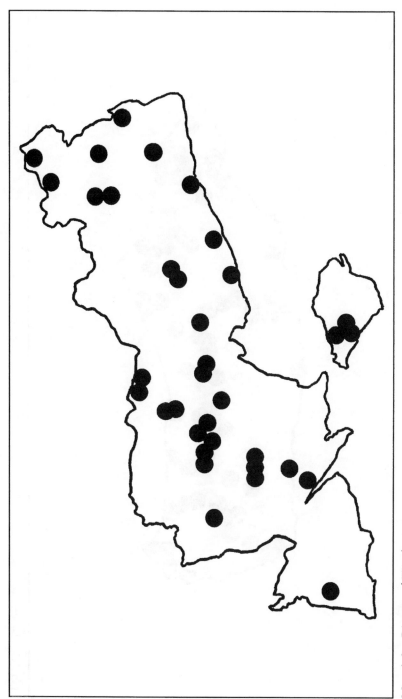

Map A.2   Diocese of Winchester

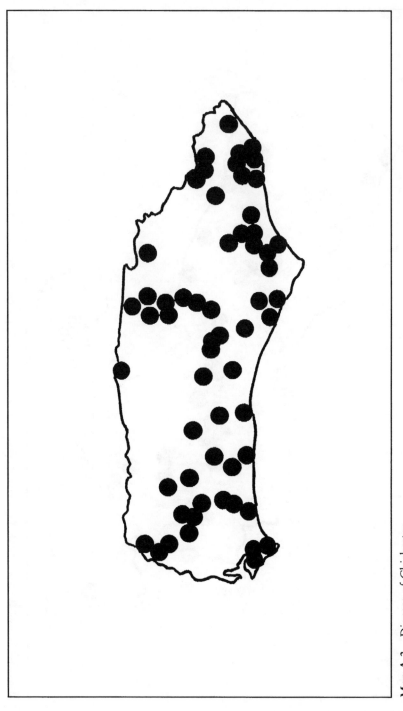

Map A.3   Diocese of Chichester

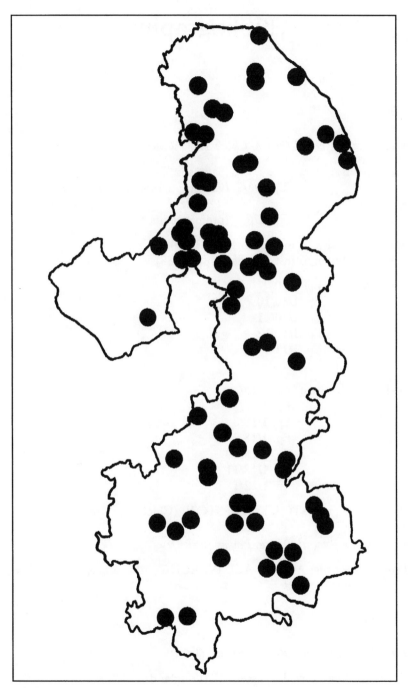

Map A.4   Diocese of Lincoln

Bibliography

Manuscript Sources

Chichester

West Sussex Record Office, Chichester (WSRO)

Episcopal Registers: Ep. 1/1/6 (Sampson, Day, Scory)
Ep. 1/1/7 (Christopherson, Barlow, Curteys, Bickley)
Ep. 1/6 (presentments to benefices)

MP 1095 (Index to Institutions, 1503–59)
MP 1096 (Index to Institutions, 1560–1658)

Court Books: Ep. 1/10/9
Ep. 1/10/10
Ep. 1/10/11
Ep. 1/10/12
Ep. 1/11/1
Ep. 2/9/1

Visitation Records: Ep. 1/18/5
Ep. 1/18/7
Ep. 1/18/8
Ep. 1/18/9
Ep. 1/18/10
Ep. 1/18/11
Ep. 1/22/1

Probate Records: STC I, STC II, STC III (Chichester Archdeaconry)

East Sussex Record Office, Lewes (ESRO)

Probate Records: ACL III, ACL IV, ACL V, ACL VI, ACL VII (Lewes Archdeaconry)

Lincoln

Lincolnshire County Record Office (LAO)

Episcopal Registers: LRO Reg. 27 (Longland)
LRO Reg. 28 (composite)

Courts Records:	Cij 2 (Lincoln Archdeaconry 1549–53)
	Cij 3 (Lincoln Archdeaconry 1553–78
	Cj 7 (Episcopal Court Book 1554–55)
	Cj 3 (Episcopal Court Book, composite)
	Box 58/1
	Box 59/1
Visitation Records	Vij 13 (1551–56)
	Vij 2 *c.* 1564
Lic/Cler/W:	Letters Testimonial for clerical wives

Probate Records

Salisbury

Wiltshire County Record Office, Trowbridge (WRO)

Episcopal Registers: Nicholas Shaxton, 1535–39
John Capon, 1539–57
John Jewel, 1560–71

Court Books, Visitation Records: D1/39/1/1
D1/39/1/2
D1/42/3
D1/42/4
D1/43/1
D1/43/2
D1/43/3
D4/3/1
D5/3/1

Probate Records: Consistory Court of Sarum
Archdeaconry of Sarum
Archdeaconry of Wiltshire
Peculiars

Winchester

Hampshire Record Office (HRO)

Episcopal Registers: 21 M 65 / A1/24–26

Court Books: 21 M 65 C1/5/1
21 M 65 C1/6
21 M 65 C1/7
21 M 65 C1/14/2
21 M 65 C/2/4–13

Depositions: 21 M 65 C3/4
                        21 M 65 C3/5
                        21 M 65 C3/7
                        21 M 65 C6/2

Visitation Records: 21 M 65 B1/6
                        21 M 65 B1/7
                        21 M 65 B1/8
                        21 M 65 B1/9
                        21 M 65 B1/10

Probate Records

Public Record Office

Wills proved in the Prerogative Court of Canterbury
E 164/31 (Pension List of Cardinal Pole, 1556)
PROB 34 / 1 (Suits for the restoration of married clergy deprived by
    Mary; London, Norwich, Ely)
PRO C/1 – Early Chancery Proceedings

British Library

Additional MSS 33, 39326–39456, 29546
Cottonian MSS Cleo E iv, Cleo E v
Harleian MSS 416, 421, 590, 3838
Lansdowne MSS 443–5, 762
Stow MSS 269

Cambridge University Library

Add. MSS 6740 (List of Sussex incumbents since the Reformation)

Corpus Christi College, Cambridge

MS 105
MS 109
MS 113
MS 119
MS 122 (Parker Returns for 1561, Lincoln and Winchester)

Printed Primary Sources

Acts of the Privy Council of England, ed. J.R. Dasent, 32 vols (1890–1907)

Aelfric (tr. M. Parker), *A Testimonie of Antiquitie, shewing the auncient fayth in the church of England touching the sacrament of the body and blooude of the Lord*, tr. Matthew Parker (1562), RSTC 159

Agrippa, C., *The Commendation of Matrimony*, tr. David Clapam (1545), RSTC 202

Angel, J., *The Agrement of the holye fathers and Doctors of the Churche upon the cheifest articles of Christian Religion* (1555), RSTC 634

Anon, *A New Dialogue called the endightment agaynste mother Messe* (1548), RSTC 20499

Anon., *Here begynneth a boke called the faule of the Romyshe churche* (1548), RSTC 21305

Anon., *A Commysion sent to the bloudy butcher byshop of London and to al conuents of Frers by the hight and mighty prince lord, Sathanas the deuill of Hell*, (1557?), RSTC 3286

Bale, J., *A Comedy Concernynge thre Lawes of Nature, Moses, and Christ* (Wesel, 1538), RTSC 1287

————, *Yet a Course at the Romyshe Foxe. A Dysclosynge or openyng of the Manne of Synne* (Antwerp, 1543), RSTC 1309

————, *The Epistle Exhortatorye of an Englyshe Christiane* (Antwerp, 1544), RSTC 1291

————, *A Mysterye of inyquyte contayned within the heretycall Genealogye of Ponce Pantolabus* (Antwerp, 1545), RSTC 1303

————, *The Actes of the Englysh Votaries*, first part (Antwerp, 1546), RSTC 1270

————, *The Second Part or Contynuacyon of the Actes of the Englysh Votaries* (1551), RSTC 1273.5

————, *The First Examinacyon of Anne Askewe, lately martyred in Smythfelde*, (Wesel, 1546), RSTC 848

————, *The lattre examynacyon of Anne Askewe, with the elucydacyon of J. Bale* (Wesel, 1547), RSTC 850

————, *An Answere to a papystycall exhortacyon, to auoyde false doctryne* (Antwerp, 1548), RSTC 1274a

————, *The Apology of Johan Bale Agaynste a Ranke Papyst* (1550), RSTC 1275

————, *The Image of Both Churches after the moste wonderful and heauenly Reuelacion of sainct John the Eua[n]gelist* (1550), RSTC 1298

————, *An Expostulation or complaynte agaynste the blasphemyes of a franticke papyst of Hampshyre* (1551), RSTC 1294

————, *Scriptorum Illustriu[m] Maioris Brytanniae quam nunc Angliam & Scotiam Vocant: Catalogus* (Basle, 1557)

————, *Acta Romanorvm Pontificum a dispersione discipulorum Christi: ad temora Pauli quarti* (Basle, 1558)

————, *A Declaration of Edmonde Bonner's Articles concerning the cleargy of Lo[n]don dyocese ... 1554* (1561), RSTC 1289

———— (tr. John Studley), *The Pageant of Popes, contayninge the lyues of all the Bishops of Rome from the beginninge of them to the yeare of Grace 1555* (1574), RSTC 1304

Barlow, W., *A Dyaloge descrybyng the orygynall grou[n]d of these Lutheran faccyons* (1531), RSTC 1461

Barnes, R., *A Supplication unto the most gracious prince Henry VIII* (1534), RSTC 1471

————, *Sentenciae ex Doctoribus Collectae* (Wittenberg, 1536)

————, *Vitae Romanorum Pontificum, quos papas uocamus summa diligentia ec fide collectae* (Basle, 1555)

Bateson, M., ed., *A Collection of Original Letters from the Bishops to the Privy Council, 1564*, Camden Society ns. 53 (1895)

Becon, T., *The Worckes of Thomas Becon whiche he hath hytherto made and published with diuerse other newe Bookes added* (1564), RSTC 1710

Bonner, E., *A Profitable and Necessarye doctrine with certayne homelyes* (1555), RSTC 3281.5

Bradford, J., *The Writings of John Bradford*, ed. A. Townsend, Parker Society (Cambridge, 1853)

Brinklow, H., *Complaynt of Roderick Mors and Lamentacyon of a Christen Agaynste the Cytye of London*, ed. J.S. Cooper, *Early English Texts Series*, extra series 22 (1874)

Bucer, M. (tr. Thomas Hoby), *The Gratulation of the moost famous clerke M. Bucer* (1549), RSTC 3963

Bullinger, H. (tr. Miles Coverdale), *The Golden Boke of Christen Matrimonye*, (1541), RSTC 4045

———— (tr. Miles Coverdale, with preface by Thomas Becon), *The Golden Boke of Christen Matrimonye* (1543), RSTC 4046

———— (tr. J. Daues), *A Hvndred Sermons vpo[n] the Apocalips of Jesu Christe* (1561), RSTC 4061

————, *A Commentary on Daniel*, 2 vols (Oxford, 1986)

———— (tr. H.I.), *Fiftie Godlie and Learned Sermons divided into fiue decades* (1577), RTSC 4056

Calendar of the Patent Rolls Preserved in the Public Record Office (1901–66)

Calendar of State Papers Domestic, Edward VI, Philip and Mary, Elizabeth, 9 vols. (1856–72)

Calvin, J. (tr. J.W. Fraser, ed. D.W. and T.F. Torrance), *The First Epistle of Paul to the Corinthians* (Edinburgh, 1960)

——— (tr. W.B. Johnstone, ed. D.W. Torrance), *The Epistle of Paul the Apostle to the Hebrews and the first and second Epistles of St Peter* (Edinburgh, 1963)

——— (tr. T.A. Smail, ed. D.W. and T.F. Torrance), *The Second Epistle of Paul the Apostle to the Corinthians and the Epistles to Timothy, Titus, and Philemon* (Edinburgh, 1964)

——— (tr. J.R.S. Reid), *The Necessity of Reforming the Church*, Library of Christian Classics, vol. 22 (1954)

Cardwell, E., *Documentary Annals of the Reformed Church of England*, 2 vols (Oxford, 1839)

Carion, J., *The Thre bokes of Cronicles whyche John Carion ... Gathered with great diligence of the beste authors* (1550), RSTC 4626

Catherine of Siena, *Here Begynneth the orcharde of Syon in the whiche is conteyned the reuelacyon of seynt Ketheryne of Sene* (1519), RSTC 4815

Cole, R.E.G., 'Chapter Acts of the Cathedral Church of St Mary of Lincoln AD 1547–1559', *Lincoln Record Society*, 15 (1920)

Concilia Magnae Britanniae et Hiberniae, ed. D. Wilkins (1737)

Councils and Synods with other Documents Relating to the English Church, ed. D. Whitelock, M. Brett and C.N.L. Brooke, 2 vols (Oxford, 1981)

Coverdale, M., *Writings and Translations of Myles Coverdale, Bishop of Exeter*, ed. G. Pearson, Parker Society (Cambridge, 1844)

———, *Remains of Miles Coverdale, Bishop of Exeter*, ed. G. Pearson, Parker Society (Cambridge, 1846)

Cranmer, T. (E.P.), *A Confutatio[n] of Unwritten verities / both bi the holye scriptures and moste auncient authors* (Wesel, 1556), RSTC 5996

Crowley, R., *A Confutation of .xiii. Articles wherunto Nicholas Shaxton late byshop of Salisbury subscribed* (1548), RSTC 6083

———, *The way to wealth, wherein is taught a remedy for sedicion* (1550), RSTC 6096

———, *Depositions and Other Proceedings from the Courts of Durham extending from 1311 to the reign of Elizabeth*, ed. J. Raine, Surtees Society, 21 (1845)

Dionysius Carthusianus, *The Lyfe of Prestes* (1533), RSTC 6894

Erasmus, D., *The Collected Works of Erasmus*, ed. R.D. Sider (Toronto, 1974–)

——— (ed. N. Udall), *The First Tome or Volume of the paraphrase of Erasmus vpon the Newe Testamente* (1548), RSTC 2854

Esquillus, P., (tr. William Baldwin), *Wonderfull Newes of the death of*

Paul the .iii. last byshop of Rome & of diuerse thynges that after his death haue happened (1551), RSTC 10532

Flacius, M., *Catalogus Testivm Veritatis, qui ante Nostram Aetatem Reclamarunt Papae* (Basle, 1566)

Foster, C.W., 'The Chantry Certificates for Lincoln and Lincolnshire, returned in 1548', *Associated Architectural Societies Reports*, 37 (1923–5), 18–106

———, 'Certificates or Returns of all Fees, Annuities, Corrodies or Pensions payable to Religious Persons, 1555–6', *AASR*, 37 (1923–5), 276–94

———, 'Lincoln Episcopal Records in the Time of Thomas Cooper, Bishop of Lincoln 1571–1584', *Lincoln Record Society*, 2 (1912)

———, 'The state of the Church in the reigns of Elizabeth and James I as illustrated by documents relating to the Diocese of Lincoln', *Lincoln Record Society*, 23 (1926)

Foxe, J., *The Actes and Monuments of these latter and perillous dayes* (1563), RSTC 11222

———, *The Actes and Monuments of these latter and perillous dayes* (1570), RSTC 11223

——— (tr. J. Bell), *The Pope Confuted. The Holy and Apostolique Church Confuting the Pope* (1580), RSTC 11241

———, ed., *The Whole Workes of W. Tyndall, Iohn Frith and Doct. Barnes, three worthy martyrs and principall teachers of this churche of Englande* (1573), RSTC 24436

Frere, W.H., *Visitation Articles and Injunctions for the Period of the Reformation*, 3 vols (Alcuin Club, 1910)

Frith, J., *A Pistle to the christen reader: The reuelacion of antichrist* (Antwerp, 1529), RSTC 11394

Furnivall, F.J., *Harrisons Description of England in Shakespeare's Youth* (1877)

Gardiner, S., *Stephani Vvinton Episcopi Angli ad Martinvm Bucerum de Impudentia euisedem Pseudologia Conquestio* (Louvain, 1544)

———, *Stephani Winton Episcopi Angli as Martinum Bvcervm epistolas qua cessantem hactenus & cunctantem ac frustratoria responsionis pollicitatione* (Louvain, 1546)

———, *Exetasis Testimoniorum quae Martinus Bucerus ex sanctis patribus non sancte edidit* (Louvain, 1554)

Gilby, A., *An Ansvver to the Deuillish Detection of Stephane Gardiner* (1547), RSTC 11884

———, *A Commentary upon the Prophet Mycha* (1551), RSTC 11886

The Grey Friars' Chronicle of London, ed. J.G. Nicholls, Camden Society o.s. 53 (1852)

Gualter, R. (tr. J. Old), *Antichrist: that is to say a true reporte that Antichriste is come* (1556) RSTC 25009

Gwynneth, J., *A declaration of the state wherein all heretikes dooe leade their liues* (1554), RSTC 12558

Harpsfield, N., *Dialogi Sex contra Svmmi Pontificatvs, Monasticae Vitae Sanctorvm, Sacrarvm Imaginum Oppugnatores et Pseudomartyres* (Antwerp, 1566)

Harrington, W., *In this boke are conteyned / the commendacions of matrymony*, (1528), RSTC 12799

Hilarie, H., *The Resurreccion of the Masse / with the wonderful vertues of the same*, (Wesel, 1554), RSTC 13457

Hooper, J., *Early Writings of John Hooper DD, Lord Bishop of Gloucester and Worcester, martyr, 1555*, ed. S. Carr, Parker Society (Cambridge, 1843)

————, *Later Writings of Bishop Hooper together with his letters and other pieces*, ed. C.H. Nevinson, Parker Society (Cambridge, 1852)

Huggarde, M., *The Displaying of the Protestantes & sondry their practises* (1556), RSTC 13558

James, T., *A Manvduction or Introduction vnto Diuinitie* (Oxford, 1625), RSTC 14460

Jewel, J., *The Works of John Jewel, Bishop of Salisbury*, ed. J. Ayre, Parker Society, 4 vols (Cambridge, 1845–50)

Joye, G., *The Letters whych Johan Ashwell Priour of Newnham Abbey ... sente secretly to the byshope of Lincolne* (Antwerp, 1531), RSTC 845

————, *The Defence of the Mariage of Preistes Agenst Steuen Gardiner* (Antwerp, 1541), RSTC 21804

————, *The Rekening and declaratio[n] of the faith of H. Zwingly* (Antwerp, 1543), RSTC 26138

————, *The Exposicion of Daniel the Prophete gathered oute of Philip Melanchthon / Johan Ecolampadius / Conrade Pellicane / out of Johan Draconite &c.* (Antwerp, 1545), RSTC 14823

Judex, M. and Wigand, J., *Ecclesiastica Historia* (Basle, 1560–74)

Latimer, H., *Sermons of Hugh Latimer, sometime bishop of Worcester*, ed. G.E. Corrie, Parker Society (Cambridge, 1844)

————, *Sermons and Remains of Hugh Latimer*, ed. E. Corrie, Parker Society (Cambridge, 1845)

The Lay Folks Mass Book, ed. T.F. Simmons, EETS, 71 (1879)

Lemaire, J., *Oeuvres de Jean Lemaire de Belges*, ed. J. Stecher, 3 vols (Louvain, 1885)

Le Neve, J., *Fasti Ecclesiae Anglicanae, 1300–1541* (12 vols), 1541–1857 (in progress), (1962–present)

Letters and Papers Foreign and Domestic of the reign of Henry VIII, ed. J.S. Brewer and R.H. Brodie, 21 vols (1862–1932)

Luther, M., *Luther's Works. American Edition*, ed. J. Pelikan and H.C. Oswald, 56 vols (St Louis, 1955–86)

Marcort, A., *A Declaration of the Masse* (1548), RSTC 17314

Martin, T., *A Treatise declaryng and plainly provyng that the pretensed marriage of priestes ... is no mariage* (1554), RSTC 17517

Martyr, P., *Defensio de Petri Martyris Vermilii Florentini divinarum literarum in schola Tigurina* (Basle, 1559)

———— (tr. A. Marten), *The Commonplaces of the most famous and renowned Diuine Doctor Peter Martyr* (1583), RSTC 24669

Melanchthon, P. (tr. George Joye), *A very godly defense full of lerning defending the mariage of preistes* (Antwerp, 1541), RSTC 17798

Mirk's Festial. A Collection of Homilies by Johannes Mirkus, ed. T. Erbe, *EETS*, 96 (1905)

Monumenta Germaniae Historiae inde ab Christi quingentesimo vsque ad annum millesimum et quingentesimum. Libelli de Lite, vol. I (Hanover, 1891)

More, T., *Utopia*, ed. E. Surtz, S.J. Hexter and J.H. Hexter, *CW*, 4 (1963)

————, *Responsio ad Lutherum*, ed. J.M. Headley, *CW*, 5 (1969)

————, *A Dialogue Concerning Heresies*, ed. T.M.C. Lawler, G. Marc'hadour and R.C. Marius, *CW*, 6 (1981)

————, *Letter to Bugenhagen, Supplication of Souls, Letter against Frith*, ed. F. Manley, G. Marc'hadour, R. Marius and C.H. Miller, *CW*, 7 (1990)

————, *The Apology*, ed. J.B. Trapp, *CW*, 9 (1979)

————, *De Tristitia Christi*, ed. C.H. Miller, *CW*, 14 (1976)

————, *The Confutation of Tyndale' Answer*, ed. L.A. Schuster, R.C. Marius, J.P. Lusardi and R.J. Schoek, *CW*, 8 (1973)

Old, J., *A Short Description of Antichrist vnto the Nobilitie of Englande* (Emden, 1555? 1557?), RSTC 673

Parker, H., *Dives and pauper* (1536), RSTC 19214

————, *Dives and Pauper*, ed. P.H. Barnum, *EETS*, 275, 280 (1976)

Parker, M., *Epistolae duae D.Volusiani Episcopi Carthaginensis ad Nicholaum papam primum, de Celibatu Cleri* (1569), RSTC 24872

———— (ed.), *A Defence of Priestes mariages agaynst T. Martin* (1567), RSTC 17519

————, *Correspondence of Matthew Parker*, ed. J. Bruce and T. Perowne, Parker Society (Cambridge, 1853)

Peckham, W.D., ed., 'A Diocesan Visitation of 1553', *Sussex Archaeological Collections*, 77 (1936), 93–105

————, 'The Acts of the Dean and Chapter of the cathedral Church of Chichester', *Sussex Record Society*, 58 (1959)

Phillipps, T., *Institutiones Clericorum in Comitatu Wiltoniae anno 1297 ad annum 1810* (1825)

Ponet, J., *A defence for the mariage of Priestes, by Scripture and Aunciente Wryters*, (1549), RSTC 20176

————, *An Apologie fully aunsweringe by Scriptures and auncea[n]t Doctors a blasphemouse book gathered by D. Steph. Gardiner* (Strasbourg, 1555), RSTC 20175

Ramsay, J., *A Plaister for a galled horse* (1548), RSTC 20662

Registra Stephani Gardiner et Johannes Poynet, Episcoporum Wintoniensium, ed. H. Chitty (Canterbury and York Society, 37, 1929–30)

Rhegius, U. (tr. William Turner), *A Co[m]parison betwene the olde learnynge & the newe* (1537), RSTC 20840

Ridley, L., *A Commentarye in Enlgyshe vpon saynte Paules epystle to the Ephysyans* (1540), RSTC 20138

Robinson, H., *Original Letters relative to the English Reformation: written during the reigns of king Henry VIII, king Edward VI, and queen Mary: chiefly from the archives of Zurich*, Parker Society, 2 vols (Cambridge, 1846–47)

Roy, W., *Rede me and be nott wrothe* (n.p. 1528), RSTC 21427

Royal Visitation of 1559. An Act Book for the Northern Province, ed. C.J. Kitching, Surtees Society, 187 (1975)

Sandys, E., *The Sermons of Edwin Sandys DD, successively Bishop of Worcester and London and Archbishop of York*, ed. J. Ayre, Parker Society (Cambridge, 1841)

Shepherd, L., *A Pore Helpe. The Buklar and defence of mother holy kyrke* (1548) RSTC 13051.7

————, *Pathose* (c.1548), RSTC 19463

Smith, R., *A Brief Treatyse settyng forth diuers truthes necessary both to be beleued of chrysten people & kepte also* (1547), RSTC 22818

————, *Defensio sacri Episcoporu[m] & sacerdotum coelibatus contra impias & indoctas petri Martyris* (Paris, 1550)

————, *A Bouclier of the catholike fayth of Christes church* (1554, 1555), RSTC 22816–7

————, *Of Unwrytten Verytyes* (1548), RSTC 22823

Strype, J., *Ecclesiastical Memorials Relating Chiefly to Religion and the Reformation of it; and the emergencies of the Church of England under King Henry VIII, King Edward VI, and Queen Mary I*, 3 vols (Oxford, 1822)

————, *Memorials of the Most Reverend Father in God Thomas Cranmer, sometime Lord Archbishop of Canterbury* (Oxford, 1812)

————, *The Life and Acts of Matthew Parker. the first archbishop of Canterbury in the reign of queen Elizabeth* (Oxford, 1821)

————, *Annals of the Reformation and the establishment of Religion and Various other occurrences during queen Elizabeth's happy reign* (Oxford, 1824)

Surrey Wills, 3 vols, Surrey Record Society (1915–29)

Sussex Wills. Transcripts of Sussex Wills in four Volumes, ed. R. Garraway Rice and W.H. Godfrey, Sussex Record Society, 91–94 (1935–41)

Swinnerton, T., *A Mustre of schismatyke bysshoppes of Rome / other wyse naming them selues popes* (1534), RSTC 23552

Tudor Royal Proclamations, ed. P.L. Hughes and J.F. Larkin, 3 vols (New Haven and London, 1964–69)

Turner, W., *The Huntynge & fyndyng out of the Romishe fox which more than seuen years hath bene hyd among the bisshopes of England* (Basle, 1543), RSTC 24354

————, *The Rescuynge of the Romishe Fox, other vvyse called the examination of the hunter* (Bonn, 1545), RSTC 24355

————, *A Breife recantation of maystres missa* (1548), RSTC 17137

————, *A New Dialogue wherein is contayned the examination of the Masse* (1548), RSTC 24364

————, *The Huntyng of the Romyshe Vuolfe* (Emden, 1554), RSTC 24356

————, *A New Booke of spirituall physik for dyuerse diseases of the nobilitie and gentlemen of Englande* (Emden, 1555), RSTC 24361

Ulric of Augsburg, *An Epistle of moche learni[n]g sent ... unto Nicholas Bysshoppe of Rome* (1547), RSTC 24514

U.V., *The Olde Fayth of great Brittaygne and the newe learnynge of Englande*, (1549)

Valor Ecclesiasticus, ed. J. Caley and J. Hunter, 6 vols (1810–34)

Veron, J., *A stronge defence of the maryage of pryestes* (1562), RSTC 24687

Visitation Articles and Injunctions for the Period of the Reformation, ed. W.H. Frere, 3 vols (1910)

Von Watt, J. (tr. William Turner), *A worke entytled of ye olde god & the newe of the old doctryne and ye newe* (1534), RSTC 25127

Whitelock, D., Brett, M. and Brooke, C.N.L., *Councils and Synods with other documents relating to the English Church*, 2 vols (Oxford, 1981)

Whitford, R., *Here begynneth the boke called the Pype/ or Tonne / or the lyfe of perfection* (1532), RSTC 25421

Wright, T., ed., *Three Chapters of Letters relating to the Dissolution of the Monasteries*, Camden Society, o.s. 26 (1843)

Wriothesley, C., *A Chronicle of England During the Reigns of the Tudors from* AD *1485 to 1559*, ed. W.D. Hamilton, Camden Society, n.s. 11 (1875)

De Worde, W., *The Birth and Lyfe of Antechryst* (1525?), RSTC 670

Printed Secondary Sources

Almasy, R.A., 'Contesting Voices in Tyndale's *The Practice of Prelates*', in John A.R. Dick and Anne Richardson, eds, *William Tyndale and the Law: Sixteenth Century Essays and Studies*, 25 (Kirksville, MO, 1994), pp. 1–12

Aston, M., *England's Iconoclasts. Laws Against Images*, vol. 1 (Oxford, 1988)

———, *Lollards and Reformers. Images and Literacy in Late Mediaeval Religion* (London, 1984)

Aveling, J.C., 'The English Clergy, Catholic and Protestant, in the Sixteenth and Seventeenth Centuries', in J.C. Aveling, D.M. Loades and H.R. McAdoo, eds, *Rome and the Anglicans. Historical and Doctrinal Aspects of Anglican–Roman Catholic Relations* (Berlin and New York, 1982), pp. 55–142

Backus, I., 'Calvin's Judgement on Eusebius of Caesarea: An Analysis', *Sixteenth Century Journal*, 22 (1991), pp. 419–437

Bagchi, D.V.N., *Luther's Earliest Opponents. Catholic Controversialists 1518–1525* (Minneapolis, 1991)

Bailey, D.S., *Thomas Becon and the Reformation of the Church in England* (Edinburgh, 1952)

Ball, B.B., *A Great Expectation. Eschatological Thought in English Protestantism to 1660* (Leiden, 1975)

Barry, J., 'Literacy and Literature in Popular Culture: Reading and Writing in Historical Perspective', in T. Harris, ed., *Popular Culture in England c. 1500–1850* (Basingstoke, 1995), pp. 69–94

Barstow, A.L., *Married Priests and the Reforming Papacy. The Eleventh Century Debates*, Texts and Studies in Religion, 12 (1982)

———, 'The First Generation of Anglican Clergy Wives: Heroines or Whores?', *Historical Magazine of the Protestant Episcopal Church*, 52 (1983), pp. 3–16

Baskerville, E.J., *A Chronological Bibliography of Propaganda and Polemic Published in English Between 1553 and 1558, from the death of Edward VI to the death of Mary I* (Philadelphia, 1979)

———, 'John Ponet in Exile: A Ponet Letter to John Bale', *Journal of Ecclesiastical History*, 37 (1986), pp. 442–7

Baskerville, G., 'Married Clergy and Pensioned Religious in the Norwich Diocese', *English Historical Review*, 48 (1933), pp. 43–64, 199–228

————, 'English Monks and the Suppression of the Monasteries', *Bedford Historical Series*, 7 (1958)

————, 'The Dispossessed Religious in Surrey', *Surrey Archaeological Society*, 47 (1941), pp. 12–28

Bauckham, R., *Tudor Apocalypse. Sixteenth Century Apocalypticism, Millennarianism and the English Reformation from John Bale to John Foxe and Thomas Brightman* (Courtenay Library of Reformation Classics no. 8, Sutton Courtenay, 1978)

Bayne, C.G., 'The Visitation of the Province of Canterbury 1559', *English Historical Review*, 28 (1913), pp. 636–77

Bennett, H.S., *English Books and Readers 1475–1557* (Cambridge, 1952)

Birch, D., *Early Reformation English Polemics* (Salzburg, 1983)

Block, J., 'Thomas Cromwell's Patronage of Preaching', *Sixteenth Century Journal*, 8 (1977), pp. 37–50

Booty, J., *John Jewel as Apologist of the Church of England* (London, 1963), pp. 106ff

Bowker, M., *The Henrician Reformation. The Diocese of Lincoln under John Longland 1521–1547* (Cambridge, 1981)

————, 'The Henrician Reformation and the Parish Clergy', *Bulletin of the Institute of Historical Research*, 50 (1977), pp. 30–47

Bradshaw, B., 'The Controversial St Thomas More', *Journal of Ecclesiastical History*, 36 (1985), pp. 535–69

Bradshaw, C.J., 'David or Josiah? Old Testament Kings as Exemplars in Edwardian Religious Polemic', in B. Gordon ed., *Protestant History and Identity in Sixteenth-Century Europe*, 2 vols. (Aldershot, 1996), II, pp. 77–90

Brecht, M. (tr. J.L. Schaaf), *Martin Luther. Shaping and Defining the Reformation 1521–1532* (Minneapolis, 1990)

Brigden, S., *London and the Reformation* (Oxford, 1989)

Brooke, C.N.L., 'Gregorian Reform in Action: Clerical Marriage in England 1050–1200', *Cambridge Historical Journal*, 12 (1956), pp. 1–21

Brooks, P.N., *Thomas Cranmer's Doctrine of the Eucharist*, second edition (Basingstoke, 1992)

Brown, A., *Popular Piety in Late Mediaeval England. The Diocese of Salisbury 1250–1550* (Oxford, 1995)

Bugge, J., *Virginitas. An Essay in the History of a Medieval Ideal* (The Hague, 1975)

Butterworth, C.C. and Alan G. Chester, *George Joye 1495?–1553. A Chapter in the History of the English Bible and the English Reformation* (Philadelphia, 1962)

Caldicott, D.K., *Hampshire Nunneries* (Chichester, 1989)

Cargill Thompson, W.D.J., 'Who Wrote *The Supper of the Lord?*', *Harvard Theological Review*, 53 (1960) pp. 79–91

————, *Studies in the Reformation. Luther to Hooker* (London, 1980)

Carlson, E., 'Clerical Marriage and the English Reformation', *Journal of British Studies*, 31 (1992), pp. 1–31

————, 'The marriage of William Turner', *Historical Research*, 65 (1992), pp. 336–9

————, *Marriage and the English Reformation* (Oxford, 1994)

Cholij, R., *Clerical Celibacy in East and West* (Worcester, 1989)

Chrisman, M.U., *Lay Culture, Learned Culture. Books and Social Change in Strasbourg, 1480–1599* (New Haven, CT and London, 1982)

Christianson, P., *Reformers and Babylon. English Apocalyptic Visions from the Reformation to the Eve of the Civil War* (Toronto, 1978)

Clair, C., 'On the Printing of Certain Reformation Books', *The Library*, fifth series, 18 (1963), pp. 275–87

Clark, F., *Eucharistic Sacrifice and the Reformation*, second edition (Oxford, 1967)

Clark, J.A., 'The Bible, History, and Authority in Tyndale's *The Practice of Prelates*', *Moreana*, 106 (1991), pp. 105–17

Clarke, G.W., *The Letters of St Cyprian of Carthage*, in *Ancient Christian Writers. The Works of the Fathers in Translation*, ed. J. Quasten, W.J. Burghardt and T.C. Lawler, 43–6 (New York, 1984)

Clebsch, W.A., *England's Earliest Protestants 1520–1535* (New Haven, 1964)

————, 'More Evidence that George Joye Wrote *The Supper of the Lord*', *Harvard Theological Review*, 55 (1962), pp. 63–6

Congar, Y., *Tradition and Traditions. An Historical and a Theological Essay* (London, 1966)

Corpus Iuris Canonici editio lisiensis secunda post Aemili Ludovici Richteri curas ad librorum manu Scriptorum et Editionis Romanae Fidem recognovit ed. Anotatione Critics Instruxit Aemilius Friedberg (Leipzig, 1879)

Craig, J. and Litzenberger, C., 'Wills as Religious Propaganda: The Testament of William Tracy', *Journal of Ecclesiastical History*, 44 (1993), pp. 415–31

Criccio, P., 'Hugh Latimer and Witness', *Sixteenth Century Journal*, 10 (1979), pp. 21–34

Crichton, A.B., '*King Johan* and the *Ludus de Antichristo* as Moralities of the State', *Sixteenth Century Journal*, 4 (1973), pp. 61–76

Cross, C., 'Priests into Ministers: The Establishment of Protestant Practice in the City of York 1530–1630', in P.N. Brooks, ed.,

Reformation Principle and Practice. Essays in Honour of Arthur Geoffrey Dickens (London, 1980), pp. 203–25

Daniell, D., *William Tyndale. A Biography* (New Haven, 1994)

Darlington, R.R., 'Ecclesiastical Reform in the late Old English Period', *English Historical Review*, 51 (1936), pp. 385–428

Davenport, J., *Notes on the Bishopric of Worcester 1547–1559* (Worcester, 1916)

Davies, C.M.F., '"Poor Persecuted Little Flock" or "Commonwealth of Christians". Edwardian Protestant Concepts of the Church', in Peter Lake and Maria Dowling, eds, *Protestantism and the National Church in Sixteenth Century England* (London, 1987), pp. 78–102

Davies, C.S.L., *Peace, Print and Protestantism. 1450–1558* (London, 1977)

Devereux, E.J., 'John Rastell's Press in the English Reformation', *Moreana*, 49 (1976), pp. 29–47

Dick, J.A.R., '"To Dig Again the Wells of Abraham": Philology, Theology, and Scripture in Tyndale's *The Parable of the Wicked Mammon'*, *Moreana*, 28 (1991), pp. 39–52

———, '"To Trye his True Frendes": Imagery as Argument in Tyndale's *The Parable of the Wicked Mammon'*, *Moreana*, 28 (1991), pp. 69–82

Dickens, A.G., 'Aspects of Intellectual Transition Among the English Parish Clergy of the Reformation Period. A Regional Example', *Archiv für Reformationsgeschichte*, 43 (1952), pp. 51–69

———, *The English Reformation*, second edition (London, 1989)

———, *Lollards and Protestants in the Diocese of York 1509–1558* (London, 1959)

———, 'The Marian reaction in the diocese of York', in Dickens, ed., *Reformation Studies* (London, 1982), pp. 93–158

———, 'Robert Parkyn's Narrative of the Reformation', in Dickens, ed., *Reformation Studies* (London, 1982), pp. 293–312

———, 'Archbishop Holgate's Apology', in Dickens, ed., *Reformation Studies* (London, 1982), pp. 353–62

———, 'Two Marian Petitions', in Dickens, ed., *Reformation Studies* (London, 1982), pp. 83–91

———, 'Robert Holgate, Archbishop of York and President of the King's Council in the North', in Dickens, ed., *Reformation Studies* (London, 1982), pp. 323–51

Dickens, A.G. and Tonkin, J., *The Reformation in Historical Thought* (Oxford, 1985)

Douglas, M., *Purity and Danger. An Analysis of Concepts of Pollution and Taboo* (London, 1966)

Duerden, R., 'Justice and Justification: King and God in Tyndale's *The Obedience of a Christian Man*', in John A.R. Dick and Anne Richardson, eds, *William Tyndale and the Law, Sixteenth Century Essays and Studies*, 25 (Kirksville, MO, 1994) pp. 69–80

Duffy, E., *The Stripping of the Altars. Traditional Religion in England 1400–1580* (New Haven, 1992)

Dugmore, C.W., *The Mass and the English Reformers* (London/New York, 1958)

Eaves, R.G., 'The Reformation Thought of Dr Robert Barnes, Lutheran Chaplain and Ambassador for Henry VIII', *Lutheran Quarterly*, 28 (1976), pp. 156–65

Eisenstein, E., *The Printing Press as an Agent of Change: Communications and Cultural Transformations in Early Modern Europe*, 2 vols (Cambridge, 1979)

Elton, G.R., *Reform and Reformation. England 1509–1558* (London, 1979), pp. 157–68

————, 'Reform and the "Commonwealth men" of Edward VIs Reign', in P. Clark, A.G.R. Smith and Nicholas Tyacke, eds, *The English Commonwealth 1547–1640. Essays in Politics and Society* (New York, 1979), pp. 23–39

Emden, A.B., *A Biographical Register of the University of Oxford to 1500*, 8 vols (Oxford, 1957)

Emmerson, R.R. and McGinn, B., eds, *The Apocalypse in the Middle Ages* (Ithaca, 1992)

Evans, G.R, *Problems of Authority in the Reformation Debates* (Cambridge, 1992)

Fairfield, L.P., *John Bale. Mythmaker for the English Reformation* (West Lafayette, Indiana, 1976)

————, 'The *Vocacyon of Johan Bale* and Early English Autobiography', *Renaissance Quarterly*, 26 (1971), pp. 327–340

————, 'John Bale and the Development of Protestant Hagiography in England', *Journal of Ecclesiastical History*, 24 (1993), pp. 145–60

Febvre, L.P. (tr. D. Gerard), *The Coming of the Book. The Impact of Printing 1450–1800* (London, 1976)

Feasey, E.J., 'William Baldwin', *Modern Languages Review*, 20 (1975), pp. 407–18

Ferguson, A.B., *Clio Unbound. Perception of the Social and Cultural Past in Renaissance England* (Durham, North Carolina, 1979)

Fines, J., 'An Un-noticed Tract of the Tyndale-More Dispute?', *Bulletin of the Institute of Historical Research*, 42 (1969), pp. 220–30

Firth, K.R., *The Apocalyptic Tradition in Reformation Britain 1530–1645* (Oxford, 1979)

Flesseman Van Leer, E., 'The Controversy About Ecclesiology Between

Thomas More and William Tyndale', *Nederlands Archief voor Kerkesgeschiedenis*, 44 (1960), pp. 65–86

———, 'The Controversy About Scripture and Tradition Between Thomas More and William Tyndale', *Nederlands Archief voor Kerkesgeschiedenis*, 43 (1959), pp. 143–64

Foster, J., *Alumni Oxonienses. The Matriculation Registers of the University, arranged, revised and annotated*, 4 vols (Oxford, 1887–88)

———, *Index Ecclesiasticus: or Alphabetical list of all the ecclesiastical dignitaries in England and Wales since the Reformation* (Oxford, 1890)

Fox, A., *Politics and Literature in the Reigns of Henry VII and Henry VIII* (Oxford 1989)

Freeman, T.S., 'Research, Rumour, and Propaganda: Anne Boleyn in Foxe's Book of Martyrs', *Historical Journal*, 38 (1995), pp. 797–819

Frere, W.H., *The Marian Reaction in its Relation to the English Clergy. A Study of the Episcopal Registers* (Church Historical Society, London, 1896)

Furcha, E.J., *The Essential Carlstadt. Fifteen Tracts by Andreas Bodenstein (Carlstadt) from Karlstadt* (Scottdale, Pennsylvania, 1995)

Gabler, U. (tr. R.G.L. Gritsch), *Huldrich Zwingli. His Life and Work* (Edinburgh, 1986)

Garrett, C., *The Marian Exiles* (Cambridge, 1938)

———, '"The resureccion of the Masse": by Hugh Latimer or John Bale?', *The Library*, fourth series 21 (1940), pp. 143–59

Gee, H., *The Elizabethan Clergy and the Settlement of Religion 1558–1564* (Oxford, 1898)

Gerrish, B.A., *The Old Protestantism and the New. Essays on the Reformation Heritage* (Edinburgh, 1982)

———, 'Priesthood and Ministry in the Theology of Luther', *Church History*, 34 (1965), pp. 404–22

Gillett, C.R., *Burned Books. Neglected Chapters in British History and Literature*, 2 vols (New York, 1932)

Gogan, B., *The Common Corps of Christendom. Ecclesiological Themes in the Writings of Sir Thomas More* (Leiden, 1982)

Gordon, B. ed., *Protestant History and Identity in Sixteenth-Century Europe*, 2 vols (Aldershot, 1996)

Grane, L., Schindler, A. and Wriedt, M., eds, *Auctoritas Patrum. Contributions on the Reception of the Church Fathers in the 15th and 16th Century* (Mainz, 1993)

Gree, L.C., 'Faith, Righteousness, and Justification. New Light on their development under Luther and Melanchthon', *Sixteenth Century Journal*, 4 (1972), pp. 65–86

Greenblatt, S., *Renaissance Self-Fashioning from More to Shakespeare* (Chicago, 1980)

Greenslade, S.L., 'The authority of the tradition of the early church in early Anglican thought', *Oecumenica* (1971–72), pp. 9–33

———, *The English Reformers and the Fathers of the Church. An Inaugural Lecture delivered before the University of Oxford 10 May 1960* (Oxford, 1960)

Gresham, S., 'William Baldwin: Literary Voices of the Reign of Edward VI', *Huntingdon Library Quarterly*, 44 (1980–81), pp. 101–16

Grieve, H., 'The Deprived Married Clergy in Essex, 1553–1561', *TRHS*, fourth series, 22 (1940), pp. 141–69

Guy, J., *Tudor England* (Oxford, 1988)

Hadfield, A., *Literature, Politics, and National Identity. Reformation to Renaissance* (Cambridge, 1994)

Hageman, E.A., 'John Foxe's Henry VIII as Justicia', *Sixteenth Century Journal*, 10 (1979), pp. 35–44

Haigh, C., 'Some Aspects of the Recent Historiography of the English Reformation', *Stadtburgertum und Adel in der Reformation. Studien zur Sozialgeschichte der Reformation in England und Deutschland* (Stuttgart, 1979)

———, *Reformation and Resistance in Tudor Lancashire* (Cambridge, 1975)

———, *English Reformations. Religion, Politics, and Society under the Tudors* (Oxford, 1993)

———, ed., *The English Reformation Revised* (Cambridge, 1990)

———, ed., *The Reign of Elizabeth* (Basingstoke, 1988)

Hale, W., *A Series of Precedents and Proceedings in Criminal Cases extending from the year 1475–1640, extracted from the Act Books of the Ecclesiastical Courts of the Diocese of London* (1847)

Hammond, G., 'Law and Love in Deuteronomy', in J.A.R. Dick and A. Richardson eds, *William Tyndale and the Law*, Sixteenth Century Essays and Studies, 25 (1994), pp. 51–58

Harris, J.W., *John Bale. A Study in the Minor Literature of the Reformation* (Urbana, 1940)

Headley, J.M., 'The Reformation as crisis in the Understanding of Tradition', *Archiv für Reformationsgeschichte*, 78 (1987), pp. 5–22

———, *Luther's View of Church History* (New Haven, CT, 1963)

———, 'Thomas Murner, Thomas More, and the First Expression of More's Ecclesiology', *Studies in the Renaissance*, 14 (1967), pp. 73–92

———, 'Thomas More and Luther's Revolt', *Archiv für Reformationsgeschichte*, 60 (1969), pp. 145–60

Heal, F., 'The Parish Clergy and the Reformation in the Diocese of Ely', *Proceedings of the Cambridge Antiquarian Society*, 66 (1976), pp. 141–63

Heal, F. and O'Day, R., eds, *Church and Society in England. Henry VIII to James I* (London, 1977)

Heath, P., *The English Parish Clergy on the Eve of the Reformation* (London, 1969)

Hirsch, R., *Printing, Selling, and Reading 1450–1550* (Wiesbaden, 1967)

Hitchcock, J., 'More and Tyndale's Controversy over Revelation. A test of the McLuhan Hypothesis', *Journal of the American Academy of Religion*, 39 (1971), pp. 448–466

Hodgett, G.A.J., 'The State of the Ex-religious and Former Chantry Priests in the Diocese of Lincoln 1547–1574. From Returns in the Exchequer', *Lincoln Record Society*, 53 (1959)

Hogg, J., *Richard Whitford's 'Pype or Tonne of the Lyfe of Perfection' with an Introductory Study on Whitford's Works* (Salzburg, 1979)

Houlbrooke, R.A., *Church Courts and the People During the English Reformation 1520–1570* (Oxford, 1979)

Hughes, C., 'Two Sixteenth Century Northern Protestants. John Bradford and William Turner', *Bulletin of the John Rylands Library*, 66 (1983), pp. 104–38

Iserloh, E., *The Catholic Literary Opponents of Luther and the Reformation*, in *History of the Church*, 5 (London, 1980), pp. 191–207

James, C., 'Ban Wedy I Dynny: Mediaeval Welsh Law and early Modern Propaganda', *Cambrian Mediaeval Celtic Studies*, 27 (1994), pp. 61–81

Jones, N.L., 'Matthew Parker, John Bale, and the Magdeburg Centuriators', *Sixteenth Century Journal*, 12 (1981), pp. 35–49

Jones, W.R.D., *William Turner. Tudor Naturalist, Physician and Divine* (London, 1988)

Jordan, W.K., *Edward VI. The Young King. The Protectorship of the Duke of Somerset* (London, 1968)

———, *Edward VI. The Threshold of Power* (London, 1970)

King, J.N., *English Reformation Literature. The Tudor Origins of the Protestant Tradition* (Princeton, 1982)

———, *Tudor Royal Iconography. Literature and Politics in an Age of Religious Crisis* (Princeton, 1989)

———, 'Freedom of the Press, Protestant Propaganda, and Protector Somerset', *Huntingdon Library Quarterly*, 40 (1976–77), pp. 1–10

———, 'Protector Somerset, Patron of the English Renaissance', *The Papers of the Bibliographical Society of America*, 70 (1976), pp. 307–31

Kitch, M.J., *Studies in Sussex Church History* (London, 1981)

Klaasen, W., *Living at the End of the Ages. Apocalyptic Expectation in the Radical Reformation* (Lanham, MD,1992)

Knox, D.B. *The Lords Supper in the Writings of the English Reformation before 1549. An Exposition and Critique* (London, 1968)

Kronenberg, M.E., 'Forged Addresses in Low Country Books in the period of the Reformation', *The Library*, fifth series, 2 (1947), pp. 81–94

Kyle, R., 'John Knox and the Purification of Religion. The Intellectual Aspects of his Crusade Against Idolatry', *Archiv für Reformationsgeschichte*, 77 (1986), pp. 265–280

Lea, H.C., *A History of Sacerdotal Celibacy in the Christian Church*, third edition (London, 1907)

Levin, C., 'A Good Prince: King John and early Tudor Propaganda', *Sixteenth Century Journal*, 11 (1980), pp. 23–32

Levy, F.J., *Tudor Historical Thought* (San Marino, California, 1967)

Lloyd, C., *Formularies of Faith Put Forth by Authority During the Reign of Henry VIII* (Oxford, 1825)

Loach, J., 'Pamphlets and Politics 1553–1558', *Bulletin of the Institute of Historical Research*, 48 (1975), pp. 31–44

————, 'Reformation Controversies', in J. McConica, ed., *History of the University of Oxford* (Oxford, 1986), vol. III, pp. 363–97

Loades, D.M., 'The Press Under the Tudors. A Study in Censorship and Sedition', *Transactions of the Cambridge Bibliographical Society*, 4 (1964), pp. 29–50

————, *The Reign of Mary Tudor. Politics, Government and Religion in England 1553–1558* (London, 1979)

————, 'The Piety of the Catholic Restoration in England 1553–1558', in J. Kirk, ed., *Humanism and Reform: The Church in Europe, England, and Scotland 1400–1643. Essays in Honour of James K. Cameron*, Studies in Church History, 8 (Oxford, 1991), pp. 289–304

————, ed., *The End of Strife. Papers Collected from the Proceedings of the Colloquium of the Commission Internationale d'Histoire Ecclesiastique*, (Edinburgh, 1984)

Lynch, J., 'A Critique of the Law of Celibacy in the Catholic Church from the Period of the Reform Councils', *Concilium*, 8 (1972), pp. 57–83

MacCulloch, D., 'Two Dons in Politics. Thomas Cranmer and Stephen Gardiner 1503–1533', *Historical Journal*, 31 (1994), pp. 1–22

————, *Suffolk and the Tudors. Politics and Religion in an English County 1500–1600* (Oxford, 1986)

————, *Thomas Cranmer. A Life* (New Haven, CT, 1996)

————, *The Later Reformation in England: 1547–1603* (Basingstoke, 1990)

Macek, E., 'Richard Smith: Tudor Cleric in Defence of Traditional Belief and Practice', *Catholic Historical Review*, 72 (1986), pp. 383–402

Macken, R., 'Denys the Carthusian, Commentator on Boethius "De Consolatione Philosophiae"', *Analecta Cartusiana*, 118 (Montpellier, 1984)

Manning, R.B., *Religion and Society in Elizabethan Sussex. A Study of the Enforcement of the Settlement of Religion 1558–1603* (Leicester, 1969)

Marius, R., 'The Pseudonymous Patristic text in Thomas More's "Confutation"', *Moreana*, 4 (1967), pp. 253–66

————, 'Thomas More and the Early Church Fathers', *Traditio*, 24 (1968), pp. 379–407

————, 'Thomas More's View of the Church', *Confutation of Tyndale's Answer*, ed. J.M. Headley, CW 8, pt. III, pp. 1269–363

————, *Thomas More* (London, 1993)

Marsh, C., 'In the Name of God. Will Making and Faith in Early Modern England', in G.H. Martin and P. Spufford, eds, *The Records of the Nation. The Public Record Office 1838–1988* (Woodbridge, 1990), pp. 215–49

Marshall, Peter, *The Catholic Priesthood and the English Reformation* (Oxford, 1994)

————, 'The Debate over "Unwritten Verities" in Early Reformation England', in B. Gordon ed., *Protestant History and Identity in Sixteenth-Century Europe*, 2 vols (Aldershot, 1996), I, pp. 60–77

Martin, J.W., 'Miles Hogarde. Artisan and Aspiring Author in Sixteenth Century England', *Renaissance Quarterly*, 34 (1981), pp. 359–83

Mayhew, C.J., 'The Progress of the Reformation in East Sussex 1530–1559. The Evidence from Wills', *Southern History*, 5 (1983), pp. 38–67

McCann, T.J., 'The Clergy and the Elizabethan Settlement in the Diocese of Chichester', in M. Kitch, ed., *Studies in Sussex Church History* (London, 1981), pp. 93–123

McCusker, H., *John Bale. Dramatist and Antiquity* (Bryn Mawr, 1942)

————, 'Books and Manuscripts Formerly in the Possession of John Bale', *The Library*, fourth series 16 (1936), pp. 144–65

McCutcheon, R.R., 'The Responsio ad Lutherum. Thomas More's Inchoate Dialogue with Heresy', *Sixteenth Century Jouranl*, 22 (1991), pp. 77–90

McGrath, A., *Iustistia Dei. A History of the Christian Doctrine of Justification*, 3 vols (Cambridge, 1986)

————, *Reformation Thought. An Introduction* (Oxford, 1988)

McKisack, M., *Mediaeval History in the Tudor Age* (Oxford, 1971)

McLean, A.M., '"A Noughtye and a false Lying Boke": William Barlow and the "Lutheran Factions"', *Renaissance Quarterly*, 31 (1978), pp. 173–86

————, '"Detestynge Thabomynacyon". William Barlow, Thomas More, and the Anglican Episcopacy', *Moreana*, 43–4 (1973–74), pp. 67–77

Messenger, E.C., *The Reformation, the Mass, and the Priesthood. A documented history with special reference to the question of Anglican Orders*, 2 vols (London, 1936)

Meyer, C.S., 'Henry VIII Burns Luther's Books 12 May 1521', *Journal of Ecclesiastical History*, 9 (1958), pp. 173–87

Morris, C., *Political Thought in England from Tyndale to Hooker* (London, 1953)

Mozley, J.F., *Coverdale and His Bibles* (London, 1953)

————, '"The Supper of the Lord": Tyndale or Joye?', *Moreana*, 3 (1966), pp. 11–16

Muller, J.A., *Stephen Gardiner and the Tudor Reaction* (London, 1926)

————, ed., *Letters of Stephen Gardiner* (Cambridge, 1933)

Mullett, C.F., 'That All May Understand: The early English Bibles as Archives of History', *The Historical Magazine of the Protestant Episcopal Church*, 44 (1975), pp. 353–64

Murray, J., 'Ecclesiastical Justice and the Enforcement of the Reformation: The case of Archbishop Browne and the Clergy of Dublin', in A. Ford, J. McGuire and K. Milne, eds, *As By Law Established. The Church of Ireland Since the Reformation* (Dublin, 1995), pp. 33–51

Obelkevich, J., Roper, L. and Samuel, R., eds, *Disciplines of Faith. Studies in Religion, Politics, and Patriarchy* (London, 1987)

Oberman, H., *The Dawn of the Reformation. Essays in Late Medieval and Early Modern Thought* (Edinburgh, 1986), pp. 289–96

———— (tr. E. Walliser-Schwarzbart), *Luther. Man Between God and the Devil* (London, 1989)

O'Day, R., *The English Clergy. The Emergence and Consolidation of a Profession 1558–1642* (Leicester, 1979)

————, *The Debate on the English Reformation* (London, 1986)

————, *Education and Society 1500–1800. The Social Foundations of Education in Early Modern Britain* (London, 1982)

O'Day, R. and Heal, F., eds, *Continuity and Change. Personnel and Administration of the Church of England 1500–1642* (Leicester, 1976)

O'Donnell, A.M., 'Scripture versus Church in Tyndale's Answer unto Sir Thomas More's Dialogue', *Moreana*, 106 (1991), pp. 119–30

Old, W.W., 'Memorials of John Old the Reformer', *TRHS*, n.s. 2 (1873), pp. 199–211

Oxley, J., *The Reformation in Essex to the Death of Mary* (Manchester, 1965)

Ozment, S., 'Marriage and the Ministry in the Protestant Churches', *Concilium*, 8 (1972), pp. 39–56

———, *When Fathers Ruled. Family Life in Reformation Europe* (Cambridge, Mass., 1983)

Palliser, D.M., 'The Reformation in York 1534–1553', *Borthwick Institute Papers*, 40 (1971)

Partner, N., 'Henry of Huntingdon: Clerical Celibacy and the Writing of History', *Church History*, 42 (1973), pp. 467–75

Patrides, C.A. and Wittreich, J., eds, *The Apocalypse in English Renaissance Thought and Literature. Patterns, Antecedents, and Repercussions* (Manchester, 1984)

Paul, J.E., 'Hampshire Recusants in the Reign of Elizabeth I, with Special Reference to Winchester', *Proceedings of the Hampshire Field Club*, 21 pt II (1959), pp. 61–81

Pelikan, J., *Obedient Rebels: Catholic Substance and Protestant Principle in Luther's Reformation* (London, 1964)

Peters, R., 'Who Compiled the Sixteenth Century Patristic Handbook *Unio Dissidentium*?', in G.J. Cuming, ed., *Studies in Church History*, 2 (London, 1965), pp. 237–50

Pettegree, A., 'The Latin Polemic of the Marian Exiles', in *Studies in Church History*, Subsidia, 8 (1991), pp. 305–29

———, *Marian Protestantism. Six Studies* (Aldershot, 1996)

Pineas, R., 'William Tyndale's Influence on John Bale's Polemical use of History', *Archiv für Reformationsgeschichte*, 53 (1962), pp. 79–96

———, *Thomas More and Tudor Polemics* (Bloomington, IL, 1968)

———, 'George Joye's "Exposicion of Daniel"', *Renaissance Quarterly*, 28 (1975), pp. 332–43

———, 'George Joye's Polemical Use of History in his Controversy with Stephen Gardiner', *Nederlands Archief voor Kerkgeschiedenis*, 55 (1972), pp. 21–31

———, 'William Tyndale's Polemical Use of the Scriptures', *Nederlands Archief voor Kerkesgeschiedenis*, 45 (1962), pp. 65–78

———, 'William Tyndale's use of History as a Weapon of Religious Controversy', *Harvard Theological Review*, 55 (1962), pp. 121–41

———, 'William Turner and Reformation Politics', *Bibliothèque d'Humanisme et Renaissance*, 37 (1975), pp. 193–200

———, 'William Turner's Polemical use of History and his Controversy with Stephen Gardiner', *Renaissance Quarterly*, 33 (1980), pp. 599–608

————, 'Thomas More's Use of the Dialogue Form as a Weapon of Religious Controversy', *Studies in the Renaissance*, 7 (1960), pp. 193–206

————, 'Some Polemical Techniques in the Nondramatic Works of John Bale', *Bibliothèque d'Humanisme et Renaissance*, 24 (1962), pp. 583–8

————, 'John Bale's Nondramatic Works of Religious Controversy', *Studies in the Renaissance*, 9 (1962), pp. 218–33

————, 'Thomas Becon as a Religious Controversialist', *Nederlands Archief voor Kerkesgeschiedenis*, 45 (1962), pp. 206–20

Plomer, H.R., 'The Protestant Press in the Reign of Queen Mary', *The Library*, n.s. I (1910), pp. 54–72

Pocock, N., 'The Condition of Morals and Religious Belief in the Reign of Edward VI', *English Historical Review*, 10 (1895), pp. 417–44

Pogson, R.H., 'Revival and Reform in Mary Tudor's Church. A Question of Money', *Journal of Ecclesiastical History*, 25 (1974), pp. 249–65

Prior, M., 'Reviled and Crucified Marriages. The Position of Tudor Bishops' Wives', in M. Prior, ed., *Women in English Society 1500–1800* (London, 1985), pp. 118–48

Redworth, G., 'A Study in the Formulation of Policy. The Genesis and Evolution of the Act of Six Articles', *Journal of Ecclesiastical History*, 37 (1986), pp. 42–67

————, *In Defence of the Church Catholic. The Life of Stephen Gardiner* (Oxford, 1990)

Reeves, M., 'History and Eschatology: Mediaeval and Early Protestant Thought in Some English and Scottish Writings', *Medievalia et Humanistica*, n.s. 4 (1973), pp. 99–123

Rex, R., 'The English Campaign Against Luther in the 1520s', *TRHS*, fifth series 39 (1989), pp. 85–106

————, *Henry VIII and the English Reformation* (Basingstoke, 1993)

Richardson, A., 'Scripture as Evidence in Tyndale's "The Obedience of a Christian Man"', *Moreana*, 106 (1991), pp. 83–104

Ringler, W.A. and Flachmann, M., *Beware the Cat by William Baldwin. The First English Novel* (San Marino, California, 1988)

Roper, L., *The Holy Household. Women and Morals in Reformation Augsburg* (Oxford, 1989)

Rupp, G., 'The Battle of the Books: The Ferment of Idea and the Beginning of the Reformation', in P.N. Brooks, ed., *Reformation Principle and Practice. Essays in Honour of Arthur Geoffrey Dickens* (London, 1980), pp. 1–19

————, *Studies in the Making of the English Protestant Tradition (Mainly in the reign of Henry VIII)* (Cambridge, 1966)

Russell, W.R., 'Martin Luther's Understanding of the Pope as Antichrist', *Archiv für Reformationsgeschichte*, 85 (1994), pp. 43–4

Ryrie, A., 'The Problem of Legitimacy and Precedent in English Protestantism 1539–1547', in B. Gordon, ed., *Protestant History and Identity in Sixteenth-Century Europe*, 2 vols (Aldershot, 1996), I, pp. 78–92

Salzman, L.F., 'Sussex religious at the Dissolution', *Sussex Archaeological Collections*, 92 (1954), pp. 24–36

Scarisbrick, J.J., *The Reformation and the English People* (Oxford, 1984)

————, 'Clerical taxation in England 1485–1547', *Journal of Ecclesiastical History*, 11 (1960), pp. 41–54

Schillebeeckx, E., *Clerical Celibacy Under Fire. A Critical Appraisal*, tr. C.A.L. Jarrott (London and Sydney, 1968), pp. 51–6

Schuster, L.A., 'Reformation Polemic and Renaissance Values', *Moreana*, 43–4 (1974), pp. 47–54

————, 'Thomas More's Polemical Career 1523–1533', in *The Confutation of Tyndale's Answer*, CW 8 pt III, pp. 1137–268

Scribner, R.W., *Popular Culture and Popular Movements in Reformation Germany* (London, 1987)

Sipos, S., *Enchiridion Iuris Canonici ad usum scholarum et Privatorum Concinnavit* (Rome, 1954)

Sloyan, G. 'Biblical and Patristic Motives for Celibacy of Church Ministers', *Concilium*, 8 (1972), pp. 13–29

Smeeton, D., 'The Wycliffite Choice: Man's Law or Gods's?', in J.A.R. Dick and A. Richardson, eds, *William Tyndale and the Law* (Kirksville, MO, 1994), pp. 31–40

Smith, L.B., *Tudor Prelates and Politics 1536–1558* (Princeton, 1953)

Southgate, W.M., *John Jewel and the Problem of Doctrinal Authority* (Cambridge, Mass., 1962)

Spielman, R.M., 'The Beginning of Clerical Marriage in the English Reformation: The Reigns of Edward and Mary', *Anglican and Episcopal History*, 56 (1987), pp. 251–263

Steinberg, S.H., *Five Hundred Years of Printing* (Harmondsworth, 1961)

Tavard, G.H., *Holy Writ or Holy Church. The Crisis of the Protestant Reformation* (London, 1959)

Thomson, J.A.F., *The Later Lollards 1414–1520* (Oxford, 1965)

Tinsley, B.S., *History and Polemics in the French Reformation. Florimund de Raemond: Defender of the Church* (Selinsgrove, PA, 1992)

Tjernagel, N.S., *Henry VIII and the Lutherans. A Study in Anglo-Lutheran Relations from 1521–1547* (St Louis, 1965)

Torr, V.B., 'An Elizabethan Return of the State of the diocese of Chichester', *Sussex Archaeological Collections*, 61 (1920), pp. 92–124

Venn, J. and J.A., *Alumni Cantabrigienses. A Biographical list of all
known students, graduates, and holders of office at the University of
Cambridge till 1900*, 6 vols (Cambridge, 1922–54)

Victoria County History, Sussex, vol. II (1907)

———, *A History of Hampshire and the Isle of Wight*, vol. II (1903)

———, *A History of Berkshire*, vol. II (1907)

———, *A History of Wiltshire*, vol. II (1956)

Walder, G., *Persuasive Fictions: Faction, Faith and Political Culture in
the Reign of Henry VIII* (Aldershot, 1996)

Walker, R.B., 'Reformation and Reaction in the County of Lincoln,
1547–1558', *Lincolnshire Architerctural and Archaeological Society
Reports and Papers*, 9 (1962), pp. 49–62

Walsh, K.J., 'Cranmer and the Fathers, especially in the *Defence*',
Journal of Religious History, 11 (1980), pp. 227–47

Welch, C.E., 'Three Sussex Heresy Trials', *Sussex Archaeological
Collections*, 95 (1957), pp. 59–70

Whiting, R., *The Blind Devotion of the People. Popular Religion and the
English Reformation* (Cambridge, 1989)

Williams, G., *The Welsh Church from Conquest to Reformation*
(Fayetteville, 1993)

———, *Reformation Views of Church History* (London, 1970)

———, *Welsh Reformation Essays* (Cardiff, 1967)

Williams, J.F., 'The Married Clergy of the Marian Period', *Norfolk
Archaeology*, 32 (1961), pp. 85–95

Wood, A., *Athenae Oxonienses: An Exact History of all the writers and
bishops who have had their education in the University of Oxford*,
third edition with additions by P. Bliss, 8 vols (1813–20)

Woolf, D.R., 'The Power of the Past. History, Ritual, and Political
Authority in Tudor England', in P.A. Fideler and T.F. Mayer, eds,
*Political Thought and the Tudor Commonwealth. Deep Structure,
Discourse, and Disguise* (London, 1992), pp. 19–49

Yost, J.K., 'Tyndale's use of the Fathers: A Note on his Connection to
Northern Humanism', *Moreana*, 6 (1969), pp. 5–13

———, 'The Reformation Defence of Clerical Marriage in the Reigns
of Henry VIII and Edward VI', *Church History*, 50 (1981), pp.
152–165

Zell, M.L., 'The use of Religious Preambles as a Measure of Religious
Belief in the Sixteenth Century', *Bulletin of the Institute of Historical
Research*, 50 (1977), pp. 246–9

———, 'The Personnel of the Clergy in Kent in the Reformation
Period', *English Historical Review*, 84 (1974), pp. 513–33

Unpublished Dissertations

Barratt, D.M., 'The Condition of the Parish Clergy Between the Reformation and 1660, with special reference to the dioceses of Oxford, Worcester, and Gloucester', Oxford D.Phil. (1949)

Callum, D., 'The Origins of Clerical Celibacy', Oxford D.Phil. (1977)

Lander, S.J., 'The diocese of Chichester 1508–1558. Episcopal Reform under Robert Sherbourne and its Aftermath', Cambridge Ph.D. (1974)

Marshall, P., 'Attitudes of the English People to Priests and Priesthood 1500–1553', Oxford D.Phil. (1990)

Peet, D.J., 'The Mid Sixteenth Century Parish Clergy, with Particular Consideration of the Dioceses of Norwich and York', Cambridge Ph.D. (1980)

Powell, M.R., 'The Polemical Literature of the English Protestant Reformers c.1534–1547', Edinburgh, Ph.D. (1984)

Sheild, I.T., 'The Reformation in the Diocese of Salisbury 1547–1562', Oxford B.Litt. (1960)

Wooding, L.E.C., 'From Humanists to Heretics: English Catholic Theology and Ideology c.1530–1570', Oxford D.Phil. (1995)

Index